The Style of Hawthorne's Gaze

The Style of Hawthorne's Gaze

REGARDING SUBJECTIVITY

John Dolis

The University of Alabama Press

Tuscaloosa & London

∞

The paper on which this book is printed meets the minimum
requirements of American National Standard for Information
Science-Permanence of Paper for Printed Library Materials,
ANSI Z39.48-1984.

Library of Congress Cataloging-in-Publication Data

Dolis, John, 1945–
    The style of Hawthorne's gaze : regarding
subjectivity / John Dolis.
        p.   cm.
    Includes bibliographical references and index.
    ISBN 0-8173-0681-1 (alk. paper)
    1. Hawthorne, Nathaniel, 1804–1864—Technique.
2. Art and literature—United States.   3. Subjectivity
in literature.   4. Narration (Rhetoric)   I. Title.
PS1891.D64   1993
813'.3—dc20   92-33475

British Library Cataloguing-in-Publication Data available

For Agnes McNeill Donohue

Contents

Acknowledgments

In gratitude: I dedicate this work to Agnes McNeill Donohue, whose presence is always and everywhere before me.

For both the "Hawthorne" of this book, as well as the very book itself, I am—in every sense of the word—*profoundly* indebted to Edgar A. Dryden, without whom neither would have appeared.

For comments and suggestions for revisions, thanks to David L. Minter; for encouragement and correspondence, thanks to C. Carroll Hollis; for advice and friendship, thanks to R. W. B. Lewis.

I also wish to express my deepest thanks to Anthony LaBranche: some things must go unsaid.

The following friends and colleagues are inextricably part of this book: Monica Apostol, Andrew Chrucky, Michael Gessner, Robert Haas, Harold Hild, Michael Kilduff, Jack Leckel, Masood Otarod, Dennis Pahl, Veronica Polk, Suresh Raval, Clyde Robbins, Robert Shearer, Rudolph Stoeckel, Jan Stryz, Thomas Tierney, and Paul Vachon.

The book was made possible in part by two fellowships from the National Endowment for the Humanities, Summer Seminars, the first directed by R. W. B. Lewis, Yale University, and the second directed by Edgar A. Dryden, University of Arizona; and a Fulbright Professorship in American Literature at the University of Turin, Italy.

Several sections—rewritten and expanded for this book—have previously appeared in article form. I'm grateful to the publishers for permission to reprint: "Hawthorne's Morphology of Alienation: The Psychosomatic Phenomenon," *American Imago* 41 (1984), 47–62 [permission of Johns Hopkins University Press]; "Hawthorne's Metonymic Gaze: Image and Object," *American Literature* 56 (1984), 362–78 [permission of Duke University Press]; "Hawthorne's Blithedale: Narrative Ethos as Absence," *Arbeiten aus Anglistik und Amerikanistik* 10 (1985), 155–64; "Hawthorne's Gentle Reader: (The Hen) House of (Family) Romance," *Arizona Quarterly* 47 (1991), 29–47 [permission of Arizona Board of Regents]; "Hawthorne's Tactile Gaze: The Phenomenon of Depth," *Modern Language Quarterly* 44 (1983), 267–84; "Hawthorne's Letter," *Notebooks in Cultural Analysis: An Annual Review* 1 (1984), 103–23 [permission of Duke University Press].

Special thanks go to Bradley L. Taylor, free-lance copy editor for The University of Alabama Press.

Provision

○

This book assumes a certain familiarity with continental thinking, its figures and configurations. In this context, "Hawthorne" will figure forth against and beyond the four sides of a (theoretical) frame: Maurice Merleau-Ponty, Jacques Lacan, Martin Heidegger, and Jacques Derrida. Some, of course, will object to this. For certain reasons (methodology, chauvinism, ignorance, IQ), they don't wish to see Hawthorne keep such company. Such people would rather starve than eat a meal with "outsiders," "foreigners" who don't belong (Brillat-Savarin, forgive them). Some will further object to the configuration itself, the eclecticism of this

In Retrospect

○

Looking A/head

dinner party. They would *exclude* mon-sewer Derrida for the sake of conversation, the flow of things around the table—that is, for the sake of consistency, on behalf of (a) system: one that might *include,* perhaps, the pre-reflexive. Others, still, would stage a different scene, would cut out Merleau-Ponty, delete him from the guest list, so that this opening now removes, perhaps, its strongest link to (the) tradition—what the "Language Club" critiques. Such people would also remove Christ from the scene of Leonardo's "Last Supper" (look at that gathering): he's simply in the way (go ahead: take another look). In this case, the exclusion of a figure for the sake of the view could only be (taken as) a frame-up. In either case, the figures of Merleau-Ponty and Derrida would seem to represent a scenario at odds with itSelf. In any case, perception and reflection are the antagonists.

In his later works, Merleau-Ponty foresees this problem, critiques this scene, the place of perception in his earlier thinking: "If my left hand is touching my right hand, and if I should suddenly wish to apprehend with my right hand the work of my left hand as it touches, this reflection of the body upon itself always miscarries at the last moment: the moment I feel my left hand with my right hand, I correspondingly cease touching my right hand with my left hand."[1] Perception erases its subject (self-perception) as the failure of perception itself: "if it is true that my body as an opacity opens up the space of my glance, then this condition of possibility of all perception also entails the impossibility of self-perception."[2] Merleau-Ponty's notion of a *hyper-reflection* will subsequently seek to fill the space of this void. As a "dialectic without synthesis," this "hyperdialectic" anticipates the operation of deconstruction, as Gasché observes; and yet the thrust of its desire would recuperate "the being that lies before the cleavage operated by reflection"—in other words, the One, Being as a whole.[3]

Derrida's early thinking begins upon this threshold; he will dismantle its frame, recite it at the site of auto-affection itSelf: "auto-affection must either pass through what is outside the sphere of 'ownness' or forego any claim to universality. When I see myself, either because I gaze upon a limited region of my body or because it is reflected in a mirror, what is outside the sphere of 'my own' has already entered the field of this auto-affection, with the result that it is no longer pure. In the experience of touching and being touched, the same thing happens. In both cases, the surface of my body, as something external, must begin by being exposed in the world."[4] Here, Derrida critiques that One-ness of Being (what Merleau-Ponty would recover) as it appears in Husserl: the desire for a reflection coincident with itSelf. For Husserl, the "voice" provides this "medium of universal signification"; it "meets no obstacle to its emission in the world precisely because it is produced *as pure auto-affection*. This auto-affection is no doubt the possibility for what is called *subjectivity* or the *for-itself*."[5] Derrida will subsequently disrupt the scene of this phantasy, subvert it with the structure of the sign. The meaning of the percept, as such, cannot be prior to reflection.

Between these two "antagonists" emerges a third: Jean-François Lyotard. His notion of the *figural* retrieves the space of Merleau-Ponty's *hyper-reflection,* but in the form of deconstruction.[6] We've neither time nor space to trace the various shapes of this configuration.[7] Suffice it to say that the figure of Lyotard provides the fifth side of that theoretical frame through which my gaze at "Hawthorne" will pass. Thus, were I to exclude either (Merleau-Ponty or Derrida) from the party, Lyotard would take that place. Let it be. He is the fifth side of the frame—silent, but there. You may not always see him.

At any rate, the "Hawthorne" set forth in this book explodes whatever frame appears to surround it, confine it—exceeds, in fact, (the view of Hawthorne) itSelf. For "Hawthorne" is a configuration of texts (so designated by the name) *further complicated* by the fact that, in those very texts, Hawthorne frequently (mis)places himSelf (puts himSelf in place, puts in place [*mise-en-scène*] himSelf, puts Hawthorne in "Hawthorne") as one of its (own) figures—and often, moreover, ahead of itSelf, beside itSelf, at the head of its self: prior to the text as its pretext (preface). This configuration of texts called "Hawthorne" is itSelf abysmal *(mise-en-abyme).* Hawthorne puts "Hawthorne" in (the) place of itSelf: "Hawthorne" puts Hawthorne in (the) place of itSelf. Thus, for the sake of a certain economy, I will—for the most part—remove the quotes that frame him. Hawthorne will speak for itSelf, will be, indeed, an envoy shuttling back and forth in the post that would send him hither, thither, and beyond (himSelf). Along the way, "Hawthorne" (now how did that frame get back in here/[there]?) will resonate those figures with whom he is invited to play. These playmates will volley a barrage of signs to which others might (co)respond: *Augenblick* (the blink of an eye), *Bestand* (standing-reserve, standing by for duty), *bord* (border, edge, margin), *coup* (cut, the "wound" [*blessure*] of desire), *das Ereignis* (the event), *das Man* (One, the "they-self"), *Dasein* (there being/being there), *eidos* (the idea[l], pure form, absolute referent), *envoi* (envoy, message, relay), *fort-da* (gone-here/there [it is], Freudian repetition), *Geist* (mind, spirit), *Ge(schick)sal* (fate, destiny, destination, sender/sent, post), *Ge-stell* (frame), *(Holz)weg* ([forest]path), *Kern* (kernel, heart, center), *mise-en-abyme* (put-in-abyss, abysmal), *mise-en-scène* (put-in-place, set-up, staging/staged), *objet petit a* (the "other" [small *(a)utre*], object of desire: to be distinguished from the "Other" [capital *(A)utre*]—i.e., let's make no bones about this: Language), *parergon* (frame), *pli* (fold, gap, nothing), *poiēsis* (making, gathering, "poetry"), *poste* (postal system, post office, station, position), *regard* (look, glance, gaze), *subjectum* (subject, [world]view, subject in subjection to its view, the world subjected to the view of a subject), *technē* (making, craft, technique [to be distinguished from technology]). The effect is often dizzying: signs playing off one another like the reflections in Hawthorne's mirrors, bouncing (things) around, a playground of echoes, vertigo, the abyss. To this montage of signs, I'll add but one of my own. I've coined it purely for the sake of economy. Whenever I use the term "itSelf," I specifically call your attention to a certain doubling, duplicity, reflexivity within the word to which it refers. For instance, "narration itSelf" refers to the "self" of narration, the very self narration constitutes. Regarding the play of this proliferation of signs, I can't go (back) over this (play)ground *(Ab-grund)*, here, in detail; I can only suggest its terrain, territory, its topography, the lay of the land. I've yet another tract to get through before we arrive at the *word* ("Hawthorne") *as such*. Should we lose the way, however, I recall you to Izaak Walton regarding a favorite conceit of the angler. One cannot lose what he never had to begin.

I leave you hovering around the table, awaiting the body of "Hawthorne," anxious for the provision(s) to be (re)past, to be under way, on the way *(weg)*. A word of caution, however: what lies (up) ahead will take some time. It's not a fish fry. The regalement will proceed as follows: an apéritif, three main courses (concluding with Hen), dessert, and a digestif. The course (of these courses) may (re)turn upon itself *(Holzweg)*: some will go back for seconds. Those impatient to finish must leave the pleasure of these delays behind. I'm behind you in this. In any case, there's no clean getaway, no bib. From here on, things get messy. Finger food is first. Bon *a(p)pétit!*

Prologue

○

The Middle Ages had conceived of a picture as "a material, impenetrable surface *on* which figures and things are depicted"; similarly, what it had called *perspectiva* was merely optics—that is, "an elaborate theory of vision which attempted to determine the structure of the natural visual image by mathematical means but did not attempt to teach the artist how to reproduce this image in a painting or drawing."[1] It was not until about 1420 that Brunelleschi defined the painting as "a plane cross section through the pencil of rays connecting the eye of the painter (and the beholder) with the object or objects seen," so that by around 1435 Alberti was able to formulate the picture as a *pariete di vetro* or "an imaginary window pane *through* which we look out into a section of space."[2] Because the Renaissance predicated its new approach to the visible upon this revolutionary definition of artistic construction *(technē)* and representation, (the space of) "the world" itself was uniformly—that is, geometrically—put in (its) place: *mis-en-scène*. Above all, this new pictorial or "artificial" perspective enabled the science of anatomy to explore the interior space of the human body with an objective precision hitherto impossible. Leonardo's *Situs* drawings, for example, not only correlate perspective images with vertical and horizontal sections, but also demonstrate the internal organs in transparency; his "serial sections" represent "a concrete, surgical application of a method of geometrical projection developed by Piero della Francesca and later adopted by Dürer: the plotting of a series of cross-sections through the human body preparatory to exact perspective construction"; in this respect, Andreas Vesalius' *De humani corporis fabrica* (1543) marks the inception of a new epoch in anatomical investigation.[3] Science had securely commenced its transparent mission: seeing *through* the world.

At the same time, another science was breaking fresh ground on a reciprocal front. In the very year Vesalius published his *Fabrica*, Copernicus had formulated the new astronomy; by placing the earth in (proper) perspective, he set up the "correct" space of the world. And like the human body, the external world demonstrated its own theory of proportions which would henceforth locate the *res extensa* within a transparent view uniformly ingressive to all by virtue of its technological constitution. To the degree that "the world" had become geometrically spatial, the subject had become an observer—the disinterested spectator of its view. And this technique—the instrumentality of a uniform space—sends science on its way *(Bestimmung)*. For what, after all, constitutes scientific observation,

Perspective and Frame

○

The Daguerreotype

9

its *destinée,* but an attitude that varies the point of view while keeping the object fixed?[4] Subject and object now rendezvous at the very point upon which they vanish. I needn't recall the "psychology" of this event. Suffice it to say that the rhetoric of alienation extends as "far back" as the Renaissance: witness Hamlet or Lear.[5] Perspective thus transposes a transparent consciousness onto "the world": the means of seeing through it. Poised "outside," the view itself hands over to the subject a picture of the whole. Copernicus' view affirms as much. Let's not be deceived by the "illusion" of displacement. For its ironic moment merely puts the subject in the center of the picture *as* its very frame—what has been "missing" from (the center) itSelf.[6] It remained for Kepler to establish this new world picture, in (the) light of its technology, with finality. But that's another story *(récit).*

Here's the one whose path *(weg)* I track. Writing to Francis Bacon in 1620, Sir Henry Wotton told of a visit to Kepler, where he saw a "draft of a landscape on a piece of paper, methought masterly done"; and to Wotton's surprise, Kepler remarked that he had made the picture from "a little black tent . . . exactly close and dark, save at one hole, about an inch and a half in the diameter, to which he applies a long perspective trunk, with a convex glass fitted to the said hole, and the concave taken out at the other end . . . through which the visible radiations of all the objects without are intromitted, falling upon a paper . . . and so he traceth them with his pen in their natural appearance."[7] Kepler's "little black tent" was, of course, a *camera obscura,* and it became his visible model for the human eye. Although Giambattista della Porta had popularized it in the sixteenth century, the first (published) account appeared in Vitruvius' *Architecture* (1521). While others before Kepler had remarked its analogies to the human eye, Kepler was the first to fully demonstrate its resemblance to vision; and it remained for Scheiner to prove the hypothesis at his exhibition in Rome, 1625, where he "cut away the coats of the back parts of eyes of sheep and oxen, and, holding objects before them, saw the images of the objects clearly and distinctly inverted upon the naked retina."[8] Descartes' geometrical vision was thus substantiated by these "pictures" painted on the eye. And many thinkers of the period entertained the notion that in the structure of the eye could be found that intermediary term, the missing link, between *cogito* and *res extensa*—a "sophisticated" rendition of the Cartesian pineal gland.

In his *Essay Concerning Human Understanding* (1690), Locke's dark-room analogy extends this (im)position toward the epistemological domain: the subject (of knowledge) itSelf—that is, "the Subject who is Supposed to Know."[9] His famous "closet-simile" recites the place of its inversion (neither-nor/neuter), the legacy to which it has always already been dispatched, posted: this "little black tent" (read, instead, its lips: this little black "box") become phallus. Here's Locke: "methinks, the *Understanding* is not much unlike a Closet wholly shut from light, with only some little opening left, to let in external visible Resemblances, or *Ideas* of things without; would the Pictures coming into such a dark Room but stay there, and lie so orderly as to be found upon occasion, it would very much resemble the Understanding of a Man, in reference to all Objects of sight, and the *Ideas* of them."[10] Leibniz, on the other hand, will have no problem with this shadow *(obscura)* in whose room *(camera)* will be enacted the *(mis en)* scene (of a crime: a body is missing). The *Discourse on Metaphysics* (1686) shows nothing but light.[11] It will require but the stroke *(coup)* of Hume to change the face of this picture once and for all, to set—in (the) place of understanding—imagination as the site of all future sights regarding the *camera obscura.*

Hume "draws" his distinction between memory and imagination in terms of their respective representational ability to produce a lively "image" or picture, to *paint* their objects.[12] Consistent with this painting metaphor, he attributes to imagination, vis-à-vis its facility to grasp the object, a certain ability to position the subject itSelf, a position, for the moment, contingent upon both time and space. The *camera obscura* is here; imagination always relates its object to the "present" (time and space). The more remote the object in time or space, the more difficult is the task for imagination, and the greater the pleasure we derive from its use. And though Hume admits "the consequences of a removal in *space* are much inferior to those of a removal in *time*," he nevertheless conceives the function of imagination primordially in spatial terms; for the removal in time is thought as a *distance* between individual successive moments; in effect, imagination positions the subject with respect to its object as a relation of perspective.[13] Something is already sliding, slipping away—from sight: fading from (the) view.

Now here's the coup (de grâce), the rub (out), the prestidigitation: before our very eyes the object disappears (a body is missing). For the greater the distance between subject and object, the nearer we approach the sublime.[14] The sublime itself recedes—indeed, will come to inhabit— the "vanishing point" of the subject. The death of the object is the birth of the subject. We're but a (side) step away from Kant, whose track we follow, and in whose image (make no mistake: this "Copernican revolution" is square, not round) "the world" will be framed—that is, made immanent in the subject, as Husserl observed.

Let's set the stage *(mise-en-scène).* Kant's distinction between empirical ("reproductive") and transcendental ("productive") imagination sets forth the object as that regarding which the subject frames an image. Extending Hume's theory of imagination from the empirical realm to the transcendental, Kant defines imagination as that faculty which not only makes "sense" of the object, enabling the subject to represent its image in the object's absence, but also determines the form of sensation *a priori*. Imaginative activity is "apprehensive"; it mediates sensation and intellection; it contributes to awareness (via representation) insofar as it frames the image. Despite the aesthetic concerns of *The Critique of Judgment* (1790), let's not forget its proposed function. The Third Critique seeks to link understanding to reason by way of judgment, specifically, the "reflective judgment," which from a particular "given" appropriates a universal.[15]

When imagination frames an image for understanding, in ordinary perception, it brings that object before the understanding as a *determinate* concept; in the perception of the object as "aesthetic," on the other hand, imagination frames an image regarding which understanding confirms its concept of the object as *indeterminate*. In aesthetic judgment, imagination is not contingent upon the laws of association; it is free to focus on the (visible) form itself, independent of a concept. Indeed, imagination is liberated from any prior concept whatsoever, and therefore able to set up, install, its own.[16] That is, imagination *freely* frames its images, independent of the determinate concepts of understanding. Here, then, is the scene (of the crime), the very "primal scene," if you will, of the Third Critique— the site upon which "apprehension" will transcend (re-site) the *limit* of "comprehension" (the sensory): a body is missing, whose recitation opens up what Kant will call the "colossal," its own perversion. But I'm ahead of myself.

Kant's further distinction, between the "beautiful" and the "sublime," depends upon the very *possibility* of the frame—on which everything now hangs, excluding the pleasure (principle) of the subject itself, who will receive no gratification as such (interest). The frame *(parergon)* will serve to bracket the subject's desire—the *objet petit a,* as Lacan defines it[17]—for the sake of the "work" itself—its transformation from (psychic) energy *(energeia)* to *ergon*. Morality assumes its place, here, on the installment principle. To be sure, the frame collapses the juncture opened up between the beautiful and the sublime at the site of its installation, the site of "formal" judgment with respect to its end (purpose): an end without (outside) its representation, "beyond" purpose. This is, of course, that very (vanishing) point, prefigured by Hume, in which the object disappears *for the sake of* the spectacle. Forget the disposition of the Real; the object (of knowledge) is gone (by the boards), gone overboard *(bord)*. The frame recovers this loss and opens up the view, installs it. It's all technique *(technē).* The frame is technically a "logic"—what structures, now, the very space of desire, and by means of whose vanishing point it recovers its technology: the technology of desire/desire of technology. What is its "end" if not this purpose: to fix its own ends?[18]

I recall you to Heidegger's critique of this event, that point of departure regarding which "the world" becomes a *view.*[19] It happens in the space of this epoch, within its frame, between the very ("perspective") lines of Kant's Third Critique. The frame equips this space. It is the space of the *subjectum,* of the subject "as" *technē (Ge-stell),* its dis-position to be (at) its own disposal, to be its (own) standing-reserve *(Bestand),* regarding which Heidegger cautions: "man everywhere and always encounters only himself."[20] In Kant, this "view" will be turned back upon the subject, will reflect itSelf, at the point where the spectacle exceeds the frame, spills over as excess, excessive, "colossal." This place is marked by the sublime.

The sublime but indicates the (place of) transfer of an object presented to reason as an indeterminate *idea.* As such, imagination is incapable (impotent) of framing an image; it has before it the form of some object beyond which no further image can be produced, no visible form created: an idea for which there is no ideal. Here is the site of transfer, the site of the subject as "view," the sight of itSelf (spectator *as* spectacle): it will be the spectacle of itSelf. For the sublime is not in nature, as such; "properly speaking, the word should only be applied to a state of mind, or rather to its foundation in human nature" (CJ:121). Here, too, arises the (empty) locus of the moral law: the will that's good in itself (that is itSelf), that knows (owes) its duty to its self, that acts out of respect for the self. (Schopenhauer will object to this subject.) Its duty is immense—and so the site removes itself from quality to quantity.[21] Upon this site, duty will "do its duty," expel the excrement of desire, and in the very name of the *sublime:* "Duty! Thou sublime and mighty name."[22] How fitting that the (proper) name of the sublime recites the place we would expect to see appear the disappearance of desire; for in the Second Critique the subject *will* be moved "objectively" by duty itself, the practical moral law.[23] The categorical imperative knows no other end than itself. It is its own end. And there is only one: the Good.

Now in the Third Critique, sublimity is set against the "colossal"— that is, in effect, the infinite. There is no limit once the site has been (re)moved to quantity: sublimity exceeds the limit of the colossal itself (CJ:91). It exceeds its very frame *(parergon)* precisely insofar as and to the extent that it is not a work *(ergon)*—belonging neither to nature nor art: neither-nor/neuter. Beyond imagination, beyond the frame, it nevertheless belongs to (the frame of) the subject itSelf—and to the subject alone:

"*the bare capability of thinking* this infinite without contradiction requires in the human mind a faculty itself supersensible" (CJ:93). The subject thus recites the site of the colossal as but the sight of itSelf, the subject as sublime, the sublime subject: "it makes us judge as *sublime*, not so much the object, as our own state of mind in the estimation of it" (CJ:94). In light of this magnitude, the object disappears from (the) view, becomes itself the *limit* of the infinitesimally small. Nature as a whole, in its totality, likewise approaches this limit *as object,* as Heidegger observes, once "man has become *subjectum* and the world a view."[24] The subject here exceeds both frame (as its view: itSelf as subject) and view (as its frame: the whole of the existent, including itSelf, as object). It is the measure of the measureless (without), the incommensurable measure (within). As such, the subject posits itSelf "as the setting, in which the existent must from now on represent itself, present itself, that is, be a view or picture. Man becomes the representative of the existent in the sense of the objective."[25] The moral (police) state has been installed. What happens here requires the incommensurate.

For "measure" read "body"; for "measureless" read "mind." In setting "out" (for) the colossal, its starting point must first set up, set before, set "in" (place) (the "average" size of) the *human* body.[26] Setting *in* (place) the colossal will require this standard, as Derrida observes: "It is to this fundamental measurer *(Grundmass)* that the colossal must be related, its excess of cise, its insufficient cise, the almost and the almost too much which holds it or raises or lowers it between two measures."[27] "In" setting *out* the colossal, on the other hand, this size must be erased, removed from its (own) foundation, the site it grounds—in sight of which the colossal now unfolds. Another substitution is in place: for "body" (measure) read "penis"; for "mind" (measureless) read "phallus." In (the) place of the subject as a "fold" *(pli)* in being, the subject now unfolds itSelf as sublime: the colossal subject. What comes of this? Its penis is nothing *(ne pas faire pli)* compared to this colossus in whose name ("sublime") the subject has always already been enfolded as the very possibility of this dimension: the phallus, the Other, the Law of the Law, the Moral Law, The Good. Nature is a midget compared to this colossal (erection of the) subject, the *subjectum* itSelf, the subject as a whole, regarding which the Third Critique now "stands" as both construction of its (own) edifice and edification of its (own) construction. Morality thus finds its home in perversion.

By definition, we're in the realm of the Imaginary. The sublime admits as much. Its simple duality inscribes a set of themes, within the duplicity of binary operations, around the centrality of the subject. The subject's here in its entirety—as a whole. The object alone is missing from this view. Deprived of—detached from—its pleasure, its own desire, the desire of the "other"—Lacan's *objet (a)*—the subject has nothing to adhere to but (the Law of) the Law itself, the Other (capital A: *Autre*). Upon this capital (Lacan) of the "column" (Derrida),[28] the colossal subject is left hanging (limp), reciting the Other, in-siting *its* pleasure in (the) place of its own (now out of sight, gone, *fort*). Thus Kant lines up with Sade: a fascination with the Other at the subject's own expense, the expense of its pleasure—(colossal) perversion.[29] I take this to be the "end," the "moral," if you will, of Derrida's *récit,* his deconstruction of the frame in Kant: the abysmal frame as ultimate frame-up.[30] The moral subject will erect itSelf, will be its own erection: submission to the Law accounts for its colossal alienation.[31] Desire is on the outside looking in (not unlike the "Wolf Man's" dream): a voyeur.[32]

Here "measure" is the rule, the ruler's edge, distance as the instance of its alienation.[33] The "view" is its *récit;* the view re-sites itSelf as story of "the world," the very "life" of the existent as a whole: "As soon as the world becomes a view or picture, the attitude of man is conceived as a world view. . . . the world became a view, as soon as man brought his life as subject into the forefront of the frame of reference."[34] The borders of the Third Critique erect this monument: "To wit: the more completely and thoroughly the conquered world stands at our disposal . . . the more inevitably do contemplation and explanation of the world and doctrine about the world turn into a doctrine of man, into anthropology. It is no wonder that humanism arises only when the world becomes a view. . . . Humanism . . . is therefore nothing but a moral-aesthetic anthropology."[35] The Third Critique itself is but pre-liminary to this border (station), this frame(up)—the subject as colossal psyche *(energeia),* inscription, (art)work, *(par)ergon:* machine: unconscious.

This colossus stands behind the subject, in whose disregard the subject's disappearance has always already been secured in advance, ahead of itSelf *(da).* What stands in front is its colossal erection, the colossal erection of itSelf, unfolded, of no consequence *(ne pas faire pli),* less than nothing, fading (from *(a)* to A) once again *(fort),* in whose regard the subject jumps in head first to take it from behind: the circular abyss of a frame *(fort-da):* without purpose: the very place the subject gets it: in the end.[36] I'll give Heidegger the last word on this:

what is new in this process by no means consists in the fact that now the viewpoint of man in the midst of the existent is simply different over and against that of medieval and ancient man. What is decisive is that man himself takes this viewpoint . . . as the basis of a possible development of humanity. Now, for the first time, there is such a thing as a viewpoint of man. . . . That type of being-a-man begins which uses the sphere of human powers as the place for measuring and accomplishing the mastery of the existent as a whole. The age which is determined by this event is not only . . . a new one . . . but it asserts itself specifically as the new one. To be new is peculiar to the world which has become a view.[37]

The scene is blank: "the world" stands (in) for this trauma: deferred action: deferred understanding: obsession: internal hysteria: (the Wolf Man's here): strangulated affect: no abreaction. The picture will be set in motion. The screen (memory) is coming.

☐

For the Eighteenth Century, the World Existed to End in a Picture[38]
("you oughta be in . . .")

☐

The nineteenth century was a time of stunning technological innovation. Among the numerous inventions of the age, Emerson lists five miracles which appeared in his own lifetime: the steamboat, the railroad, the telegraph, the application of the spectroscope to astronomy, and the photograph.[39] A little ditty expresses what must have been a common sentiment:

> Oh, the world ain't now as it used to was,
>   The past is like a dream, sirs.
> Every thing's on the railroad plan,
>   Though they don't all go by steam, sirs.
>
> Expresses now are all the rage,
>   By steamboat and balloon, sirs,
> In a year or two we'll get the news
>   Directly from the moon, sirs.
>
> The electric telegraphs are now
>   Both time and distance mocking,
> But then, the news which they convey
>   Is really very shocking. . . .
>
> Short hand is now quite out of use,
>   For when the ministers preach, sirs,
> Or politicians rise to spout,
>   They "Daguerreotype" the speech, sirs.[40]

Over and above this surplus of innovation, one technique *(technē)* stands out beyond the rest, and articulates the general technological bias. As

Richard Rudisill remarks, more than any other invention, the daguerreotype became the very metaphor for technology in the public consciousness: "Along with the railroad and the electric telegraph, it had taken
hold of popular imagination as an example of technology. Distinct from
the railroad and the telegraph, the daguerreotype had implications of
symbolic insight which made it an ideal agency for such use. It seemed
to epitomize new means of reaching truth in a form acceptable to
everyone.["41]

Erwin Panofsky incisively summarizes the technological history that
stretches out between the Renaissance and the nineteenth century: "It is
no exaggeration to say that in the history of modern science the advent of
perspective marked the beginning of a first period; the invention of the
telescope and the microscope that of a second; and the discovery of
photography that of a third."[42] Technologically, the "daguerrean view"
reinforced the bias of perspective and its concomitant pictorial orientation insofar as it helped to verify the "location" of both the subject and its
object world. As that which is "real" only to the extent that it is set before
a subject, the world becomes entirely accessible, so it seems, when technology can finally frame an image irrespective of position, an image,
moreover, which appears to coincide with the object perfectly, thus guar-
anteeing both its object space and space of "the world" as a continuous,
uniform *view.* Ensnared by the machine—what seems a "purely" objective technology, divorced from the partial subjectivity inherent in microscopic and telescopic instrumentation—the existent is assumed to be
there, in (the) view, once and for all, and to be so "rationally." This is no
small task. Indeed, given the cumbersome mechanical apparatus atten-
dent upon its birth, the daguerrean machine did, it seems, secure its
capture of the existent within the space of a single "take," in (nothing—
less than) the blink ("click") of an eye *(Augenblick).* Or should I say
"kaboooom?" Yet this duration *is* its very alterity (open/closed), the
condition for (re)presentation in general.[43] (I needn't remind you that, in
its early days, the "blink" was of considerable length.) Let's take another
look at its punctuality.

In 1849, Samuel Dwight Humphrey sent one of his plates of a multiple exposure of the moon to Jared Sparks, then president of Harvard
University, who replied: "We here perceive the apparent motion of the
Moon, or rather the actual motion of the Earth on its axis, distinctly
measured for half a minute's time, within the space of one-tenth of an
inch."[44] Insomuch as time and space are now represented as entirely
measurable functions, as that which can be placed in rational perspective,
they are demonstrated to be calculable and manipulable; they are, in fact,

proven to be exclusively objective, and to be so "really." The daguerreo-type's ability to record a direct image of the subject's location with respect to the moon and stars reasserted its presence in the universe and pushed it further into the forefront of that frame (of reference) by which the existent as a whole would henceforth be envisioned, manipulated, and constituted. The daguerreotype made explicit the central thought of the age; once the subject no longer considers its configuration in the world, but rather proposes itSelf both central figure and frame in terms of which the truth of the world is solely determined and appropriated—that is, insofar as it coincides with its representation—perception is no longer an issue. The world becomes an idea whose essence is nothing short of Newtonian (Euclidian) space. Technology now guarantees it. Henceforth the world "records" the subject as it goes about the business of manipulating and calculating the existent (an imaginary business). If the subject continues to "see" at all, it is to represent that which is looking back. Everything bears witness to the subject's actions, and history becomes its narcissistic image, the universal notebook of its presence. The traces of idealism—to wit, Kant's "Copernican revolution"—bear down upon this new t(r)ack: it is the burden of history, whose own birth as "science" will but partially eclipse the seemingly omnipotent truth of the daguerrean image. It happens as no accident that technology envisions the photograph as the very instrument that frees history (being) from myth (subjectivity), that frees it *for* the object (objective history). With the advent of the photograph, history itself becomes a technique. Here history links up with its envoy (anthropology as "science") of the Third Critique. Heidegger traces the path: "It is because history as research projects and objectifies the past in the sense of a nexus of events which can be explained and surveyed that it requires the critique of sources as the instrument of objectification."[45] The daguerreotype ensures the "source" at its origin: nature.

Edward Hitchcock expresses this connection without reserve: "Men fancy that a wave of oblivion passes over the greater part of their actions. But physical science shows us that those actions have been transfused into the very texture of the universe, so that no waters can wash them out, and no erosions, comminution, or metamorphoses, can obliterate them. . . . *Our words, our actions, and even our thoughts, make an indelible impression on the universe.*"[46] He further envisions the universe as one "vast picture gallery," and defines the universe, in essence, as nothing less than a huge daguerreotype of history which "encloses the *pictures* of the past, like an indestructible and incorruptible record, containing the purest and the clearest truth"; considering the implications that all nature is pervaded by this photographic influence, he observes: "We do not know but it may imprint upon the world around us our features, as they are modified by various passions, and thus fill nature with daguerreotype impressions of all our actions that are performed in daylight."[47] Here Hitchcock perceives history in photographic terms. For all future generations, the "truth" of history will be directly accessible. History and truth will coincide with what can be pictorially apprehended and accurately recorded. As Heidegger suggests, the (true) story of the subject (history) depends upon nature as the site/cite of its inscription.[48] The Third Critique is here as well. Only the represented "fact" is true, and it is true to the extent that its objectivity coincides with the rational. A clandestine affair is at stake.

This collusion between (human) being and nature is strikingly evident in Emerson's *Nature,* where Nature coquettishly acknowledges a human presence in the universe. The essay originally appeared in 1836, and discloses to what extent the stage had been set for its latest technological performance. Like Romanticism, Transcendentalism is largely the product of post-Kantian idealism; and as Romanticism could talk about the truth of nature as a reflection or image of the mind, so too could Transcendentalism speak of a spiritual "insight" based on close observation of nature. For Emerson, each moment is uniquely transcendent in the perception of the object; and if we see it "correctly" we are led to the truth of nature itself. Yet Emerson was no more liberated in his thinking than Coleridge. And though it seems that he "sincerely" envisioned himself as a counter-gradient to the perceptual bias of his age, his thinking remains inextricably tied to the age's most fundamental prejudice—one whose paradigm had been secured by Kant.

In *Nature,* Emerson mirrors this tradition, privileging the visual image—that is, picture and frame. Describing the correspondence between "visible things and human thoughts," he remarks, "Every natural fact is a symbol of some spiritual fact. Every appearance in nature corresponds to some state of the mind, and that state of the mind can only be described by presenting the natural appearance as its picture."[49] And elsewhere: "To the attentive eye, each moment of the year has its own beauty, and in the same field, it beholds, every hour, a picture which was never seen before, and which shall never be seen again" ("Beauty":18). That Emerson uses the word "picture" to such excess suggests he recognizes the moment of vision as a fixed, organized image—anticipating the daguerreotype by three years.[50] Years later, in a journal entry for June, 1862, he returns to this epistemological metaphor, "picture" and its facility for representation: "Two things in picture; 1. representation of nature, which a photograph gives better than any pencil, and a *camera obscura* better than a photograph, and which is a miracle of delight to every eye. 2. an ideal representation, which, by selection and much omission, and by adding something not in nature, but profoundly related to the subject, and so suggesting the heart of the thing, gives a higher delight, and shows an artist, a creator."[51] Already in 1836 this "ideal representation" carries the weight: in order to see nature correctly, "I become a transparent eyeball; I am nothing; I see all; the currents of the Universal Being circulate through me" ("Nature":10). Seeing all, the perceiver becomes a transparent eyeball, thereby escaping the frame of the body as well as the situation of perception itself; such a disembodied being is clearly "nothing," as Emerson would have it. Even so, before this transparent eyeball becomes a nothingness in order to discern the reciprocal transparency of nature and universe, it must condescendingly address the "forms" of nature. As an object of the intellect, "The beauty of nature re-forms itself in the mind, and not for barren contemplation, but for new creation" ("Beauty":23). And again: "The eye is the best of artists. By the mutual action of its structure and of the laws of light, perspective is produced, which integrates every mass of objects, of what character soever, into a well colored and shaded globe, so that where the particular objects are mean and unaffecting, the landscape which they compose is round and symmetrical" ("Beauty":15). Nature is thus "the integrity of impression made by manifold natural objects. . . . There is a property in the horizon which no man has but he whose eye can integrate all the parts" ("Nature":8). Once more, that specific property of the eye able to unify the manifold, to integrate the objects of nature into a continuously uniform space, is characterized by perspective. We've seen this before: the existent is becoming to the subject: it becomes (as pretty as) a picture.

Spatial perspective so permeates his thinking that he defines memory in similar terms: "Visible distance behind and before us, is respectively our image of memory and hope" ("Language":26). The figure echoes Hume. Yet Emerson rhetorically espouses an all-inclusive posture; he facilely accommodates all other systems insofar as they contain a partial truth, a kind of mental "aspect" of nature. Because idealism glibly negotiates all angles simultaneously, sees *through* the angular opacity of matter in terms of a perspective somehow beyond perspective, Emerson judiciously concedes all points of view: "The dawn is my Assyria; the sunset and moonrise my Paphos, and unimaginable realms of faerie; broad noon shall be my England of the senses and the understanding; the night shall be my Germany of mystic philosophy and dreams" ("Beauty":17). Although this remark appears to oblige both empiricism and idealism, truth nonetheless reposes ultimately in the mind. Imagination mediates between reason and sensation in order to arrive at the transparency of the world: "The Imagination may be defined to be the use which Reason makes of the material world" ("Idealism":52). In a passage somewhat reminiscent of Kant's sublime, Emerson speaks of the "eye" of reason, although it seems a pure "vision" of reason is beyond form—a transparency that approximates Kant's formlessness: "When the eye of Reason opens, to outline and surface are at once added grace and expression. These proceed from imagination and affection, and abate somewhat of the angular distinctness of objects. If the Reason be stimulated to more earnest vision, outlines and surfaces become transparent, and are no longer seen; causes and spirits are seen through them" ("Idealism":49–50).

Regardless whether he has Kant's concept distinctly in mind, it's obvious that Emerson's thinking, here, is dominated by the desire to see "through" the world. We can only arrive at reason's vision by cutting down the angular distinctness of matter as it shapes and forms the object; but to do this, imagination must somehow alter the point of view. By changing the point of view we get a new perspective, one whose ultimate totality de-realizes nature amid its fleeting variety of shapes and forms: "Nature is made to conspire with spirit to emancipate us. Certain mechanical changes, a small alteration in our local position, apprises us of a dualism. . . . The least change in our point of view gives the whole world a pictorial air. A man who seldom rides, needs only to get into a coach and traverse his own town, to turn the street into a puppet-show. The men, the women, the boys, the dogs, are unrealized at once, or, at least, wholly detached from all relation to the observer, and seen as transparent, not substantial beings" ("Idealism":50–51). Changing the point of view idealizes the world insomuch as the vision is "wholly detached from all relation to the observer"; Emerson's observer ideally perceives the object from everywhere at once. In theory, only when imagination presents the object from *every* point of view is reason then disposed to see the transparency of nature. No longer "in the world," the vanishing point now nebulously inheres in the formlessness of the "truth" of nature as a whole. "Every universal truth which we express in words, implies or supposes every other truth. *Omne verum vero consonat.* It is like a great circle on a sphere, comprising all possible circles; which, however, may be drawn and comprise it in like manner. Every such truth is the absolute Ens seen from one side. But it has innumerable sides" ("Discipline":44). From the outside looking in (the voyeur is here), only thus does the subject perceive the truth of the existent as a whole: "A fact is the end or last issue of spirit. The visible creation is the terminus or the circumference of the invisible world" ("Language":34–35).

Emerson's reason would thereby define its scope in terms of the infinite; failing to acknowledge the situation, it dislocates itself from the world it seeks to know and, henceforth, ascribes to mind alone what belongs to the body as well. Indeed, to the extent that truth *is* mind, what is set before the subject is, in fact, itSelf. Only because mind expropriates the mirror of truth can nature, in turn, become a "discipline." At times, Emerson's essay reads like a gloss on Kant: when the subject's thoughts equal nature—indeed, exceed it—then, and only then, "the frame will suit the picture. A virtuous man is in unison with her works, and makes the central figure of the visible sphere" ("Beauty":22). Nature thus frames the subject, who in turn frames (the truth of) the world.

In general, idealism doesn't do away with the distinction between subject and object, but rather makes the subject the object of its own observation. Like the seventeenth-century portrait, which gazes in full view upon the observer, idealism establishes a psychological vanishing point in the viewer.[52] "We are taught by great actions that the universe is the property of every individual in it. Every rational creature has all nature for his dowry and estate. It is his, if he will. He may divest himself of it; he may creep into a corner, and abdicate his kingdom, as most men do, but he is entitled to the world by his constitution. In proportion to the energy of his thought and will, he takes up the world into himself" ("Beauty":20). Reason determines the world, constitutes the world, indeed creates the world; through it, we learn the lesson of the subject: "man has access to the entire mind of the Creator, is himself the creator in the finite. This view . . . carries upon its face the highest certificate of truth, because it animates me to create my own world through the purification of my soul" ("Spirit":65). Here "the world" belongs to those who think it best, and existence becomes the thinking of history or, better, the history of thought; for only the rational (perspective) is correct: "In inquiries respecting the laws of the world and the frame of things, the highest reason is always the truest" ("Prospects":66). The manifold in unity, *il piu nell' uno* (Plato's "One": the "Hen") subsequently exists as something "tacked onto" reason whereby nature itself becomes but "an appendix to the soul" ("Idealism":56). This attitude represents a logical extension of Cartesian metaphysics, wherein the existent as a whole is set before the subject insofar as it loses its opacity, becomes transparent.[53] Adding an invisible *quale* over and above the quantum, the epistemology of demand insists upon the consolation of transparency.

In effect, Emerson no more wished to address the structure of vision than did Descartes. Rather than investigate the phenomenon, he would chase the specters of Reason, negotiating formless, objectless perceptions "on the edge of a world that doesn't equivocate"; like Descartes' *Dioptric,* Emerson's *Nature* represents "the breviary of a thought that wants no longer to abide in the visible and so decides to construct the visible according to a model-in-thought."[54] The subject thus secures itself from doubt. By calculation and manipulation, this metaphysics of power determines the existent as subservient:

> The exercise of the Will, or the lesson of power, is taught in every event. From the child's successive possession of his several senses up to the hour when he saith, "Thy will be done!" he is learning the secret that he can reduce under his will not only particular events but great classes, nay, the whole series of events, and so conform all facts to his character. Nature is thoroughly mediate. It is made to serve. It receives the dominion of man as meekly as the ass on which the Saviour rode. It offers all its kingdoms to man as the raw material which he may mould into what is useful. Man is never weary of working it up. . . . One after another his victorious thought comes up with and reduces all things, until the world becomes at last only a realized will,—the double of the man. ("Discipline":39–40)

Let's get this straight: nature is an ass, in whose disregard the subject takes it from the rear (reason as sodomist). This *discipline* or "exercise of the Will" identically re(a)sembles the entirety of Kant's Third Critique, specifically the notion of purposiveness that structures reflexive (aesthetic) judgment in its totality—the subject is the final end of nature: "*if* we assume that men are to live upon the earth, then the means must be there without which they could not exist as animals, and even as rational animals . . . ; and thereupon those natural things, which are indispensable in this regard, must be considered as natural purposes" (CJ:214–15). That is to say, nature as a (w)hole is indispensable (since nothing is dispensable) regarding the subject whose very being (reason) is given to determine its own end(s): "The only being which has the purpose of its existence in itself is *man,* who can determine his purpose by reason. . . . This *man* is, then, alone of all objects in the world, susceptible of an ideal of *beauty,* as it is only *humanity* . . . that is susceptible of the ideal of *perfection*" (CJ:69–70). In this regard *(droit),* the subject is bequeathed full license (freedom) to mess around with nature, to screw it. The propriety of the view now guarantees this inalienable right *(de regard):* nature is the rightful property of the subject who frames it. Nature must con-form to reason. The results, of course, are predictable, as Emerson hastens to observe: "The greatest delight which the fields and woods minister is the suggestion of an occult relation between man and the vegetable. I am not alone and unacknowledged. They nod to me, and I to them. . . . Nature always wears the colors of the spirit" ("Nature":10–11). Nature recognizes the subject, reassures its presence. The subject needs this kind of formal acknowledgment once it locates itself outside the existent as an observer.

Hitchcock's definition of the universe as a vast picture gallery—and history as the all-inclusive daguerreotype—merely constitutes the daguerrean "exposure," if you will, of Emerson's description of idealism, which "beholds the whole circle of persons and things, of actions and events, of country and religion, not as painfully accumulated, atom after atom, act after act, in an aged creeping Past, but as one vast picture which God paints on the instant eternity for the contemplation of the soul" ("Idealism":60). The present of presence/presence of the present is here, beyond the shadow of a doubt. The daguerreotype terminated the emphasis which the age placed on visual representation and its correlative ability to arrive at the truth of nature and reality in general. Consciousness thus comes to be determined by its visual "data," a collection of mental contents. Idealism here shares the very same epistemological assumptions as empiricism. Like pictoral perspective, symbolic insight is fated to remain irreparably divorced from the phenomenon. In this regard, the daguerreotype accommodated both the "realistic" and "transcendental" posture; for over and above its ability to record accurately the object as it appears, the daguerreotype simultaneously articulated the symbolic demand that we see in the object something beyond—that is, that we see "more."

Axiomatically, the daguerreotype was quick to seize the "content" of (perspective) painting as most germane to its own purpose and potential. That very content is, as McLuhan reminds us, another medium *(techne):* the *camera obscura.* Photography's domain, its self-placement *(mise-en-scène),* the arrangement of its room *(camera),* will henceforth be haunted by this paternal ghost *(obscura).* Barthes observes as much: "The first man who saw the first photograph (if we except Niepce, who made it) must have thought it was a painting: same framing, same perspective. Photography has been, and is still, tormented by the ghost of Painting . . . ; it has made Painting, through its copies and contestations, into the absolute, paternal Reference."[55] By means of its *techne* (perspective) photography envisions itself as full, complete, uniform. This (imaginary) presence will repress the "ghost" of painting which inhabits its very frame *(techne),* the trace of what is marginal to itself: the detail. For at the heart *(kern)* of the spectacle is the specter, the return of the dead, what Barthes will call its "punctum," its hole—that which doesn't belong to the context ("studium"), to the image as a whole.[56] The punctum is "out of place," missing; it's (not) a part of the spectacle as a (w)hole: an absence which usurps the (fullness of the) whole. It is, in effect, a writing effect (affect) that doesn't belong to the image (spectacle) as such. The punctum (detail) is the wound, the very "text" of desire: the *objet (a)*. Thus Barthes remarks it as a "supplement," and not "intentional"; the detail (punctum) is timely: "*that* is dead and *that* is going to die."[57] Yet this is marginal, beyond the edges of the *view* (spectacle), belonging to the frame *(technē):* regarding which technology itself is blind. The punctum functions like a particle, a quantum (matter: *res*), an "object" of discourse; it "occupies" a dual, a doubled, a duplicitous space: "detail is offered by chance and for nothing."[58] It is a point of contingency, an "affect."

In itself, the spectacle forecloses this event, to which the history of photography attests. For at its very birth, "daguerrean" idealogy (continuity/uniformity/the whole/the "view") has always already supplanted Fox Talbot's fascination with its specter (contiguity/fragmentation/the part/the "gaze").[59] To wit: the camera as machine *(technē)* dis-figures, decapitates, desire—beside whose fallen figure "lies" only impotence and aggression.[60] And in its "place" appears the literal, the line, the continuous, the uniform, the view. Foreclusion: no slippage *(glissement):* it seeks the one-to-one (Plato's "hen" is back) relation—that is, no relation—between the image and its referent, between signifier and signified. It seeks the literal: this is its "Good" (Kant is back as well). The disappearance of the affect is the disappearance of the body, a "unary" space: the studium devoid of the punctum, the image void of nothing.[61] Nothing *is* missing: to which the spectacle now hands us over. The inside of its view will have no outside, no without, and hence no intimacy, no response.

The photographic image is the guarantor of Being; to its uniform space (perspective) the subject will always already have been bequeathed. Its paternity, the *camera obscura,* authorizes this continuity (genealogy) by means of whose presence, whose (instru)mentality, the image is fully present to itSelf. The "product" is guaranteed, now, by its very process, a process—as Fox Talbot puts it—"by which natural objects may be made to delineate themselves."[62] Technology "authenticates," as it were, (the space of) painting (perspective/*camera obscura*) as both its origin and end. It therefore happens as no coincidence that painting and photography will declare an initial fraternity, that—within a year of its invention—Samuel Morse will have already remarked the daguerreotype's enormous possibility as a determining factor in the art world. In 1840, as president of the National Academy of Design, Morse declared: "The daguerreotype is undoubtedly destined to produce a great *revolution* in art, and we, as artists, should be aware of it and rightly understand its influence. This influence, both on ourselves and the public generally, will, I think, be in the highest degree *favorable* to the character of art."[63] In light of its claim to represent the existent in itself, the daguerreotype supported the realistic function of painting, a function not only endorsed by many painters, but also shared by a large portion of the general public.[64] "Working men and artisans over the country formed a keenly critical audience able to spot an inaccuracy or a distortion of what they knew from experience; in this kind of image recording even more than with landscapes, Americans believed that a picture was 'good' if it was 'true.' Perhaps more than any other form of visual record, the genre paintings illustrated a climate of interest that was favorable for the introduction of photography. Like the panoramas, these pictures prefigured a need for the recording accuracy of the daguerreotype."[65]

In Paris, however, when Daguerre produced his first "sun-paintings," audience response was somewhat qualified; Daguerre's early pictures reflected a magical aura, most notably in terms of their acutely represented detail. The initial rejoinder to the daguerreotype evinced a feeling that something was "missing." The very accuracy of these pictures ironically intensified this magical mood, the eerie representation of Paris, for instance,

> as a city complete to every brick yet totally devoid of life. Since even the most carefully detailed paintings of the age—such as those of David or Ingres—were still oriented to a central concern with humanity, people were used to thinking of pictures as centering on man. Since it was also the period of Romantic painting, pictures were expected to idealize the world by addition or suppression or interpretation. Now, suddenly, people in one of the most art-conscious cities of the world were confronted with pictures that were uncompromisingly acute in itemizing the details of the world but which simultaneously removed all trace of human life. The absence of color in such otherwise perfect representations further stressed this effect, as did the curious negative-positive character of the image on a perfect mirror surface that turned realistic scenes into ghostly negative images with the slightest change of viewing angle.[66]

What's missing, this "ghostly negative image," is nothing short of the subject itSelf. To compensate for this apparent void in the photographic "still-life," its ghostly absence, the "subject" will again (re)position itSelf in the forefront of the frame, declaring the daguerrean process an art. The daguerreotypist becomes an "artist," a maneuver especially necessary for an audience which could only think in terms of visual conditioning centered around (a human) presence, particularly so in painting; by comparison, the daguerreotype must have seemed peculiarly, if not frighteningly, devoid of the human "touch." Ironically, the painters were among the first to recognize the daguerreotype's artistic significance: Delacroix, for example, made elaborate use of the photographic medium for his own drawings; and Paul Delaroche, in a remark singularly pertinent to the over-worked comparison to Rembrandt's etchings, said of the daguerreotype, "Color is translated with so much truth that its absence is forgotten."[67] Whatever mysterious meaning Delaroche may have intended, comparison with Rembrandt immediately became a general touchstone "for discussing the monochromatic continuous-tone subtleties of light and dark which had never been seen before, and the medium's acuteness of rendering of atmospheric conditions was a constant marvel."[68]

Already, in 1839, the year of its birth, N. P. Willis, the "sunshine and summer" columnist as S. G. Goodrich called him in contradistinction to the "chill, dark, and wintry" Hawthorne,[69] said of the daguerreotype: "All nature shall paint herself—fields, rivers, trees, houses, plains, mountains, cities shall all paint themselves at a bidding, and at a few moment's notice. Towns will no longer have any representative but themselves. Invention says it. It has found out the one thing new under the sun; that, by virtue of the sun's patent, all nature, animate and inanimate, shall be henceforth its own painter, engraver, printer, and publisher."[70] Fittingly, Willis would be counted among Hawthorne's bunch of "scribbling women"; he nevertheless prefigures, here, the terms in which the daguerreotype generally would be discussed. Rather than deny the daguerreotypist his "art," Willis' comment merely points to the difference between the European and American attitude toward painting at the time. Unlike the European reaction which focused on the creativity of the individual artist, the American attitude tended to emphasize the objects of nature as the "formal" constituents of art. In this respect, American painting principally attended to nature rather than the artist. Behind the theoretical divergence, however, one constant emerges: the daguerreotype must tell the truth; it cannot lie.[71]

In 1840, expressing a desire for this kind of absolute certainty, one of the great "rationalists" of the nineteenth century, Edgar Allan Poe, unequivocally stated the daguerreotype's superiority in this respect: "In truth the daguerreotype plate is infinitely more accurate than any painting by human hands. If we examine a work of ordinary art, by means of a powerful microscope, all traces of resemblance to nature will disappear—but the closest scrutiny of the photographic drawing discloses only a more absolute truth, more perfect identity of aspect with the thing represented."[72] Poe's "more perfect identity of aspect with the thing represented" best describes the nineteenth-century technological attitude in general, a bias grounded in "rational" perspective, the correspondence between subject and object. And whether that view focused outward upon the object or inward upon the subject—as an object of "study"—it invariably employed imitation (correspondence) as its criterion for truth, the resemblance between image and object. The daguerreotype conferred a finality upon the existent in the sense that certainty no longer depended upon, or con-formed to, a physical organ or mental faculty. Released from the subjectivity inherent in microscopic or telescopic instrumentation, as well as the extreme "inaccuracies" inherent in a painting or drawing, the mirror-image "correctly" reflected the existent in its absolute truth: "A painting may omit a blemish, or adapt a feature to the artist's fancy, but a reflected image must be faithful to its prototype."[73]

Paradoxically, this attitude likewise decreed the daguerreotype a medium capable of symbolic "insight": the photographic image could apprehend the object in the truth of its "form." Insofar as idealism demands resemblance between external and internal "world," phenomena always already disclose a pre-existent "reason"; formal identity de-problematizes the maximum coherence of "the world"; it is, instead, the very condition of its possibility (Kant).[74] Symbolic "insight" illuminates the world to the extent that it *projects* the internal in the external, or vice versa. In the same way, the daguerreotype's symbolic function enhanced its potential to define and perpetrate a national image which at once became "historical" and "true," a symbolic reality. The possibility of publicly recording, for all time and place, an event or personality instigated a national or group consciousness: "When bodies of people taking part in noteworthy events were so deliberately involved with pictorial situations, a form of group consciousness of communication with later generations was activated. . . . The commonality of public experience in the picture-making situation from one part of the United States to another tended to universalize the responses of the people into national behavior and attitudes held in general"; public response to the daguerreotype consequently revealed a sense of historic iconology: "Merely by its presence, such a body of pictures conditioned the process of visual perception along particular lines of development so that people came to conceive of certain kinds of visual images as being true, or permanent, or typical."[75] Here, "the value attached to the subject of a picture was often transferred to the picture itself in a way that allowed the picture not only to reflect attitudes or feelings but to affect them in terms of what people saw and how they saw it."[76]

Nothing substantiated the symbolic function of the daguerreotype more than its relation to light. In *Nature,* Emerson had likewise remarked the efficacy of light in perception: "And as the eye is the best composer, so light is the first of painters. There is no object so foul that intense light will not make beautiful. And the stimulus it affords to the sense, and a sort of infinitude which it hath, like space and time, make all matter gay" ("Beauty":15). With the daguerreotype, however, nature could immediately paint itself; as the direct and absolute image of light, its very *body,* these "sun-paintings" represented a "shadow" cast across the instant eternity. And here, as Barthes suggests, a second *technē* informs the photograph in more essential ways than painting: "It is often said that it was the painters who invented Photography (by bequeathing it their framing, the Albertian perspective, and the optic of the *camera obscura*). I say: no, it was the chemists. For the *noeme* 'That-has-been' was possible only on the day when a scientific circumstance (the discovery that silver halogens were sensitive to light) made it possible to recover and print directly the luminous rays emitted by a variously lighted object."[77] Barthes echoes Morse, who called the products of this process *fac-simile* sketches of nature; as such, these images "painted by Nature's self with a minuteness of detail which the pencil of light in her hands alone can trace . . . cannot be called copies of nature, but portions of nature herself."[78] Where nature inscribes itself, the "text" is (literally) true. Photography verified the Newtonian "divinity" of light. Much was made of the truth of this direct image, and the daguerreotype machine became a kind of mystical medium capable of asserting its own agency in the production of truth—as though the machine itself could capture the real, independent of its image (perception). Speaking of his own machine, James F. Ryder expressed the sentiment ingenuously: "The box was the body, the lens was the soul, and an 'all-seeing eye,' and the gift of carrying the image to the plate."[79] It would be stretching the point to see a difference, here, between this "eye" and Emerson's: even Clark Kent's stopped at lead. We are recalled, of course, to the *camera obscura,* whose "physiology" reflected the same (sexual) features: a sexless being whose (w)hole has been plugged for good (truth).

Symbolic insight here is impotent, blind, a reified version of Emerson's transparent eyeball which, in its ability to capture the general effect as well as the specific detail, sees through the world to its ultimate meaning, a transcendental signified. This claim to truth (universality) but mirrors the heart of its bourgeois desire.[80] Now the photographer, due to his superior "selective understanding" of the existent and in conspiracy with the "penetrating power of the camera-eye," unabashedly guarantees the truth of his presentation. The photograph no longer even represents the object, but becomes the representation of how well the photographer understands the object before he objectifies it. This "pat on the back" *(coup)* in no way cuts; there is no loss to be recuperated. Barthes observes as much of this inversion: "In an initial period, Photography, in order to surprise, photographs the notable; but soon, by a familiar reversal, it decrees notable whatever it photographs."[81] The image is thereby set in (its) place, set before us, "brought to light" (reason) in (the) place of the real. Regarding truth, there's no room left for the shadow. Its own historian, light reveals nature as some sort of mysterious agent in subtle and unexpressed complicity with being. The ironic moment here reveals its familiar reversal: once the object exists in the mind of the subject (artist) before it's "taken" or captured, photography has always already inverted its original aesthetic. Light itself is left behind. Reality no longer appears. Disenfranchised from the object (of vision), the image defenestrates the scene of perception.

In its initial stage, light does all the work. The object itself is pregnant, full of meaning. Blinded, missing from the scene of the object, the subject takes up its (sun) glasses in order to acknowledge, to recognize, to record the image of (itself reflected in) (the mirror of) nature— Niepce's "heliography," for instance: something is/was "really" "out" there, "in" the world, as though we never "imagined" it in the first place. Photography's later date (with the object) will turn this scenario on its head—a tale of fullness once again; but now the subject (artist) is pregnant (with meaning): the object itself is missing from (the scene of) the subject who sees into it, *through it,* as the site/sight of the concept, the idea *(eidos).* The subject (artist) throws out his camera and reels it back in *(fort-da):* yet it's no longer the representation (image) itself which makes present the (missing) subject (object), but rather the *act* of representation which, in its semblance as subjectivity (art), would (dis)guise the (dis)appearance of the object. In either case, initial or later scene, the subject's encounter with the object is simply a *"rendez-vous,"* as Duchamp puts it—a *rendezvous,* I need hardly add, with itSelf.[82] It is, in fact, always and everywhere, a blind date: the scene of the voyeur: the subject who sees (knows) but is not seen. Its ironic moment but constitutes the subject's disappearance from the scene (of) itSelf.

As the site of ("pregnant") meaning, moreover, both these scenes ("seeing"/"more") again suggest a crime. For what is "seeing more," this "surplus" of the essence of things, if not an ethos (Kant) of vision—an essentialist moment directed against (that is, the [subl(im)ated] murder of) the time of the subject: a (sublime) *memento mori?*[83] This in-sight buys it time, hands the subject over to its "proper" place (site): an imaginary coincidence of real and ideal (surreal). Idealism becomes the lure of the specular—the mirror image regarding which the subject (artist) deflects its capture in the scopic drive. The image thus forecloses on the real, the thing-in-itself. Displaced by the *subjectum,* the image not only represents the subject's understanding of the object, but likewise represents the subject as the object of knowledge: who is (sup)*posed* to know. That is, the "subject" (matter) of the image becomes the "object" of the subject's knowledge (of the object)—the very object of knowledge itself. The view again will guarantee as much. There's nothing abysmal here; it is a matter of coincidence. Fully present (identical) to itSelf, the subject (artist) thereby escapes the question of (formal) identity. It coincides with the Real: it *is* itSelf. Having placed itself "in the picture" (as the picture), the subject tenaciously holds to this image by which it constitutes "the world" (understood as a view). The more it pursues the calculation, manipulation, and objectification of the existent, the more prominently it places itSelf in the forefront of the frame. I recall you to Heidegger: "That the world becomes a view is one and the same process with that by which man, within the existent, becomes a *subjectum.*"[84] We've seen (the scene of) this crime before: a body is missing. I defer, once more, its (dis)solution.

It therefore happens as no accident that (human) being, already ahead of itself, becomes the subject of its own picture. The daguerrean portrait "objectively" places the "subject" in the picture, literally terminating the anthropological tangent of nineteenth-century hero worship. Emerson's early thinking, for instance his lectures on *Biography* (1835), reiterates Carlyle's *On Heroes, Hero-Worship, and the Heroic in History,* and the nineteenth-century approach to history in general. And his *Representative Men* (1850), though somewhat tempered by a growing emphasis on dialectic so that society as well as the individual is given a positive role in the historical synthesis, denotes a contiguous attitude insofar as the individual abides *as* "representative."[85] Subjectivity *represents* the determination of historical events, the age, and does so in terms of a fixed and static vision, a moment in time. Even if that moment now resides in either the dialectical thesis or antithesis, which taken as a relation is always "moving" toward synthesis, the vision itself remains permanently fixed in its truth. In other words, the "face" of the subject, if you will, represents the existent as a whole in no less a dogmatic sense than Swedenborg's theory of correspondences. And though it seems fair to say with Charles Feidelson that Swedenborg "was Emerson's favorite whipping boy" regarding the stasis of Swedenborg's doctrine of symbolism,[86]

Emerson's view in *Representative Men* is equally retrospective or static insomuch as it discovers the dynamics of an age by looking back at an individual as representative—and frames that perspective, moreover, as one which will be correct and true for all future generations who subsequently look back.

In such a way, the meaning of history never belongs to the present, much less the future, but remains the counterfeit property of the past, "an object of tender regard."[87] The interpretation of history is in no way "subject" to change because the subject has become an object for study, a "discipline." Anchored in the past, these fixed lines of force secure the subject's position in the future with finality. The future (perfect) is its past. *Geist* worships in (the place of) the photographer's studio: once upon a time, it will have been (in) a photo album. Of course, by its very nature, as a *view* into the past, the portrait frames or isolates a moment which represents the "subject" of history as a timeless object, an object out of time. It was only with the photographic *technē* (mechanical reproduction), however, that "everyman" could become a hero—though, to be sure, this is no return to medieval non-perspectivism. Rather, the daguerreotype offered the subject every opportunity to "own" (nothing short of capitalism is on the line here) itSelf as (public) object (a commodity)—to have, in its keeping, this most precious of all possessions, a perspective on its (private) life, exhibited at will, and thereby sustaining the claim that *every* life participates in the existent significantly. In turn, daguerreotype calling cards became the latest social currency.[88]

In its ironic moment, therefore, the daguerrean portrait levels down the very notion of the hero as representative of an age (a double leveling, in fact)—a *technē* which double-crosses itself, as Kierkegaard observes: "With the daguerreotype everyone will be able to have their portrait taken—formerly it was only the prominent; and at the same time everything is being done to make us all look exactly the same—so that we shall only need one portrait."[89] With this reversal, technology undoes the heroic thread of history: "great men" no longer represent its story (myth). The portrait no longer pictures or brings to life the past as present ("living" history), but rather consigns the present to the past, to the grave, before it is lived (history "in the making"). As Barthes observes, the photographic image has no future: "Motionless, the Photograph flows back from presentation to retention."[90]

Unlike the portrait painting, "regarding" which the subject projects itSelf as an "authentic" moment of the future (the "spirit" of the age lives on), daguerrean portraiture bequeaths the subject ("matter") to the past (dead meat) as an object of future consumption ("look here; remember when . . . "). It does this, moreover, in the disguise of the "present," the subject's presence to itSelf. Its need to possess this souvenir of itSelf, itSelf as spectacle, betrays its desire to be immortal, outside time—that is, spatial: (part of) a collection that now stands (in) for (represents) the (second-hand) experience of its owner. Its "life" is its most treasured *possession.* The proof is in this (re)collection, which here attests to the subject's understanding of itSelf as unrepeatable—no longer "subject" to repetition (recollection), to time (the return of the repressed)—with memory having gone by the boards, over the edge *(bord),* overboard. Its being *(das Ereignis)* is an album of unique events, and hence its need for souvenirs. These portraits will remind it of itSelf.[91] And if the subject *is* (its) past, surpassing itself in having passed itSelf by, it is the same for everyone: the subject matter is The Past. By means of technology, (the subject of) history is always already dead, a corpse, meat for the freezer. History is wrested, set free, from its myth (the Hero), the image divorced from its narrative, the scene from its scenario. As McLuhan suggests, the daguerrean portrait transformed people into things insofar as it extended and multiplied the human image to the proportions of mass-produced merchandise.[92] Daguerrean technique made everyman the subject of history and history the object of everyman. Regarding this democratization, Melville's *Pierre* already does Kierkegaard one better: "instead of, as in old times, immortalizing a genius, a portrait now only *dayalized* a dunce. Besides, when every body has his portrait published, true distinction lies in not having yours published at all."[93]

In "no time" whatsoever, the portrait became the mainstay of the daguerreotypist's trade, and portrait galleries arose in every major city. While the European tradition of daguerrean portraiture emphasized aesthetic composition, the American portrait, ironically, stressed a central figure (everyman as hero). The typical method presented the subject in direct light against a dark background. This, in effect, toned down the purely realistic or compositional aspect of the portrait while playing up the symbolic. Thus, European daguerreotypes, in general, seem more "self-contained than is the immediate moment hacked out of the passing scene often shown in American pictures. This sort of jagged directness tends to emphasize the 'truth and reality' of the American picture in a way suggesting that the picture is less a distinct entity than a view *into* the world beyond it in an almost Emersonian sense."[94] Daguerrean portraiture, presenting the high-lighted subject set off against a dark background, again recalls Rembrandt's own technique. Similarly, at the photographic exhibit for the London World's Fair, the jury reported: "America stands alone for stern development of character, her works, with few exceptions, reject all accessories, present a faithful transcript of the subject and yield to none in excellence of execution. . . . The portraits stand forward in bold relief upon a plain background. The artist, having placed implicit reliance upon his knowledge of photographic science, has neglected to avail himself of the resources of art."[95] Rather than paint in a scene or background ("the resources of art"), American daguerreotypists preferred the more direct contrast between light and dark as a significant commentary on the subject. Concerning his own technique, Gabriel Harrison explained: "In daguerreotyping, as well as in painting, the artist should endeavor to secure three distinct and marked peculiarities that can hardly fail of making his production a superior work of art. These three points are the high lights, the middle tints, and the shadow"; he further remarked that when tonal gradations define the effect in this way, the daguerreotypist will ensure himself a picture "whose deep and Rembrandt-like shadow contrasts finely with the clear distinct tone of the high light, while the middle tints exhibit an elasticity of appearance so pure and lifelike, that the flesh seems imbued with motion, and the dull, frosty, death-like representation, that is so detestable in a work of art, is studiously avoided."[96]

Upon this very point ("punctum")—that is, (a)voiding the void of "death-like representation"—I now return you to the scene of the crime: (1) in which a body is missing, and (2) regarding which the (dis)solution of this murder is itself self-evident. As we'd expect, a certain violence inhabits this (primal) scene respecting whose ghost it will remain photography's t(r)ack to repress. The scene is Paris, 1855, the Universal Exposition. Its scenario, indeed, exposes the violation of itSelf: a technique for retouching the photographic image. And for the very first time, it's understood the photograph can "lie" *(touché):* its very *technē* retouches (encounters) itSelf. And so the spectacle of the image is always already handed over to this scene, the spectral: its ghost. So too, the photographer (artist) now enters the scene as the agent of death—has always already been its agent insofar as the image *can* (always) *be* touched (up), has always been (re)touched with respect to (vis-à-vis) an "other" scene "as if by chance"—that is, the Real. Regarding this encounter, the photographic image re-verses itself, re-turns the "negative" (original) to "positive" (a copy).[97] The Real is a cliché, itself untouchable: it "lies" behind the return: is always missed. The image (phantasy) conceals ("screens") this trauma. Unlike a painting, for instance, the photograph cannot transcend its content.[98] And yet the realization of its "content" will never be sufficient to "memorize," to re(a)semble, itSelf.[99] In s(p)ite of this encounter, the spectacle will defer the specter (negative) that inhabits the spec(tac)ular (positive), that which unnerves (tic) the spectacle itself, its very (un)doing. This *is* its punctuality. The technique of en-largement will only exacerbate its (dis)order: the real-ization of greater detail (the limit, here, is nothing short of infinite: desire) undoes, "in itself," the very image as a whole. This very *technē* will post the image toward its future: the time of the image subverts the phantasy of its timelessness. In this event, the *motion* picture will halt, delay, disrupt this day-dream: yet only for the instant (post-haste).[100] It but returns, again the self-same scene. In this epoch, the photograph will (re)enact the (primal) scene of the crime.[101] Here it comes apart at the seam *(parergon)*—the image bereft of a body, the post bereft of a material document for transport.[102] Its *technē* now "anticipates" computerized production of the image and its transmission (post). Repressing the ghost of what remains outside its frame, the photographic image looks forward *(regarder)* to everything but itSelf *(se regarder):* it cannot see itself, just as it "cannot convey all the linguistic senses of *se regarder,* namely that it can-not show two people looking into each other's eyes."[103] Vis-à-vis itself, it's blind. This blind spot is the way in which it stands outside, escapes, the ghost of the gaze, the specter of the specular, the obliquity of the scopic drive; this blind spot is the "part" it plays *(fort-da)* in the fullness of itself, the oneness of its whole, the presence of its present: the very circuit of the (partial) drive.

In the "mean time," photography conceals what's missing, represses the (missing) body by means of its focus and—yes—its vanishing point, through whose instrumentality everything is present in the picture and beyond which nothing *is* missing: a continuous, uni-form, uni-versal space, a view beyond which nothing can op-pose it. Everything is here—nothing outside, not even the subject: who is now frame and view at once. There is (nothing outside) the spectacle. Thus by a curious inver-sion, Barthes' remark makes sense: the photograph is closer to theatre than to painting.[104] Let's push it further: the "outer limit" of the spectacle inscribes its paranoia. Barthes draws the line at the (vanishing) point of the spectator who intentionalizes the referent—"the *necessarily* real thing which has been placed before the lens."[105] I would say, rather, that in the spectacle, the spectator becomes the referent, becomes One with (the view) itSelf; the spectator itSelf becomes spectacular: identification is complete. Reciprocally, Guy Debord remarks the inversion or inner limit of the spectacle regarding society as a whole, its schizophrenia: "The spectator's consciousness, imprisoned in a flattened universe, bound by the *screen* of the spectacle behind which his life has been deported, knows only the *fictional* speakers who unilaterally surround him with their commodities and the politics of their commodities. The spectacle, in its entirety, is his 'mirror image.' Here the stage is set with the false exit of generalized autism."[106] Cut off from the Other, this form of alienation underscores the subject's phantastic structure. Being One with the image *is* Being itself—that is, no one in particular: neither subject of nor subject to desire. Hence Sontag's brilliant *coup:* the camera eye makes everyone a tourist in reality.[107]

The image, here, is not without its economics (the desire not to desire); for nothing short of consumerism is at stake. "The spectacle results only in speculation."[108] In "the Age of Mechanical Reproduction," the circuit of distribution approaches the limit of saturation, a vicious circle: "Mass reproduction is aided especially by the reproduction of masses."[109] Forget "aided especially by": I see no difference between this scene and that which represses enlargement of the image, its detail. The view remains continuous, uniform, anonymous, its objects interchangeable; the limit of circulation/saturation is but the "point" at which identity breaks down, becomes "identical" (to). As Benjamin observes, "In big parades and monster rallies, in sports events, and in war, all of which nowadays are captured by camera and sound recording, the masses are brought face to face with themselves. This process, whose significance need not be stressed, is intimately connected with the development of the techniques of reproduction and photography. Mass movements are usually discerned more clearly by a camera than by the naked eye. A bird's eye view best captures gatherings of hundreds of thousands."[110] While this process may be "intimately" connected to techniques of reproduction, there's nothing intimate here; for if the masses are brought "face to face with themselves," the image (bird's eye), the view, will guarantee they are faceless. Finder's keeper's: the viewfinder negotiates property. Though such a view, Benjamin continues, "may be as accessible to the human eye as it is to the camera, the image received by the eye cannot be enlarged the way a negative is enlarged"; here Benjamin is on the money: "With the close-up, space expands. . . . The enlargement of a snapshot does not simply render more precise what in any case was visible, though unclear: it reveals entirely new structural formations of the subject."[111] The space of the camera thus stands (in) for the unconscious itself. As I have argued, however, regarding this "development," it's toward the suppression of detail, of desire, of the *objet petit a*—at its expense (this is the price)—that the photographic image secures the spectacle. If it imag(in)es anything, it is itself *as* (the) Real.

This I take to be the (end of the) end (purposiveness) of the frame in Kant. Mechanical reproduction not only "does in" the original image, the artisanal production, [112] but its referent as well—that is, the "real" to which it refers. The spectacle is *more alive* than "what" it represents. The spectacular subject is the very object of the image. Here nothing "matters." Regarding this view without affect (desire), "the world" is an indifferent "place." By a similar reversal of "logic," the age of mechanical reproduction projects the subject in the mode of the image. The image (of the body) is the body (of the image). Only thus does the "thing" become ghostly "in" and "of" itself, the revenant of the real. This event still waits for (psycho)analysis to trace the ghost of the subject insofar as its "reality" appears in the Imaginary. The real itself remains, no longer even re-membered: to see, to perceive, to look upon the "real thing" is, in effect, to disbelieve it, to take it as false—for what it's not. Reality is an illusion, the delusion of "the world." Susan Stewart observes as much:

> the body of lived experience is subject to change . . . death. The idealized body implicitly denies the possibility of death—it attempts to present a realm of transcendence and immortality, a realm of the classic. This is the body-made-object . . . as potential commodity, *taking place* within the abstract and infinite cycle of exchange.
>
> Within the development of culture under an exchange economy, . . . the lived relation of the body to the phenomenological world is replaced by a nostalgic myth of contact and presence. . . . In this process of distancing, the memory of the body is replaced by the memory of the object, a memory standing outside the self and thus presenting both a surplus and lack of significance. The experience of the object lies outside the body's experience. . . . the seriality of mechanical modes of production leads us to perceive that outside as a singular and authentic context of which the object is only a trace. [113]

Such is the (perspective) space of "the world" (reproduced) as a view (spectacle).

It's not for nothing that, *in* the spectacle, death itself becomes unreal: that exception which must be "captured" to prove it "exists." If, and for as along as, I (try to) imagine death, I am exempt from it. Death is always already a thing of the past: I have passed it by—have overtaken the very thing for which there is no longer any wait. No wonder that the image of death itself becomes a favorite subject in the epoch of the spectacle. [114] This "subject" is, in turn, ("becoming" to) the death of photography: its self-consuming moment. Barthes pushes this notion to its extreme. The very "spectrum" or referent *(eidolon)* of the photograph is death: "Ultimately, what I am seeking in the photograph taken of me (the 'intention' according to which I look at it) is Death: Death is the *eidos* of that Photograph." [115] This is the trick: "imagine" death. No longer marginal, the subject and its time are now outside response, without deferment. Spectacular consciousness no longer experiences its life as passage.[116] Time is (no longer) on the line: its "space" aligns itself as inter-exchangeable commodity. No longer eye to eye (vis-à-vis), spectacular consciousness knows only a disrespect to, disregard for, the regard itself *(se regarder):* an eye for an eye, view for view—a capital production. Circulation takes (up its) place *(mise)* within the very scene that will efface it: it is on track: the railroad, here, begins the process of eliminating space itself—and (at the same) time. This ironic moment (reversal) illustrates its own inversion. The epoch which eliminates geographical distance reproduces distance internally as spectacular separation: "In a society where no one can any longer be *recognized* by others, every individual becomes unable to recognize his own reality. Ideology is at home; separation has built its world."[117] Having jumped the track, consciousness side-steps the very border(s) of its being: the spectacular subject is *(part* of) the public domain. By means of its *technē,* the "view" now guarantees as much: transparency but opens onto secret surveillance, exploitation, policing the subject from behind *(manque d'égards)* the veil of the voyeur.[118]

Thus treating the subject as "part" of its single, uniform, continuous object-space, technology lays claim to the authority of its truth *(trait)*—the truth of its authority. That vision can take *(viser/s'arbitrer)* an ultimate form (of authority) but mirrors the way in which technology assumes its pose, retraces the path on which technology and history both implicate the scene (as the crime), send being (subjectivity) on its way, a way, away *(da/fort: weg:* "go away"). Destruction will bring the point home regarding which the camera-eye will always already have seen, have held, this end (purpose) in (its) view (finder: *parergon).* As Steinbeck observed in World War II, "The camera is one of the most frightening of modern weapons, particularly to people who have been in warfare, who have been bombed and shelled, for at the back of a bombing run is invariably a photograph. In back of ruined towns, and cities, and factories, there is aerial mapping or spy mapping, usually with a camera."[119] In light of this (transparent) view, its pose (perspective), its placement *(Ge-stell),* technology pro-poses to frame *(parergon)* "the world," im-poses this *technē* as the very zero-point of the *sub-jectum:* there is nothing to see, to hear, to sup-pose *(poiēsis).*[120] It therefore threatens to foreclose, close down, those stations *(le poste)* of the post that open onto and beyond the frame (out-posts) of what's staked out, its (proper) domain *(droit de regards),* its territory. In this disguise *(poste de police)* it promises to overtake its envoys from behind, from the rear: posterior. A police state menaces the very freedom of the post. This is the issue: its posterity.

We are inveterately deceived should we think technology had ever been—"once upon a time"—the handmaiden of science. It is the other way around, that path *(weg)* whose traces I promised to track at the head of this journey, whose (circuitous) destination is now in view, whose tale is now in sight, whose (de)tail is now in site (point blank), and at whose end (insight) we now take aim—a final moment organized, not unlike the Kantian frame itself, in view of an end ("purpose") whose end is never in view *(but en blanc),*[121] and regarding whose destiny the critique of the spectacle can only defer. To wit: the *camera obscura* (perspective) created the very possibility of (an "objective") science. The subsequent development of all the sciences during the Renaissance was directly contingent upon this revolutionary *technē*. As Panofsky observes, perspective laid the foundation for advances in botony, palaeontology, physics, zoology, and both projective and analytical geometry.[122] Leonardo's *Situs* drawings and the attendant science of anatomy were predicated on this new pictorial technique which could now describe/proscribe/prescribe/subscribe/inscribe the interior of the body as well as "the (external) world" itself. Telescope and microscope had further magnified this object-space. But with the photograph, the technological mission *(envois)* had entered a new epoch(ē) that would extend the transparency of the camera-eye to the "end" of the twentieth century (and beyond). In "so far as" the photograph was able to capture the interior gestures of both matter and mind, it constituted the foundation not only for particle physics, but for the "world" of psychopathology as well.[123] The critique which goes beyond the spectacle must know how to wait.[124] Meanwhile, it has always already gathered its emissaries, its strength *(poiēsis).*

The
World of
Hawthorne's
Work

○

For the nineteenth century, the daguerreotype securely located the subject within the perspective coordinates of the world understood as a view. Yet, as McLuhan remarks, violent technical innovation engenders alienation and the pain of

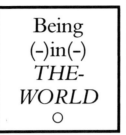

isolation in any age.[1]

Hawthorne's fiction ex-   presses the alienation and
pain of isolation which   his own age experienced,
and does so only because   he was eminently aware
of the condition of his en-   vironment. His fiction
condemns the uncon-   scious bias of perception
in his own culture, and   thus opens the possibility
of new perceptions with   respect to the counter-
environments of the fic-   tional world itself. In this

respect, McLuhan observes, "Ordinary human instinct causes people to recoil from these new environments and to rely on the rear-view mirror as a kind of repeat or *ricorso* of the preceding environment"; the artist, on the other hand, has the power to discern the current environment created by the latest technology: "The function of the artist in correcting the unconscious bias of perception in any given culture can be betrayed if he merely repeats the bias of the culture instead of readjusting it. In fact, it can be said that any culture which feeds merely on its direct antecedents is dying. In this sense the role of art is to create the means of perception by creating counterenvironments that open the door of perception to people otherwise numbed in a nonperceivable situation."[2] Although it is difficult to assess the degree to which Hawthorne was consciously aware of himself as the creator of counter-environments, his fiction clearly speaks against the age, and does so with remarkable consistency.

Perhaps what he most generally reproved about his age was its attitude toward the visual sense, an attitude which overwhelmingly reflected the major bias of his day as it appeared vis-à-vis technology—specifically, the "daguerrean" world-view. His use of mirrors, for example, counterbalances the transilluminated image of the daguerrean plate; rather than perfectly reflect the world, his mirrors obliquely demonstrate its perceptual opacity prior to reflection itself. The mirror translates the reflexivity of the sensible, that in which my own externality completes itself, as Merleau-Ponty has remarked: "More completely than lights, shadows, and reflections, the mirror image anticipates, within things, the labor of vision."[3] The body image transcends itself to become a specter in its own right: the double or "other" of the self. Vision already contains within its very structure this "doppelganger technique." Above all else, the mirror teaches us the lesson that re-flection is always already re-moved from its origin. "Monsieur du Miroir," for example, ironically illustrates

43

the futility of any attempt to capture "the picture or visible type of what I muse upon, that my mind may not wander so vaguely as heretofore, chasing its own shadow through a chaos, and catching only the monsters that abide there."[4] For Hawthorne, the gaze itself might function as a mirror, provoking one's double or shadow—as with Hester Prynne: "Once, this freakish, elfish cast came into the child's eyes, while Hester was looking at her own image in them . . . and, suddenly, . . . she fancied that she beheld, not her own miniature portrait, but another face in the small black mirror of Pearl's eyes. It was a face, fiend-like, full of smiling malice, yet bearing the semblance of features that she had known full well, though seldom with a smile, and never with malice, in them" (I:97). Furthermore, like many painters who use the mirror to paint themselves in the act of painting, Hawthorne's narrators frequently employ "mirrors" in order to write themselves into the writing. Indeed, on an aesthetic level, the mirror "mirrors" Hawthorne's maieutic narrative method. Often his "socratic" narrator not only questions the subject-matter and audience, but repeatedly interrogates himself. In so doing, he places a "counter" image before himself, an opaque alternative which re-creates the ambiguous dialectic of "within" and "without." This primordial ambiguity sets the tone throughout much of the oeuvre, for the self-interrogative narrator is often the source of the irony as well. Like Matisse, Hawthorne enjoyed drawing the self into the very structure of the work: "Farewell, Monsieur du Miroir! Of you, perhaps, as of many men, it may be doubted whether you are the wiser, though your whole business is REFLECTION" (X:171).[5]

Inescapably, Hawthorne's fiction is predominantly visual; but to the extent that it is visual at all, it is always counter-visual: its perception runs antithetical to the public bias. Throughout his life, Hawthorne remained half-convinced that the "reflection" was indeed the reality (VIII:360). In this respect, he was a traitor to society, as Jean Normand remarks, "for he was refusing to play the game. He had therefore forfeited all his rights, his identity, indeed all reality, and even in his own eyes."[6] Thus Hawthorne acquired what Malcolm Cowley calls his "compulsive habit," for he adorned "his imagined rooms and landscapes with mirrors of every description—not only looking-glasses but burnished shields and breast-plates, copper pots, fountains, lakes, pools, anything that could reflect the human form."[7] Yet, insofar as the "reality" to which Hawthorne's eyes fell forfeit remained solely constituted by the technological frame of his age, he "lost" nothing more than the static certitude of its world-view.

It is commonly accepted that he sought what was hidden beneath appearances, and that his fiction plays out a variation on the theme of transcendental idealism. Evidence suggests that this is not the case, that in fact Hawthorne continually made attempts in both the fiction and the notebooks *to recover the appearance itself.* Indeed, his descriptive passages run counter to the imperative of the age, the demand for the whole, a totalizing vision. Instead, Hawthorne's description sets forth the perceptual phenomenon itself, the temporal aspect of the object as it's "intended" in consciousness. In *The American Notebooks,* for example, he says of his daughter Una's appearance: "Her beauty is the most flitting, transitory, most uncertain and unaccountable affair, that ever had a real existence; . . . if you glance sideways at her, you perhaps think it is illuminating her face, but, turning full round to enjoy it, it is gone again" (VIII:413). Grounded in finitude, Hawthorne's gaze never gives us the "whole picture" any more than the mind is able to grasp the meaning of being within a single and systematic equivalent. In fact, after 1837, the notebooks reveal a marked shift in his own perceptual habits, a shift toward minute observation of the appearance of things, as Normand observes: "His eye became a faceted mirror reflecting a reality fragmented into elements of microscopic size."[8] His emphasis on feeling, sensibility, and interiority reflects his reaction to the prevalent transparency of his day, and appropriates, in its place, the changing aspects of each object with respect to the temporality of perception.

His fiction proclaims a new moment in its discovery of the "real," a moment liberated for itself in order to become *apparent*—that is, transitory and opaque[9]—and encourages, as Thoreau put it, "the discipline of looking always at what is to be seen."[10] As Hawthorne remarked in *The English Notebooks,* "I doubt if anybody ever does really see a mountain, who goes for the set and sole purpose of seeing it. Nature will not let herself be seen in such cases. You must patiently bide her time; and by and by, at some unforeseen moment, she will quietly and suddenly unveil herself and for a brief space allow you to look right into the heart of her mystery. But if you call out to her peremptorily, 'Nature! unveil yourself this very moment!' she only draws her veil the closer; and you may look with all your eyes, and imagine that you see all that she can show, and yet see nothing."[11] While it compels us to reorient ourselves to a world previously envisioned as familiar, Hawthorne's gaze simultaneously reveals the primordial opacity of being in general. The changing technological milieu forcibly brought this point home, for in the mechanistic utilitarianism of contemporary science he apprehended the very ground of the transparently fixed idea which dominated his own century as it had shaped the distinctive contour of Western civilization since the Renaissance.

Very few writers reacted more critically to the nineteenth-century scientific view than Hawthorne. An unsigned review of 1860, in *The Times,* expressed a typical utilitarian response to his fiction:

> There is a peculiar type of the American mind which is strongly in revolt against American utilities, and which is predisposed by the very monotony of its surroundings to hues of contrast and attitudes of antagonism. . . . It is emphatically the desire of idealists like . . . Mr. Hawthorne to escape from the 'iron rule' of their country and the 'social despotism' of their generation. They disdain to be parts of a complicated scheme of progress, which can only result in their arrival at a colder and drearier region than that they were born in, and they refuse to add to 'an accumulated pile of usefulness, of which the only use will be, to burden their posterity with even heavier thoughts and more inordinate labour than their own.'[12]

Rather than paint the time in which he lived, Hawthorne chose to attack its fundamental beliefs. In science he recognized the mechanical illustration of ready-made truths about the meaning of life in which only a mind imbued with the most rigid principles could take delight.[13] And like his scientists, Hawthorne's intellectuals and reformers similarly display the same conceptually sterile fixation so characteristic of the age. Thus all three groups seek not so much to discover but to *verify.* Accomplished "anatomists," Hawthorne's villains attempt to penetrate the ambiguity of appearance, to see through the illusive opacity of both body and mind in order to substantiate their own transparent views. Aylmer, Rappaccini, Chillingworth, Westervelt, Hollingsworth, and even Holgrave—as I would argue—all represent men with minds conditioned by inflexible concepts, the single perspective of a rational and fixed idea. Obsessed by the absolute invariability of its belief, this mentality is forced to use any means to prove its truth, for without proof its whole intellectual super-structure would collapse. The scientific frame of reference provided Hawthorne with images which enabled him to interiorize the world afresh in order to communicate with it, and to rediscover its primordial texture rather than describe its popularly accepted fixation in physical, chemical, and biological laws, as it was by such naturalists as Zola in France, and Dreiser and Crane in the States.[14]

Because his concerns were wholly other than those expressed by the popular literature of his day, in conflict with public sensitivity, he was condemned to failure from the start. As one critic put it: "Mr. Hawthorne, we are afraid, is one of those writers who aim at an intellectual audience, and address themselves mainly to such. We are greatly of opinion that this is a mistake and a delusion, and that nothing good comes of it. The novelist's true audience is the common people—the people of ordinary comprehension and everyday sympathies, whatever their rank may be."[15]

In the critical vocabulary of the time, Hawthorne's fiction apportioned too much "shadow" and insufficient "sunshine." In an age when the general truths of the world were supposed to inhere in the unambiguous divinity of light, the daguerrean view came to represent the scientific certitude of reason itself. In typically ironic fashion, Hawthorne discussed this aesthetic obstacle in his preface to *The Marble Faun:* "No author, without a trial, can conceive of the difficulty of writing a Romance about a country where there is no shadow, no antiquity, no mystery, no picturesque and gloomy wrong, nor anything but a common-place prosperity, in broad and simple daylight" (IV:3). Poe's disapprobation of Hawthorne's propensity toward the dark and hidden articulated the common sentiment of the age, and its naive faith in the ultimate guarantee of reason: "let him mend his pen, get a bottle of visible ink."[16] Like Baudelaire, Hawthorne was compelled to limit his audience to a few select readers who might understand him. One such reader was John Lothrop Motley, who had written to Hawthorne in praise of *The Marble Faun:* "I like those shadowy, weird, fantastic, Hawthornesque shapes flitting through the book. I like the misty way in which the story is indicated rather than revealed; the outlines are quite definite enough from the beginning to the end to those who have imagination enough to follow you"; on 1 April 1860, Hawthorne replied: "You are certainly that Gentle Reader for whom all my books were exclusively written. . . . It is most satisfactory to be hit upon the raw, to be shot straight through the heart. It is not the quantity of your praise that I care so much about (though I gather it all up most carefully, lavish as you are of it), but the kind, for you take the book precisely as I meant it. . . . You work out my imperfect efforts, and half make the book with your warm imagination; and see what I myself saw, but could only hint at. Well, the romance is a success, even if it never finds another reader."[17]

Unfortunately, for Hawthorne, the cheery optimism indigenous to the scientific "sunshine" of the age imbued its literature also, where it came to represent an essentially feminine talent as opposed to the masculine strength of scientific inquiry. While Hawthorne observed this impoverished spectacle, he was simultaneously "consumed with fury at having to watch a damned mob of scribbling women reaping a harvest of easy popularity at his expense, while the most enlightened critics of the age were for their part awaiting the appearance of the male genius, America's poetic Jupiter."[18] He had, of course, arrived. The general public, however, lacked the sophisticated sensitivity Hawthorne would have liked it to cultivate; unfortunately, "it was not even responsible for the quality of its emotions—emotions that those with the necessary astuteness make it their business to provoke. . . . His inward themes could reach the ear of a lazy public only with great difficulty."[19] As one critic so aptly described the technological prejudice for transparency, and Hawthorne's subsequent lack of recognition by the general public: "Taste and culture, in fact, the outgrowths of educated thought, are drawbacks to popularity, so far forth at least as they tend to add angles reflective and refractive to the media through which people see works of art. The law is, the more transparent the medium, the more instinctive the recognition."[20] Richard Holt Hutton equally recognized the obliquity of Hawthorne's gaze and specifically applied it to the thematic treatment of the tales: "For the secret of his power lies in the great art with which he reduplicates and reflects and re-reflects the main idea of the tale from the countless faces of his imagination, until the reader's mind is absolutely saturated by it."[21]

☐

Lighting had always beguiled Hawthorne, and *The American Notebooks* repeatedly reveal this preoccupation. Unlike the daguerrean preoccupation, however, his interest in light primarily derives from its ability to cast a shadow, to elucidate some new perceptual aspect of an obscurely darkened world, or to transform, rather than accurately record the thing itself or "bring it to light."[22] Thus, rather than light his objects by the constancy of the sun, Hawthorne illumines his scenes by the ambiguous flicker of the lantern, the torch, the fire, the moon. Such partial and intimate lighting subtly discloses its objects, previously envisioned as familiar, in strange and new disguises: "Moonlight, in a familiar room, falling so white upon the carpet, and showing all its figures so distinctly,— making every object so minutely visible, yet so unlike a morning or noontide visibility,—is a medium the most suitable for a romance-writer to get acquainted with his illusive guests. . . . whatever, in a word, has been used or played with, during the day, is now invested with a quality of strangeness and remoteness, though still almost as vividly present as by daylight" (I:35–36). Like Verlaine, Hawthorne's description appropriates the principle, "Pas la couleur, rien que la nuance."[23] Margaret overlooks the street scene from her window, where a lantern momentarily reddens the foreground surrounded by the deluge of darkness which envelops every other object (XI:195); Robin finds his kinsman amid the labyrinthian procession illuminated by the dense multitude of torches which temporarily disrupts the chilly detachment of the moonbeams (XI:229); Goodman Brown discovers his fellow townsmen assembled at the black mass in the forest around the grotesque blaze of the fire, just as the ambiguous moonlight originally allowed him access to that clearing (X:84–85);

Ethan Brand stands virtually hypnotized before the dazzle of the lime-kiln to which he surrenders (XI:99–100); the indistinct moonlight dimly reveals the body of Dorcas' son lying dead upon the bones of her father (X:360).

Unlike the sun-drenched world of scientific objectification, Hawthorne depicts an ambiguous world of shadow. As he remarks, for example, of *Twice-told Tales,* "The book, if you would see anything in it, requires to be read in the clear, brown, twilight atmosphere in which it was written; if opened in the sunshine, it is apt to look exceedingly like a volume of blank pages" (IX:5). Like the child, science would paint a world transparently clear, as Hawthorne observed of his daughter Una, who "wants there to be all sunshine and no shadow, like a Chinese picture" (VIII:418–19). Hawthorne, on the other hand, was steadfastly aware that the truth of consciousness inheres in the subject's primordial interrogation of the world, replete with doubt and contradiction. Thus, the dark shadow of ambiguity falls across every page of his work: "Hawthorne could not prevent himself from seeing darkness even at high noon."[24] Whereas his age demanded that the new American psyche be white, just as its literature be pure, Hawthorne fearlessly discerned beneath its facade the monadic truth of black: "That blue-eyed darling Nathaniel knew disagreeable things in his inner soul. He was careful to send them out in disguise."[25] Hawthorne's gaze perceived the void that subjectivity inhabits between affective poles of transformation, the "black, impenetrable nothingness" which awaits all who would wander from the security of their familiar surroundings into the "obscurity that hems them in" (IX:427, 429). Similarly, we often find in his descriptive sketches the variously achromatic shades of black-on-black, as in the opening scene of *The Scarlet Letter* where "the wooden jail was already marked with weather-stains and other indications of age, which gave a yet darker aspect to its beetle-browed and gloomy front" (I:47), or in the public square where the "snake-like black eyes" of the Indians (I:246), whose gaze upon Hester's bosom figures forth the scarlet of the Letter, both prefigure and paradoxically displace the black back*ground* of the tombstone escutcheon itself. Sometimes the dark ambiguity of one shadow merely comes to be replaced by that of another which casts its indistinctive gloom through the surrounding field, piercing the image more severely than light: thus, the prison-house ominously intersects the clearing "long after the fall of the gigantic pines and oaks that originally overshadowed it" (I:48).

Even Hawthorne's portraits elude their daguerrean likenesses, which would freeze them in their being, to become "a ground of perceptual metamorphosis under cover of dim shadows."[26] As the narrator of "The

Prophetic Pictures" observes, "In most of the pictures, the whole mind and character were brought out on the countenance, and concentrated into a single look, so that, to speak paradoxically, the originals hardly resembled themselves so strikingly as the portraits did" (IX:170). Set in relief by varying degrees of darkness, the faces emerge to touch us with their glance, just as the pale but unfaded Madonna, "who had perhaps been worshipped in Rome now regarded the lovers with such a mild and holy look that they longed to worship too"; simultaneously these faces recede into the surrounding darkness, like the two old bearded saints who had nearly vanished "into the darkening canvas" (IX:170). The portrait "completes" the spectator's gaze while the spectator's gaze, in turn, completes the portrait: "They hung side by side, separated by a narrow panel, appearing to eye each other constantly, yet always returning the gaze of the spectator" (IX:176). Often these portraits paradoxically light the rooms they inhabit, as with the pictures of Walter and Elinor which, "concealed for months, gleamed forth again in undiminished splendor, appearing to throw a sombre light across the room, rather than to be disclosed by a borrowed radiance" (IX:181). Like the incomplete silhouette of Hepzibah, framed by "the dusky, time-darkened passage" into which she steps, "a tall figure, clad in black silk" (II:32),[27] the portraits of Walter and Elinor are variously completed in accordance with the individual gaze which perceives them: "Such persons might gaze carelessly at first, but, becoming interested, would return day after day, and study these painted faces like the pages of a mystic volume. . . . they sometimes disputed as to the expression which the painter had intended to throw upon the features; all agreeing that there was a look of earnest import, though no two explained it alike" (IX:176–77).

By virtue of his indirect lighting, Hawthorne's gaze suggests the incomplete contours of a world primordially articulated by the perceiving subject. It explodes the predetermined objectification of a reality transparently and uniformly illuminated by the scientific vision—a vision, moreover, that would impose its own inflexibly rigid structure in order to dominate the content of its (fixed and sterile) view. The world of Hawthorne's fiction defrays the inordinate cost of an objectively "neutered" universe, and its bankrupt vision, in favor of a polar and metamorphic reality situated in the individual glance of a perceiver. Amid this "sexually" ambiguous world, the gaze regards the "interiority" (desire) of its objects as they in turn reconstruct the consciousness perceiving them. Like the echoes in "The Hollow of the Three Hills,"[28] Hawthorne's objects rebound from various external surfaces to strike our eyes only insofar as they are deflected, reflected, and re-reflected in the gaze which temporarily beholds them. Grounded in the mutability of time, the object refuses the absolute determination assigned it by the formal and spatial priority of the world (understood as a) view. Hawthorne's ambiguous lighting enables the object to escape the scientific schematization to which the daguerrean view would subject it: the Letter ricochets off the armor in fragmented form in order to be completed a different way in the "shape" of Pearl, who in turn perceives a similar image in the head-piece, "smiling at her mother, with the elfish intelligence that was so familiar an expression on her small physiognomy. That look of naughty merriment was likewise reflected in the mirror, with so much breadth and intensity of effect, that it made Hester Prynne feel as if it could not be the image of her own child, but of an imp who was seeking to mould itself into Pearl's shape" (I:106). The inter-play of light and shade, of reflected and refracted light against an obscure backdrop of black, allows Hawthorne to populate his universe with objects imbued with the opacity of human consciousness. These ambiguously changing figures defy the reflection which would petrify them as they appear in the pool (IX:203), the fountain (IX:214), and the well (II:88), and then just as suddenly disintegrate back to the mutably indeterminate form whence they originally came.

Among the shadowy folds of darkness which encompass it, the House of the Seven Gables acquires its "concentration of intimacy";[29] via the forces which beseige it, the House becomes human. It even reciprocates Hepzibah's desire to decorate her hat with ribbons by growing flowers on its rook, and imitates her frown with its "meditative look," its "impending brow," its "thoughtful gloom," its "rusty" and "battered visage" (II:27, 28, 12, 56, 81). In the same way, regarding the interior life of the House, the dim looking-glass that used to hang in one of the rooms "was fabled to contain within its depths all the shapes that had ever been reflected there" (II:20). Yet, Hawthorne no more needs this apparently lost device than the inhabitants of the house, for his own descriptive gaze invests the objects within the house, as it does all the significant objects of his oeuvre, from the very walls to the portraits which adorn them, with the "human" or expressive space by which they come to life. His radical perception indirectly illuminates the objects of its gaze from within; it permits, in fact, the objects to enlighten us, just as Beatrice's face "positively illuminated the more shadowy intervals of the garden path" (X:102). Moreover, once the object is brought to prominence in this way, the world "becomes once more what it really is, the seat and as it were the *homeland* of our thoughts. The perceiving subject ceases to be an 'acosmic' thinking subject, and action, feeling, and will remain to be explored as original ways of positing an object."[30] Thus each object discloses itself insofar as a subject gropingly enowns it in perception, just as the Great Carbuncle refuses to unveil its light to anyone who would seek it "objectively"—that is, as a detached observer in search of absolute truth—and instantaneously mutates to "opaque stone, with particles of mica glittering on its surface" (IX:165). Hawthorne's Faustian gaze dared to see reality differently than his age would have him view it; rather than intellectually codify the images of experience, he ventured into their intrinsic chaos in order to resurrect the very body of the world, a body whose physical and opaque carnality had long since been discarded by the disembodied image of pictorial-daguerrean representation, the flat projection of the scientific-technological world-view.

Whatever constancy accrues to the objects within the world of Hawthorne's work does so because the objects themselves appear against a double horizon: the embodied perceiver articulates the general setting. Here perception implies the dilation of a subject's presence within the structures of an indeterminate field; the body "takes up room" among the objects which surround it without ever becoming an object in itself. The physical presence of a perceiver thus "makes room" for the world by virtue of a space neither entirely subjective nor objective, and which accommodates its objects only to the extent that they reciprocally call each other into being. The meteor punctuates the surrounding darkness just as surely as the darkness "creates" the meteor (I:153–54); the lime-kiln reveals the night just as the night "illuminates" it (XI:85); the people on "the other side" of the veil "wear" it just as fittingly as the minister (IX:52). Each makes the other possible and contemporaneously exists only because it "touches" the *affective* surface of the gaze. In this sense, every object becomes a metaphor; must be, in fact, a metaphor before it can become an object as such. Language, here, inosculates the very "being" of the object—that is, the subject's desire. The gaze exhibits this configuration of image and object.

Although, at the outset, the Letter measures precisely three and one-quarter inches on each side, its (affective) significance remains dormant without a factical subjectivity that calls it into being. Thus, Hawthorne's initial description of the Letter engages its immediate qualities, those aspects which arrest the gaze, and not its geometric properties: "But the point which drew all eyes, and, as it were, transfigured the wearer,—so that both men and women, who had been familiarly acquainted with Hester Prynne, were now impressed as if they beheld her for the first time,—was that SCARLET LETTER, so fantastically embroidered and illuminated upon her bosom. It had the effect of a spell, taking her out of the ordinary relations with humanity, and inclosing her in a sphere

by herself" (I:53–54). Similarly, the Letter has yet to become a significant sensory experience because it remains to be "lived" by the reader-
perceiver throughout the course of the novel. Each perceiver must
discover a way in. Hawthorne implicitly understood this and re-created
the perceiver's ingress into the thing itself. Rather than confer a notional
meaning on the object, his inosculation of light and shade inherently
organizes a structural field in which the object *is* only insofar as perception
disrupts into it; experience of the world can only transcend itself in the
objects of that world because it is born amid the situation. Here the
conspicuous absence of color in Hawthorne's oeuvre invites further investigation.

In perception, the reflection of light functions incidentally; its presence confers life upon the objects it illumines, whereas its absence deprives
them of all "expression." Similarly, lighting "is not presented to our
perception as an objective, but as an auxiliary or mediating element. It is
not seen itself, but causes us to see the rest."[31] Because lighting constitutes
an aspect of the field, lingering in the background without drawing specific attention to itself, it encourages or guides the gaze toward maximum
determinateness, and hence reveals the way in which the gaze takes up its
objects in perception. The transparency of the daguerrean view posits the
framed prospectus of a world uniformly illuminated from without along
each of its objectively indivisible "points." In perception, on the other
hand, the gaze engages its objects gropingly. Like the incomplete light of
the candle which shows up certain objects at the expense of others, the
gaze attests to a phenomenal body already "alongside" the objective body
as such, and which initially allows it to take up an object at the cost of
forfeiting those other objects in the field.

Now an object primordially announces itself in terms of its immediate "expression," its contours as they strike a kinaesthetic displacement of
the phenomenal body. As Max Scheler observes, perception goes straight
to the thing, "and by-passes the colour, just as it is able to fasten upon the
expression of a gaze without noting the colour of the eyes."[32] Conversely,
color may appear in modes other than the fixed quality of a reflective
attitude. Thus, the dark-green moss which covers the burial-stone of
Parson Hooper appears to the receptive eye as black (IX:53), as does the
verdure of the forest in "Young Goodman Brown" (X:83). Reciprocally,
to certain eyes the Letter may appear "freshly green, instead of scarlet"
(I:178). Indeed, the "blackness" which persists beneath the scarlet of the
Letter is less a sensible quality than a lugubrious power which affectively
emerges from the object, constantly insinuating its presence even while
"sensibly" absent from sight. Moreover, whether it is seen in the direct

light of the sun or the reflected and refracted light of the polished armor, the Letter affectively retains its constancy in modes other than the "sensory." It is visible primarily in the sense that moral blackness is visible.[33] Thus, the scarlet of Hester's embroidered letter "is but the *shadow*" (I:255, italics mine) of the red stigma inscribed upon Dimmesdale's own breast; similarly, the "A" of the tombstone inscription, which gules upon a sable field, is "gloomier than the shadow" (I:264) itself.

In this respect, Hawthorne's descriptive gaze anticipates the elemental function of lighting anterior to the distinction between colors as such. His lighting directs the gaze so that it discovers the object and "completes" it in accordance with the spectacle previously fore-"shadowed," just as Sir William Howe discerns his own image beneath the cloaked figure which unexpectedly issues from the shadow and then recedes before the spectators are able to catch a glimpse of it (IX:254). Set in relief by the folds of darkness which surround them, Hawthorne's figures surface to the gaze by virtue of the suggestive lighting which nudges them forth, redistributing whatever color "qualities" they possess back to the neutrality or "neutral territory" whence they initially emerged according to the variable level of lighting: "A child's shoe; the doll, seated in her little wicker carriage; the hobby-horse;—whatever, in a word, has been used or played with, during the day, is now invested with a quality of strangeness and remoteness, though still almost as vividly present as by daylight. Thus, therefore, the floor of our familiar room has become a neutral territory, somewhere between the real world and fairy-land, where the Actual and the Imaginary may meet, and each imbue itself with the nature of the other" (I:35–36). So too the red of the roses is lost to the "dark and glossy curls" of the two youths encompassed within the ring of monsters at the maypole (IX:56); the motley colors of the clearing are neutralized by the Puritans, invisibly watching the spectacle, who compare these revelers to the darksome evil that populates the "black wilderness" (IX:56); the richly colored garments of the figures, which emerge atop the staircase of the Province-House during the masked ball, gradually fade to dusk so that the shapes "appeared rather like shadows than persons of fleshly substance" (IX:251); the passionate colors of the plants in the garden reflect the artifice of man's depraved fancy, "glowing with only an evil mockery of beauty" (X:110). Hawthorne's black and white vision significantly outweighs his color-daubing, but only because his descriptive gaze inclines toward the primary constitution of the perceptual operation prior to its thematization. When colors do appear, he utilizes bold and primary ones—like Rousseau—engagingly set off against a tenebrous background which averts attention from itself because it creates the elemental space of perception: "in the momentary gloom, the fire seemed to be glimmering amidst the vagueness of unenclosed space" (X:448).

Already alongside an objective "eye," the phenomenal space of an expressive bodily "eye" opens onto the object and makes it visible insomuch as it seizes the interplay of light and shade without recognizing the light and shade as such. Lighting always lingers hidden in the background as a structural phenomenon whenever it makes an object visible, for in order to see the object "it is necessary *not* to see the play of shadows and light around it."[34] The shadows of the tree boughs, for example, which flicker over the dead figure of Judge Pyncheon amid the gloomy room articulate the slumping object while they simultaneously interrogate the birth of the perceiving subject. Conversely, these shadow-branches which reach out to touch us by reason of their unique space appear *doubly there* as they synchronously suggest an actual counter-part, beyond the window frame, presented in profile against the object they embody. The lighting thus directs our gaze toward the lifeless shape in the chair as "one" who has already been there, and leads us to the object to the extent that we submit or entrust ourselves to it. Affectively situated, we perceive the spectacle in conformity with the light which surrounds the body and permits the object to confront us. The lighting itself is "neutral"; only later, once the object has become determinate, do colors as such appear.

By reason of Hawthorne's indirect lighting, then, which gravitates toward the absence of color, objects apportion color among themselves. The quality of color in an object becomes determinate only after its renitency to some variable level of lighting. Initially, Hawthorne's lighting is always on the side of the subject, and not the object. Prior to the distinction between colors, the effect of lighting is precisely what gives us access to the perceptual situation; for example, when a painter wishes to portray some striking object, "he does so less by applying a bright colour to that object than by a suitable distribution of light and shade on surrounding ones."[35] Hawthorne's description of the dead Judge poignantly exemplifies this perceptual phenomenon:

> Meanwhile the twilight is glooming upward out of the corners of the room. The shadows of the tall furniture grow deeper, and at first become more definite; then, spreading wider, they lose their distinctness of outline in the dark, gray tide of oblivion, as it were, that creeps slowly over the various objects, and the one human figure sitting in the midst of them. The gloom has not entered from without; it has brooded here all day, and now, taking its own inevitable time, will possess itself of everything. The Judge's face,

indeed, rigid, and singularly white, refuses to melt into this universal solvent. Fainter and fainter grows the light. It is as if another double-handfull of darkness had been scattered through the air. Now it is no longer gray, but sable. There is still a faint appearance at the window; neither a glow, nor a glimmer—any phrase of light would express something far brighter than this doubtful perception, or sense, rather, that there is a window there. Has it yet vanished? No!—yes!—not quite! (II:276)

Moreover, just as the harmony of a piece of music may structure itself around a dominant tone, Hawthorne's descriptive gaze orders its objects around a variable level of lighting which, in itself, always tends toward the dominant "color" inherent in his oeuvre. This elemental constancy within the world of the work, and which sustains the very setting of that world, uniformly *appears* as black. Thus, the twilight glooming upward in the room where Judge Pyncheon motionlessly slumps obtains from this pre-dominant darkness and ultimately subsists within it. Ontologically, of course, this perceptual "dominant" constitutes nothing less than temporality, the horizon of nothingness which threatens at any moment to annihilate our perceptual consciousness and all the other forms of consciousness as well: "And there is still the swarthy whiteness—we shall venture to marry these ill-agreeing words—the swarthy whiteness of Judge Pyncheon's face. The features are all gone; there is only the paleness of them left. And how looks it now? There is no window! There is no face! An infinite, inscrutable blackness has annihilated sight! Where is our universe? All crumbled away from us; and we, adrift in chaos, may hearken to the gusts of homeless wind, that go sighing and murmuring about, in quest of what was once a world!" (II:276–77). Hence, Hawthorne's lighting suggests an ontological significance far beyond its descriptive surface and returns us to the subject of perception. In the sense that lighting corroborates the perceptual situation, spontaneously guiding the gaze toward an object which can only become determinate to the extent that it comes into being amid a general setting whose structure "surrounds" both subject and object, the subject-object dichotomy coalesces to a dialectic of inside and out.[36] Just as the meteor and the darkness are mutually impossible without each other, the perceptual subject can experience neither without the phenomenon of lighting which allows them to appear. Hawthorne's descriptive gaze accommodates this "double" space within the single image because it is willing to forfeit the visual frame of perspective, which merely expropriates the object, in favor of the ambiguous experience of "the world."

Furthermore, Hawthorne's darkness situates us at an interior "center," although that central "point" can never be located geographically or geometrically, but only phenomenally. Unlike the detached observer, such as Coverdale or Kenyon, whose preconceived perspective constitutes a world uniformly illuminated from without, Hawthorne's dark creates a specific, situated point of view by means of which the observer participates in the perceptual bequeathment of the object; the surrounding blackness dissolves the "objective" distance between spectator and world which the spiritualized Paul Pry takes for granted (IX:191–98) since it situates us toward an intentional "where" and not the spatial "where" of scientific objectification. Hawthorne's image encourages the percipient to disrupt or merge into the "content" of the gaze by virtue of the surrounding darkness which, at every moment, threatens to obliterate this world "like the archway of an enchanted palace, all of which has vanished but the entrance into nothingness and empty space" (VIII:133). In order to transcend or overcome the dark, this world must be continually reappropriated by a subject who, in fact, must turn itself inside-out with each successive image which appears. Every new image thus guarantees a primordial coherence between subject and object; the percipient sensibly *participates* in the being of this world. Hawthorne implicitly understood this pre-objective structure of perception, and descriptively endeavored to bring us back in touch with our inaugural perception of the world prior to objectification. By reason of its indirect lighting, the image *suggests* the object through certain operations which already begin to function cinematically.

In order to create this "motion," Hawthorne's oeuvre required a constant setting by which the world of his work would phenomenally cohere. If his indirect lighting were to articulate the objects of an emblematic gaze so that they virtually protrude to touch us, he would have to project an affective field which interpenetrates every experience of his world, and concomitantly allows for the inter-sensory unity of every "thing." In other words, Hawthorne's gaze required a means at its disposal by which he could sustain the reality of the world of his vision, and he unearthed that key in the diorama. Normand brilliantly explores this notion in depth: "If Hawthorne continued after his illness was over to shut himself away in order to look at things in the dark, if he displayed an interest in magic lantern shows and fairground dioramas, he did so in no dilettante spirit but with deliberate intent. It was upon a foundation of shadow that he built up his technique of indirect lighting. Light came for him, as it did for Van Gogh, through darkness."[37] This all-encompassing darkness which informs Hawthorne's vision, and which Melville so brilliantly acknowledged at the center of his art, not only structures our experience of that vision but also suggests its ontological ground. Here

Hawthorne's fascination with the confessional parallels his predilection for the dark, for it was the psychological as well as the visual phenomenon that excited his imagination.[38] Yet, however much the confessional might attract him, the diorama most consistently structures his descriptive technique. What best characterizes the dioramic experience of darkness is its ability to absorb self-consciousness—the very precondition for involvement. Regarding this effect in contemporary cinema, V. F. Perkins has observed: "In the (ideally) comforting, self-forgetting darkness of the movie-house we attain faceless anonymity, a sort of public privacy, which effectively distances the real world and our actual circumstances. That the darkness is an essential insulator will have been realized by any reader who has had to watch films in an insufficiently darkened cinema. The deterioration of the image on the screen matters far less than the absence of the 'shield' which darkness customarily offers. The erection of the shield seems to be the precondition of involvement."[39] Darkness makes this possible. Darkness is *immanence*.[40] It recreates the "interior" of being, the site *(mise-en-scène)* upon which the world makes its first appearance in consciousness.

To speak in these terms is not to place the subject perceptually or ontologically prior to the world, for Hawthorne's darkness engages the reader by surrounding him, and thus establishes the specific situatedness by which a percipient makes the birth of being possible. Because it encloses the spectator within the immediacy of its "distanceless" depth, dioramic darkness generates a self-sufficient world.[41] In fact, the reader has already been put into the situation by virtue of the presence of those images which spontaneously appear against this ground of chaos and are already on the way toward a determinate order. Amid the enclosing dark, the image "takes shape" and prematurely stands out, as Jules Supervielle has expressed it, against this indeterminate field "like someone on the screen when the film is half over and one has only just walked into the darkness of the cinema. . . . the image, before one's eyes, is already in the present indicative."[42]

Hawthorne's description of the dead Judge, for example, intimately engages the reader in this active, interior moment. From the twilight glooming upward, toward the swarthy whiteness of the Judge's face, and finally to that inscrutable blackness which annihilates all traces of any world "out there" beyond the window—Hawthorne's description transforms the transparency of an objective world "without" into the ambiguous opacity of an interior space which paradoxically locates the subject at the center of a world that is, ironically, the subject itself. Like the cinematic vision, defined by George-Michel Bovay as "la vision intérieure d'un monde,"[43] Hawthorne's diorama-like technique eliminates the traditional or daguerrean frame and enables us to perceive and complete the image insofar as we are situated—that is, engulfed by the surrounding dark. Here, a commonplace event, the coming of night, "is transformed into apocalyptic revelation through description that conveys the internal vantage point of diorama—that conveys the sense of immersion in a changing scene in which real time expands into dioramic time, into dream time."[44] This physical blackness therefore points to a primordial correspondence between subject and object within the world of Hawthorne's work, for being is always situated. As Lautréamont remarks: "It is only by admitting the night physically that one is able to admit it morally."[45] Thus, through the interplay of light and shade, grounded in dioramic darkness, Hawthorne was able to create "a total ambiguity that would enable him to achieve the freest possible interplay of substance, identities, and physical, moral, and psychological realities."[46] At the interior of this ambiguous vision, Hawthorne explores the affective depth by which an expressive space superannuates the perspective distance of the daguerrean view. Through his dioramic gaze, the world no longer stands before the spectator as a representation, but becomes visible in its interior immediacy. The world is born anew.

Since the daguerrean frame supports a view upon the outside in terms of its *optical* relation to the world, it always represents a spectacle of something else—something "beyond" itself. As Hawthorne observed of his journey up Green Mountain:

> As we ascended the zig-zag road, we looked behind, at every opening through the forest, and beheld a wide landscape of mountain-swells, and vallies intermixt. . . . Over this wide scene, there was a general gloom; but there was a continual vicissitude of bright sunshine flitting over it; now resting for a brief space on portions of the heights, now flooding the vallies with green brightness. . . . But we, who stood so elevated above mortal things, and saw so wide and far, could see the sunshine of prosperity departing from one spot and rolling towards another; so that we could not think it much matter which spot were sunny or gloomy at any one moment. (VIII:129)

Indeed, from such a "godly" vantage point, nothing *matters;* it is all the same: a matter of mind. This remote perspective, divorced from all affective aspects ("we could not think it much matter"), is indifferent to time as well ("at any one moment"). Whenever seen in perspective, the external world looms somehow always beyond time; for ultimately everything can and will be located in its proper, uniform place. Even history arrays itself before us in fastidious chronological order.[47] At the other end of daguerrean objectification, the diorama initially investigates the spectacle for its own sake: "The spectacle is first of all a spectacle of itself before it is a spectacle of something outside of it."[48] In Hawthorne, the image is able to exist for its own sake because it spontaneously emerges from a universal blackness which circumscribes the percipient. Dioramic darkness engages us from a situated point of view, one in which the thing acquires a specific carnality and, at the same time, engenders an affective world.

The lighting in general achieves this effect: each part of the spectacle contributes to the whole insomuch as it de-realizes the objectivity of the object. The image no longer stands over and against us as a representation, but rather "trans-substantiates," as it were, the very reality of the thing; it can at any moment be swallowed once again by the surrounding dark: "Be pleased, therefore, my indulgent patrons, to walk into the show-room, and take your seats before yonder mysterious curtain. . . . the lamps are trimmed, and shall brighten into noontide sunshine, or fade away in moonlight, or muffle their brilliancy in a November cloud, as the nature of the scene may require; and in short, the exhibition is just ready to commence" (XI:49–50). Hawthorne's image illustrates the intrinsic way in which the thing belongs to no-thing, how dis-appearance, too, befits the very nature of the apparition and structures the phenomenon of consciousness: "Therefore, by my control over light and darkness, I cause the dusk, and then the starless night, to brood over the street; and summon forth again the bellman, with his lantern casting a gleam about his footsteps, to pace wearily from corner to corner, and shout drowsily the hour to drowsy or dreaming ears" (XI:67). Here the visual image inosculates a field beyond sight itself, where darkness belongs to the deaf and silent "ear" of the dream.

Within the interior of its space, Hawthorne's image confers upon perception a facticity which daguerrean objectification merely relegates to the sun-drenched status of the factual. Indeed, once the factual is abolished, perception gravitates toward a world entirely devoid of objects: the dioramic world prior to the appearance of its first image. It retrieves the night, that pure and simple being-in-the-dark. Analogously, it is the night which brings me back in touch with my contingency: "Night is not an object before me; it enwraps me and infiltrates through all my senses, stifling my recollections and almost destroying my personal identity. I am no longer withdrawn into my perceptual look-out from which I watch the outlines of objects moving by at a distance. Night has no outlines; it is itself in contact with me and its unity is the mystical unity of the *mana*. Even shouts or a distant light people it only vaguely, and then it comes to life in its entirety; it is pure depth without foreground or background, without surfaces and without any distance separating it from me."[49] If the reflective attitude sustains its space by thinking the illuminated relation of its parts, the interior of dioramic darkness, on the other hand, unites me to an affective space precisely because it intimately merges with the surface of my body, and threatens to absorb that reflective identity which can always disperse it by "turning on the lights." Darkness mirrors the affective depth of the perceptual situation. Without anchor in externally objective coordinates, Hawthorne's dioramic gaze recites the world of his work upon the ambiguous site of affectivity—that zone of "not-being-in-front-of" where things initially come to light—and, on the descriptive level, provides the very darkness necessary in the cinema in order to show up the performance.[50] As he expressed it in *The French and Italian Notebooks:* "darkness, to objects of sight, is annihilation, as long as the darkness lasts" (XIV:205).

□

The daguerrean artist assumes the fixed transparency of a world uniformly illuminated by light in its primordial constitution. Whatever "shadow" the daguerreotype secures represents merely an artistic "effect" in the reproduction of an absolutely accessible truth. In this respect, art often impersonated the nineteenth-century scientific vision itself, a viewpoint appropriate to the time, "that individual differences in artistic renderings indicate flaws in perception, at least for the recording arts."[51] Even the sophisticated aesthetic of a daguerreotypist such as Albert Southworth betrays this desire to fix the object in its inflexible truth, though it appears deceptively attractive at first sight. In the attempt to capture the essence of his "subject," the daguerreotypist, as Southworth remarks, "feels its expression, he sympathizes with its character, he is impressed with its language; his heart, mind, and soul are stirred in its contemplation. It is the life, the feeling, the mind, the soul of the subject itself."[52]

Ultimately, however, the daguerreotypist can procure the desired representation only insofar as his sympathetic facility enables him to see *through* the appearance into the heart of its transparent reality, its contemplatively universal significance—its "soul." Holgrave, for example, epitomizes the primary manifestation of this attitude; he dares the existent to stand still and show itself worthy of representing not only the truth of itself, but the truth of the existent as a whole. As the translator and divine agent of light, the daguerreotypist cannot err to the extent that he appropriates this insight or view through the world. Holgrave's willingness to challenge the existent derives from this belief, and the attendant belief in the absolute disclosability of nature. His naive trust in the ability of light to elucidate the truth of the world equally sustains his confidence in its transparency: "Most of my likenesses do look unamiable; but the very sufficient reason, I fancy, is, because the originals are so. There is a wonderful insight in heaven's broad and simple sunshine. While we give it credit only for depicting the merest surface, it actually brings out the secret character with a truth that no painter would ever venture upon, even could he detect it" (II:91). His daguerreotype of Judge Pyncheon, despite numerous efforts to make it more agreeable, similarly reveals the judge as a morally despicable person. Indeed, Holgrave's desire to fix the truth of nature in general, to catch it in the act, to hold or capture permanently the existent amid its fleeting variety of form and shape, reminds us of Emerson's transcendental posture. Like Emerson, Holgrave challenges nature to hold still, to prove itself. In this respect, his powers alarm Phoebe: "He made her uneasy, and seemed to unsettle everything around her, by his lack of reverence for what was fixed; unless, at a moment's warning, it could establish its right to hold its ground" (II:177). Thus, despite Holgrave's apparent "lack of reverence for what was fixed," we are mistaken should we construe him to figure as the representation of modernism and change in the novel. For though he seemingly argues against the kind of permanence suggested by the house, he no sooner prepares to leave it than he expresses the desire to preserve the exterior while altering the interior to suit the individual's taste.[53]

Hawthorne was especially intrigued by technological advances in media, and it was only natural that the daguerreotype fascinated him. Throughout his life, his work was continually discussed in reference to daguerrean technique. As early as 1842, in a brief review of *Twice-told Tales,* Lewis Gaylord Clark had compared his mind to "the plates of the Daguerreotype";[54] and in 1850, George Ripley said of *The Scarlet Letter,* "The introduction, presenting a record of savory reminiscences of the Salem Custom House, a frank display of autobiographical confessions, and a piquant daguerreotype of his ancient colleagues in office, while surveyor of that port, is written with Mr. Hawthorne's unrivalled force of graphic delineation."[55] E. A. Duyckinck, in a review of 1852, remarked of *The Snow-Image:* "It is no Chesterfieldian vacuum of politeness, but a world of realities, a camera obscura of the outer world delicately and accurately painted on the heart."[56] And in 1864, the year of Hawthorne's death, George William Curtis said of him that he "treated his companions as he treated himself and all the personages in history or experience with which he dealt, merely as phenomena to be analyzed and described, with no more private malice or personal emotion than the sun, which would have photographed them, warts and all."[57] Even today, critics continue to analyze him with respect to the aesthetic catchword of his own age, "chiaroscuro." For instance, Harry Levin discusses Hawthorne in terms of "that obsessive dark room which is always behind the focus of his vision"; and he says of the interplay between light and dark—"la feuille blanche, le roman noir"—that, in the twelve years of solitude at Salem, "His mind itself became a *camera obscura,* a dark room which sensitively registered the infiltration of light from outside."[58]

True enough, Hawthorne often emphasized the interaction of high-light, middle tint, and shadow, as Gabriel Harrison had defined the daguerrean method; but most critics have predominantly failed to see how the effect of Hawthorne's lighting obscures a more profound percep-tual principle. His description of the drowned girl in *The American Note-books,* for example, later used in *The Blithedale Romance* to depict the death of Zenobia, reveals an exceptionally stark realism, dramatically highlighted by lantern as in a Goya painting:

> When close to the bank, some of the men stepped into the water and drew out the body; and then, by their lanterns, I could see how rigid it was. . . . They took her out of the water, and deposited her under an oak-tree; and by the time we had got ashore, they were examining her by the light of two or three lanterns.
>
> I never saw nor imagined a spectacle of such perfect horror. The rigidity, above spoken of, was dreadful to behold. Her arms had stiffened in the act of struggling; and were bent before her, with the hands clenched. She was the very image of a death-agony; and when the men tried to compose her figure, her arms would still return to that same position. . . . The lower part of the body had stiffened into a more quiet attitude; the legs were slightly bent, and the feet close together. But that rigidity!—it is impossible to express the effect of it; it seemed as if she would keep the same posture in the grave, and that her skeleton would keep it too, and that when she rose at the day of Judgment, it would be in the same attitude. (VIII:263–64)

Like many others, Hawthorne's wife misperceived the essential quality of his descriptive dynamic, mistaking the above passage for photographic realism. Editing her husband's notebooks for publication, Sophia wrote to James T. Fields in 1867, inquiring whether they should publish "this wonderful photograph of the terrible night" (VIII:685). And when the passage first appeared—in Julian Hawthorne's biography of his parents, *Nathaniel Hawthorne and His Wife* (1884)—it thoroughly shocked one reviewer, Thomas Wentworth Higginson, who considered it "almost too frightful to put into words,—certainly to put into types"; had there been introduced "a series of photographs from the Paris morgue, the result would not have been more horrible."[59]

However, beneath the daguerrean appearance of the description of the drowned girl lurks the hidden drama of an expressiveness inaccessible to the photographic medium itself. For the image is initially disclosed insofar as it is discovered or intended in consciousness, revealing the movement inherent in the perceptual operation of a situated subject, and not as the elucidation of an invariable object. The photograph objectively fixes its content by virtue of a single and constant external horizon. Hawthorne's description, on the other hand, subjectively unfolds in time; the variable constitution of the image reflects an affective "distance" between scene and spectator. We perceive the changing "aspects" of the drowned girl at various distances which more or less *express* the designated "figure" Hawthorne would have us "complete" against the indeterminate periphery of the "field." "Near" and "far" are not determined by the continuity of perspective, but rather appear as functions of an ambiguous situation, the way in which each detail establishes itself in consciousness. Thus, the clenched hands, for instance, which perspectively figure to be smaller than the arms, appear, in fact, much larger; they loom beyond their graphic relation to the arms and come to designate, in themselves, the general rigidity of the entire image. Here Hawthorne's gaze reveals his habitual inclination toward contiguous relationships, relations which "logically" digress from a continuously uniform setting in space and time. Like the cubists, he transforms the object into a set of synecdochic oscillations (arms/hands/arms/legs/feet) whereby visual orientation strives toward maximum determinateness. The object obtains only insofar as the reader-perceiver "completes" it himself. Again, this technique is cinematic and prefigures the changing angle, variable perspective, and repertoire of variously focused "shots" indicative of the highly sophisticated motion picture of the twentieth century. The close-ups or "tight shots" of the drowned girl momentarily fill the visual field no less affectively than the revolutionary metonymic "set-ups" in the productions of D. W. Griffith.[60]

A remarkable passage in "Ethan Brand"—gleaned also from an entry in *The American Notebooks* (VIII:130), though nearly seven years prior to that of the drowned girl—corroborates this technique. Indeed, it concludes with an image that rivals Griffith's original cinematic close-up which caused such panic in the theatre—a huge "severed" head smiling at the public for the first time.[61] Having placed his diorama in proper position, the German Jew "invited the young men and girls to look through the glass orifices of the machine," where he exhibited cracked and wrinkled pictures of "cities, public edifices, . . . ruined castles, . . . Napoleon's battles, and Nelson's sea-fights"; in the very midst of these would be seen "a gigantic, brown, hairy hand—which might have been mistaken for the Hand of Destiny, though, in truth, it was only the showman's—pointing its forefinger to various scenes of the conflict" (XI:95). At the conclusion of this exhibit, "the German bade little Joe put his head into the box. Viewed through the magnifying glasses, the boy's round, rosy visage assumed the strangest imaginable aspect of an immense, Titanic child, the mouth grinning broadly, and the eyes, and every other feature, overflowing with fun at the joke. Suddenly, however, that merry face turned pale, and its expression changed to horror; for this easily impressed and excitable child had become sensible that the eye of Ethan Brand was fixed upon him through the glass" (XI:95). The sequence of tight shots (hand/forefinger/head/face/mouth/eye/ . . . eye) annuls any perspective image of the whole; rather, its variable depths create an affective space—in this instance, a discontinuous movement from joy to horror. All "objective" distance has vanished. In dioramic effects, Hawthorne had discovered the space of subjectivity, a logic of contiguity (montage) which disrupts the uniform distance of perspective and objectivity in general.

So too Hawthorne's description of the drowned girl manifests this affective "distance" as an expressive function of the gaze—of subjectivity itself: his image alters the discovery of the object according to the changing situatedness of the perceiver. Here's the passage as it appeared in *Blithedale:*

> Her wet garments swathed limbs of terrible inflexibility. She was the marble image of a death-agony. Her arms had grown rigid in the act of struggling, and were bent before her, with clenched hands; her knees, too, were bent, and—thank God for it!—in the attitude of prayer. Ah, that rigidity! It is impossible to bear the terror of it. It seemed . . . as if her body must keep the same position in the coffin, and that her skeleton would keep it in the grave, and that when Zenobia rose, at the Day of Judgment, it would be in just the same attitude as now!
>
> One hope I had; and that, too, was mingled half with fear. She knelt, as if in prayer. . . . But her arms! They were bent before her, as if she struggled against Providence in never-ending hostility. Her hands! They were clenched in immitigable defiance. Away with the hideous thought! The flitting moment, after Zenobia sank into the dark pool—when her breath was gone, and her soul at her lips—was as long, in its capacity of God's infinite forgiveness, as the lifetime of the world. (III:235)

Once again, synecdochic oscillations (arms/hands/knees/arms/hands) designate the "whole" of Hawthorne's image, although the hands explicitly express "more" than the sum of the parts. What descriptively appears last is foremost in expressive value, for it has previously emerged at the conclusion of the preceding chapter where Hawthorne skillfully pre-"figures" the affective significance of this aspect (the hands) as it is intended in consciousness. Here he sets up the aspect of the hands in a series of tight shots repeated again and again:

" . . . Here is my *hand!* Adieu!"

She gave me her *hand,* with the same free, whole-souled gesture as on the first afternoon of our acquaintance; and being greatly moved, I bethought me of no better method of expressing my deep sympathy than to carry it to my lips. In so doing, I perceived that this white *hand*—so hospitably warm when I first touched it, five months since—was now cold as a veritable piece of snow.

"How very cold!" I exclaimed, holding it between both my own, with the vain idea of warming it. "What can be the reason? It is really deathlike!"

"The extremities die first, they say," answered Zenobia, laughing. "And so you kiss this poor, despised, rejected *hand!* Well, my dear friend, I thank you! You have reserved your homage for the fallen. Lip of man will never touch my *hand* again. . . . Once more, farewell!"

She withdrew her *hand,* yet left a lingering pressure, which I felt long afterwards. (III:227–28, italics mine)

In passing, I would suggest this "lingering pressure" not only affects the narrator, but the reader-perceiver as well, producing a kind of "after-image" which remains on the "mind's eye" long after the original image has disappeared from "view" (cf. III:156).

While these examples re-enact the object as an image of the narrative consciousness, that consciousness is sometimes performed "outside" itself. In the striking description of the death of Judge Pyncheon, it is a fly that does the work, tracing out the substitution of one aspect for another in a series of metonymic set-ups which this time takes the following form: forehead/chin/nose/eyes—"And there we see a fly—one of your common house-flies, such as are always buzzing on the window-pane—which has smelt out Governor Pyncheon, and alights now on his forehead, now on his chin, and now, Heaven help us, is creeping over the bridge of his nose, towards the would-be chief-magistrate's wide-open eyes" (II:283). Amid these discontinuous spatial aspects, the affectivity of the object emerges first, and not its logical or notional signification. In the passage from *Blithedale,* for example, Zenobia's hand is but the emotional silhouette, as it were, of Coverdale's own state of mind. So too with the Judge's empty stare: it corresponds to the vacancy of his existence, his meaningless impact on all whose lives he touched. This upsurge of expression heralds an ambiguously shifting relation between subject and object, the way in which the subject "inhabits" the object, and not the representational determination of an object as such. At the threshold of Hawthorne's world, distance expressively designates a variable figure-ground relation, and not the static and fixed pictorialism of photographic perspective. The descriptive image re-creates the discovery of an object according to the changing situatedness of a subject; that is, the image postpones "identifying" the object as objective, as that which stands over and against a subject in reflection. Our proximity to any given figure is predicated solely upon the way in which we affectively take it up, so that the unity of the object is decisively "intentional."

Because Hawthorne's fiction questioned the certainty which its public ascribed to the external world, it required a commonly accepted ground whence it could thereafter proceed to undermine that very foundation. If anything, what has been traditionally called his allegorical method often constitutes nothing more than a front or "masque" to catch the public off-guard, a ceremonial way of getting the reader into the more significant fictional "vision"—a convenient method of fixing things in a superficial form both accessible and acceptable to his general public.[62] Understood as such, and so reduced to a single "optical" appearance, allegory imprisons its content, its objects, within the confines of an abstraction that doesn't equivocate, a theoretically fixed and static frame—a completed view that is always and everywhere an illusion. Hawthorne's objects, on the other hand, consistently defy their abstracted "allegorical" frame: the letter, the house, the faun, the serpent, the ribbon, the maypole, the veil, the lime-kiln—these objects function expressively and shape the significance of the narration itself. They correspond to an interior resonance, elements of an affective configuration grounded in the structural "gestalt" of a perceiver.

For Hawthorne, an object "objects" only to the extent that it partially informs a "field." By definition, furthermore, a field of vision is never in the object. As such, the object is fated to remain ultimately ambiguous insomuch as we can never "trace it out" in its entirety. As Merleau-Ponty has suggested,

> the edge of the visual field is not a real line. Our visual field is not neatly cut out of our objective world, and is not a fragment with sharp edges like the landscape framed by the window. We see as far as our hold on things extends, far beyond the zone of clear vision, and even behind us. When we reach the limits of the visual field, we do not pass from vision to non-

vision. . . . Conversely, what we see is always in certain respects not seen: there must be hidden sides of things, and things 'behind us', if there is to be a 'front' of things, and things 'in front of' us, in short, perception. The limits of the visual field are a necessary stage in the organization of the world, and not an objective outline.

Similarly, the different parts of the whole possess an importance beyond the particular qualities of its individually determinate figures: "Already a 'figure' on a 'background' contains . . . much more than the qualities presented at a given time. It has an 'outline', which does not 'belong' to the background and which 'stands out' from it; it is 'stable' and offers a 'compact' area of colour, the background on the other hand having no bounds, being of indefinite colouring and 'running on' under the figure."[63] So it is with Hawthorne's most suggestive symbol, the scarlet letter.

In the most basic sense of the term, all of Hawthorne's symbols are, in fact, emblems. They exist within a spatial configuration, and appear as figures against an ambiguous ground. The woodcut emblems of the *New England Primer* had indelibly engraved themselves upon his consciousness. What constitutes his emblematic technique, then, is not so much an allegorical content supplemental to the visual image as the affective apprehension of a figure on a ground. His fiction abrades the traditional descriptive distance; we find ourselves in a unique landscape where the immediate encroaches so entirely, so expressively, upon our "perceptual attention" that we can scarcely obtain a perspective at all.[64] Though few critics have recognized the importance of Hawthorne's emblematic technique and its incomplete external contours, an anonymous commentator remarked in 1863 that the English sketches delineate "outlines not drawn from notes or from reminiscences painfully recalled, but phototyped from the very retina of the inward eye, and filled in with the very hues and shadings supplied at the moment by the author's taste, wit, sympathy, or disgust."[65] Although both Newtonian and "daguerrean" presuppositions are apparent in the critical terminology, at least the passage underscores the perceptual demands exacted of the reader. Charles Webber had expressed a similar observation:

> One of his finest traits is a sort of magical subtlety of vision, which, though it sees the true form of things through all the misty obscurations of humbug and cant, yet possesses the rare power of compelling others to see their naked shapes through a medium of its own. . . . It is a favorite expression with regard to Hawthorne, that he '*Idealizes*' everything. Now what does this Idealization mean? Is it that he *improves* upon Nature? Pshaw! this is a Literary cant which it is full time should be exploded! . . . Now, Haw-

thorne does not endeavor to improve upon the Actual, but with a wise emulation attempts—first to reach it, and then to modify it suitably with the purpose he has to accomplish. Of course he is led by his fine taste to desire to see it himself, and make you see it in precisely that light in which it shows best—in which its highest beauty is revealed. . . . We can't get away from the physical, and just as our material vision informs the inner life will that life know Wisdom.[66]

In *The American Notebooks*, Hawthorne likewise had remarked: "An innate perception and reflection of truth gives the only sort of originality that does not finally grow intolerable" (VIII:358). For Hawthorne, then, description corresponds to subjectivity; it recuperates the affect, the expressive accommodation of an object as it initially appears to consciousness. Unlike Emerson's symbolism, which represents the looking-glass raised to its highest "objective" power,[67] its transcendental or transparent omniscience, Hawthorne's symbolism re-creates a situated, emblematic point of view, an origin-al moment in the perception of the object rather than a derivative conceptual resemblance or representation. By erasing the noumenon from the topography of consciousness, Hawthorne thus inscribes the phenomenon itself as the very *texture* and structure of his descriptive landscape. In effect, his fiction cancels the subject-object dichotomy, as Charles Feidelson has observed: "there is no longer any question of subjective expression or objective description."[68]

Consequently, this moment is metamorphic, grounded as it is in temporality; or as Hawthorne expressed it: "Were we to sit here all day, a week, a month, and doubtless a lifetime, objects would thus still be presenting themselves as new, though there would seem to be no reason why we should not have detected them all at the first moment" (VIII:247). Perhaps this event is best expressed in the description of Pearl, the very embodiment of the object upon which all eyes in the novel gaze in order to discover the "shape" of its meaning: "The child could not be made amenable to rules. In giving her existence, a great law had been broken; and the result was a being, whose elements were perhaps beautiful and brilliant, but all in disorder; or with an order peculiar to themselves, amidst which the point of variety and arrangement was difficult or impossible to be discovered" (I:91). The peculiar order of Pearl's "arrangement" derives from the metamorphic nature of the perceptual operation; imbued with indeterminacy, she indicates the temporal aspect of the Letter itself: "This outward mutability indicated, and did not more than fairly express, the various properties of her inner life. Her nature appeared to possess depth, too, as well as variety" (I:90). As an emblem in her own right, her "figure" subsequently stands out against "an absolute circle of radiance around her, on the darksome cottage-floor. . . . Pearl's aspect was imbued with a spell of infinite variety; in this one child there were many children, comprehending the full scope between the wild-flower prettiness of a peasant-baby, and the pomp, in little, of an infant princess" (I:90). She is, of course, the rose itself, and figures as the wild-flower emerging from the prison-house of Puritanism. Over and against the static representation of an object in perspective, Pearl's figuration unfolds in time; its multiple configurations open up the possibility of meaning, just as the ambiguous embellishment of the Letter against its own darksome ground is variously interpreted by those who see it to stand for anything from "Adultery" to "Angel" to "Able" (I:158, 161).

What Hawthorne most admired in the Rembrandt-like achromaticism of the daguerreotype was its ability to *suggest* a hidden psychological drama or intuition. As Hilda remarks in *The Marble Faun:* "Nobody, I think, ought to read poetry, or look at pictures or statues, who cannot find a great deal more in them than the poet or artist has actually expressed. Their highest merit is suggestiveness" (IV:379). The portrait genre particularly accommodated this interest in dramatic expressiveness: "What he looked for in a portrait was expression, pathos, the hidden drama of a Beatrice Cenci; what interested him in a still life was the materiality of the objects."[69] The portrait of Beatrice exemplifies this effect: "It is a peculiarity of this picture, that its profoundest expression eludes a straightforward glance, and can only be caught by side glimpses, or when the eye falls casually upon it; even as if the painted face had a life and consciousness of its own, and, resolving not to betray its secret of grief or guilt, permitted the true tokens to come forth only when it imagined itself unseen" (IV:204–5). Of portraits in general, Hawthorne commented in *The American Notebooks:* "The pursuit has always interested my imagination more than any other; and I remember, before having my first portrait taken, there was a great bewitchery in the idea, as if it were a magic process" (VIII:492–93). In order to capture this moment, however, the portrait painter was forced to wrestle with time, "casting quick, keen glances at me, and then making hasty touches on the picture, as if to secure with his brush what he had caught with his eye" (VIII:498). Elsewhere, the narrator of "The Prophetic Pictures" observes: "Nothing, in the whole circle of human vanities, takes stronger hold of the imagination, than this affair of having a portrait painted. Yet why should it be so? The looking-glass, the polished globes of the andirons, the mirror-like water, and all other reflecting surfaces, continually present us with portraits, or rather ghosts of ourselves, which we glance at, and straightway forget them. But we forget them, only because they vanish. It is the idea of duration—of earthly immortality—that gives such a mysterious interest to our own portraits" (IX:173). Yet, less than two months after *The Scarlet Letter* first appeared in print, Hawthorne had remarked in a notebook entry of 5 May 1850: "In fact, there is no such thing as a true portrait; they are all delusions. . . . A bust has more reality" (VIII:491).

Ten years later, not only the bust but the entire body as well would come to life in Donatello. Hawthorne's fascination with moonlight, for example, already prefigures this disposition: "Moonlight is Sculpture:— Sunset, and sunlight generally, Painting."[70] Here Hawthorne would seem to agree with Cornelius Agrippa's estimation of painting in general: "there is more vnderstoode, and iudged, then seen."[71] Despite frequent critical attacks on Hawthorne's ability to appreciate sculpture, evidence suggests quite the opposite and points to the "material" quality of his descriptive gaze. A notebook entry for 10 August 1842 already reveals his visual proclivity toward the tactile and tangible qualities of sculpture, anticipating the marvelously ironic work of Hans Arp in our own century: "Summer squashes are a very pleasant vegetable to be acquainted with;—they grow in the forms of urns and vases, some shallow, others of considerable depth, and all with a beautifully scalloped edge. Almost any squash in our garden might be copied by a sculpture, and would look beautifully in marble, or in china-ware; and if I could afford it, I would have exact imitations of the real vegetable as portions of my dining-service" (VIII:329).[72] In a letter to her father, 1853, Sophia observed as much of Hawthorne's *style:* "Mr. Hawthorne hates exclamations and all sorts of expletives. He likes pure sculpture in talk, as you may suppose from his style of writing."[73] Indeed, just as Donatello's sylvan dance suggests "the realization of one of those bas-reliefs . . . twined around the circle of an antique vase" (IV:88) or "the sculptured scene on the front and sides of a sarcophagus" (IV:88), the very structure of *The Marble Faun* is like a sculptured frieze-in-the-round: "It moves by way of brief and brisk episodes in a circle—'as all things heavenly and earthly do'—from the opening chapter . . . to the similarly titled final chapter."[74] The eye delights in the tangible, that around which it can playfully "feel" in order to investigate the various aspects of an object; its operation mirrors the intentional configuration of the perceptual object itself, the opaque appropriation of the object as a whole. For Hawthorne, the portrait was "false" to the extent that it presumed to "complete" an expressiveness entirely disproportionate to a predetermined objectification, for "expression" inheres in the perceptual situation and not the objectivity of the object.

Thus Hawthorne's own technique often reveals a natural affinity for the sketch or "trace" which, like sculpture, invites completion by virtue of its opaque suggestivity. Perceptually speaking, his gaze always seeks to inform the partial contours of an obscure design: "There was formerly, I believe, a complete arch of marble, forming a natural bridge over the top of the cave; but this is no longer so" (VIII:100); "We climbed to the top of the arch, in which traces of water having eddied are very perceptible" (VIII:133); "Sometimes the image of a tree might be almost traced; then nothing but this sweep of broken rainbow" (VIII:158); "The foundation of a spacious porch may be traced on either side of the central portion; some of the stones still remain; but even where they are gone, the line of the porch is still traceable by the greener verdure" (VIII:160). An entry in *The French and Italian Notebooks,* 21 May 1858, underscores the immanent value Hawthorne places on the incomplete or unfinished design: "Here were pen-and-ink sketches, and pencil-drawings, on coarse and yellow paper of centuries ago, often very bold and striking; the 'motives,' as artists say, or first hints and rude designs, of pictures which were afterwards painted, and very probably were never equal to these original conceptions. Some of the sketches were so rough and hasty that the eye could hardly follow the design; yet, when you caught it, it proved to be full of fire and spirit. Others were exceedingly careful and accurate, yet seemed hardly the less spirited for that; and in almost all cases, whether rough or elaborate, they gave me a higher idea of the imaginative scope and toil of artists than I generally get from their finished pictures" (XIV:221).[75] Neither the portrait nor the daguerreotype provided Hawthorne with the kind of situated, temporal gestalt he demanded of description for, in themselves, both are condemned to remain fixed and dead.[76] Like the portraits that continually haunt the painter's imagination in "The Prophetic Pictures," his description allows us to complete the object as a "lived" experience, to dwell affectively amid the network of intention: "Whenever I look at the windows or the door, there it is framed within them, painted strongly, and glowing in the richest tints—the faces of the portraits—the figures and action of the sketch" (IX:180).

The *frame,* which figures so prominently in Hawthorne, accordingly provides an emblematic background against which the possibility of an expressive delineation first appears; like the portrait painter of "The Prophetic Pictures," Hawthorne seldom felt an impulse "to copy natural scenery, except as a frame work for the delineations of the human form and face, instinct with thought, passion, or suffering" (IX:178). His perceptual figures uniquely stand out against an emblematic context that alters their significance by virtue of a situated gaze, a gaze that undermines the very structure of the transcendental vision. Rather than delimit its content, the frame enables Hawthorne to define the object contextually. His frames never constitute the traditionally isolated and uniform view by which the object had previously been envisioned for centuries, for when he specifically uses the word "frame" it nearly always means the background by which a foreground figure affectively comes to be set off, and not the optical representation of a perspective section of space. In itself, the Hawthornian frame most clearly approaches what, today, Gestalt theory calls a field of vision. For evidence of this perceptual configuration, despite the apparent contradiction in terminology, one need only consult *The American Notebooks,* that indispensable record of his observational techniques: "this gentle picture strangely set off by the wild mountain frame around it" (VIII:132); "On the slope of Bald Mountain, a clearing, set in the frame of the forest on all sides" (VIII:138); "Towards the dimness of evening, a half-length figure appearing at a window:—the blackness of the back ground and the light upon the face cause it to appear like a Rembrandt picture" (VIII:259); "Monument Mountain stands out in great prominence, with its dark forest-covered sides, and here and there a large white patch, indicating tillage or pasture land;—but making a generally dark contrast with the white expanse of the frozen and snow-covered lake at its base, and the more undulating white of the surrounding country" (VIII:305); "I saw the face and bust of a beautiful woman gazing at me from a cloud. . . . The vision lasted while I took a few steps, and then vanished. I never before saw nearly so distinct a cloud-picture—or rather sculpture; for it came out in alto relievo on the body of the cloud" (VIII:311); "an open eye in earth's countenance" (VIII:320); "There are broad and peaceful meadows, which, I think, are among the most satisfying objects in natural scenery; the heart reposes on them, with a feeling that few things else can give, because almost all other objects are abrupt and clearly defined; but a meadow stretches out like a small infinity, yet with a secure homeliness, which we do not find either in an expanse of water or of air" (VIII:321–22); "it seems as if the picture of our inward bliss should be set in a beautiful frame of outward nature" (VIII:366); "The fireplace had a white marble frame about it, richly sculptured with figures and reliefs" (VIII:490). Perhaps the narrative intention of "The Story Teller" expresses it best: "With each specimen will be given a sketch of the circumstances in which the story was told. Thus my air-drawn pictures will be set in frames, perhaps more valuable than the pictures themselves, since they will be embossed with groups of characteristic figures, amid the lake and mountain scenery, the villages and fertile fields, of our native land" (IX:492).

Concerning its design, moreover, the Letter is by far Hawthorne's most appropriate emblem indicative of subjectivity, for it locates the ground of existence in language. By 1839, he had already insinuated such ontological implications in a journal entry explicitly dealing with perception: "Letters in the shape of figures of men, &c. At a distance, the words composed by the letters are alone distinguishable. Close at hand, the figures alone are seen, and not distinguished as letters. Thus things may have a positive, a relative, and a composite meaning, according to the point of view" (VIII:183). Generally speaking, Hawthorne's use of the frame purveys a supralogical background or field in order to *embody* the object, and yet by virtue of its subjectively situated constitution, the field extends beyond the edges of whatever particular device he chooses as the frame itself. His emblematic field allows the image to be reflected and re-reflected off its surrounding surfaces, just as the entire surrounding scene bounces off the many-faceted sides of Endicott's armor (IX:434), or Zenobia's gaze rebounds from Westervelt's "courteous visage, like an arrow from polished steel" (III:173), or the scarlet letter, in the transformed shape of Pearl, is reflected off the polished, convex mirror of the breastplate in "exaggerated and gigantic proportions, so as to be greatly the most prominent feature of her appearance. In truth, she seemed absolutely hidden behind it" (I:106). Hawthorne's gaze lures the object out of its perspective depth and toward the *surface,* where it leaves the artificial confines of its optical frame to enter that affective field we call "the world." Via this emblematic articulation of consciousness, both image and object implicate the scene of subjectivity. Thus, as Holgrave unveils the recess in the wall, disclosing the ancient deed, the debilitated portrait, "frame and all, tumbled suddenly from its position, and lay face downward on the floor" (II:315–16).

With the scarlet letter, the "ontological" blackness of its emblematic frame indeterminately extends beyond the precisely embroidered figure of the "A" which measures, as we're told in "The Custom-House," exactly three and one-quarter inches on each side (I:31). I needn't remind you that the blackness surrounding the concluding tombstone image constitutes not only an ontological "ground" but an aesthetic ground as well, for when Hawthorne "discovers" the Letter in the Custom-House it has no ground whatsoever. The narrative text of the romance becomes the very ground of what, at first glance, is but an isolated and solitary "figure." It's not by chance that Hester's weave and Hawthorne's *textile* conceit for narration itself are one and the same. The Letter points to Hawthorne's perceptual labyrinth and how it differs so radically from traditional description or representation, for in embroidery Hawthorne discerned a felicitous tactile analogy for the gaze itself. Unlike the visual content of perspective, which resides somewhere "in back of" the pictorial surface at an invisibly inaccessible "location," its vanishing point, the visual content of an embroidery extends outward, "in front of" its optical surface, toward a tangibly tactile space. The embroidered emblem virtually protrudes to *touch* our eye. It thus reciprocates the sculptural quality of the gaze, and approximates the general situatedness of perception. Hawthorne intuitively understood the situation as the reciprocal basis of perception as well as being. Like the painting which Ishmael encounters at the Spouter Inn, whose ambiguous "something" in the middle evades definitive articulation, the perceptual "shape" of the "A" is likewise variously apprehended according to the situation of the individual perceiver and therefore destined to remain ultimately opaque; we can never get an absolute perspective on it.

And herein emerges a veritable key to the nature of Hawthorne's lighting and his descriptive affinity for the "power of blackness" which Melville attributed to him, rather than the light and sunshine of his own age. As Henry James expressed it, Hawthorne's fiction exposes his cat-like facility for seeing in the dark, which Emerson, "as a sort of spiritual sun-worshipper, could have attached but a moderate value to."[77] Taking his lead from Bacon, with whose writing he was well acquainted, Hawthorne solidified his basic emblematic habit. In "Of Adversity," Bacon had written: "We see in needleworks and embroideries, it is more pleasing to have a lively work upon a sad and solemn ground, than to have a dark and melancholy work upon a lightsome ground: judge therefore of the pleasure of the heart by the pleasure of the eye."[78] Melville was one of those rare critics who immediately understood Hawthorne's counter-visual response to the prejudice of his age—and its concomitant emphasis on the absolute efficacy of light—in favor of this darkness which gives "more effect to the ever-moving dawn, that for ever advances through it, and circumnavigates his world"; indeed, Melville seems to have been the only one to perceive the gestalt dimension of "this black conceit" which "pervades" Hawthorne "through and through": "You may be witched by his sunlight . . . but there is the blackness of darkness beyond; and even his bright gildings but fringe and play upon the edges of thunder-clouds. In one word, the world is mistaken in this Nathaniel Hawthorne. He himself must often have smiled at its absurd misconception of him. . . . this blackness it is that furnishes the infinite obscure of his back-ground."[79]

Thus, unlike pictorial-daguerrean representation, which seeks to bring into sharp focus the entire content of its frame, Hawthorne's emblematic field, grounded in darkness, merely suggests the incomplete outlines of its figures as they are "illuminated" by the perceptual intention to take them up. In the same way, Goodman Parker's lantern gleams along the street, "bringing to view indistinct shapes of things, and the fragments of a world, like order glimmering through chaos, or memory roaming over the past" (XI:196). Similarly, Dimmesdale is greeted by a lantern "which, at first a long way off, was approaching up the street. It threw a gleam of recognition on here a post, and there a garden-fence, and here a latticed window-pane, and there a pump, with its full trough of water, and here, again, an arched door of oak, with an iron knocker, and a rough log for the door-step" (I:149–50). Whatever objects this gaze takes up ambiguously appear set off against an indeterminate surrounding. For every object the gaze investigates, it simultaneously forfeits its hold upon the other objects in its field; they in turn slip away or fade back toward the obscure periphery whence they came, "in harmony with the low relief and dimness of outline of the objects that surrounded them."[80] The rose momentarily appears in relief against the gloom of the prison (I:48); the blurred meteor temporarily disrupts the vacant regions of the night sky (I:154); the lime-kiln juts out from the surrounding darkness to swallow us (XI:89); the stark fir-tree punctuates the desolate landscape, covered with its solitary growth of living branches from the middle up (IX:70); the Great Stone Face emerges against the perpendicular side of a mountain (XI:27); the "lightsome couple" spontaneously issues forth from the band of gothic monsters, this crew of Comus, to relieve the darksome face of the English priest, shaded by the maypole (IX:56–57); the Letter itself writhes and twists its contorted shape upon the sable field which provides an ambiguous backdrop for the ocular metamorphoses of this illuminated manuscript (I:106).

Hawthorne's gaze approaches the object gropingly; it must feel around it as a blind man runs his hands over the features of another's face—thus, its peculiar sculptural or tactile quality. It brings the object out from its surroundings, from its perspective depth, toward an affective or "bodily" depth uniquely born amid the situated structure of perception. For Hawthorne, being is carnal throughout, the image made flesh between the double horizon of physico-geometric and expressive-bodily space, the cold marble resuscitated in the warmth of the Faun. His gaze inaugurates the discovery of a material world, the "outsidedness" of the self, where objects encroach upon our vision, touching the "fingertips" of the eye.[81] The world seen from "within" magnifies the body to infinity, reversing the traditional perspective on an object; the vanishing point hurtles toward me as I simultaneously explode the boundaries of its frame. To emphasize transparency is to ignore the world's body; similarly, Hawthorne shunned the ubiquitous view of his age which pretended to ignore the ambiguous carnality of being. Beseiged by an encompassing blackness that threatens to devour us at any moment, we are no longer disinterested spectators of the scene.

In opposition to the uniform continuity of perspective,[82] Hawthorne sketches his most dramatic scenes *palpably close* because they are perceptually inquisitive, re-creating the ambiguous network of affective intention.[83] An osmosis transpires between subject and object which obliterates the objectification of pictorial-daguerrean representation in favor of the situation. Hawthorne brings the object out of its predetermined location and to the surface, just as the mountain prefigures Ernest's face upon its side. Thus "man rediscovers himself through topography," as Levin observes.[84] In this sense, Hawthorne never "paints" or "pictures" his most affective scenes, but rather disrupts them from the inside out; his gaze engages the object insomuch as it seduces it outward and away from the familiar security of its perspective depth. As Melville incisively remarked in a letter to Hawthorne, "We think that into no recorded mind has the intense feeling of the visable [*sic*] truth ever entered more deeply than into this man's. By visable truth, we mean the apprehension of the absolute condition of present things as they strike the eye of the man who fears them not, though they do their worst to him."[85] The image no longer represents a constituent whole; its structure enacts the perceptual intention, the inaugural situation in which the object ceaselessly recommences itself. Each aspect compresses within it the (w)hole of existence. Unlike the portrait, the painting, or the photograph, whose being precedes its significance by virtue of its *finished* design, the trans-figuration of Hawthorne's image projects significance and being as one and the same phenomenon. And so with the meteoric lighting which temporarily illuminates the scaffold during the minister's vigil; it sets off each of its figures with a "singularity of aspect." "So powerful was its radiance, that it thoroughly illuminated the dense medium of cloud betwixt the sky and earth. The great vault brightened, like the dome of an immense lamp. It showed the familiar scene of the street, with the distinctness of mid-day, but also with the awfulness that is always imparted to familiar objects by an unaccustomed light. . . . all were visible, but with a singularity of aspect that seemed to give another moral interpretation to the things of this world than they had ever borne before" (I:154).

Hawthorne's "alien" lighting, his inosculation of light and dark, thus commences the perceptual intention, for the familiar is that which, paradoxically, has fallen into obscurity, that which we no longer notice. In this beginning, the object reveals its "syntax," the form of its emergence to consciousness as a series of synecdochic oscillations, a sequence of discrete aspects. Hawthorne's tactile gaze re-creates the temporality of this event within the descriptive image itself, the way in which the subject "holds" the object, the way in which each con-forms to the other. His image shatters the purely external space of the pictorial-daguerrean tradition and representation in general—the ideal "view" of a consciousness without "ground," without (a) body, outside desire. Over and against the age's demand for transparency, in which the object remains forever closed off to doubt, invariably complete as a determinate whole, Hawthorne's oeuvre addresses the opacity of the object as a part-icular structure of consciousness, a lived experience whose numerous aspects discontinuously surface to the touch of the gaze. This phenomenon, in turn, discloses the reciprocity between subject and object in a world common to both—a world, moreover, which makes the birth of being possible in the first place.[86] "They stood in the noon of that strange and solemn splendor, as if it were the light that is to reveal all secrets, and the daybreak that shall unite all who belong to one another" (I:154).

□

Because visual experience naturally pushes objectification further than the tactile, as Merleau-Ponty suggests, "it presents us with a spectacle spread out before us at a distance, and gives us the illusion of being immediately present everywhere and being situated nowhere"; tactile experience, on the other hand, "adheres to the surface of our body; we cannot unfold it before us, and it never quite becomes an object."[87] It's through the body that I am able to open onto the object as a constant in itself, what geometry calls a "solid." Hawthorne's descriptive technique recuperates this tactile, pre-objective contour of the object for, within the expressive space of its interior, his image makes the object determinate only to the extent that it disrupts the objective dimensions of "location." Here the spectator assumes a spatial relation to the thing in terms of his restricted situation and not the "ubiquitous" position of optical perspective which merely treats the body as another object in external space. Hawthorne appreciated the aspect of the thing and employed a descriptive technique that engages us with every new appearance of the image.[88] "Aspectivity" substantiates the limited ability of the gaze at all times and constitutes the Rubicon which can never be crossed perceptually; it always puts "solidity" or objectivity on the hither side of the distinction between affective and rational space. The aspect itself inaugurates the primordial depth of the visible. The fragmented character of Haw-

thorne's image recovers this depth, a depth prior to the interval of perspective. Rather than place the object in a matrix of geometric space
extrinsic to and independent of all point of view, his descriptive technique
announces a radically different kind of location. By means of partial and
deflected images, the object comes to occupy a certain place only insofar
as it eclipses or envelopes other objects in the field. In this way, depth is
initially understood as a kind of imbrication in the visual field: objects
mutually implicate one another.

Once depth is no longer conceived as an invisible, third dimension
(as breadth viewed in profile, or from the side), all dimensions in space
are thereafter understood as reversible expressions of volume. The location of the object is no longer "external" to the perceiver. Hawthorne
knew what Cézanne was to discover, and what cubism would repeat:
"that the external form, the envelope, is secondary and derived, that it is
not that which causes a thing to take form, that this shell of space must be
shattered, this fruit bowl broken."[89] At the same time, however, pure
forms, possessing an apparent solidity internally determined, can never
disclose this interstitial or bodily aspect of depth, for the space in which
perception transpires can never be given to us as an intention *to know*.
During his middle period, Cézanne experimented in this direction, "and
came to find that inside this space, a box or container too large for them,
the things began to move, color against color; they began to modulate in
instability. Thus we must seek space and its content *as* together."[90] Only
between the double horizon of physico-geometric and bodily-expressive
space does the object begin to secure its constant dimensions. Aspectivity
thus confirms the reciprocity between subject and object, makes non-
sense of each apart from the other. Rather than portray an optical relation
to the world, as that which is outside the percipient, Hawthorne's gaze
presents us with an internal animation of the image, one which interrogates the image for its own sake: it is first and foremost autofigurative,
invested with a logic of its own.

Linear perspective presents the illusion of a world outside us inasmuch as it fixes the object by means of a visible outline; it locates the
thing in its objective position with reference to a uniform mental space.
The line thus seeks to imitate the border between things. Perception, on
the other hand, shows us that the space between things is in no way
formative of the thing in itself much less visible as a self-evident boundary; for example, the line which circumscribes the objects in a painting is,
in reality, implicated between and behind that upon which we focus: it's
not a physical thing but rather an "inflection," as it were, and forms a
system relative to every other line in the composition, each line possess-

ing a diacritical value, a certain disequilibrium, another aspect of the line's relation to itself.[91] In the same way, if we follow the linear development of Hawthorne's "compositions," we discover within the image the axes of a system which simultaneously renders the dual horizons of bodily (expressive) and physical (geometric) space; taken as a (w)hole these discontinuous aspects express the "tension" of the visual image, its in-tension and ex-tension which together inaugurate the temporality of the thing to consciousness as pre-tended in vision. In Hawthorne, the descriptive object initially appears as that which beckons us to coordinate its internal discord as an image, just as the body performs a similar task in perception.

When Hester discards the Letter beside the brook, for example, Hawthorne describes the scene as follows: "But Pearl, not a whit startled at her mother's threats, any more than mollified by her entreaties, now suddenly burst into a fit of passion, gesticulating violently, and throwing her small figure into the most extravagant contortions. . . . *Seen in the brook,* once more, *was the shadowy wrath of Pearl's image,* crowned and girdled with flowers, but stamping its foot, wildly gesticulating, and, in the midst of all, still pointing its small forefinger at Hester's bosom" (I:209–10, italics mine). Once again, synecdochic oscillations (head/foot/ arms/finger) fragment the image into a series of separate aspects, each aspect demanding a new focus in order to count as a figure against its ever-changing ground. But even more, the image is grasped in its dual syntax. In the first "place," there is the figure of Pearl whose contortions undergo a series of displacements in external space alone; in the second "place," however, and at the same time, there is the figure of Pearl decomposed or deflected in the brook—an image which no longer reflects the thing as an extension in external space, but as an *expressive counterpart:* her "shadowy wrath." Indeed, this image is nothing less than the inversion of a previous one in which the expression or in-flection, if you will, of the water reflection prepares us for quite the opposite: "And beneath, in the mirror of the brook, there was the flower-girdled and *sunny image* of little Pearl, pointing her small forefinger too" (I:209, italics mine). Furthermore, Hawthorne's deployment of the image here reveals an internal disjunction; its "linear development" is contiguous, not continuous, and discloses "between" the appearance of each aspect a kind of emptiness or void whose task it is to gouge out the thing as it is ceaselessly renewed in perception. Rodin, in fact, defined the function of the line in sculpture precisely this way, and for this very reason declared, "It is the artist who is truthful, while the photograph is mendacious; for, in reality, time never stops cold."[92]

To put it another way, the perceived contains "gaps"; the perceptual phenomenon gives us the object with no guarantee whatsoever in being. Only in the world, taken objectively, does the unity or "solidity" of the object become a problem. The visual *field,* on the other hand, like the body itself, is that zone "in which contradictory notions jostle each other because the objects . . . are not, in that field, assigned to the realm of being, in which a comparison would be possible, but each is taken in its private context as if it did not belong to the same universe as the other."[93] Similarly, with the individual object, its various aspects can never be simultaneously present; they emerge contiguous to each other precisely because they are temporal. The configuration of Hawthorne's image reveals a more primordial notion of depth.

But how are we to understand this "depth" since, as Sartre defines it, for example, the imaginary itself lacks depth; it fails all effort to vary the point of view?[94] For Sartre, imagination constitutes the negation of perception; it posits the unreal as an end in itself. Moreover, insofar as the imaginary constitutes an "object," it belongs to the very same *perspective* as being. If, on the other hand, we understand the imaginary as a field or dimension of being—its immanent prefiguration—then clearly it possesses a certain depth which belongs not to *what* is imagined, but to the composition of the image itself: a depth in intention. As Mikel Dufrenne observes, even the unreal is never entirely aberrant; there is an unreal which is pre-real, an anticipation of the real of which it is the essential function of imagination to pre-form: "To imagine is first of all to open up the possible, which is not necessarily realized in images. Imagination is to be distinguished from perception as the possible is distinguished from the given, not as the unreal is from the real. ... . If imagining produces anything, it is the possibility of a given. Imagining does not furnish the content as perceived but sees to it that something *appears.*"[95] Likewise, the "unity" of Hawthorne's image, its apparent solidity and constancy in depth, originates in an immanent arrangement of its "field," a pre-objective depth which foreshadows a determinate form. The image emulates what Husserl calls "operative intentionality," and not its thematization. This movement postpones "identifying" through representation in favor of "expression," for the object is neither copied nor reproduced but rather *composed.* Here depth belongs to the point of view itself and not the thing; it is not an objective relation but an *organization* in the field. As Merleau-Ponty suggests, depth expresses an intentional distance without reference to objective size, an enlargement of the field in which the distant thing begins to fade or slip away from the gaze. In order to continue holding it, the field reorganizes itself toward a more perfect symmetry in which the phenomenon of depth constitutes a moment of stabilization, a movement toward determinate form. The thing is therefore never actually achieved, but remains always that transcendent synthesis whose discontinuous presence arises amid the continuous absence toward which it unceasingly withdraws.

Hawthorne's close-ups, for example, destabilize the organization of the field; synecdochic oscillation breaks up the object into a momentary mosaic of disparate planes which destroys the organization in depth. Here, an equidistant distribution of the gaze demands that the gaze recuperate its focus. The object begins to disappear not only as a function of "far," but also "near." Just as I lose sight of the object at a very great distance, so too I lose it at a very close one; it becomes an indistinguishable mass, something alien and strange. Hawthorne's synecdochic technique enacts this perceptual orientation toward an appropriate depth, as in the following description of Pearl:

> Hester . . . saw that, owing to the peculiar effect of this convex mirror, the scarlet letter was represented in exaggerated and gigantic proportions, so as to be greatly the most prominent feature of her appearance. In truth, she seemed absolutely hidden behind it. Pearl pointed upward, also, at a similar picture in the headpiece; smiling at her mother, with the elfish intelligence that was so familiar an expression on her small physiognomy. That look of naughty merriment was likewise reflected in the mirror, with so much breadth and intensity of effect, that it made Hester Prynne feel as if it could not be the image of her own child, but of an imp who was seeking to mould itself into Pearl's shape. (I:106)

The fragmented image, through the course of its various aspects up close (letter/finger/smile), disorients the reader-perceiver. In order to reorient the gaze, Hawthorne's image motivates the subject to regather its focus— that is, to make one of the aspects count *as a figure,* and therefore seem "nearer" than the other aspects in the field.

His gaze is most intriguing whenever he applies this technique specifically to the human face in order to disclose the "person." In the above example, Pearl's smile figures forth her elfish essence. Elsewhere, the face of the dead Judge, for instance, invites a closer scrutiny: "And there we see a fly—one of your common house-flies, such as are always buzzing on the window-pane—which has smelt out Governor Pyncheon, and alights now on his forehead, now on his chin, and now, Heaven help us, is creeping over the bridge of his nose, towards the would-be chief-magistrate's wide-open eyes" (II:283). Again, we are no longer in possession of a single horizon which unambiguously inheres "in the picture," but a multiplicity of horizons, of planes, nudging the reader-perceiver's own body. Amid this oscillation of aspects (forehead/chin/nose/eyes), there emerges a specific organization of the field, a *configuration* of variable figure-ground relations which express the ultimate vacancy of the Judge's character as it was in life. In fact, Hawthorne's technique displaces or substitutes figure and ground as interchangeable; here, as with Pearl's elfish smile, it is the final focus in the sequence which counts. Far from determining a certain size, this original depth, prior to all objective relations of geometric perspective, expresses the phenomenal grasp the body has on its surroundings—how "near" and "far" but designate the *affective* interface of image and object within the world of the work.

Hawthorne's description of Westervelt further exemplifies this phenomenon: "In the excess of his delight, he opened his mouth wide, and disclosed a gold band around the upper part of his teeth; thereby making it apparent that every one of his brilliant grinders and incisors was a sham. This discovery affected me very oddly. I felt as if the whole man were a moral and physical humbug; his wonderful beauty of face, for aught I knew, might be removeable like a mask; and, tall and comely as his figure looked, he was perhaps but a wizened little elf . . . with nothing genuine about him, save that wicked expression of his grin" (III:95). As with Pearl's elfish smile and Judge Pyncheon's vacant stare, the sham of Westervelt's grin most prominently stands out—indeed, trans-figures him. Here too Hawthorne's gaze zooms to the single aspect, the lonely detail which not only counts as a figure but expresses the whole of his "person" as well—the moral decrepitude which belies that wonderful beauty of all the other features his face would im-personate. Amid the synecdochic structure (mouth/gold band/teeth), the tight shot of Westervelt's grin stays with us; it is a means of "recognizing" him again in the future. Thus, when Coverdale spies him from the window of his boarding-house in Boston, the renewed oscillations of the gaze (forehead/smile/teeth) once again reduce the whole to its single-most affective part, its expression: "Westervelt approached the window, and leaned his forehead against a pane of glass, displaying the sort of smile on his handsome features which, when I before met him, had led me into the secret of his gold-bordered teeth. Every human being, when given over to the Devil, is sure to have the wizard mark upon him, in one form or another. I fancied that this smile, with its peculiar revelation, was the Devil's signet on the Professor" (III:158).

Here the gaze hits upon the very "heart" of the appearance, and co-responds to what the aspect signifies. Hawthorne's use of the term "signet" for this dynamic appropriately characterizes the emblematic quality of the gaze, the way in which the expression of the thing etches itself in consciousness, its pre-objective inscription in the flesh. The same is true of Old Moodie's *patch,* for instance, or the Model's obscured *eyes.* These particular aspects of the human face express the "significance" of the person as a whole, just as the thing itself initially appears as an affective reply to the questioning gaze. Thus, Hawthorne's attention to the human face not only underscores the metonymic structure of the gaze but also the expressive quality of perception in general. The thing presents itself under the sign of a certain physiognomy, a familiar "face" invested with a living significance toward which we move with a peculiar style. As Kurt Koffka observes, an object looks attractive or repulsive before it looks black or blue, circular or square.[96] So too with the human face: perception goes straight to the expression. This dynamic enables Hawthorne to "identify" his characters in *The House of the Seven Gables,* for example, with the simple epithets the "scowl" and the "smile" (II:223ff.).

The geometric space of pictorial-daguerrean representation is always and everywhere indifferent to its content; the rules of perceptual syntax, on the other hand, precede all objective relations, revealing its affective significance. Although perception, as such, is strictly a third-person operation in which the subject as a "person" (reflexive consciousness) is absent, it nevertheless partakes of significance by means of its intentionality. The meaning of the percept, its irreducible configuration, is performed against the background of the human body. Hawthorne's image enacts this dimension. It trans-"figures" an indefinite series of discontinuous aspects into a project (intention) which is the object itself, an object whose claim to "objectivity" must be perpetually recaptured in a fresh act that is itself temporal. As Merleau-Ponty remarks, "In every focusing movement my body unites present, past and future, it secrets time, or rather it becomes that location in nature where, for the first time, events, instead of pushing each other into the realm of being, project around the present a double horizon of past and future and acquire a historical orientation. . . . But every act of focusing must be renewed, otherwise it falls into unconsciousness."[97] The unity of the object is therefore never complete or "finished" but endures, as such, only so long as it is taken up by the subject and invested with a "living" significance. The style of Hawthorne's gaze thus bypasses a geometry of the line in favor of a contour which shows up the object in its expressive physiognomy; its "plenary" appearance is but the project of the reader-perceiver's own existence. Hawthorne's image constitutes the visible "reply" to those interrogations which the object inaugurates. In this way, the descriptive object "speaks" to us from out of the depths of its expressive configuration. Indeed, it is this expression which confers upon the object its self-evidence.

If at the level of perception subjectivity is not the self-consciousness of reflection but rather temporality itself, objectivity in turn is not the self-subsistence of the thing but rather that dimension in which the thing initially appears as a form of behavior expressing a certain style. Prior to all objectification, Hawthorne's image points to the *emblematic* value of existence, the way in which emotion, passion, and desire originally imbricate experience. As Merleau-Ponty observes, "If I say that in disappointment I am downcast, it is not only because . . . I discover between the objects of my desire and my desire itself the same relationship as exists between an object placed high above me and my gesture towards it. The movement upwards as a direction in physical space, and that of desire towards its objective are mutually symbolical, because they both express the same essential structure of our being, being situated in relation to an environment."[98] Here the object is linked to its significance insofar as it expresses the "direction" of the subject's existence, the affective vector which stands between it and things as a means of projecting the world. That is to say, the object is not an invariant conglomeration of perspectives, but rather the expressive con-figuration of aspects. Regarding the proximity of Hawthorne's gaze to the object, his tight shots function as a means of focusing upon the most significant aspect by which an object announces itself—that expressive space of the world.

In this way, the object possesses a "figurative" significance beyond its figure-ground relation; it is first of all a "figure" of speech, a metonymy. Here the thing is grasped as the configuration of desire; it already holds within the "materiality" of the apparition a symbolic form, as Cassirer observes: "The essence does not recede behind the appearance but is manifested in it. . . . The expressive meaning attaches to the perception itself, in which it is apprehended and immediately experienced."[99] This emblematic inosculation of apparition and expressive physiognomy guarantees the "interior" of the world, its affective structure, just as the scarlet letter initially transports the subject by means of its own affective spell, taking Hester "out of the ordinary relations with humanity, and inclosing her in a sphere by herself" (I:54). Hawthorne's spatial relations are initially figures of human relations, the space of desire, the "soul" of things—what transports the reader-perceiver to the *heart* of all appearance: "The 'soul' of things signifies here the pure expressive meaning with which they seize upon consciousness and draw it into their sphere."[100] Hawthorne's image reveals how we are simultaneously rooted in two horizons, the human (expressive) space of the body and the natural (geometric) space of the thing. Both open onto the single space of the world.[101]

The drama which transpires within the structure of this space articulates an affective "locale" wherein the object virtually comes to life: Hawthorne's Ovidian universe announces itself to the degree that it becomes expressive, that it *figures*—indeed, trans-figures—itself. The letter, the house, the faun, the ribbon, the pipe, the oaken lady, the mountain, the forest, the lime-kiln—these figures touch us insofar as they correspond to an affective configuration. The controlling consciousness at the center of Hawthorne's vision is thus discovered amid the interval of both human and natural space; here alone we unearth that intimate bearing toward the object as a (w)hole. The image holds within it the inward landscape of the world, its "figured" texture, the space of desire: an icon of vision that enables affective experience to transcend itself, a means of co-existence with the phenomenon. In effect, Hawthorne's descriptive technique provides a "syntax" of the object—its very language—which integrates into a single "life" each aspect as its emblem, a symbolic system of human life: "That is why we say that in perception the thing is given to us 'in person', or 'in the flesh'. Prior to and independently of other people, the thing achieves that miracle of expression. . . . Thus the thing is correlative to my body and, in more general terms, to my existence. . . . and if we try to describe the real as it appears to us in perceptual experience, we find it overlaid with anthropological predicates"; as a form or style of behavior, moreover, "The thing is inseparable from a person perceiving it, and can never be actually *in itself* because its articulations are those of our very existence, and because it stands at the other end of our gaze or at the terminus of a sensory exploration which invests it with humanity. To this extent, every perception is a communication or a communion."[102]

To understand better the form of this communion, we need recall the absence of (self)reflection in the perceptual operation—its impersonal structure. Just as in the visual field the line constitutes a certain emptiness, a way of gouging out the thing, so too in perception the subject "delineates" the object against the absence of the "self"—that is, against the background of the body alone. As a mode of the impersonal or, better, pre-personal, the subject constitutes nothing less than a gap in the existent as a (w)hole, a discontinuity by which the perceptual operation and all subsequent forms of consciousness, as well, remain forever open; the eye accomplishes this dehiscence: "Vision is not a certain mode of thought or presence to self; it is the means given me for being absent from myself, for being present at the fission of Being from the inside—the fission at whose termination, and not before, I come back to myself."[103] Hawthorne's image re-creates this lacuna at the origin of all appearance by means of elision. Amid the absence of the object as a final and determinate "whole," the affective aspect reduces the thing to its expressive "persona." Here consciousness links up to the thing as a kind of mask or anti-self, yet prior to any sense of self-"identity."

At the same time, this dynamic helps explain Hawthorne's apparent disregard for in-depth characterization; for as an "object" of description the human person-ality is likewise first encountered simply as an expressive feature of the face—that single, most prominent aspect of the whole. Indeed, with Hawthorne's villains this initial encounter characterizes them entirely, and with an emblematic permanence that no amount of further knowledge can ever revise: witness, for example, Westervelt's grin. His visage remains the same, closed off to change and growth, indelibly characterized by the im-personation in which it is fixed. Beyond the villains, moreover, nearly all of Hawthorne's characters are inscribed to consciousness by means of a single expression and betray his passion, in general, for "masquerade." Faithfulness to the appearance constitutes one of the most striking dynamics of his oeuvre, and everywhere exhibits the reduction of personality to its single most affective aspect: its "face" or *persona,* as it were. Here again, synecdochic substitution of part for whole provides the pre-personal basis for all subsequent personality, as with the Model's eyes, Hepzibah's scowl, Mr. Hooper's smile, Old Moodie's patch, and Westervelt's grin, to cite only a few instances. This abolition of personality at the advent of being to consciousness illustrates the way in which the image is given to us "anonymously."

Accompanying this elision of the subject to *persona* we find a complimentary dynamic: the significance of the thing itself, its expressive physiognomy—that is, the object transfigured in *personification.* The House, for example, reciprocates Hepzibah's scowl with its "meditative look," its "impending brow," its "thoughtful gloom," its "rusty" and "battered visage" (II:27, 28, 12, 56, 81). The forest of *The Scarlet Letter* assumes "the kindest of its moods" to welcome Pearl (I:204). Similarly, the letter, the faun, the Great Stone Face, the oaken lady, the hollow, the rosebud, the red cross, the mantle, the fountain, the bell, the ring, the Old Manse, the great carbuncle, the birth-mark, the mirror—nearly all of Hawthorne's objects are "figures" (personification), "symptoms" of desire. Insofar as his descriptive technique reconstructs the topography of consciousness, it collapses the reflective distance between subject and object upon a middle term or "point" where they meet. Here image and object are but reciprocal expressions of that fissure in being from which the world emerges. As with the object in perception, so too the apprehension of Hawthorne's image requires that the reader occupy a self-less point between aspect (origin) and whole (terminus), an emblematic relief or epiphany understood as the confrontation of a subject with an-Other (perhaps demonic)—the drama of the very masque of the body of the thing, the object "in person" or "in the flesh." Its inversion constitutes the very drama of the mask itself: so it is with "The Minister's Black Veil."[104]

Elision of the person thus accomplishes a kind of "zero-value" juncture, that gap or fissure in the existent wherein subjectivity lodges prior to all objectification and which, enacted by means of Hawthorne's synecdochic oscillation of the image, allows the world of his work to rise up before us as a temporal intention.[105] Hawthorne's image delineates this lacuna in the existent in terms beyond or other than the personal; in a sense, it is the archetype of subjectivity, that absence against which self, object, other, and ultimately "the world" are able to appear, and yet is never "in the picture." It is the site and very possibility of personality itSelf.

☐

If Hawthorne's gaze reveals an indeterminate world no longer constituted by the pictorial or daguerrean frame, it simultaneously structures a consciousness which is itself ambiguously circumvoluted. Because the image projects a space which comes and goes, it subsequently creates an iconology whose jagged edges split and tear the image rather than seal it off.[106] Insofar as these images which shift and fade occupy an haptic foreground, emerging to touch the surface of the gaze, they are, as it were, emphatic. Vision in high definition always discourages empathy,[107] whereas this fragmented vision encourages participation by virtue of the indefinite edges of its "field," a field which affectively enters onto the space of the narrative world itself. At the interior of this disconnected, unenclosed vision, Hawthorne's work heuristically interrogates the significance of those apparitions which inhabit its world. Left to its own devices, the visual sense always seeks to outrage the ambiguous opacity of appearances by seeking "reality" elsewhere; indeed, the rift between appearance and reality is already built into that kind of seeing which pictures the world as a view. The world of Hawthorne's work, on the other hand, pre-views the purely apparitional space of cinema and its irreverent disregard for objectivity by reincorporating appearance and reality. In order to escape the rationalism of the visual frame which had dominated Western civilization for centuries, his oeuvre recovers an iconography whose interior vision once again involves the spectator as a participant. Amid the mosaic of appearances, Hawthorne's world refuses the spectator the possibility of escaping those questions which it raises; he can deny them, but he must address them first. Grounded in contingency, the image is therefore formal only insofar as it is phenomenal; because it has no framework fixed in a physical or pictorial space, but merely structures the reticulation of intention, it thus asserts, as its primary characteristic, a virtual present, an order of direct apparition.[108] It *is* in the mode of "dream."

Dream parallels the spatio-temporal structure of perception *at the level of sensation;* here too the subject is absent from its "self": "Every sensation carries within it the germ of a dream or depersonalization such as we experience in that quasi-stupor to which we are reduced when we really try to live at the level of sensation."[109] Hawthorne characteristically evokes a dream mode, one which brings its elements equally into the foreground as Susanne Langer has remarked: "The most noteworthy formal characteristic of dream is that the dreamer is always at the center of it. Places shift, persons act and speak, or change or fade—facts emerge, situations grow, objects come into view with strange importance, ordinary things infinitely valuable or horrible, and they may be superseded by others that are related to them essentially by feeling, not by natural proximity. But the dreamer is always 'there,' his relation is, so to speak, equidistant from all events. Things may occur around him or unroll before his eyes; he may act or want to act, or suffer or contemplate; but the *immediacy* of everything in a dream is the same for him."[110] The dream is thus essentially iconic, and not pictorial: the psychiatrist forms the story line.[111] Similarly, the dreamed reality can move forward or backward because it constitutes a virtual present.[112] The dream provides a diastolic counterbalance to the systole of rationalism and its retro-(per)spective "view." As Freud observed, the dream is disclosable precisely to the degree that it is "over-determinate"; the principles of "over-determination" and "condensation" allow the dream expressively to transpose disparate and discontinuous elements or moments in time. Hawthorne implicitly understood this dynamic, and explicitly reconstructed the logic of dream in order further to undermine the certitude of objectification, undercutting the heart of the subject–object dichotomy. As the narrator in "P.'s Correspondence" remarks: "More and more I recognize that we dwell in a world of shadows; and, for my part, I hold it hardly worth the trouble to attempt a distinction between shadows in the mind, and shadows out of it. If there be any difference, the former are rather the more substantial" (X:367). In *The American Notebooks,* Hawthorne said it another way: "students ought to be day-dreamers, all of them—when cloud-land is one and the same thing with the substantial earth" (VIII:122–23). Hawthorne typically adopted this stance.[113] Against the rational transparency of the age, his fiction asserts the ambiguity of truth, recites its epistemological problematic in pre-objective phenomena. His most effective efforts addressing the problem of knowledge derive from the threshold of consciousness as it matriculates the subject into self, other, and world. Dream (re)enacts certain dimensions of this liminal structure.

By establishing the primacy of the phenomenon, Hawthorne's dream-like vision returns to the immediate order of apparitions as they make their first "intrusion" in consciousness, and by which the world, in turn, originally announces itself. The dream enabled Hawthorne to structure a vision of the world essentially grounded in appearance, a vision indistinguishable from the "reality" it is presumed to represent. The vague phantasms which inhabit the world of Hawthorne's work are no less real than its perceptions. Over and against the scientific-technological objectification of the existent, Hawthorne's dream consciousness secures the reality of the phenomenon itself and likewise rescues it from its "invisible" fixation in the mind; reality becomes the oblique transfiguration of appearances, as Lessing had observed, a lived-through structure in which the subject's facticity constantly announces itself anew.[114] Hawthorne recognized that the "worldly" character of truth implies the (w)hole of consciousness: "Truth often finds its way to the mind close-muffled in the robes of sleep, and then speaks with uncompromising directness of matters in regard to which we practice an unconscious self-deception, during our waking moments" (X:40).

Since neither truth nor beauty subsist "objectively" within the whole of being, they must be sought on the hither side of an artificial distinction between subject and object. Both physical and metaphysical inquiry often ignore their own relation to the "nature" they so obdurately seek to disclose by virtue of the theoretical frame they employ, and which subsequently places the content of their investigation outside the inquiring subject itself.[115] For Hawthorne, on the other hand, the dream mode cancelled out the abstract and theoretical logic of objective consciousness; the truth of the world no longer obtains from its non-contradictory agreement within a fixed and sterile mental perspective of "correct" ideas. Indeed, dream even distorts the "probable," that quantitative security blanket with which the masses pacify their lives mathematically.[116]

Hawthorne's "interior world" translates the dream into the realm of metaphysics as an analogous model of logic. In contrast to the mediate, reflexive consciousness of the rational attitude, this "inner" consciousness reveals a logic directly "in touch" with subjectivity. Insofar as it "occupies" a finite middle between two extremes, the subject, here, reposes at the center of itSelf, a sphere whose circumference is nowhere. As Pascal observes: "For in fact what is man in nature? A Nothing in comparison with the Infinite, an All in comparison with the Nothing, a mean between nothing and everything. Since he is infinitely removed from comprehending the extremes, the end of things and their beginning are hopelessly hidden from him in an impenetrable secret."[117] Thus, for instance, Owen Warland, whose butterfly becomes a heap of glittering fragments, at last enowns the object of his life-long labors only when it ceases to be *objective:* "the symbol by which he made it perceptible to mortal senses became of little value in his eyes, while his spirit possessed itself in the enjoyment of the Reality" (X:475). Only "outside" the existent does the subject objectify the object; within the solicitous sphere of itSelf, the object is objective only insomuch as it ob-jects.

Hawthorne's turn toward the interior of being discloses a logic which converts objective consciousness into what Heidegger calls "the heart's innermost region."[118] Within this intimate space—the space of the desire of reason itself, the very reason of desire (itSelf)—subject and object mutually implicate each other as they proximally express the "nearness" of being. Here exploitation of the dream parallels the function of the body in sensation; it seeks to recuperate a space prior to that of the perceived world. Dream does not "take place" in the intersubjective world where the thing abides fully "in itself"; the apparition in no way corresponds to an actual environment, but rather articulates an "other" world, a configuration (co)responding to bodily sensation. This disorienting proximity of the dream landscape, like hallucination, does not produce the kind of depth and duration of the thing as it is given in perception, but re-creates the way in which corporeality itself strikes the subject in its affective being—it is to be "read" as the inscription of the *being of feeling*. In dream, the apparition is purely an affective entity.[119] Indeed, that the remoteness of being, which the perspective of the scientific-technological attitude takes for granted, represents the most pressing dilemma of a visual culture is already indicated in the growing sense of division between appearance and reality, a rift which, since the Renaissance, betrays an ever-burgeoning obsession with the problem of hypocrisy. Rather than reflect what McLuhan calls "the Baroque quest for depth through duality,"[120] Hawthorne's oeuvre, like the mirrors which populate it, seeks to deflect consciousness away from the reflection of itself and back to that absence or lack we call "desire," what Scheler calls the "emptiness of the heart," in which consciousness dwells—that existential tide which runs through all the forms of space.[121] Here, the dream apparition expresses the world in its inaugural physiognomy: the absence of the self against the presence of desire.

More often than not, Hawthorne considered life itself a dream. He did so with the implicit recognition that those passing apparitions which besiege the life of consciousness, especially those which assail the "Haunted Mind" somewhere between waking and slumber, bespeak a reality at odds with the noonday certitude of everyday experience, and yet constitute a significant aspect of that experience. As Heidegger has remarked, existence itself provokes this confrontation, "the difficulty of going over from the . . . still covetous vision of things, from the work of the eyes, to the 'work of the heart.'"[122] The world of Hawthorne's work begins with this event: the trans-position from objective representation to the logic of the heart. Like the narrator of "The Celestial Rail-Road," it's easy to dismiss the affective dimension of consciousness with the facile cliché, "it was only a dream" (X:206). For Hawthorne, however, this cliché represents the ultimate, bathetic gesture in escape from (self) knowledge.[123] Hawthorne's work attests the bankruptcy of that intelligence which denies its own apparitions; his oeuvre articulates a "physics of the exception"[124] rather than the rule—it takes the subject beyond the protective rule of uniformity toward that discontinuous space which bears the affective stamp of being. At Blithedale, for example, Coverdale's ultimate failure is already prefigured on one of his first nights in the community by his dismissal of a dream: "Had I made a record of that night's half-waking dreams, it is my belief that it would have anticipated several of the chief incidents of this narrative, including a dim shadow of its catastrophe" (III:38).[125] In the preface, Hawthorne had observed that his own experience at Brook Farm was "essentially a day-dream, and yet a fact . . . offering an available foothold between fiction and reality" (III:2). His oeuvre addresses an audience whose sensibility, as he said of his daughter Una, "is more readily awakened by fiction than reality" (VIII:415). Similarly, with the Pyncheons, "rejection of dream at cost to their humanity is characteristic. . . . Haughtily as the Pyncheons bear themselves in the noonday streets, however, they are 'no better than bondservants to these plebian Maules, on entering the topsy-turvy commonwealth of sleep.'"[126] In this regard, those who reject dream inevitably find themselves cut off from their own humanity and the world which they inhabit—witness Goodman Brown: "A stern, a sad, a darkly meditative, a distrustful, if not a desperate man, did he become, from the night of that fearful dream" (X:89).

Throughout his life, everything predisposed Hawthorne to daydreaming, toward unfocused diversions of the mind and senses;[127]

single-mindedly, his work accomplished this oneiric transformation of reality, projecting a world prior to "without" and "within."[128] As Normand suggests, Hawthorne's fiction reclaims the Ovidian universe as its primordial homeland: "We find ourselves on the borders of the region of primitive romance, of the supernatural, of dreams. We are entering a land of chimeras where everything is possible, where everything is capable of metamorphosis: houses transformed into vegetables, human trees, wooden figureheads with faces of flesh—we stand once again in the province of magic—in which objects and beings are simultaneously themselves and other than themselves, change their faces, their forms, their colors, appear and disappear . . . the country in which things become animate, in which living beings suddenly become statues, in which the dead move, in which man is on the same scale as nature."[129] Against the scientific world-view, which makes the subject "larger" than nature, its "measure," dream inscribes the subject within the ambiguous texture of the existent. In this respect, Hawthorne's iconic imagery re-creates the expressive labyrinth of a world whose ownmost image is itself to be discovered at the interior of the heart's inner space. Each image being a hermeneutic sphere or circle, the interwoven fabric of "the world" finds its reciprocal convexity and concavity enclosed by opposing mirrors which constantly reflect the ambiguous image of being back upon itself:[130] the echoes which ricochet from the hills are mutually supported by the hollow, perpetually drawing them back to its center (IX:201); the images of the past which circle around Hester are inclusively maintained within the silent present of the pillory (I:58–59); the scenes which evolve inside the showman's box are ultimately grounded in its finite, temporal center (XI:49–50); the interior labyrinth which Goodman Brown discovers in the forest paradoxically encloses that which it reveals, as the forest itself reciprocally revolves about him (X:83–84).

This dream-like contour of the image actively provokes the antagonism of the straight line and the acute aggressive angle.[131] Here dream opposes all reflective distance by which the subject "knows" its world of objects. Like the reverie of images which revolve around Hester on the pillory, dream puts us directly in touch with a world immediately our own: the reality of immediate appearance. As Werner Wolff points out: "Most investigators of the dream acknowledge that the dream is a reflection of waking experiences, but none has stated that our waking experiences are also reflections of our dreams"; and though in dream the subject searches for the fulfillment of reality, the opposite is equally the case: "in reality, man searches for the figures of his dream."[132] Similarly, Hawthorne's narrator often questions the very reality of the *récit:* "Had Goodman Brown fallen asleep in the forest, and only dreamed a wild dream of a witch-meeting? Be it so, if you will" (X:89). The ambiguous references to illusion and reality accommodate Hawthorne's opaque technique without having to define the objective nature of that experience—for example, whether it is "actual" or "imaginary." If anything, the superimposed questioning voice central to many of Hawthorne's narratives constitutes the rhetorical negation of all certitude whatsoever. For instance, the "supered" interrogation attending his description of the dead Judge—"Has it yet vanished? No!—yes!—not quite!" (II:276)—reflects the epistemological ambiguity of his entire oeuvre. In dream, objects of the conceptual mind become but nebulous shadows; the image is returned to the logic of a carnal wor(l)d. "The Haunted Mind" defines the oneiric urgency of this moment: "*Passion and Feeling assume bodily shape,* and the things of the mind become dim spectres to the eye" (IX:306, italics mine). The haunted mind relinquishes its will to will in favor of a sensibility more or less entirely passive—a "negative capability," to use Keats' phrase, which invites "the world" to *appear:* "In an hour like this, when the mind has a passive sensibility, but no active strength; when the imagination is a mirror, imparting vividness to all ideas, without the power of selecting or controlling them; then pray that your griefs may slumber, and the brotherhood of remorse not break their chain" (IX:306).

For centuries, the ontical world of science had contented itself with "observation," a manipulative procedure which Hawthorne found at best superfluous. Insofar as scientific observation merely "takes note of" the conspicuous, it is redundant. For this kind of "seeing," the world, as merely the sum of individual entities, becomes a concept in the mind. For Hawthorne, however, "to see" is to perceive the inconspicuous, to discover the phenomenon of form. At the Old Manse, for example, he once observed: "The trees have a singular appearance in the midst of waters; the curtailment of their trunks quite destroys the proportions of the whole tree; and we become conscious of a regularity and propriety in the forms of Nature, by the effect of this abbreviation" (VIII:381). In the same way, dream presents a mode of being in which all its forms phenomenally cohere. Unlike the objective analytic of the scientific-technological "view," which "subjects" the world to a determinate number of discrete entities, dream expresses the indeterminate structure of the existent. As Freud observed: "Dreams are particularly fond of reducing antitheses to uniformity, or representing them as one and the same thing."[133] Paradox, oxymoron, and ambiguity in general are therefore central to dream logic. Thus, the Letter comes to mean things opposite to the Puritan conception of sin.[134] Indeed, dream is generally that

mode which best lends itself to "burrowing . . . into the depths of our
common nature" which Hawthorne found most suitable to the purposes
of "psychological romance," as he expressed it in his preface to *The
Snow-Image,* and whosoever pursues his researches in such a dusky region
must necessarily do so as much "by the tact of sympathy as by the light
of observation" (XI:4).

While dream often reveals that which most affectively "lies" closest
to us, it always does so in disguise, disclosing what is most "closed off"
from the reflective self, including its attitudes about itself. Coverdale's
"central" dream, for example, refutes the abstract, reflective logic of his
waking moments, the logic of his *récit,* while it confirms the logic of his
heart, that feeling which the narration itself denies. Although he constantly refers to himself as a minor figure in the drama of Blithedale, his
intermediate position between Zenobia and Hollingsworth, as they stand
on either side of the bed reaching across to exchange a kiss amid the
torment of his dream, reveals in fact that he considers himself central to
both their lives; indeed, as he beholds this passionate exchange between
the two, the image of Priscilla entirely fades so that the dream itself
discloses what even his final confession conceals: he was in love with
Zenobia and not Priscilla (III:153, 247).[135] Similarly, if Goodman
Brown's experience in the forest was only a dream, "alas! it was a dream
of evil omen" (X:89), for in denying his own evil, he henceforth severs
himself from both his wife and the remainder of humanity as well—
"severs," that is, in every way but one, for he is followed to his grave, I
would remind you, by "children and grandchildren, a goodly procession" (X:90).

In its deployment of images, moreover, the dream mode likewise
functions cinematically. Even those works which don't explicitly concern
themselves with dream often appropriate its technique, collapsing the
border between the phantasm and the real: "Hawthorne was simply consciously exploiting the cinematic resources of the soul. He was one of the
first to discover, and to demonstrate in dazzling fashion, that the cinema
had always existed potentially in our imagination, and that it is part of
our mental activity."[136] To the extent that Hawthorne's descriptive technique visually dis-locates "reality," it adhibits the hypnagogic as well,
those images "subsisting on the borderland of the unconscious which
surrealism has seized for its peculiar domain"; indeed, Hawthorne's image, as Eisenstein says of cinema itself, draws the spectator into a creative
act "in which his individuality is not subordinated to the author's individuality, but is opened up throughout the process of fusion with the author's intention."[137]

The interior landscape of "Young Goodman Brown," for example, engages us with its urgency. Through the cinematic play of light and shade, this ambiguous nightmare arrests our attention at the very surface of its dramatic "screen": up front and center. It is intrinsically immediate. Likewise, the action of "My Kinsman, Major Molineux" refutes a "public" space and time; it (re)arranges its materials by means of montage as in a dream: "Indeed, in the sense of the rapid succession of images that the story gives us and in the definite effect of condensation and acceleration involved . . . we almost seem—as though we were Robin—to dream rather than read the story."[138] The focus of Robin's gaze alters in proportion to its discoveries, and with an alacrity that immediately reflects the dramatic situation; rooftops become walls become mansions become balconies become pillars become a gothic window (XI:221). Montage, however, disappears abruptly at the end. The procession fades out first, leaving the scene by itself; the sense of location goes last as the procession moves on, bequeathing a silent street behind: out of this silence, there comes the break in the fabric of the dream.[139] Hawthorne's sharp focus at the conclusion further punctuates the solitary "privacy" of this vision, and re-situates us toward the public space and time outside the labyrinthian interior from which Robin has emerged. While Robin's perception of his kinsman at the conclusion is diametrically opposed to his previous impression in the country, these "faces" of interpretation are neither self-evident nor mutually exclusive. So too Robin's laughter at the end transfigures the double-visaged figure, ironically suggesting the inherent paradox of being.

In addition to nightmare and dream, however, the "Haunted Mind" accommodates reverie as well; indeed, "it contains the entire cinema of consciousness, with its methods, its technique, its screen, its camera."[140] "You sink down in a flowery spot, on the borders of sleep and wakefulness, while your thoughts rise before you in pictures, all disconnected, yet all assimilated by a pervading gladsomeness and beauty"; or, to vary the figure, "you find yourself, for a single instant, wide awake in that realm of illusions, whither sleep has been the passport, and behold its ghostly inhabitants and wondrous scenery, with a perception of their strangeness, such as you never attain while the dream is undisturbed" (IX:308, 304). A world of fragmented images arises before the haunted mind within "the space of a summer night" (IX:305)—images which reveal the depths of the heart; it is the present moment of a time thoroughly detached from all biographical perspective, a time without past or future: "Yesterday has already vanished among the shadows of the past; to-morrow has not yet emerged from the future. You have found an intermediate space, where the business of life does not intrude; where the passing moment lingers, and becomes truly the present; a spot where Father Time, when he thinks nobody is watching him, sits down by the way side to take a breath" (IX:305). It is the time of "conscious sleep" (IX:307). Like the images that engage us before a fire, each lingers in the mind's eye long after the darkness has swallowed the reality (IX:308). Around the principle of the haunted mind, Hawthorne thus structures his most affective tales. Harassed by the phantasms which arise before him, Goodman Brown struggles forward through the gloom of the forest (X:81); plagued by the panorama of her past, Hester momentarily displaces the anguish of the pillory with that of another (I:58); compelled by his curious sense of unreality, the adventurer of the "Night Sketches" hastens through the darkness guided only by an occasional flicker of light—a reverie of street-lamps rather than fire (IX:428, 431). And so the consciousness of reverie articulates a parallel between human life and itself: "In both you emerge from mystery, pass through a vicissitude that you can but imperfectly control, and are borne onward to another mystery" (IX:309).

Before the blaze of the fire, Ethan Brand struggles against those images that besiege him, recalling the smoldering panorama of his life within a single instant. More than anything, fire invites reverie. As Bachelard observes: "If fire, which, after all, is quite an exceptional and rare phenomenon, was taken to be a constituent element of the Universe, is it not because it is an element of human thought, the prime element of reverie?"[141] Hawthorne's own life reveals a marked fascination, if not obsession, with this phenomenon. In Salem, as a child, he often went to watch the fires that broke out; and if one occurred late at night, he used to send his sister to investigate, reporting back to him whether it was worth getting out of bed to see.[142] Both the notebooks and the fiction abound with references to the fireside. Distinct from the attention of observation and contemplation, reverie occasions transformation. Thus Ethan Brand "sat listening to the crackling of the kindled wood, and looking at the little spirts of fire that issued through the chinks of the door. These trifles, however, once so familiar, had but the slightest hold of his attention; while deep within his mind, he was reviewing the gradual, but marvelous change, that had been wrought upon him by the search to which he had devoted himself" (XI:98). The fire reflects this change, the withering of a heart having "ceased to partake of the universal throb" (XI:99). Hawthorne here conjoins this transformation to both the minimal life of the fire and the plenary life of the lime-kiln, a world unto its own, as Ethan ascends the hill toward the top of the structure. In its own way, reverie has already accomplished this task. As Bachelard suggests, "Fire is for the man who is contemplating it an example of a sudden change or development and an example of a circumstantial development. Less monotonous and less abstract than flowing water . . . fire suggests the desire to change, to speed up the passage of time, to bring all of life to its conclusion, to its hereafter. In these circumstances the reverie becomes truly fascinating and dramatic; it magnifies human destiny; it links the small to the great, the hearth to the volcano, the life of a log to the life of the world. The fascinated individual hears *the call of the funeral pyre*. For him destruction is more than a change, it is a renewal."[143]

Thus Ethan, through identification, surrenders the cold marble of his heart to the heart of the flame. Unlike the mayfly, however, this incomplete lesson in eternity leaves a trace—the shape of his heart endures upon the surface of the lime: once the lime-burner crushes the remains, returning Ethan to the anonymity of humanity's common bond, the lesson is complete. Ironically, death in the flames is the least lonely of deaths; through it, Ethan attains the cosmic: a microcosm is reduced to nothingness.[144] Only the dream endures: "That night the sound of a fearful peal of laughter rolled heavily through the sleep of the lime-burner and his little son; dim shapes of horror and anguish haunted their dreams, and seemed still present in the rude hovel when they opened their eyes to the daylight" (XI:100).

Insofar as it thus accommodates nightmare, dream, and reverie, the haunted mind evades objective time and space. Within this ambiguous and opaque abode, the transparent "cogito" gets thrown back upon its equivocal adherence in pre-objective phenomena. Like the gothic edifice in "The Hall of Fantasy," the haunted mind admits the light of "heaven" or reason "only through stained and pictured glass, thus filling with many-colored radiance, and painting its marble floor with beautiful or grotesque designs; so that its inmates breathe, as it were, a visionary atmosphere, and tread upon the fantasies of poetic minds" (X:172). This edifice of fantasy remains the subject's lasting homeland, for though it superficially gives "the impression of a dream, which might be dissipated and shattered to fragments, by merely stamping the foot upon the pavement," yet, "with such modifications and repairs as successive ages demand, the Hall of Fantasy is likely to endure longer than the most substantial structure that ever cumbered the earth" (X:172–73).

Hence, the logic of the haunted mind is nothing less than poetic; it articulates the "interior" of the world, that uncharted region we are prone to isolate from "reality," either to grant it an immaterial existence apart or to deny its existence altogether. Indeed, the world of Hawthorne's work converts poetic consciousness into an organ, a thing of flesh and blood "whose substance may be tenuous but which can also become extremely dense and weigh down with a great weight in the physical world"; insomuch as the haunted mind incorporates the image, in all its manifestations, it always already inheres in the world it projects: "consciousness awake and consciousness asleep—consciousness questing or fleeing, following its own arabesques, mingling with itself, fighting against itself without cease."[145] The haunted mind scorns any and all objectification whose schemes for "fixing the reflections of objects in a pool of water, and thus taking the most life-like portraits imaginable" (X:178) must always go awry. Reflection thus penetrates the dream-like opacity of the haunted mind only to the extent that it mirrors those interior voids or subjectivities that dwell within its fold, those impenetrable gaps in the texture of the existent which both disclose and conceal its world. As P. remarks: "The reality—that which I know to be such—hangs like remnants of tattered scenery over the intolerable prominent illusion. Let us think of it no more" (X:371).

Hawthorne's haunted mind recuperates, moreover, the *imaginative* site upon which narration itself recites this scene, returning the clarity of the concept back to the pre-objective text of experience; it accommodates a plethora of (human) spaces prior to the rational, those ambiguous forms that reveal the way in which the subject both "figures" and "projects" the world anterior to objectification. Dream, nightmare, and reverie provide a veritable theatre of the re-sources of consciousness, modes of existence wherein the subject's contingency repeatedly returns to haunt it, modes by which the world itself is put in doubt, yet simultaneously put in place *(mise-en-scène)*. Hallucination, too, expresses this abysmal structure *(mise-en-abyme)*. P.'s correspondent explains it thus: "My unfortunate friend P. has lost the thread of his life, by the interposition of long intervals of partially disordered reason. The past and present are jumbled together in his mind, in a manner often productive of curious results. . . . The poor fellow . . . meets, in his wanderings, a variety of personages who have long ceased to be visible to any eye save his own. In my opinion, all this is not so much a delusion, as a partly wilful and partly involuntary sport of the imagination" (X:361). In having lost the "thread" of his life, P.'s imagination disrupts the temporal knot of existence. The unorthodox logic of P.'s "irrational" mind returns the idea(l) to the affect, the carnal *text*ure of being. Similarly, this unorthodox logic consolidates itself "into almost as material an entity as mankind's strongest architecture. It is sometimes a serious question with me, whether ideas be not really visible and tangible, and endowed with all the other qualities of matter" (X:362). Here, "the world" cannot be taken for granted. Insomuch as sensation already contains within it the material affect, the haunted mind reveals to what extent "reality" accommodates both the phenomenon and its form. As Merleau-Ponty has observed, "Clear space, that impartial space in which all objects are equally important and enjoy the same right to existence, is not only surrounded, but also thoroughly permeated by another spatiality thrown into relief by morbid deviations from the normal."[146] The haunted mind reveals this "other" spatiality insofar as dream, nightmare, reverie, and hallucination carry within themselves the value of reality. Hawthorne's fiction recuperates the haunted mind in order to secure the world's inner space, the space of the heart where every apparition expresses the reciprocity of subject and object—the very body of the world.[147]

By reason of its own logic, dream discloses those aspects of the subject and (its relation to) the world which observation would deny. Hawthorne's world expresses the bankruptcy of an objective view grounded in reason alone, the *ordo* of the ordinary. The logic of the heart, of the affective life, is extraordinary insofar as it takes the subject beyond the protective and "self"-defensive bounds of objectification. Only within the exposition of the heart is the subject secured. Speaking of Shelley's later works, P. expresses it thus: "The author has learned to dip his pen oftener into his heart, and has thereby avoided the faults into which a too exclusive use of fancy and intellect was wont to betray him" (X:373). In an age still oriented toward moral analysis, Hawthorne's fiction brought about a psychological revolution in American literature, "a revolution that in no way prefigured the introduction into the average American's everyday life of a psychoanalysis imbued with a superstitious regard for the social norm, but, on the contrary, that upheld both the rights of the outstanding individual and the rights of the poet."[148] Through its dream-like vision, recouping the re-sources of the subject, "the world" of Hawthorne's work opens a phenomenal ingress to the question of being, without which consciousness would leave that very world behind. Here dream provides an intrinsic link between the "dual" spatiality of subject and object within the structure of the world, as Merleau-Ponty suggests: "though it is indeed from the dreamer that I was last night that I require an account of the dream, the dreamer himself offers no account, and the person who does so is awake. Bereft of the waking state, dreams would be no more than instantaneous modulations, and so would not even exist for us. During the dream itself, we do not leave the world behind: the dream is segregated from the space of clear thinking, but it uses all the latter's articulations; the world obsesses us even during sleep, and it is about the world that we dream."[149] The haunted mind enacts a consciousness whose fluid interior equivocates the transparent picture objectivity demands, a space wherein free and multiple forms of consciousness provoke the bodily reality of a world beyond the edges of an objective frame. Its figures mean *other* than the literal— exceed, escape the logic of the scientific-analytic that would contain them, frame them, just as the figures of Phoebe's mesmerized vision will enter the narrative space of, merge with the text of, *The House.* The haunted mind thus figures figuration itself; its affective logic embodies the very body of Hawthorne's text, its sexual ambiguity. "What a strange, incongruous dream is the life of man" (X:373).

Similarly, this affective link between subject and object obtains in everyday experience as well and returns us, in every instance, to the configuration of that space we call "the world." The affect is its *body.* Within the haunted mind, appearance and reality are one and the same. Here consciousness admits of no separation between the apparent and the real; there is only the phenomenon.[150] "Personal" time, which holds the past and future in the present, is put in abeyance: a single, all-pervasive present abides. As "lived," Hawthorne's poetic consciousness structures the self-less realm of the percept, the way in which the reader-perceiver loses its self in the (descriptive) image—its synecdochic oscillation and affective proximity. Like Giacometti's sculptures that represent a foot, a leg, "but so huge that one no longer thinks of the body to which they lead up," Hawthorne's dialectic of detail confers upon the depth of space its heart: "Part becomes bigger than whole; whole becomes smaller than the smallest part."[151] I recall you to Lacan: desire is a metonymy. The differential detail exists as that expressive correspondence between subject and object, what generates the very space of "the world." This world precedes objectification. Within the thickness of the present, Hawthorne's haunted mind sets up *(mise)* that ambiguity and ambivalence from which consciousness can never be completely extricated. Freed from the bonds of causality, the various forms of antepredicative space procure an "opening," exploding that frame of representation by means of which the subject objectifies the existent as a whole. As Piaget observes, causality is but the intellectual elaboration of this primordial spatiality of the world and not its *a priori* form.[152] "The world," here understood, is neither a view nor a matter of inference, but rather the "theatre" *(scène)* of experience; it accommodates both object and image without discrimination because an "individual" consciousness embraces everything. The world is not a collection of objects linked by causal relations. To perceive, to dream, to hallucinate, and—more generally—to *imagine* "is to exploit this tolerance on the part of the antepredicative world, and our bewildering proximity to the whole of being in syncretic experience."[153]

□

Nevertheless, the imagined isn't mine alone, but opens onto that world in which other subjects likewise appear, take (up a) place—those discontinuous breaches in the existent as a (w)hole which enable being itSelf to figure forth. To the extent that Hawthorne's image opens the subject onto the phenomenal, the haunted mind (synecdochic syntax/ dream ["poetic"] logic) provides those variations in consciousness which enable reflection to transcend the appearance, bequeathing to consciousness that possibility we call the "self." Within the structure of this world, this possibility appears as a hiatus in the "language" of the existent, a region of silence (it needs to be called forth, provoked). Here consciousness reveals itself as an "anonymous" form of the world, a mode of being beneath the personal which "signals" the existence of an inborn complex—regarding whose "significance" reflection gives the name *repression*.[154] Only insofar as the subject is always already given over to this structure can it erect a superstructure of ideas beyond (the world of) sensory experience—express it(Self).[155] In perception, the (out)line (re)constitutes this gap between seer and seen, this "absence" in the image. It is the image's own technique by means of which desire inhabits the imaginary, *inscribes* the subject, from the outset—its own colossal excess, the exer-"cise" of within/without, the very citation (of the subject) of perception: "Line is the common bond between man and things; the modulations of line constitute a language. And here it is necessary to take the word 'literally' literally: the identity of human language and the language of things occurs at the level of the alphabet."[156] The "line" between objects, what "frames" them in perception, that very line which represents the object in a composition, is—*at the level of reflection*—(always already) narration (itSelf). Upon this site, the subject recites its self, composes itSelf.

The narrative line will frame the play of figuration at its heart—the subject's attempt to make sense, to figure itSelf (out)—just as *The House* configures those figures central to (the heart of) the House, including the figure of the House as a heart. At the same time, however, narration will frame those figures in which it (itSelf) figures, in which it figures itSelf. The House as a heart is (at) the heart of *The House*, just as the affect is (at) the heart of Hawthorne's House of Fiction. Narration recites the House by heart, takes it to heart: the House is but a figure for the narrative "frame" *(The House)*, a figure of the frame of its figures, its narrative "body." Narration is the frame that figures itSelf, its own frame. The narrative frame stands (in) for itSelf, stands in (for) itSelf, stands (up) as the very figure it embodies, the body of itSelf. No longer missing (from the [primal] scene of the crime), the body is a frame (up).

In effect, the affect is a writing effect, an inscription, a detail (metonymy) which figures the figure of detail (desire): desire inscribes (the body of) the text itSelf. Thus, for example, the figure (body) of Hepzibah exceeds the figuration of itself as frame, the frame of its figure. Awaiting Clifford's arrival, in preparation for this figure, "there had been a constant tremor in Hepzibah's frame; an agitation so powerful, that Phoebe could see the quivering of her gaunt shadow, as thrown by the firelight on the kitchen-wall, or by the sunshine on the parlor-floor. Its manifestations were so various, and agreed so little with one another, that the girl knew not what to make of it" (II:101). This interchange of figure and frame, its doubling, the ghostly image of each within the other, in turn, mirrors the affect, commemorates it, memorizes it. Regarding these various "manifestations" of Hepzibah's frame, the "constant tremor" of her figure,

> Sometimes, it seemed an ecstacy of delight and happiness. . . . The next moment, without any visible cause for the change, her unwonted joy shrank back, appalled, as it were, and clothed itself in mourning; or it ran and hid itself, so to speak, in the dungeon of her heart, where it had long lain chained. . . . She often broke into a little, nervous, hysteric laugh, more touching than any tears could be; and forthwith . . . a gust of tears would follow; or perhaps the laughter and tears came both at once. . . . Towards Phoebe, as *we* have said, she was affectionate . . . yet with a continually recurring pettishness and irritability. She would speak sharply to her; then . . . ask pardon, and, the next instant, renew the just forgiven injury. (II:101–2, italics mine)

As with the House, narration here secures that figure at the heart of Hepzibah's frame, its own heart. I alert you to the pronoun "we," the "tremor" at the very heart of this narration, its divisiveness within the space it claims as proper to itSelf, its own (proper-ty): "ran and hid itself" indeed—and "so to speak" (no less). Narration doesn't miss a beat. Or is it, rather, that the *récit* conceals its own arrhythmia, that here and there ([Da]*sein*) it skips a beat *(fort-da)*? In Hawthorne, there is always this chance—this duplicity, this doubling, trebling, multiplicity of affect, the excess of the subject. Narration frames its (ghostly) desire: the desire to frame itSelf, to embody its own body. The frame, however, can no more contain its figures than its figures configure the frame. Figures are "subject" to frames, including the figure of framing (the figure of framing [the figure of framing . . .]), just as, in *The House*, the railroad car will frame those figures at the heart of its interior, those passengers, those readers, who "had plunged into the English scenery and adventures of pamphlet-novels, and were keeping company with dukes and earls" (II:257). These figures, in turn, will frame the figures in the books they read (those "dukes" and "earls") by way of allusion.[157] The very figure of reading, moreover, will frame the reading of figures, the problematic of narration in general: "Figures are subject to reading, but reading can lead only to other figures, including figures of reading."[158] Indeed, figuring the frame transfigures the figure itself. This (ex)change exceeds any sense of totality, makes nonsense of the whole.

If the affect takes a figure-ground gestalt, this configuration but signifies the image of its own desire, its locus in the imaginary. Narration will undo this (self)reflection, unravel, unthread the knot of this phantasy. While narration frames the figure (of detail), outlines the affect, its frame is—in itself—a detailed figure, a body without a tail, a tale without a tail, without an end, outside it, outside its own end, its "purpose" (I recall you to the frame in Kant), beside itSelf. The end of the narrative line is its (k)not, the very figure of its absence (to itSelf), its (absence to) self. At "heart," the figure-frame configuration in Hawthorne is abysmal.

The frame, at best, will figure a configuration of frames. Thus Hawthorne often frames a story within a story: witness, for instance, both Zenobia's legend of "The Silvery Veil" and old Moodie's sketch of "Fauntleroy" in *Blithedale*. So too, the tale of "Alice Pyncheon," embedded within the larger frame of *The House,* suggests the abyss that structures the origin of any story. This "wild, chimney-corner legend" (II:197), which Holgrave recites to Phoebe, induces a "remarkable drowsiness" (II:211)—to which the reader is also susceptible. Those who stay awake, however, experience something more akin to vertigo. The succession of narrative frames seduces the reader into its abyss, just as Alice Pyncheon's father appears to be absorbed "in the contemplation of a landscape by Claude, where a shadowy and sun-streaked vista penetrated so remotely into an ancient wood, that it would have been no wonder if his fancy had lost itself in the picture's bewildering depths" (II:203).

If Hawthorne's frames implode toward an abysmal interior, they likewise explode their exterior. Consequently, at the end of *The House,* Colonel Pyncheon's portrait, "frame and all, tumbled suddenly from its position, and lay face downward on the floor" (II:315–16). With their departure from the House, its central figures disfigure those figures that framed them, confined them. And with the disappearance of figure, the frame collapses also. Now free of the peripheral figure that framed them from out of the past (Colonel Pyncheon), and the figure that framed them in the present (Judge Pyncheon: and literally so, regarding Clifford), the central figures now pass beyond the frame that figured them at the outset of this *récit*—the dialogue between Dixey and the anonymous townsman upon the threshold of Hepzibah's "Shop-Window," the very threshold of the story. But what's to become of these figures—Clifford, Hepzibah, Phoebe, Holgrave?

It's not by chance—in a text which figures its figures reading (figures), which figures the reading of figures, which figures the figure of reading—that Hepzibah will read to Clifford a story whose ending prefigures the "happy" ending of the story that frames it: "Hepzibah then took up Rasselas, and began to read of the Happy Valley, with a vague idea that some secret of a contented life had there been elaborated, which might at least serve Clifford and herself for this one day. But the Happy Valley had a cloud over it" (II:134).[159] Judge Pyncheon's death will serve to clear things up, so that the end of *The House* both returns its figures to this interior "shot" of the House—this internal frame of *The House*—and simultaneously opens them upon another frame external to the space of both the House and *The House,* opens onto an "other" end ("purpose" vis-à-vis the [primal] scene of a crime) that frames them as those figures who live happily ever after—that is, without an end. The "ever after" of *The House,* however, first enters the space of another text—and from the rear no less, its "end" (*The House* will take this other text from behind)— where the final chapter of *Rasselas* sets out its "Conclusion, in which Nothing is Concluded." There, in fact, its figures are still confined to a house at the end. Here Hawthorne does Johnson one better.

By opening onto/into the space of another text by way of allusion, *The House* affirms the abysmal structure of (inter)textuality (intersubjectivity) in general. In itself, allusion is always abysmal: its entry into another text *is* that text's entry into it. Allusion is the very figure of reading (itSelf) in Hawthorne: it figures the abyss of reading (figures). The ending of *The House* thus figures the end of its figures as endless. So too of (the narrative frame) itSelf. *The House* will bring its figures outside itself (the House), beyond its own frame, to enter the frame of another house (text) whose frame (end) itself collapses in the (frame) end (of *The House*), sinks into the abyss (Poe's not far away: I know, neither is madness). There's no place to go but down—or up. *The House* will opt for the latter. It's but a short climb to heaven, whither the narration itSelf passes (away): "And wise Uncle Venner, passing slowly from the ruinous porch, seemed to hear a strain of music, and fancied that sweet Alice Pyncheon—after witnessing these deeds, this by-gone woe, and this present happiness, of her kindred mortals—had given one farewell touch of a spirit's joy upon her harpsichord, as she floated heavenward from the *House of the Seven Gables*" (II:319): "The End" (II:319): whooah, not so fast! Let's get this straight: *The House,* here, enters the end of another (its *jouissance* begins here: the pleasure of [the text] itSelf) in order to (don't start what you can't) finish nothing—in order not to finish or, better, to go on forever. This is that (happily) "ever after" of the frame without an "end." This is its conclusion—the conclusion not to conclude: to leave everything up (a/head), in the air ("heavenward" indeed). The inconclusiveness of *The House* returns with a vengeance in *The Faun,* where it will serve to conclude the entirety of Hawthorne's oeuvre. In the meantime *(Blithedale),* and in sight of the abyss itself *(The Letter),* Hawthorne's gaze will turn its own world inside out.

In his preface to *Twice-told Tales,* Hawthorne remarks:

> The sketches are not, it is hardly necessary to say, profound; but it is rather more remarkable that they so seldom, if ever, show any design on the writer's part to make them so. They have none of the abstruseness of idea, or obscurity of expression, which mark the written communications of a solitary mind with itself. They never need translation. It is, in fact, the style of a man of society. Every sentence, so far as it embodies thought or sensibility, may be understood and felt by anybody, who will give himself the trouble to read it, and will take up the book in a proper mood.

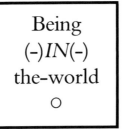

> This statement of apparently opposite peculiarities leads us to a perception of what the sketches truly are. They are not the talk of a secluded man with his own mind and heart, (had it been so, they could hardly have failed to be more deeply and permanently valuable,) but his attempts, and very imperfectly successful ones, to open an intercourse with the world. (IX:6)

To open an intercourse with the world: whatever "significance" accrues to the world of Hawthorne's work comes about on the fringe of those consciousnesses that open onto it: that is, as a consequence of a dimension which is reflection itSelf. If the existential *tex*ture of an intersubjective world obtains only so long as it is "lived,"[1] the text itSelf must be *read.* And it is in this sense that Hawthorne's most demonstrable villains are principally defined. They have failed to "live," to read, to interpret, to open onto and into the "other." Here, intersubjectivity and intertextuality are one and the same phenomenon. Aylmer, Rappaccini, Chillingworth, Hollingsworth, Westervelt—all represent men with minds conditioned by inflexible concepts, the objective transparency of a fixed idea. Rather than unfold toward the interstice of discourse, of dialogue, of solicitude, Hawthorne's villains disregard the naked vulnerability of the subject. They refuse to regard the other, refuse the other's regard. They objectify the other's gaze, in fact, and thus close off the very possibility of communication.[2] Like the gaze of the crowd which interrogates Hester on the pillory, "a thousand unrelenting eyes, all fastened upon her, and concentrated at her bosom" (I:57), the careless gaze of Hawthorne's villains has already objectified, determined, and in fact judged the other as an ontically observable quantity. The transparency of such a view obscures the contingency of (its own) being, as Merleau-Ponty suggests: "the other's gaze transforms me into an object, and mine him, only if both of us withdraw into the core of our thinking nature, if we both make ourselves into an inhuman gaze, if each of us feels his actions to be not taken up and understood, but observed as if they were an insect's. This is what happens, for instance, when I fall under the gaze of a stranger. But even then, the objectification of each by the other's gaze is felt as unbearable only because it takes the place of possible communication."[3]

So it is, for example, with the exquisite pain which Hester experiences upon the pillory under public exposure: "Another peculiar torture was felt in the gaze of a new eye. When strangers looked curiously at the scarlet letter,—and none ever failed to do so,—they branded it afresh into Hester's soul" (I:85–86). Not only the gaze of a stranger, however, but even that of an acquaintance might carelessly bring before her this vivid self-perception, this estrangement, "like a new anguish, by the rudest touch upon the tenderest spot" (I:84); for in the ability of the gaze to violate the other, "an accustomed eye had likewise its own anguish to inflict. Its cool stare of familiarity was intolerable. From first to last, in short, Hester Prynne had always this dreadful agony in feeling a human eye upon the token; the spot never grew callous; it seemed, on the contrary, to grow more sensitive with daily torture" (I:86). The Indians too "were affected by a sort of cold shadow of the white man's curiosity, and, gliding through the crowd, fastened their snake-like black eyes on Hester's bosom" (I:246). Time itself cannot alleviate this alienating presence of the other's gaze, for "the inhabitants of the town (their own interest in this worn-out subject languidly reviving itself, by sympathy with what they saw others feel) lounged idly to the same quarter, and tormented Hester Prynne, perhaps more than all the rest, with their cool, well-acquainted gaze at her familiar shame" (I:246). Yet even this refusal to communicate, this absence of dialogue beneath the cold, objectifying stare, constitutes a *form* of communication, for as soon as existence gathers itself together and commits itself to some line of conduct it inscribes the scene of intersubjectivity, recites the texture of itSelf—its intertextuality: "Vision alone makes us learn that beings that are different, 'exterior,' foreign to one another, are yet absolutely *together*, are 'simultaneity'"—the other is not so much "a freedom seen *from without* as destiny and fatality, a rival subject for a subject, but he is caught up in a circuit that connects him to the world."[4]

It is this double-edged dimension of the visible, of seeing and being seen, which mirrors the essential structure of all relations—the simultaneous facility of the gaze both to familiarize and estrange, as with Chillingworth's "regard" of Hester: "A gaze that made her heart shrink and shudder, because so familiar, and yet so strange and cold" (I:72). This power is poignantly wrought out in Chillingworth's relation to Dimmesdale: "It mattered little, for his object, whether celestial, or from what other region. By its aid, in all the subsequent relations betwixt him and Mr. Dimmesdale, not merely the external presence, but the very inmost soul of the latter seemed to be brought out before his eyes, so that he could see and comprehend its every movement. He became, thenceforth, not a spectator only, but a chief actor, in the poor minister's interior world. He could play upon him as he chose" (I:140). As it applies to all of Hawthorne's villains, Chillingworth's objectification of the other accomplishes the "infernal" task of analysis: "In a word, old Roger Chillingworth was a striking evidence of man's faculty of transforming himself into a devil. . . . This unhappy person had effected such a transformation by devoting himself, for seven years, to the constant analysis of a heart full of torture, and deriving his enjoyment thence, and adding fuel to those fiery tortures which he analyzed and gloated over" (I:170).

The gaze possesses, within itself, this force of division, estrangement, alienation; it holds before it the power to violate, to utterly expose the other, as Dimmesdale acknowledges: "the shame!—the indelicacy!—the horrible ugliness of this exposure of a sick and guilty heart to the very eye that would gloat over it" (I:194). So, too, he is opened upon all eyes that would look, "overcome with a great horror of mind, as if the universe were gazing at a scarlet token on his naked breast, right over his heart" (I:148). Upon the pillory, Hester likewise experiences "this intense consciousness of being the object of severe and universal observation" (I:60). In this way, the gaze confers upon vision a concrete manifestation of the "universal visibility" of being, as Jacques Lacan has remarked: "I see only from one point, but in my existence I am looked at from all sides."[5] The paradox of vision teaches how the "evil eye" of an "other" can transform the innermost limits of the subject into the ubiquitous transparency of an object.

Above all, this dynamic informs the very heart of Hawthorne's oeuvre, the fear of transgressing the precinct of the subject, of violating the human heart itSelf—what might be called the "Paul Pry complex." From the outset, Hawthorne's work addresses this issue. In his 1831 tale, "Sights from a Steeple," having climbed to the top of his remote vantage point, the narrator observes: "The most desirable mode of existence might be that of a spiritualized Paul Pry, hovering invisible round man and woman, witnessing their deeds, searching into their hearts, borrowing brightness from their felicity, and shade from their sorrow, and retaining no emotion peculiar to himself" (IX:192)—where "The full of hope, the happy, the miserable, and the desperate, dwell together within the circle of my glance" (IX:196). It is the keenest dilemma of the artist. Here the narrator is forced to conclude: "But none of these things are possible; and if I would know the interior of brick walls, or the mystery of human bosoms, I can but guess" (IX:192).

Nonetheless, the power of the eye to pry into the secret recesses of another remained for Hawthorne a pressing and permanent reality, one which is nowhere more acutely interrogated than in the psychological nuances which structure both the narrative and the drama of *The Blithedale Romance*. Coverdale hastily sets forth the issue in the first chapter: "Now-a-days, in the management of his 'subject,' 'clairvoyant,' or 'medium,' the exhibitor affects the simplicity and openness of scientific experiment; and even if he profess to tread a step or two across the boundaries of the spiritual world, yet carries with him the laws of our actual life, and extends them over his preternatural conquests. Twelve or fifteen years ago, on the contrary, all the arts of mysterious arrangement, of picturesque disposition, and artistically contrasted light and shade, were made available in order to set the apparent miracle in the strongest attitude of opposition to ordinary facts" (III:5–6). In other words, by means of its claim to scientific transparency, mesmerism has utterly abolished the ambiguity of vision, the asymmetrical relation between "seeing" and "being seen." This, in fact, is Coverdale's initial blunder—to assume the unequivocality of seer and seen, the "uni-vocality" of the eye and the gaze (though in reality they do not, as it were, speak the same language): "It is really impossible to hide anything, in this world, to say nothing of the next" (III:163). According to this faulty premise, that final frontier—the mystery and opacity of the subject—is now as equally accessible as the rat's behavior to the laboratory "technician." By means of this new *technē*, the veil (hymen) of being—be it the Lady's *(Blithedale)*, the cleric's ("The Minister's Black Veil"), or the mind itself ("P.'s Correspondence")—has been inexorably rent; indeed, the invisible itself has disappeared, has been eradicated by the absolute insight of the scientific-analytic "view." The daguerreotype, of course, did little to dispel this new mythology. Ironically, Coverdale's position at Blithedale represents a similar attempt to bring the whole of being to light, to erase the subject's limited *point of view,* repeating the narrative desire previously repudiated in "Sights from a Steeple." Only this time, Hawthorne traces its consequences to their inevitable conclusion.

Whenever one "subjects" another to analysis, he reverses the very dimensions of subjectivity, revealing how subject and object are but different aspects of the same phenomenon. As the object might *object,* so too the subject *subject*. Here subject and object articulate the reversible, "reflexive" forms of existence for each is both noun and verb, thing and activity within the realm of the visible. At the same time, however, these reciprocal dimensions secure an inversely proportionate relation, for when the subject subjects the other to its gaze as an object—that is, *magnifies* it as an insect beneath the microscope—it simultaneously *reduces* its "self." Perhaps the telescope provides a more accurate analogy. Seen from the side of the enlarged object, the subject is, in turn, proportionately diminished—and this, ironically, at the expense of a lucidity which increasingly distances the subject from the object the closer he would draw it toward focus. The scope of visibility depends upon the power of the lens, a two-way (reversible) apparatus whose function relies upon a distance between one lens and another. From this very "distance between," this vacuum, this empty space, emerges that in which the visible is given over to vision. Within the constitution of the lens we find the structure of the gaze itself: thus, Coverdale's recurrent disappearing act, his powerlessness to bring himself within the scope of the other—and this, in spite of his repeated attempts to force the other into perfect clarity. The greater the enlargement in the scopic field, the further he recedes.[6] In the domain of the visible, the eye (I) finds both its origin and end in the gaze, that empty "space between" which holds before it both the power of the near and the far, solicitation and estrangement—the reversibility of "seer" and "seen," self and other. The gaze figures this reversibility, and is itself a figure (of speech)—an oxymoron.

Merleau-Ponty succinctly explores the spatiality of this "arrangement" in the visual field, this crossing over of self and other, with his felicitous analogy of the glove:

Reversibility: the finger of the glove that is turned inside out—There is no need of a spectator who would be *on each side*. It suffices that from one side I see the wrong side of the glove that is applied to the right side, that I touch the one *through* the other (double "representation" of a point or plane of the field) the chiasm is that: the reversibility—

It is through it alone that there is a passage from the "For Itself" to the For the Other—In reality there is neither me nor the other as positive . . . subjectivities. There are two caverns, two opennesses, two stages where something will take place—and which both belong to the same world, to the stage of Being

. . . They are each the other side of the other. This is why they incorporate one another: projection-introjection—There is that line, that frontier surface at some distance before me, where occurs the veering I-Other Other-I—

The axis alone given—the end of the finger of the glove is nothingness—but a nothingness one can turn over, and where then one sees *things*—The only "place" where the negative would really be is the fold, the application of the inside and the outside to one another, the turning point . . . the things, realized by the doubling up of my body into inside and outside—and the doubling up of the things (their inside and their outside).[7]

The gaze enacts this "fold." Here vision returns us to the "fullness" of being at the very point where something is *missing,* for in the solicitation of the gaze I am both "completed" by the other and made absent from, or doubled in, myself. Regarding this dynamic, I refer you to a most remarkable passage in Kierkegaard: "There is an engraving that portrays the grave of Napoleon. Two large trees overshadow the grave. There is nothing else to be seen in the picture, and the immediate spectator will see no more. Between these two trees, however, is an empty space, and as the eye traces out its contour Napoleon himself suddenly appears out of the nothingness, and now it is impossible to make him disappear. The eye that has once seen him now always sees him with anxious necessity. . . . there is not a single brush stroke to suggest Napoleon. Yet it is this empty space, this nothingness, that conceals what is most important."[8] Similarly, with the gaze, which offers to the subject a reflection of itSelf, there is given to consciousness that which is itself absent. Precisely in this sense, the subject constitutes a gap or fold within the texture of the existent.

Lacan pursues this notion in its psychoanalytic context, where consciousness discerns its own configuration in the inside-out structure of the gaze—that point where vision itself is able to emerge amid the ambiguity of what is inscribed within the register of the scopic drive: here the gaze is that initial point of annihilation, "in which is marked, in the field of the reduction of the subject, a break—which warns us of the need to introduce another reference, that which analysis assumes in reducing the privileges of the consciousness. Psycho-analysis regards the consciousness as irremediably limited, and institutes it as a principle, not only of idealization, but of *méconnaissance,* as—using a term that takes on new value by being referred to a visible domain—*scotoma.* . . . In the scopic relation, the object on which depends the phantasy from which the subject is suspended in an essential vacillation is the gaze."[9] It betokens that locus of an absence in the subject to which we give the name *desire.* The gaze informs that "empty space" which establishes itself, using Kierkegaard's observation, in the eye of the perceiver.

To the degree that desire is always already articulated in the domain of vision, repression is given over to a structure that mirrors perception, that self-revealing/self-concealing phenomenon of "lighting" to which Heraclitus ascribes Being itself.[10] In the same way, Heidegger interprets the famous Epicurean admonition, "live in hiding," as the way in which one presences to others: "The fundamental trait of presencing itself is determined by remaining concealed and unconcealed."[11] It is the subject's co-respondence to the question (its) being both inaugurates and exposes: "How can one hide himself before that which never sets?"[12] Can we not discern, in this very mode of being, the way in which perception, repression, and desire inosculate the human situation—the inaccessibility of that object outlined in its absence beneath the ever-present scrutiny of the gaze, the desire to make oneself present in the field of the other by hiding?

Similarly, *Blithedale* secures the trace of that which the narrative itself erases: what Coverdale covers. Here one might decipher, in Coverdale's final confession of love for Priscilla, the inscription of an absence whose silhouette but frames the contour of Zenobia herself, the very "negative" or, better, double *exposure* of that central image in his dream which places Priscilla on the margin of this "scopic" text—that is, on the outside, looking in: "It was not till I had quitted my three friends that they first began to encroach upon my dreams. In those of the last night, Hollingsworth and Zenobia, standing on either side of my bed, had bent across it to exchange a kiss of passion. Priscilla, beholding this—for she seemed to be peeping in at my chamber-window—had melted gradually away, and left only the sadness of her expression in my heart" (III:153).[13] Thus we are never for a moment deceived, amid the ceaseless flurry of Coverdale's voyeuristic enterprise, that he is, above all, hiding from himself. Precisely because desire is established here, in the domain of seeing, can he make it vanish.[14]

□

From his tree-turret observatory, Coverdale inaugurates that mode of existence which accomplishes the final abolition of all human relation— even that relationship to "self" which the Blithedale community defers: "At my height above the earth, the whole matter looks ridiculous" (III:100). In its purest form, this Paul Pry attitude delineates the extremes of isolation and alienation between self and other uncompromisingly characterized by Hawthorne in "Ethan Brand" as the *unpardonable sin*. It is nothing less than the self set before *(mise)*, set up against, itself, its ownmost enemy, "The sin of an intellect that triumphed over the sense of brotherhood with man . . . and sacrificed everything to its own mighty claims! The only sin that deserves a recompense of immortal agony" (XI:90). To make of the subject an object of "psychological experiment" (XI:94)—"he was now a cold observer, looking on mankind as the subject of his experiment, and, at length, converting man and woman to be his puppets, and pulling the wires that moved them to such degrees of crime as were demanded for his study. Thus Ethan Brand became a fiend. He began to be so from the moment that his moral nature had ceased to keep the pace of improvement with his intellect. And now . . . he had produced the Unpardonable Sin" (XI:99). Coverdale likewise comes perilously close to this end in the degree to which he persistently strives to violate the recesses of the human heart. And if his manipulative power is somewhat underplayed, lacking the uncompromising condemnation given to Ethan Brand, it is perhaps because the narrative itself sets forth the ominous dilemma of the artist.

Coverdale himself has moments of insight:

> It is not, I apprehend, a healthy kind of mental occupation, to devote ourselves too exclusively to the study of individual men and women. If the person under examination be one's self, the result is pretty certain to be diseased action of the heart, almost before we can snatch a second glance. Or, if we take the freedom to put a friend under our microscope, we thereby insulate him from many of his true relations, magnify his peculiarities, inevitably tear him into parts, and, of course, patch him very clumsily together again. What wonder, then, should we be frightened by the aspect of a monster, which, after all—though we can point to every feature of his deformity in the real personage—may be said to have been created mainly by ourselves. (III:69)

Yet he immediately obscures this intuition by his iron-willed obsession to analyze the members of the community, to solve and resolve the intricate puzzlement of its human relations: "Thus, as my conscience has often whispered me, I did Hollingsworth a great wrong by prying into his character, and am perhaps doing him as great a one, at this moment, by putting faith in the discoveries which I seemed to make. But I could not help it. Had I loved him less, I might have used him better. He—and Zenobia and Priscilla, both for their own sakes and as connected with him—were separated from the rest of the community, to my imagination, and stood forth as the indices of a problem which it was my business to solve" (III:69). It is the drive of a consciousness best characterized in *Blithedale* by the compulsion to pry, to spy—a consciousness reiterated and structured in the ironic avowal of Coverdale: "I determined to remove myself to a little distance, and take an exterior view of what we had all been about" (III:140).

"A little distance": this seemingly innocent litotes reveals the essential frame of mind in which the narrative consciousness discerns its ownmost situation for, in the world itself, being is understood as an indecent exposure—that which shows itself only to those who would *peep*: "I should have recommended a site further to the left, just a little withdrawn into the wood, with two or three peeps at the prospect, among the trees" (III:80); "Ascending into this natural turret, I peeped, in turn, out of several of its small windows" (III:99); "I could not resist the impulse to take just one peep beneath her folded petals" (III:125); "Had it been evening, I would have stolen softly to some lighted window of the old farm-house, and peeped darkling in" (III:207); "I looked on all sides out of the peep-holes of my hermitage" (III:208). To Coverdale, existence is but the occasion of the voyeur, and being itself is but the victim of its own incurable tendency to hide—the very obverse of his own repressed propensity toward exhibitionism. The universe in turn reciprocates Coverdale's voyeurism, bears witness to himself (I recall you once again to the daguerrean [world]view)—the world becomes the projection of his own isolation and thus peeps back: "his black eyes sparkled at me, whether with fun or malice I knew not, but certainly as if the Devil were peeping out of them" (III:94); "you shall hear the very latest incident in the known life—(if life it may be called, which seemed to have no more reality than the candlelight image of one's self, which peeps at us outside of a dark window-pane)" (III:108); "'How do you find yourself, my love?' said Zenobia, lifting a corner of the gauze, and peeping beneath it, with a mischievous smile" (III:116); "Priscilla, beholding this—for she seemed to be peeping in at the chamber-window—had melted gradually away" (III:153); "'Some profane intruder!' said the goddess Diana. 'I shall send an arrow through his heart, or change him into a stag, as I did Actaeon, if he peeps from behind the trees!'" (III:211). Even the pigs reflect the image of Coverdale back upon himself, "Peeping at me, an instant, out of their small, red, hardly perceptible eyes" (III:144).[15] It is the narcissistic vision of the child encapsulated by the image of itself.

He who would be all-seeing sees the same thing everywhere. Coverdale remains "invisible" (covered) beyond the *jouissance* of his manipulative vision precisely to the extent that what he sees is always and everywhere an illusion: himself (seeing himself) seeing. Not that he is playing *(fort-da)* with himself—for what he would have come (to him) is nowhere (to be found). It is already lost, precluded by the voyeuristic enterprise which ensures his presence as an absence. The Christian myth, for example, repeats this paradox of being as it is inscribed in vision. Here the world is the mirror, and humanity the image, of God—who sees all but *is not seen.* The subject can avoid its own subjection only at the cost of hiding itself from the other. Yet even this refusal to meet the other's eye turns back upon itself. Peeping gives Coverdale over to himself exactly at the point where the gaze reflects its otherness—where the seer is reflected in the seen. And so the world, too, peeps at him—a role in which he is at last exhibited despite (in spite of) himself. The invocation of the gaze thus reveals the plastic way in which the voyeur mirrors himself, the repetition of his own absence: "it is not at the level of the other whose gaze surprises the subject looking through the keyhole. It is that the other surprises him, the subject, as entirely hidden gaze."[16] What Coverdale desires is (not) himself (its perpetual absence); what he is looking for is always this *lack*—the way in which he is cut out of (castrated by) the field of the other: a talking cardboard figure. So too, we suspect the same of his "minor" voice as a poet; it reveals the absence of "dialogue"—his inability to reflect the other—as his reply to Zenobia suggests: "I hope . . . now, to produce something that shall really deserve to be called poetry—true, strong, natural, and sweet, as is the life which we are going to lead—something that shall have *the notes of wild-birds* twittering through it, or *a strain like the wind-anthems* in the woods, as the case may be" (III:14, italics mine). It happens as no accident that Coverdale desires the inarticulate sounds of "dumb" animals. Little wonder that this poet in search of "material" should end up writing prose.

At the boundary of this world, at the very limit of consciousness as a peephole, Hawthorne sets that which both prefigures and originates the misconstruction of the psychoanalytic enterprise: mesmerism. It represents the abolition of any limit whatsoever, negating not only the otherness of the gaze but the subjectivity of the subject as well: "the movement of the Veiled Lady was graceful, free, and unembarrassed, like that of a person accustomed to be the spectacle of thousands. Or, possibly, a blindfold prisoner within the sphere with which this dark, earthly magician had surrounded her, she was wholly unconscious of being the central object to all those straining eyes. . . . Sitting there, in such *visible obscurity,* it was . . . *like the actual presence of a disembodied spirit,*" where "the limitations of time and space have no existence within its folds" (III:201, italics mine). In this aethereal region, the Veiled Lady "beholds the Absolute" (III:201). Yet, this infinite distance between scene and spectator, this absolute "visibility," is itself but an illusion. Thus, just as the spectators imagined she was about to take flight into that invisible sphere, Hollingsworth had mounted the platform,

> and now stood gazing at the figure, with a sad intentness that brought the whole power of his great, stern, yet tender soul, into his glance.
> "Come!" said he, waiving his hand towards her. "You are safe!"
> She threw off the veil, and stood before that multitude of people, pale, tremulous, shrinking, as if only then had she discovered that a thousand eyes were gazing at her. Poor maiden! How strangely had she been betrayed! Blazoned abroad as a wonder of the world, . . . in the faith of many, a

seeress and a prophetess . . . she had kept, as I religiously believe, her virgin
reserve and sanctity of soul, throughout it all. . . . And the true heart-throb
of a woman's affection was too powerful for the jugglery that had hitherto
environed her. She uttered a shriek and fled to Hollingsworth, like one
escaping from her deadliest enemy, and was safe forever. (III:202–3)

The will is shaken by the touch! So too, vision hearkens to the invocation. It is the solicitation of the gaze itself.

Coverdale's compulsion to pry and peep reflects the converse, a
failure to find "completion" in the gaze of the other. It is not the failure of
Dimmesdale to look the other in the face—"he seldom, now-a-days,
looked straightforth at any object, whether human or inanimate"
(I:131)—but something far different indeed. Dimmesdale's evasive glance
signals his awareness of the other, his very need, his recognition, of the
other in the face of a shame which hides him from relation to both Hester
and the community at large—an awareness which unceasingly calls him
back to what is lacking in himself. Thus it is that Hester's provocation
recalls him to the solicitation of the gaze, to what was once "between
them"—at least momentarily. "Hester would not set him free, lest he
should look her sternly in the face" (I:194). "Here, seen only by his eyes,
the scarlet letter need not burn into the bosom of the fallen woman! Here,
seen only by her eyes, Arthur Dimmesdale, false to God and man, might
be, for one moment, true" (I:195–96). The gaze itself opens onto this
sympathetic union, reciprocating in turn the possibility of dialogue:
"Thou little knowest what a relief it is, after the torment of a seven years'
cheat, to look into an eye that recognizes me for what I am" (I:192). Both
voice and vision inosculate the intersubjective phenomenon, the genuine
re-sponsibility of the gaze as a structure of sympathetic co-respondence,
just as Hollingsworth's *voice* dispels the evil *eye* of Westervelt's mesmeriz-
ing gaze in the face of Priscilla. Coverdale, on the other hand, forecloses
on that very thing the other withholds—that is, holds forth to him as a
holding with, a holding together. Arrested by the image of himself, he
exclusively inhabits that narcissistic reflection he encounters everywhere.
While Dimmesdale's "guarded" gaze prolongs his isolation from the
other, Coverdale's plunderous vision reveals a more primordial form of
alienation. Against this rapacious facade, he refuses to be seen.

It is the paradox of his abysmal situation that, in the field opened up
by vision, Coverdale experiences in the gaze a constant occasion for
aggression: thus, his continual frustration as well. For in the ironic perplexity of this bind, ensnared between the reversible though asymmetrical desire to see and be seen, he sustains the very lack he seeks to
eradicate—his ownmost sense of deprivation as exclusion. Here the

structure of narcissism converges with the psychoanalytic phenomenon of jealousy. As Merleau-Ponty observes, the narcissistic image superimposes upon the affective subject a constructed subject, an imaginary one visible "at a distance"—what psychoanalysis calls the *super-ego:* "this alienation of the immediate *me,* its 'confiscation' for the benefit of the *me* that is visible in the mirror, already outlines what will be the 'confiscation' of the subject by the others who look at him."[17] This too accounts for the preponderance of value judgments throughout the course of Coverdale's narration. To the extent that (the lack of) the other's gaze deprives him of "himself," Coverdale seeks to live solely in the despotism of his own "constructed" image, an image which fails to reflect the other as exclusively as it outlines its own "invisibility." At the same time, he is present to himself only as an observer—that is, whenever his presence is brought home to him by virtue of its absence in the field of the other. This is why, on the one hand, he must continually espy the other while hiding himself and, on the other hand, encounter—in fact, un-cover—his own image everywhere.

Obsession with—indeed, possession by—the other is merely the flip-side of Coverdale's relation to himself: his peeping offers the most economical means of making his own absence present, if only as a lack. What's missing is, in every instance, the intersubjective dynamic—that is, the subject in relation to another. The gaze itself reveals how, in the complimentarity of "seeing" and "being seen," the logic of affective situations is at all times dialogical. Without the "dialogue" of self and other—outside it—the self would both see and be seen by itself at once. This decidedly pathological dimension characterizes Coverdale's dilemma: his effort to master the situation by seeing all is but the suppressed desire to be seen by all. Here, the reversibility of vision reveals the facility of the gaze as a means of repression. Beneath the voyeur may "lie" the exhibitionist. While Coverdale secretly watches his "victims," he would like to be watched. How else are we to understand his reply to Zenobia? "'Is it irksome to you to hear your own verses sung?' asked Zenobia, with a gracious smile. 'If so, I am very sorry; for you will certainly hear me singing them, sometimes, in the summer evenings.' 'Of all things,' answered I, 'that is what will delight me most!'" (III:14–15). He thus paradoxically falls prey to losing himself in the other and finding himself where he is not, the very structure so brilliantly defined by Hegel in his explication of the master-slave relationship.

In vision, we find the contour of this drama played out within the gaze, for in its naive beginnings it would be its own victim. Vision gives to being the exemplary mode in which the subject is able to *subject* (dominate) its object-world. In its arrested development, Coverdale's gaze uncovers to what degree his desire to hide reflects a corresponding need to cover the other as well, to obscure what others see of him—his patent failure to co-exist. In his masterful violation of the other's secrecy, he feels deprived of recognition. He cannot cover over this "other" of whom he is jealous, however—cannot, in his utter isolation, do away with it, make it disappear—since the dispossession of the other would force him to be master of himself, a function he can never perform insofar as he would, in fact, *not be* outside this thralldom to the other. Thus he *is* only to the extent that he is mirrored in the other, doubled by the invasion of an all-inclusive presence which both *excludes him from it* and yet *includes him in his absence.* Coverdale's observation of Zenobia, amid the luxury of her Boston lodging, ironically reflects this plenary presence in which nothing is missing—not even his own absence:

> I was dazzled by the brilliancy of the room. A chandelier hung down in the centre, glowing with I know not how many lights; there were separate lamps, also, on two or three tables, and on marble brackets, adding their white radiance to that of the chandelier. The furniture was exceedingly rich. Fresh from our old farm-house, with its homely board and benches in the dining-room, and a few wicker-chairs in the best parlor, it struck me that *here was the fulfilment of every fantasy of an imagination, revelling in various methods of costly self-indulgence* and splendid ease. Pictures, marbles, vases; in brief, more shapes of luxury than there could be any object in enumerating, except for an auctioneer's advertisement—*and the whole repeated and doubled by the reflection of a great mirror, which showed me Zenobia's proud figure, likewise, and my own.* (III:164, italics mine)

How ironic, therefore, is her preceding remark to Coverdale: "it must be a very circumscribed mind that can find room for no others" (III:164). For in the presence of Zenobia, Coverdale makes room for everyone but himself. Indeed, this "circumscript" gaze which cuts him off from those around him, which by seeing through a peephole leaves "no room" in the vision for being seen, inscribes a void that can be said to be only insofar as it avoids itSelf.

Coverdale cannot *abide* himself, living solely in the domination of the other's presence which cancels him out, (a)voids him. A slave to seeing and what it *represents,* he ceaselessly repeats the doubt inherent in the Cartesian *cogito,* the very doubt indigenous to its methodological "reflection" in the visible: I saw myself seeing (myself).[18] It is the posture of the slave, the primordial form of self-abasement—self-effacement, removal, eradication; it is this absolute recognition of himself as all-seeing (and therefore never seen) that puts in question his own existence,

that blots it out inasmuch as he beholds without ever being beheld—
what is withheld from him at every point. He would be both picture and
frame (of reference). Like the child, moreover, Coverdale interprets any
show of interest toward him as a mark of weakness in the other; and from
the despotism of this double image emerges all the jealousy in which
the confusion (identification) of self and other is made manifest.[19] "It
cost me, I acknowledge, a bitter sense of shame, to perceive in myself a
positive effort to bear up against the effect which Zenobia sought to
impose on me. I reasoned against her, in my secret mind, and strove so to
keep my footing. In the gorgeousness with which she had surrounded
herself—in the redundance of personal ornament, which the largeness of
her physical nature and the rich type of her beauty caused to seem so
suitable—I malevolently beheld the true character of the woman, passionate, luxurious, lacking simplicity, not deeply refined, incapable of
pure and perfect taste" (III:164–65). It is the jealous voice within—one
without which the narrative consciousness is nevertheless lost.

And with it we discern the shame which Sartre defines as a particular
form of recognition, that structure of consciousness conscious of itself *as
shame:* "it is a shameful apprehension *of* something and this something is
me. I am ashamed of what I *am.* Shame therefore realizes an intimate
relation of myself to myself. Through shame I have discovered an aspect
of *my* being."[20] For Coverdale, this shame holds within it the possibility
of a recognition which refers him to himself against the outline of the
other; he nevertheless denies it, flees it, hides it behind a bad faith which
is itself nothing less than his narration. Thus in the "present" of the
narration, Coverdale's "past" (shame) reveals to us that he *is* this being—
not in the mode of "was" or "having-to-be," but "in itself"[21]—this
being of whom he is (no longer?) ashamed (of being ashamed), and
which the narrative itself *repeats.* (It is the very meaning of his final
"confession"—one, in fact, which likewise hides him from the jealousy
he disavows.) Immediately compelled to (dis)qualify his words, to dis-
claim himself, Coverdale reclaims this provocative image of Zenobia:
"But the next instant, she was too powerful for all my opposing
struggles. I saw how fit it was that she should make herself as gorgeous as
she pleased, and should do a thousand things that would have been
ridiculous in the poor, thin, weakly characters of other women" (III:165).

Here, too, we find something of the double bind in which Coverdale
encounters the field of the other, for what "reduces" him to shame is not
the presence of the other—that other whose gaze gives back to us our
being as *seen*—but rather that shadow presence nowhere to be found, that
other who surprises him by its absence: himself. It is the gaze itself as

desire. Thus, with the erasure of himself, he can so easily make his own desire, as well, disappear. Similarly, when from his Boston lodgings he returns Zenobia's stare, he is immediately rebuked by a single gesture which comprises both his recognition and dismissal simultaneously:

> Westervelt looked into the depths of the drawing-room, and beckoned. Immediately afterwards, Zenobia appeared at the window, with color much heightened, and *eyes which,* as my conscience whispered me, *were shooting bright arrows,* barbed with scorn, across the intervening space, directed full at my sensibilities as a gentleman. If the truth must be told, far as her flight-shot was, *those arrows hit the mark.* She signified her recognition of me by a gesture with her head and hand, comprising at once a salutation and dismissal. The next moment, she administered one of those pitiless rebukes which a woman always has at hand, ready for an offence, (and which she so seldom spares, on due occasion,) by letting down a white linen curtain between the festoons of the damask ones. It fell like the drop-curtain of a theatre, in the interval between the acts. (III:158–59, italics mine)

Even this, however, does not sufficiently exhaust the tension of the scopic drive—which admits of no adequation—for Coverdale relentlessly pursues what is not there, *what cannot be seen.* In psychoanalytic terms, Lacan explains: "What occurs in voyeurism? At the moment of the act of the voyeur, where is the subject, where is the object? . . . the subject is not there in the sense of seeing, at the level of the scopic drive. . . . *The object,* here, *is the gaze—the gaze that is the subject,* which attains it, *which hits the bull's eye in target-shooting.* . . . The gaze is this object lost and suddenly refound in the conflagration of shame, by the introduction of the other. Up to that point, what is the subject trying to see? What he is trying to see, make no mistake, is the object as absence" (italics mine).[22]

In the same way, regarding his previous discovery in the eyes of Westervelt and specifically in terms of this exposure, Coverdale refuses to relinquish his role as seer: "Perhaps I ought to have blushed at being caught in such an evident scrutiny of Professor Westervelt and his affairs. Perhaps I did blush. Be that as it might, I retained presence of mind enough not to make my position yet more irksome, by the poltroonery of drawing back" (III:158). Even this refusal to hide in the face of the other signals the denial of himself as having been seen. For at the moment when the instrumentality of the other reveals he *can* be seen, he apprehends it by means of a decision *not* to give up his "post of observation" (III:158), his "hiding place," his very "subjectivity"—and this, ironically, above all else, because it is "too risky." As Sartre suggests, "Thus in the shock which seizes me when I apprehend the Other's look, this happens—that suddenly I experience a subtle alienation of all my possibilities, which are now associated with objects of the world, far from me in the midst of the world."[23] In this way, too, Coverdale denies that he is apprehended *in the other.* Rather than recognize himself as seen by Westervelt, he opts for the reverse: seeing himself seeing Westervelt. This is more than a simple grammatical inversion; it constitutes the (lack of) relation in which he (un)covers his ownmost being. The other nevertheless surpasses him while, through the instrumentality of the gaze, the situation again escapes him—the way in which the other both transcends and confers upon his being the very possibility of hiding inasmuch as he can be discovered (seen). Momentarily caught in this embarrassment, he rationalizes the event: "It must be owned, too, that I had a keen, revengeful sense of the insult inflicted by Zenobia's scornful recognition, and more particularly by her letting down the curtain; as if such were the proper barrier to be interposed between a character like hers, and a perceptive faculty like mine. For, was mine a mere vulgar curiosity? Zenobia should have known me better than to suppose it" (III:160). Unable to admit he is no longer (nor was he ever) master of the situation, Coverdale now pursues his scopic obsession to its inevitable end: "I sat in my rocking-chair, too far withdrawn from the window to expose myself to another rebuke. . . . All at once, it occurred to me how very absurd was my behavior, in thus tormenting myself with crazy hypotheses as to what was going on within that drawing-room, when it was at my option to be personally present there" (III:161–62).

The ensuing confrontation discloses the full effect of his transgression, his own effacement in the very face of the other: "I determined to make proof if there were any spell that would exorcise her out of the part which she seemed to be acting. She should be compelled to give me a glimpse of something true; some nature, some passion, no matter whether right or wrong, provided it were real" (III:165). When Zenobia at last responds with "cheeks flushed" and eyes that "darted lightning," Coverdale concludes: "My experiment had fully succeeded. She had shown me the true flesh and blood of her heart, by thus involuntarily resenting my slight, pitying, half-kind, half-scornful mention of the man who was all in all with her" (III:166). Ironically, her defense of Hollingsworth not only confirms Coverdale's secret jealousy, but removes him once again to the realm of the invisible: "I dared make no retort to Zenobia's concluding apothegm. In truth, I admired her fidelity. It gave me a new sense of Hollingsworth's native power, to discover that his influence was no less potent with this beautiful woman, here, in the midst of artificial life, than it had been, at the foot of the gray rock, and among the wild birch-trees of the wood-path, when she so passionately pressed his hand against her heart. The great, rude, shaggy, swarthy man! And Zenobia loved him" (III:167). In covering his own desire, however, it is condemned to reappear elsewhere:

> "Did you bring Priscilla with you?" I resumed. "Do you know, I have sometimes fancied it not quite safe, considering the susceptibility of her temperament, that she should be so constantly within the sphere of a man like Hollingsworth? Such tender and delicate natures, among your sex, have often, I believe, a very adequate appreciation of the heroic element in men. But, then, again, I should suppose them as likely as any other women to make a reciprocal impression. Hollingsworth could hardly give his affections to a person capable of taking an independent stand, but only to one whom he might absorb into himself. He has certainly shown great tenderness for Priscilla." (III:167)

Thus when Zenobia allows Coverdale the interview, he is already dismissed before it begins—prefiguring the ironic title of this final episode: "They Vanish." It is they, in fact, who by their own removal make him disappear. Coverdale, in turn, is left alone to that lack he would perpetuate, "excluded from everybody's confidence, and attaining no further, by my most earnest study, than to an *uncertain sense of something hidden from me*" (III:174, italics mine). By confronting the other, moreover, Coverdale is re-covered in that very situation he would avoid. As Sartre observes, "being-seen constitutes me as a defenseless being for a freedom which is not my freedom. It is in this sense that we can consider ourselves as 'slaves' in so far as we appear to the Other. . . . I am a slave to the degree that my being is dependent at the center of a freedom which is not mine and which is the very condition of my being."[24]

Likewise, this phenomenon returns us to the gaze as a means of repression. If Coverdale's vision seeks to master the situation by seeing all, it similarly structures a jealousy which ravages the surface of that illusory picture, and shows to what extent he is a slave to that desire to be part of the picture from which he is constantly excluded—a slave to the other to whom he attributes the very void he fails to recognize in himself. As he reflects on Zenobia, and the "knot of dreamers" in general: "She should have been able to appreciate that quality of the intellect and the heart, which impelled me (often against my own will, and to the detriment of my own comfort) *to live in other lives,* and to endeavor—by generous sympathies, by delicate intuitions, by taking note of things too slight for record, and by bringing my human spirit into manifold accordance with the companions whom God assigned to me—*to learn the secret which was hidden even from themselves*" (III:160, italics mine). Such is the nature of Coverdale's desire: between the spectacle of the other, and his

admiration for it, he reveals to what extent he would like to be acknowledged. Why else recount this catalogue of his "generous sympathies" and
"delicate intuitions?" It is exposure for the sake of attention. His desire is
not so much a positive feeling as one of deprivation and exclusion. As
Merleau-Ponty observes: "One might say that the jealous person sees his
existence invaded by the success of the other and feels himself dispossessed by him, and that in this sense jealousy is essentially a confusion
between the self and the other. It is the attitude of the one . . . who does
not define himself by himself but in relation to what others have."[25] This
too accounts for the fact that Coverdale identifies with the spectacle
precisely at the point where something is missing; in so doing, he permits
himself to be inwardly articulated by the one who plunders him: "Having, all told, nothing of his own, he defines himself entirely in relation to
others and by the lack of what the others have"; here jealousy returns us
to the psychoanalytic notion of the voyeur, where voyeurism merely
represents an extreme of jealousy itself: "The jealous person allows himself to be trapped or captured by the other and, inversely, moreover, he
would like to trap or capture the other in his turn. In his mind he plays all
the roles of the situation he finds himself in and not only his own role, of
which he has no separate notion."[26]

Appropriately, this role is frequently played out amid the anxiety
of the "trio," a structure which not only permanently organizes the experience of jealousy, but heightens and intensifies the sexuality of the
situation by means of a third person who functions as the occasion; this
third-person rival provides the "presence" necessary for the hidden meaning of the spectacle—its very lack: "It is thus with the jealous person. He
likes to make himself suffer. He manipulates his investigations, he seeks
information, he forms hypotheses that are always designed to stimulate his
anguish or uneasiness."[27] At the same time, this structure accounts for
what many read as an element of homosexuality in Coverdale's relation to
Hollingsworth, an element common to all the forms of jealousy—as
Freud observed—for the jealous person lives in the experience of the
other.[28] It should come as no surprise that in the trio, therefore, Coverdale establishes all sense of relationship: Coverdale-Westervelt-Zenobia,
Coverdale-Hollingsworth-Zenobia, Coverdale-Hollingsworth-Priscilla,
Coverdale-Zenobia-Priscilla. That he perceives his role as mediator con-
fuses no one but himself, to whom befalls the task—indeed, duty—of
untying this tangled "knot of dreamers." His conscience speaks eloquently
on this point. And yet, ironically, this knot is one which he alone has tied,
one which allows him to enter the sphere of the other as its (dis)solution.

The puzzle endures, however, only insofar as he is never master of the situation, but rather mastered by it—that in the hidden depth of its mysteries, he exists as its over-seer: the one to whom the other must look if it is to be resolved. His gaze, in turn, reflects this bind, returns him to the other as its slave. No wonder that his conscience holds him morally responsible for the solution of this intricate knot, for he is everywhere its missing link: *without him, nothing would be missing.* The trio thus sustains his role as an interchangeable part—an absolute signifier: he is the master key whose ubiquitous insertability fits every lock. In this way, he unlocks the truth for everyone, thereby escaping the very responsibility of which he claims his individual conscience speaks. He speaks for everyone but himself.

□

This too structures the pervasive tone of the book, the narrative ethos which is able to exist only as something absent to itself—as purely and exclusively another. Between the equi-vocation of Coverdale's conscience and his duty (Kant is back), there is outlined what the narrative obsessively repeats—a way of inscribing an ethos by means of self-*justification.* When he decides to confront Zenobia in Boston, for example, his voice betrays this tone: "My relations with Zenobia, as yet unchanged—as a familiar friend, and associated in the same life-long enterprise—*gave me the right,* and made it no more than *kindly courtesy demanded,* to call on her. Nothing, except *our habitual independence of conventional rules,* at Blithe-dale, could have *kept me from* sooner *recognizing this duty.* At all events, *it should* now *be performed*" (III:162, italics mine). And again: "*If I had any duty whatever,* in reference to Hollingsworth, *it was,* to endeavor *to save* Priscilla from that kind of personal worship which her sex is generally prone to lavish upon saints and heroes" (III:71, italics mine). By taking on these social conventions as his own, Coverdale reveals to what degree his conscience belongs to everyONE *(das Man)*—that· is, no one in par-ticular.[29] It in no way speaks for itSelf, as Zenobia remarks of Coverdale's departure from Blithedale: "'Ah, Zenobia,' I exclaimed, 'if you would but let me speak?' 'By no means,' she replied; 'especially when you have just resumed the whole series of social conventionalisms, together with that straight-bodied coat'" (III:142). Such speaking merely outlines the lacuna it would cover. Similarly, here as everywhere, when Coverdale speaks, he does so for the other—in place of the other—for how else could he understand Zenobia's existence as *belonging to his own* "life-long enterprise?" In what approaches a Messianic vision, Coverdale discloses

to what extent this ethos fails to find itSelf—and this in the very face of a
rhetoric which pronounces its reluctance to pass judgment. The passage
is worth quoting at length:

> Of all possible observers, methought, a woman, like Zenobia, and a man,
> like Hollingsworth, should have selected me. And now, when the event has
> long been past, I retain the same opinion of my fitness for the office. True; I
> might have condemned them. Had I been judge, as well as witness, my
> sentence might have been stern as that of Destiny itself. But, still, no trait of
> original nobility of character; no struggle against temptation; no iron neces-
> sity of will, on the one hand, nor extenuating circumstance to be derived
> from passion and despair, on the other; no remorse that might co-exist with
> error, even if powerless to prevent it; no proud repentance, that should claim
> retribution as a meed—would go unappreciated. True, again, I might give
> my full assent to the punishment which was sure to follow. But it would be
> given mournfully, and with undiminished love. And, after all was finished, I
> would come, as if to gather up the white ashes of those who had perished at
> the stake, and to tell the world—the wrong being now atoned for—how
> much had perished there, which it had never yet known how to praise.
> (III:160–61)

Other passages abound—value judgments grounded in self-
justification; it is the voice of convention: "A bachelor always feels himself defrauded, when he knows, or suspects, that any woman of his
acquaintance has given herself away. Otherwise, the matter could have
been no concern of mine. It was purely speculative; for I should not,
under any circumstances, have fallen in love with Zenobia" (III:48); "If I
had any duty whatever, in reference to Hollingsworth, it was, to endeavor to save Priscilla from that kind of personal worship which her sex
is generally prone to lavish upon saints and heroes" (III:71); "Had I been
as cold-hearted as I sometimes thought myself, nothing would have
interested me more than to witness the play of passions that must thus
have been evolved. But, in honest truth, I would really have gone far to
save Priscilla, at least, from the catastrophe in which such a drama would
be apt to terminate" (III:72); "It now impresses me, that, if I erred at all,
in regard to Hollingsworth, Zenobia, and Priscilla, it was through too
much sympathy, rather than too little" (III:154); "It suits me not to
explain what was the analogy that I saw, or imagined, between Zenobia's
situation and mine; nor, I believe, will the reader detect this one secret,
hidden beneath many a revelation which perhaps concerned me less. In
simple truth, however . . . it seemed to me that the self-same pang . . .
leaped thrilling from her heart-strings to my own. Was it wrong, therefore, if I felt myself consecrated to the priesthood, by sympathy like this,

and called upon to minister to this woman's affliction, so far as mortal could" (III:222); "I exaggerate my own defects. The reader must not take my own word for it, nor believe me altogether changed from the young man, who once hoped strenuously, and struggled, not so much amiss" (III:247). Similarly, Coverdale's final confession seeks to inscribe him within his own text as an after-word, or post-script, though it rhetorically functions as an effacement, an erasure: "It remains only to say a few words about myself . . . for I have made but a poor and dim figure in my own narrative, establishing no separate interest, and suffering my colorless life to take its hue from other lives. But one still retains some little consideration for one's self; so I keep these last two or three pages for my individual and sole behoof" (III:245).

While Coverdale's sense of duty persistently strives to justify the "otherness" of his narration, Zenobia's interpretation once again hits the mark: "Oh, this stale excuse of duty! . . . I have often heard it before . . . and I know precisely what it signifies. Bigotry; self-conceit; an insolent curiosity; a meddlesome temper; a cold-blooded criticism, founded on a shallow interpretation of half-perceptions; a monstrous scepticism in regard to any conscience or any wisdom, except one's own; a most irreverent propensity to thrust Providence aside, and substitute one's self in its awful place—out of these, and other motives as miserable as these, comes your idea of duty" (III:170). This "public" sense of duty and responsibility reveals the way in which Coverdale is ultimately false to himself, the inherent contradiction of his simultaneous self-inscription and self-erasure. Though he appropriates the other's life as *his* story, his jealousy yet forces him to create a "voice" for himself, a voice which despite its relentless self-justification can in no way be called his own; it is, at every turning, *borrowed*.

This "otherness" overflows the textuality of his narration to such an extent that it virtually drowns him: a neat parallel to Zenobia's death. If, in the history of Blithedale, Coverdale so often refers to the experience as an illusion, a text without substance—"it appears all like a dream" (III:165)—is it not because the past he would reclaim is but itself an artifice, a fiction which compresses the text of his life into a single form: a play? So, too, he repeatedly perceives his "cast" of characters as actors and actresses while he subordinates himself to playing the role of Chorus:

> My own part, in these transactions, was singularly subordinate. It resembled that of the Chorus in a classic play, which seems to be set aloof from the possibility of personal concernment, and bestows the whole measure of its hope or fear, its exultation or sorrow, on the fortunes of others, between whom and itself this sympathy is the only bond. Destiny, it may

be—the most skilful of stage-managers—seldom chooses to arrange its scenes, and carry forward its drama, without securing the presence of at least one calm observer. *It is his office to give* applause, when due, and sometimes an inevitable tear, to detect the final fitness of incident to character, and distil, in his long-brooding thought, *the whole morality of the performance.* (III:97, italics mine)

This is his calling, the avocation whereby, in singing the song of Blithedale, he is *called away from himself;* he is its bard: "When we come to be old men . . . they will call us Uncles, or Fathers . . . and we will look back cheerfully to these early days, and make a romantic story for the young people . . . out of our severe trials and hardships. In a century or two, we shall every one of us be mythical personages, or exceedingly picturesque and poetical ones, at all events. . . . What legends of Zenobia's beauty, and Priscilla's slender and shadowy grace. . . . In due course of ages, we must all figure heroically in an Epic Poem" (III:129). Here, in fact, Coverdale recants the singer to become the Muse itself—mysteriously absent: "and we will ourselves—at least, I will—bend unseen over the future poet, and lend him inspiration, while he writes it" (III:129). From classical tragedy to epic poetry—the performance is the same: a sustained *illusion.*

It is, of course, the dilemma of Hamlet—a dilemma, however, which is fated to draw Coverdale into the void of his own con-formity, as Zenobia so insightfully observes: "I should think it a poor and meagre nature, that is *capable of but one set of forms, and must convert all the past into a dream,* merely because the present happens to be unlike it" (III:165, italics mine). Indeed, this single set of forms in which Zenobia discerns the leading principle of Coverdale's existence is but his narrative conformity to *literary convention*—thus, Zenobia's most poignant observation: "You are turning this whole affair into a ballad" (III:223). Insofar as he lives solely in the lives of others, Coverdale is therefore compelled to create a legendary past for himself. Without this "history," he has no story to tell; outside this illusory past, he would not be. In the same way, the very text of his narration sustains a "mythical" past by means of *allusion*—the illusion of a past in the narratives of others.

It is, indeed, by converting the past into a dream-like "story" that Coverdale confers upon himself an inextricable reality, the illusion of continuity as a continuous part of the "knot" (of dreamers). He is its thread. Yet to the degree that Coverdale uncovers his speaking voice by means of allusion, the thread of this dream-like story is never his own. Rather, it structures the trans-figuration of his characters to legendary and mythical figures amid a world no less grand in its unbounded scope

and scale. The Blithedale community enacts "The curse of Adam's posterity" (III:206) where abides a time for jollity as well, "as if Comus and
his crew were holding their revels" (III:209) within this "Modern May-
day Arcadia" (III:58) dedicated to Maia, the mother of Mercury. The
story of Blithedale itself, like Zenobia's life, transacts a long day's
journey—"You have been turning night into day" (III:229)—back into
night, which "needs a wild steersman when we voyage through Chaos"
(III:142). Westervelt's power becomes bounded by "the verge of the pit of
Tartarus, on the one hand, and the third sphere of the celestial world, on
the other" (III:188), where Westervelt himself transforms to "a bearded
personage in Oriental robes, looking like one of the enchanters of the
Arabian Nights" (III:199). Priscilla runs "as if no rival less swift than
Atalanta could compete with her" (III:73); and as the Veiled Lady her
hidden face assumes the features of "a monstrous visage, with snaky
locks, like Medusa's, and one great red eye in the centre of the forehead" (III:110). Zenobia metamorphoses between an "Oriental princess"
(III:213) and "Pandora, fresh from Vulcan's workshop, and full of the
celestial warmth by dint of which he had tempered and moulded her"
(III:24); even in death, her absence is present to Coverdale in its legendary outline, "thrown . . . into the remotest and dimmest back-ground,
where it seemed to grow as improbable as a myth" (III:234). Hollingsworth is "wrought like a Titan" (III:136) and figures as Vulcan himself,
"massive and brawny, and well befitting his original occupation, . . .
that of a blacksmith" (III:28); it is, in fact, he who fires the destiny of his
Pandora/Zenobia—she who is forged in the workshop of his single-
minded being. Coverdale, too, expands to epic proportions, cursing his
illness "as bitterly as patient Job himself" (III:40), struggling with a fixed
idea "like the nail of Sisera's brain" (III:38), hearkening to the disquietude
of his heart—"this Cassandra of the inward depths" (III:139), singing the
extent of his "Orphic wisdom" (III:143), and bearing—like the stones he
carries off with Hollingsworth—the impossible narrative burden he has
set for himself, Samson with "the gates of Gaza on my back" (III:136),
Sisyphus against himself.

   Amid the radiance of this mythical textuality, this forged world,
Coverdale becomes the new Vulcan, displacing Hollingsworth by the
superior strength of his *breath* (as singer of the tale)—thus the "double
entendre" of Silas Foster's remark: "Your lungs have the play of a pair of
blacksmith's bellows" (III:138). Here his poetic facility becomes the
"equal" of Hollingsworth's brute (and therefore "dumb") physical appeal, Coverdale's way of being present to the illusive gaze of Zenobia. Its
pro-vocation is, however, more than mere artistic sublimation, for in

the substitution of himself he becomes the mere shadow of Hollings-worth, a "limp" (empty) insertion in the void he seeks to fill—a shadow destined to leave the workshop of Vulcan only to reappear beneath the darkness of Zenobia's watery grave.

Coverdale fore-shadows this desire in a previous conversation with Hollingsworth:

> But I do long for cottages to be built, that the creeping plants may begin to run over them, and the moss to gather on the walls, and the trees—which we will set out—to cover them with a breadth of shadow. This spick-and-span novelty does not quite suite my taste. It is time, too, for children to be born among us. The first-born child is still to come! And I shall never feel as if this were a real, practical, as well as poetical, system of human life, until somebody has sanctified it by death. . . .
>
> I wonder, Hollingsworth, who, of all these strong men, and fair women and maidens, is doomed the first to die. Would it not be well, even before we have absolute need of it, to fix upon a spot for a cemetery? Let us choose the rudest, roughest, most uncultivable spot, for Death's garden-ground; and Death shall teach us to beautify it, grave by grave. By our sweet, calm way of dying, and the airy elegance out of which we will shape our funeral rites, and the cheerful allegories which we will model into tombstones, the final scene shall lose its terrors; so that, hereafter, it may be happiness to live, and bliss to die. (III:129–30)

Beneath this cheerful rhetoric of allegory, drama, and "smiling pathos" (III:130), it is ironically fitting that death comes not in its "airy elegance," but in the darkness of water. Sitting next to Hollingsworth amid the silence of the boat, the solitary role of witness, of observer, once again befalls Coverdale: "Hollingsworth at first sat motionless, with *the hooked-pole elevated in the air.* But, by-and-by with *a nervous and jerky movement,* he began to *plunge it into the blackness* that upbore us, setting his teeth, and making precisely such *thrusts,* methought, as if he were *stabbing* at a deadly enemy. . . . And there, perhaps, *she lay, with her face upward,* while the shadow of the boat, and *my own pale face peering downward,* passed slowly betwixt her and the sky" (III:233, italics mine). Again the impotent outsider, Coverdale can do nothing more than observe the passion of this primal scene,[30] the sexual fury of Hollingsworth's de-sire—what casts the very shadow of his own:

> The drift of the stream had again borne us a little below the stump, when I felt—yes, felt, for it was as if the iron hook had smote my breast—felt Hollingsworth's pole strike some object at the bottom of the river. He started up, and almost overset the boat. . . .
>
> Putting a fury of strength into the effort, Hollingsworth heaved amain,

and up came a white swash to the surface of the river. It was the flow of a
woman's garments. A little higher, and we saw her dark hair, streaming
down the current. Black River of Death, thou hadst yielded up thy victim.
Zenobia was found. (III:234)

From the "Black River of Death" emerges the shadow of Coverdale's "denial," his desire for the lack (of a lack), his "fading" or disappearance in the lack of the subject itself wherein desire and not wanting to
desire articulate the (self)same thing.[31] If, as Lacan observes, the subject
is a "nothing" at the level of the drive, at the level of desire it *is* the desire
of the other. How brilliantly Hawthorne's image herein re-creates this
structure of Coverdale's desire in its shadowy duplicity, the "castration"
of the subject in the field of the other. What "belongs" to Hollingsworth
is thereby cut up within the very scope of Coverdale's gaze.[32] And might
we not discern, beneath the topography of Hawthorne's descriptive technique in general, the substitution of a shadow for the phallus?

Moreover, if the illusion of Coverdale's past is "forged" in the
legendary furnace of Vulcan, trans-figuring the epic dimension of his
narrative to mythological allusion (that is, continuous to an origin other
than his own making, his own fiction or story), it is equally trans-formed
in its conventional allusion to the literary texts of others. And precisely
insofar as, and to the extent that, it belongs to the other, it is a "forgery."
A brief comparison of Coverdale's counterfeit "signatures" against the
verso of this rectified text refers us to the following indebtedness: Fuller
(III:52), Emerson (III:52), Carlyle (III:52), Sand (III:52), Fourier (III:52),
Milton (III:60, 209), Coleridge (III:64), Voltaire (III:64), Shakespeare
(III:64, 91), Virgil (III:64), Burns (III:66, 210), Goldsmith (III:75), Defoe
(III:98), Cromwell (III:98), Spenser (III:99, 209), Perrault (III:226), Bun-
yan (III:243), and Griswold (III:246). To include all these "names," in fact,
represents nothing less than a failure to nominate himself. His *récit* is
everywhere the illusion of "other" relations; it merely recites the other.
Here we are returned to the "anxiety of influence" in its form as denial.
As Edward Said remarks, both quotation and allusion embody constant
reminders that writing itself is a form of displacement: "the quoted passage symbolizes other writing as encroachment. . . . The greater the
anxiety, the more writing appears to be quotation, the more writing
thinks of itself as, in some cases even proclaims itself, rewriting."[33] Indeed, Coverdale himself is entirely rewritten—removed—in this "homeless" narration: a displaced person without (outside) his own author-ity.

And as we would expect of a narration so implicated in impersona-
tion and fraudulence, so extensively in mortage to the other that it forecloses on itSelf, the imposture of the text is but a swindle of any and

all "signature": every major character is designated by a common de-
nominator, a *pseudonym*. For example, Coverdale begins his recitation of
Old Moodie's "history" thus: "Five-and-twenty years ago, at the epoch
of this story, there dwelt, in one of the middle states, a man whom we
shall call Fauntleroy" (III:182)—immediately preceded by the following:
"my subsequent researches acquainted me with the main facts of the
following narrative; although, in writing it out, my pen has perhaps
allowed itself a trifle of romantic and legendary license, worthier of a
small poet than a grave biographer" (III:181). And of a character in Zenobia's legend, "The Silvery Veil," she remarks: "It is essential to the purposes of my legend to distinguish one of these young gentlemen from his
companions; so, for the sake of a soft and pretty name, (such as we, of
the literary sisterhood, invariably bestow upon our heroes,) I deem it fit
to call him 'Theodore'" (III:109). Both instances, moreover, exemplify
the type of "abysmal" *(mise-en-abyme)* situation in which Coverdale's
narration is brought to light, its infinite regress in second-hand, third-
hand, fourth-hand information, its inaccessible ground: a story (fiction)
within a story (fiction) within a story (fiction). . . . Priscilla admits her
own concealed identity: "Pray do not ask me my other name—at least,
not yet—if you will be so kind to a forlorn creature" (III:29); and as the
Veiled Lady unveiled (the very "fetish" of the *récit*), she transforms to a
pale and shadowy maiden whose presence amid this "knot of visionary
people" even occasions an anonymous effect: "a nameless melancholy"
(III:114). Westervelt, too, is but en-titled a sham, in keeping with his
ultimate character: "He offered me a card, with 'Professor Westervelt'
engraved on it . . . as if to vindicate his claim to the professorial dig-
nity, so often assumed on very questionable grounds" (III:96). And
"Zenobia," as we are told from the outset, "is merely her public name; a
sort of mask in which she comes before the world" (III:8)—and again:
"This . . . was not her real name. She had assumed it, in the first instance, as her magazine-signature" (III:13).

Even Blithedale itself (as both "community" and "text") is suspect
to the problematics of nomination at its origin:

> The rest of us formed ourselves into a committee for providing our infant
> Community with an appropriate name; a matter of greatly more difficulty
> than the uninitiated reader would suppose. Blithedale was neither good nor
> bad. We should have resumed the old Indian name of the premises . . . but
> it chanced to be a harsh, ill-connected, and interminable word. . . . Zeno-
> bia suggested 'Sunny Glimpse,' as expressive of a vista into a better system
> of society. This we turned over and over, for awhile, acknowledging its
> prettiness, but concluded it to be rather too fine and sentimental a

name. . . . I ventured to whisper 'Utopia,' which, however, was unanimously scouted down, and the proposer very harshly maltreated, as if he
had intended a latent satire. Some were for calling our institution 'The
Oasis,' in view of its being the one green spot in the moral sand-waste of the
world; but others insisted on a proviso for reconsidering the matter, at a
twelvemonth's end; when a final decision might be had, whether to name it
'The Oasis,' or 'Saharah.' So, at last, finding it impracticable to hammer out
anything better, we resolved that the spot should still be Blithedale, as being
of good augury enough. (III:37).

Thus, ironically, from beginning to end, the name itself remains purely
temporary—provisional (a pseudonym, moreover, for what, of course,
in actuality was Brook Farm). And need we mention, in passing, the
origin-ality of Coverdale's own suggestion for naming the community
"Utopia," its utterly borrowed significance? And what of Coverdale himself, a man whose name exactly echoes the *original translator* (the oxymoron underscores the contradiction and equivocation of Coverdale's
récit) of the Bible with Apocrypha into English in 1535? Indeed, nothing
escapes this dream-like, equi-vocal, anonymous vacillation between private Veil and public Mask which at all times and everywhere shows
up the Blithedale enterprise as "an illusion, a masquerade, a pastoral, a
counterfeit Arcadia, in which we grown-up men and women were making a play-day of the years that were given us to live in" (III:21). In other
words, this innominate discourse inscribes the narrative ethos of Coverdale's absence (a-tone-ment) within the very same register as the ethical
voice of his conscience (at-one-ment). He is everyONE *(das Man);* he is
no one (in particular).

Just as his peeping offers the most economical means of being present in his absence—that is, on the outside looking in—so too the fabric
of allusion merely inscribes him in the margin of other texts as a
"commentary" (annotation) outside the "notation" itself. That is to say,
we are not to read the textuality of Coverdale's narration as "being-with"
the other, a dialogue or con-textuality played out amid the interval of
intersubjectivity, but rather as "being-outside" the other—a contextuality which locates him on the point of a circumference insofar as it
excludes him from its field of demarcation (and even from himself). To
the extent that he demands the (w)hole of this circum-ference in view
(what is "missing" in *other* human relations—"the secret which was hidden even from themselves") in order to in-fer himself, his *récit* most
simply circumscribes him at the center of an absence to which he is at all
times re-ferred. In this circum-locution, forever closed off to both the
being of his text and the text of his being, he is brought to bear upon

himself as its "eternal re-turn"—the "singer" who "versus" himself (self-re-ference), whose verses not only *turn* "night into day" (III:229) but also resurrect or re-verse that "dawning" as his very own death (annihilation). How else are we to understand the ending of this text—his "final confession"—which itself self-destructs? Thence would Coverdale arise from these ashes: a nothing—"But what, after all, have I to tell? Nothing, nothing, nothing" (III:245)—a meaningless mark, a period (of recuperation) whence issues forth the pre-text of this text of which he is but its insignificant postscript—"It remains only to say a few words about myself" (III:245). Or are we to decipher this postscript as *the text* itself for which *The Blithedale Romance* is but a pretense (pre-text)?

In either case, this "appendix" functions as the supplement to a proscription—"More and more, I feel that we had struck upon what *ought* to be a truth" (III:245–46, italics mine)—which inscribes Coverdale at the center of what ought to be the truth about himself as well: that in the domain of human relations the imperative (ought) but stands for aught. With the collapse of Coverdale's narrative technique—his failure to master the situation by seeing and understanding all (least of all himself)—his discourse teaches us that every *technē* imposes an inherent limit: to be (outside) this boundary is to be superimposed upon nothing. The "story" of one's self can never and in no way be objectified as an explicit intention. Coverdale's attempt to justify himself by means of *conventional* ethics (ought) here underscores the anonymity he seeks to avoid. He is but One of "them" *(das Man)*. That is, in the form of the imperative, the "subject" forecloses on its own *voice* (both active and passive)—and this, precisely to the extent that the speaker is denied, excluded from, the "object" (the other). Any discourse which takes the imperative "mood" precludes the subject itSelf.

Here, too, this narrative mood of "demand" underscores the structure of repression. What so abysmally characterizes Coverdale's "final confession"—"I—I myself—was in love—with—Priscilla " (III:247)—is neither confessional nor final, for by expressing this "one foolish little secret" (III:247) he represses the very secret he so desperately sought at Blithedale, "the secret which was hidden even from themselves." Indeed, this void within the k(not) of these others has always been, in fact, the not of himself—the "lack" or emptiness of his own desire. By filling in the missing part of *his* story, *its* "secret," Coverdale's final narrative act ensures that "nothing" *will be* missing, for he has now expressed all—except, of course, the (k)not of his own desire, what is missing from himself: the unbearable burden of the "other." Insofar as the narration inaugurates a mode of repression, it erases this "signifier" that stands before it. Furthermore, despite its obvious pose as "recall" (the re-membrance of him-self past), Coverdale's story further accomplishes the prodigious task of self-effacement by seeking to inscribe the past as the *source* of its meaning—and this, at the expense of a future which it willfully obliterates: "There is . . . one foolish little secret, which possi-bly may have had something to do with these inactive years of meridian manhood, with my bachelorship, *with the unsatisfied retrospect that I fling back on life, and my listless glance towards the future.* Shall I reveal it?" (III:247, italics mine).

What is this source which Coverdale's idle talk obscures by means of his "poetic scribbling," which his superficial reading of the text of his own life drowns out, which his average understanding refuses to under-score or stand under because it would understand everything? It is nothing less than the ground whence his narration obtains the very meaning it would circum-vent in this long-winded recursion into the past. Here Coverdale's narration leaves himself "undone" inasmuch as he attempts to tie this knot of dreamers to himself: there is no *dé-nouement* with which he might commence a knot of his own—a story facing forward, an authentic intention to secure a beginning in (and for) the future. Coverdale reminisces in order to bear him-"self" back (refer) to its original illusion, its "source" in time, the way in which he is "comple-ted." To this origin he would ascribe the *meaning* of his narration (exis-tence), ever oblivious of the ek-static structure of existence (narration) itSelf—the manner in which it stands out only against the horizon of its own not-being, its future, its ultimate de-sign. And to this degree alone, he is forever circum-stantial to what he means: he simply stands *around*— rather than *under*(stands)—this lack with*in* (himself). He is without ground, with nothing to stand on: the whence and whither of his "going around" is always in circles—beating around the bush (Zenobia's). What appears to be a mode of "making" his past present by means of remem-bering is, in actuality, a mode of "forgetting" his future (*not* being). The self can never be envisioned as a total transparency, for the meaning of narration, and of existence as a (w)hole, arrives out of the future—and not the past. That Coverdale forecloses on his future returns us once again to the structure of repression. Lacan succinctly expresses it thus: "what cannot be remembered is repeated in behavior."[34]

As a form of behavior, Coverdale's narration stands at the crossroads of two convergent avenues whereby the reflective subject is able to tra-verse the past as present. Using Kierkegaard's terminology, "The one sustains recollection negatively directed backwards in opposition to the movement of life; the other sustains recollection directed forwards in its emanation in actuality."[35] Coverdale fixes upon the former whereby the gaze toward his past remains directed backward, in its finality, as something which *has* always already *been accomplished*—as re-call. This hyperopia, however, seals off his present as something which doesn't belong— a kind of "remainder," a postscript. In this way, he is doomed to repeat himself the same way each time he "goes over" his past, this tangle from which he thinks he has been extricated (untied) and yet bestows upon him(self) the meaning and (non)direction of his future—in which *he has* forever *been* (undone). That is to say, Coverdale envisions himSelf as something accomplished—a "fact." In this, of course, he is "done in," "done for." Authentic existence (narration), on the other hand, repeats in forward re-collection a past which has already been preceded by the future—a past to which the future gives rise as its "origin," a past which arrives out of the future in anticipation, one which can be changed precisely because *there is* time. Here time bequeaths to the subject both the manner and meaning of being itSelf. Existence thus rehabilitates its meaning, its very possibility, from its "fictivity" or *thread:* it is, of its own "making" *(poiēsis),* fated—as any "story"—to end. In time, it will (k)not be.

In the "mean time," the subject is its (own) *récit.* Its tale depends upon this tail ("The End") from which it hangs, suspended. To disregard this site, as Coverdale does, condemns the subject to repeating itSelf the same way *(weg)* each time it goes over this ground, recollecting (backward) the scene of itSelf as but a "rear view" (mirror), a picture of the whole of itSelf as (the) past: a timeless object. In so doing, however, its story (scenario) has likewise passed away—its destiny s(p)ent, its existence pre-fabricated by the technique of (its) recall: the memorization of itSelf. Regarding (vis-à-vis) this site, on the other hand, the subject's recitation will inscribe the meaning of being (itSelf), the (k)not of being as a (w)hole. Fabrication, here, looks forward to its future (end), holds it at the front—by means of which the subject will re-vise itSelf, recollect (forward) the scene of itSelf while there's time, figure itSelf (out) in its (own) time, its own way, make up its destiny (scenario) as it goes along. And so the frame *(récit)* will need to be dismantled once again, opened onto another horizon. Hawthorne's oeuvre will repeat this scene, the very "script" to which Coverdale has appended himself as its "post," but in a different way *(weg),* along a different route. Coverdale's narration sends him back; it holds the scene of itSelf behind him (up ahead), heading into the past (retrospect as prospect). The *récit* is mere technique, a frame that turns its back on what's ahead (nothing): the subject (who is supposed to) knows: everything. Hawthorne will rewrite this scene ahead of itSelf, will bury in the crypt of its post (postscript) the very One (Plato's "Hen") (who is supposed to know), will lay (to rest) the (scene of the) Author for (the sake of) the scenario itSelf. This makes *(poiēsis)* the subject timely: once upon a time, it will not be. Narration, here, turns inward toward the heart *(kern)* of (being) itSelf, the inversion of the subject as an instance of the Other: its ways of being (sent, posted, destined, dispatched) beyond (the frame of) itSelf. The narrative frame undoes (the) sense (of) itself, undoes (the sense of) itSelf. Rather than avoid (repress) the void of itSelf, narration will express it, will void itSelf. In "The End," the frame itSelf will figure nothing, the nothingness of the subject who recites it. To the demarcation of this precinct wherein the mark of subjectivity is first mapped out in Hawthorne's world (its horizon as "figure," its meaning as "signification," its structure as "language") I now turn, directing your regard toward that being for whom the meaning of Being itself (being itSelf) becomes an issue in the first place[36]—and toward the fold *(pli)* of this being as it figures Hawthorne's work: the work of figuration as the disfiguration of itSelf.

Because it revokes the frame of objectivity, Hawthorne's oeuvre turns the misappropriation of the existent away from what Heidegger calls the "invisible region of the merely producing consciousness" and toward its interior, the space of the heart: "Only what we thus retain in our heart (*par coeur*), only that do we truly know by heart."[1] Those figures which populate Hawthorne's world metonymically express the (w)hole of existence at its most affective depth, a depth whose meaning obtains from an opposing "ob-," that factical subjectivity which initially calls the ob-ject into being.[2] Against the scientific-technological frame, which distances being by virtue of its "view," Hawthorne's "interior logic" of the heart configures the existent, redraws its lines, draws subject and object near to one another.[3] The dichotomy between *head* and *heart* thus structures the "nearness" and "farness" of being within a larger metaphysical picture, a picture whose referential surface Hawthorne's oeuvre sets out to destroy. On its own, the "ratio" of reason knows only the "one" (Plato), manipulates the existent for the sake of this whole, the Good (Kant) of itSelf. Such is the case with all of Hawthorne's villains. Chillingworth sets up Dimmesdale from the detached perspective of a behavioral psychologist observing the reactions of his guinea pigs (I:129–38); Westervelt controls both Zenobia and Priscilla with a dispassion equaled only by his monomaniacal attachment to his own dark schemes (III:158–59, 201–2); Aylmer tinkers with an insignificant imperfection in his wife only to discover that in curing the "disease" he has killed the patient (X:56); Rappaccini experiments on his daughter with no more concern than he displays toward the noxious plants within the encapsulated garden, a garden which not only isolates them from the world, but from each other as well—that is, he treats her ob-noxiously (X:114); even Hollingsworth, whose philanthropy has turned inward and back upon itself to the point of madness, obsessively envisions mankind as one vast body in desperate need of reform (III:70–71).

Hawthorne's villains unanimously deny the supplications of the heart; the heart itself becomes an object of investigation. Because they separate the self from the investigation as a whole, Hawthorne's villains sever the "self" from its affective relations in the world. The nature of their inquiry has always already determined this in advance. Insofar as they "undertake" the subject in order to discover it objectively, they have already "killed" it, have placed themselves outside the solicitous sphere of being. Indeed, the infinite remoteness necessary for holding the "object"

at bay precludes their ownmost freedom to take it up affectively. Since they cannot hold it in regard, Hawthorne's villains disregard the subject. Its "reality" henceforth becomes a necessary evil, an evil whose existence must be tolerated in order to transfer it theoretically to the mind where its "resistance" ceases to be an ob-stacle entirely. A theory thus becomes the world—the world, at last, "becoming" to the subject. Even the healthy, speculative mind displays this propensity: "It is remarkable, that persons who speculate the most boldly often conform with the most perfect quietude to the external regulations of society. The thought suffices them, without investing itself in the flesh and blood of action" (I:164). Hester, too, is not exempt from this inclination: "Much of the marble coldness of Hester's impression was to be attributed to the circumstance that her life had turned, in a great measure, from passion and feeling, to thought"; standing alone in the world, "she cast away the fragments of a broken chain. The world's law was no law for her mind" (I:164). Her concern for Dimmesdale, however, recoups her from the total isolation experienced by Hawthorne's villains, who "by an iron framework of reasoning" (I:162) obdurately seek to *verify* their "intellectual" convictions. Similarly, by imposing the self upon what is "other" to it, both scientist and reformer "religiously" usurp the freedom of the other. They become, in other words, fanatics. As Pascal—with whose writing Hawthorne's oeuvre provides a continuous commentary—so forcefully points out, "Men never do evil so completely and cheerfully as when they do it from religious conviction."[4]

Chillingworth deceptively begins his initial investigation "with the severe and equal integrity of a judge, desirous only of truth, even as if the question involved no more than the air-drawn lines and figures of a geometrical problem, instead of human passions, and wrongs inflicted on himself" (I:129). Yet such a naive attitude is easily distorted since it neglects its own facticity: "But, as he proceeded, a terrible fascination, a kind of fierce, though still calm, necessity seized the old man within its gripe, and never set him free again, until he had done all its bidding" (I:129). Dimmesdale's natural bent exhibits similar tendencies, for his entire bearing toward the world has been "etherealized" by extended years of weary toil among his books; all he lacked "was the gift that descended upon the chosen disciples, at Pentecost, in tongues of flame; symbolizing, it would seem, not the power of speech in foreign and unknown languages, but that of addressing the whole human brotherhood in the heart's native language" (I:141–42). Like Hester, however, the burden of guilt and complicity tempers his intellectual tendencies, ironically bestowing upon him that very faculty the pentecostal flame ignites: "But this very burden it was, that gave him sympathies so intimate with the sinful brotherhood of mankind; so that his heart vibrated in unison with theirs, and received their pain into itself, and sent its own throb of pain through a thousand other hearts, in gushes of sad, persuasive eloquence" (I:142). It is, of course, this brotherhood which Goodman Brown rejects. Nevertheless, so long as Dimmesdale denies the other, this guilt continues to gnaw at his heart, while even his eyes reflect the deep secret at his interior; thus, "it was the clergyman's peculiarity that he seldom, now-a-days, looked straight-forth at any object, whether human or inanimate" (I:131). What subsequently differentiates Dimmesdale, however, from the genuine villain, is that his human complicity, though hidden, interpenetrates the solicitous sphere of (inter)subjectivity, whereas Goodman Brown, for instance, deliberately chooses to stand apart from the existent *as a whole:* he would be the whole (in) itSelf, the whole (in-itself).

This self-imposition isolates all of Hawthorne's villains. They lack heart; "they would not make a friend of it."[5] Instead, they seek to penetrate its secrets, to analyze its operations, to rationalize its "reasons," to objectify its logic. Hawthorne's villains are thus chronically deceived in their obsessive endeavors, for though a disease of the heart may very well affect the body, it can never be transparent to a rationally comprehensive view. Although the propositions of the intellect are inferred, the principles of the heart are always intuited, as Pascal so brilliantly observed: "it is as useless and absurd for reason to demand from the heart proof of her first principles, before admitting them, as it would be for the heart to demand from reason an intuition of all demonstrated propositions before accepting them."[6] Reason's desire *is* the desire of reason. Dimmesdale suggests as much to Chillingworth: "There can be, if I forebode aright, no power, short of the Divine mercy, to disclose, whether by uttered words, or by type or emblem, the secrets that may be buried with a human heart" (I:131). Ironically, the secret buried within Dimmesdale's own heart discloses itself emblematically; as an affective phenomenon, this tell-tale icon emblazoned on his bosom inscribes a figure, (dis)figures itSelf: the symptom is a metaphor. Even after the physician discovers the burning token on Dimmesdale's breast, stealing into the room while he sleeps, it only encourages Chillingworth's curiosity the more. His compulsion forces him to delve deeper and deeper into an investigation which has no perceptible end in view. Like the vanishing point of perspective, its end is infinitely remote. It is, in fact, "sublime." The "reasons" of the heart can never array themselves before reason within a single, uniform view: the heart's own reason is reason's very heart, the heart of reason itSelf.

Insomuch as it equivocates the objectification to which Hawthorne's villains would subject it, the heart throws reason back upon itSelf, further frustrates its desire to know both the "other" and itSelf. The villain becomes his ownmost enemy. Trusting no "one" (in particular) but the "ratio" *(das Man)* of himSelf—his reason(s) alone—the subject no longer recognizes the enemy when he appears. By treating the other as an object in an object-world, the villain thereby loses itSelf. We've seen this before. Having once created this affective void at the center of its being, the villain, bereft of the other, must thereafter depend upon the *object* of his investigation for his own existence. In effect, he becomes its slave. Hence, with Dimmesdale's death, Chillingworth is doomed as well: "All his strength and energy—all his vital and intellectual force—seemed at once to desert him; insomuch that he positively withered up, shrivelled away, and almost vanished from mortal sight, like an uprooted weed that lies wilting in the sun. This unhappy man had made the very principle of his life to consist in the pursuit and systematic exercise of revenge; and when, by its completest triumph and consummation, that evil principle was left with no further material to support it,—when, in short, there was no more devil's work on earth for him to do, it only remained for the unhumanized mortal to betake himself whither his Master would find him tasks enough, and pay him his wages duly" (I:260).

Similarly, all of Hawthorne's villains maniacally attach themselves to the disembodied transparency of a fixed idea; and all are equally destined to forfeit the object of their solitary pursuit: governed by the obsession to eliminate the crimson imperfection on Georgiana's cheek, Aylmer employs his utmost energy only to lose her in the end (X:56); encouraged by his feeble curiosity and the dispassionate desire to see Beatrice transcend the sphere of ordinary women, Rappaccini rears his daughter amid the poisonous experiments of his garden only to behold her death at the hands of an ironically fatal antidote (X:128); haunted by the quest to discover the Unpardonable Sin, Ethan Brand searches throughout the world only to destroy himself in impotent surrender to the blaze of the lime-kiln (XI:100); driven by his will to power, Westervelt deploys his hypnotic skills on Zenobia and Priscilla only to squander both (III:203, 234).[7] Like Mr. Lindsey in "The Snow-Image," Hawthorne's villains utilize a dispassionate, intellectual frame by means of which they view the world without exception. In this sense, they are uniformly unexceptional.

Furthermore, the reformer is often the most dangerous, for since his object of concern is always the other, the sphere of his power frequently runs away from the very responsibility his view professes. What the narrator concludes of Mr. Lindsey holds equally true for all of Hawthorne's reformers, and would make profitable reading in a curriculum for social workers: "it behoves men, and especially men of benevolence, to consider well what they are about, and, before acting on their philanthropic purposes, to be quite sure that they comprehend the nature and all the relations of the business in hand. What has been established as an element of good to one being, may prove absolute mischief to another" (XI:25). Regarding this "transcendental" disposition, R. W. B. Lewis observes, "if anyone was certain that men were not in any respect like angels, it was Nathaniel Hawthorne."[8] Perhaps Hollingsworth's character best expresses that ironic extreme to which the "benevolent" attitude is most disposed—"the terrible egotism which he mistook for an angel of God" (III:55): "Admitting what is called Philanthropy, when adopted as a profession, to be often useful by its energetic impulse to society at large, it is perilous to the individual, whose ruling passion, in one exclusive channel, it thus becomes. It ruins, or is fearfully apt to ruin, the heart; the rich juices of which God never meant should be pressed violently out, and distilled into alcoholic liquor, by an unnatural process; but should render life sweet, bland, and gently beneficent, and insensibly influence other hearts and other lives to the same blessed end. I see in Hollingsworth an exemplification of the most awful truth in Bunyan's book of such;—from the very gate of Heaven, there is a by-way to the pit!" (III:243). The novels of Henry James will subsequently recite this self-same scene: the ideal makes monsters of us all. Within the finite realm of being, those who would be God would be Satan as well, for the other side of Angel is Devil. Pascal has said it another way: "Man is neither angel nor brute, and the unfortunate thing is that he who would act the angel acts the brute."[9]

Hawthorne's reformers are not alone in this respect; for both the scientist and the "intellectual" in general are precariously poised above this egocentric "pit." Since, by definition, the monomaniacal enterprise undertakes its mission with its gaze fixed solely on an isolated "objective"— one which constitutes the infinitely remote vanishing point of its view—it ignores that which lies closest to it. In other words, it avoids, at all cost, the responsibility for itSelf. Because it hasn't questioned its own reason(s), its very *raison d'être,* it simultaneously denies itself the possibility of self-reproach—especially for the failure it encounters. If ever, the lesson is learned too late. Thus Ethan Brand's final, "involuntary recognition of the infinite absurdity of seeking throughout the world for what was the closest of all things to himself, and looking into every heart, save his own, for what was hidden in no other breast" (XI:87), ironically terminates eighteen years of futile, blind volition. What is left to will but his own death? Similarly, years after his experience at Blithedale, Hollingsworth has yet to reform a single criminal (III:243); after seven years of uninterrupted observation, Chillingworth has yet to whole-heartedly entrap his prey (I:256); after complete surrender to an ideal quest, the artist of the beautiful has yet to permanently materialize the aim of his original intention (X:475); after a twenty-year leave of "absence" from his wife in order to observe her, Wakefield has yet to discover that the final joke is on him (IX:140). We may assume a similar failure on the part of Aylmer, Rappaccini, and Westervelt. Even Dimmesdale exhibits the egotistic tendencies of Hawthorne's villains, but at the opposite extreme. His perception of the Letter against the darkened night sky is thus imputed solely to the disease of his own eye and heart: "Not but the meteor may have shown itself at that point, burning duskily through a veil of cloud; but with no such shape as his guilty imagination gave it; or, at least, with so little definiteness, that another's guilt might have seen another symbol in it" (I:155). The narrator further comments: "But what shall we say, when an individual discovers a revelation, addressed to himself alone. . . . In such a case, it could only be the symptom of a highly disordered mental state, when a man, rendered morbidly self-contemplative by long, intense, and secret pain, had extended his egotism over the whole expanse of nature, until the firmament itself should appear no more than a fitting page for his soul's history and fate" (I:155). Paradoxically, then, the "intellectual" attitude inclines toward both extremes of consciousness: in its quest for the "objective" this attitude implicitly places itself above all "others," and therefore *beyond* even *itself,* while at the opposite extreme it may turn in upon itself so that the "self" explicitly becomes its own "object." In either case, the self becomes divine.

The ruinous effects of egotism—or the "bosom-serpent"—are nowhere more pronounced than in Roderick Elliston. Tortured by the void of his own heart, Roderick must socialize his "disease" in order to maintain any sense of individuality—he must show himself to the world. In his nothingness he henceforth becomes the supreme egotist, for he cannot bear the emptiness of his heart alone: "All persons, chronically diseased, are egotists, whether the disease be of the mind or body; whether it be sin, sorrow, or merely the more tolerable calamity of some endless pain, or mischief among the cords of mortal life. Such individuals are made acutely conscious of a self, by the torture in which it dwells. Self, therefore, grows to be so prominent an object with them, that they cannot but present it to the face of every casual passer-by . . . for it is that cancer, or that crime, which constitutes their respective individuality" (X:273). Thereafter, Roderick draws his misery around him, looking triumphantly down upon all whose interior nourishes no such deadly monster (X:274). Indeed, it is this very emptiness (alienation) that operates as an antidote against any who would attempt a cure, for no-thing (and only nothing) can come up to it. It is incomparable. Like a "black hole," it blindly swallows all "other" intentions in its own intentional void. Its only remedy is in forgetting that which it cannot forget (its self) and in remembering that which it has purposely forgotten (the other): "Could I, for one instant, forget myself, the serpent might not abide within me. It is my diseased self-contemplation that has engendered and nourished him" (X:282–83). Unlike most of Hawthorne's villains, however, Roderick learns his lesson in time; with the appearance of his estranged wife, Rosina, the cure is affected. He nevertheless typifies the extremity of those two qualities which Pascal universally ascribes to the self: "it is unjust in itself since it makes itself the centre of everything; it is inconvenient to others since it would enslave them; for each Self is the enemy, and would like to be the tyrant of all others."[10]

Isolated from the world they seek to know—to master—Hawthorne's villains are necessarily forced, in these two forms, to turn back upon themselves as the *ultimate object* of their own consciousnesses, for in having refuted (inter)subjectivity in favor of the absolute truth of their "objective," they unwittingly deny themselves the very objectivity they so obsessively wish to impose upon the world:

> This is always true of those men who have surrendered themselves to an overruling purpose. It does not so much impel them from without, nor even operate as a motive power within, but grows incorporate with all that they think and feel, and finally converts them into little else save that one principle. When such begins to be the predicament, it is not cowardice, but wisdom, to avoid these victims. They have no heart, no sympathy, no reason, no conscience. They will keep no friend, unless he make himself the mirror of their purpose; they will smite and slay you, and trample your dead corpse under foot, all the more readily, if you take the first step with them, and cannot take the second, and the third, and every other step of their terribly straight path. They have an idol, to which they consecrate themselves high-priest, and deem it holy work to offer sacrifices to whatever is most precious, and never once seem to suspect—so cunning has the Devil been with them—that this false deity, in whose iron features, immitigable to all the rest of mankind, they see only benignity and love, is but a spectrum of the very priest himself, projected upon the surrounding darkness. And the higher and purer the original object, and the more unselfishly it may have been taken up, the slighter is the probability that they can be led to recognize the process, by which godlike benevolence has been debased into all-devouring egotism. (III:70–71)

By (self)negating the objectivity they seek, Hawthorne's villains commit one of the two most all-inclusive of human errors enumerated by Pascal:

either "to take everything literally," or "to take everything spiritually."[11] The first of these intellectual over-simplifications applies to the scientist, the second to the reformer. Within the frame of this objective consciousness, Hawthorne stages the drama of its "interior," the scene of its affective logic. That mode of consciousness proper to the "head" corresponds to what Heidegger calls "the logic of calculating reason": Descartes' consciousness of the *ego cogito;* that mode of consciousness proper to the "heart" corresponds to what Heidegger calls "the world's inner realm": Pascal's logic of the heart.[12] It is this metaphysical (logical) dichotomy itself which Hawthorne's oeuvre sets out to destroy. His work inaugurates this subversion at the level of the psychosomatic.

□

That Hawthorne anticipated psychoanalysis is all the more impressive when we consider the oeuvre's constant desire to make moral "diseases" *appear* as corresponding physical diseases. As Malcolm Cowley has observed, "What happened in the heart became manifest in the flesh; and, conversely, one could arrive at inner truths by scrutinizing appearances or by watching their reflections in a mirror."[13] A notebook entry for 27 October 1841 already reveals Hawthorne's fascination with this problem: "To symbolize moral or spiritual disease by disease of the body;—thus, when a person committed any sin, it might cause a sore to appear on the body;—this to be wrought out" (VIII:222)—and again, on 1 June 1842: "A physician for the cure of moral diseases" (VIII:235). The idea, of course, is exquisitely "wrought out" in *The Scarlet Letter.*

In his exhortation to Dimmesdale to deal with Hester, the Reverend Wilson ironically betrays the issue most central to Dimmesdale's own conscience: "Truly, as I sought to convince him, the shame lay in the commission of the sin, and not in the showing of it forth" (I:65–66). From the outset, Chillingworth detects some dark secret fatally lodged within the "heart" of Dimmesdale's breast: "Wherever there is a heart and an intellect, the diseases of the physical frame are tinged with the peculiarities of these. In Arthur Dimmesdale, thought and imagination were so active, and sensibility so intense, that the bodily infirmity would be likely to have its groundwork there" (I:124). While Chillingworth figures (out) his plan of attack, the narrative itself prefigures the outcome: "A man burdened with a secret should especially avoid the intimacy of his physician" (I:124). The investigator (analyst), however, is no more immune from the disease than his object (analysand), so that Chillingworth's own physical aspect undergoes a reciprocal change. Moreover, the crowd is disposed to perceive this trans-position (counter-transference) only insofar as it "forms its judgment, as it usually does, on the intuitions of its great and warm heart," whereas whenever it "attempts to see with its eyes, it is exceedingly apt to be deceived" (I:126).

Dimmesdale likewise senses the change transpiring within and without, and rightfully understands both its origin in the psyche and its affective consequences upon consciousness: "so Mr. Dimmesdale, conscious that the poison of one morbid spot was infecting his heart's entire substance, attributed all his presentiments to no other cause" (I:140). The heart not only "colors" consciousness, but "speaks" a language of its own, a language whose "presentiments" subvert the logic of the head. So it is with Dimmesdale's final sermon before the "revelation": "But even when the minister's voice grew high and commanding . . . still, if the auditor listened intently, and for the purpose, he could detect the same cry of pain. What was it? The complaint of a human heart, sorrow–laden, perchance guilty, telling its secret, whether of guilt or sorrow, to the great heart of mankind; beseeching its sympathy or forgiveness,—at every moment,—in each accent,—and never in vain! It was this profound and continual undertone that gave the clergyman his most appropriate power" (I:243–44). The heart thus "knows" in advance of the head—amasses its "reasons" while reason stumbles. Here Hawthorne will recite Pascal by heart: the heart has reasons of which reason itself knows nothing. Hence even in his sermon, Dimmesdale is already alongside what must follow by "reason" of a logic more swift and subtle than any reason could provide.

Figured by a context that both logically and psychologically "completes" the central scaffold scene, Dimmesdale approaches the pillory where Hester had encountered the world's ignominious stare some seven years before. After an anxious delay, he at last consummates the central image of the novel, bringing it full circle as he ascends the scaffold, supported on the one hand by Hester's arm, while clasping the tiny hand of Pearl with the other. Having displaced Pearl as the central figure of the triad, he reveals the "final" secret of the heart (in) itself: inscribed upon his flesh, the scarlet letter gleams. Those best able to appreciate the minister's sensibilities, and the reciprocal operation of the heart upon the body, "whispered their belief, that the awful symbol was the effect of the ever active tooth of remorse, gnawing from the inmost heart outwardly" (I:258). In typically ambiguous fashion, however, the narration leaves even this phenomenon open to doubt; for others, who professed never once to have removed their eyes from Dimmesdale, "denied that there was any mark whatever on his breast, more than on a new-born infant's" (I:259). Yet the narrator concludes: "Without disrupting a truth so momentous, we must be allowed to consider this version of Mr. Dimmesdale's story as only an instance of that stubborn fidelity with which a man's friends—and especially a clergyman's—will sometimes uphold his character; when proofs, clear as the mid-day sunshine on the scarlet letter, establish him a false and sin-stained creature of the dust" (I:259). As Alfred Marks has said of this uncertain resolution: "Clear as the mid-day sunshine on the scarlet letter," to the twentieth-century reader who notices what Hawthorne does with sunshine, on the one hand, and the scarlet letter, on the other, means "clear as mud."[14]

While Hawthorne's fascination with the psychosomatic is nowhere more in evidence than in its meticulously detailed exploration in *The Scarlet Letter,* other tales examine this phenomenon from variously acute angles. In her complexion, for example, Beatrice betrays a marked similarity to the plants; she is the semblance of but another flower, "the human sister of those vegetable ones, as beautiful as they . . . but still to be touched only with a glove, nor to be approached without a mask" (X:97). Even her voice betrays an all-too-vivid bloom, "a voice as rich as a tropical sunset, and which made Giovanni, though he knew not why, think of deep hues of purple or crimson, and of perfumes heavily delectable" (X:96–97). Herkimer remarks that Roderick's complexion "had a greenish tinge over its sickly white, reminding him of a species of marble out of which he had once wrought a head of Envy, with her snaky locks" (X:269). And as with Dimmesdale, Roderick's symptoms produce an endless perplexity and speculation among the crowd: "They knew not whether ill health were robbing his spirits of elasticity; or whether a canker of the mind was gradually eating, as such cankers do, from his moral system into the physical frame, which is but the shadow of the former" (X:271). Similarly, among the guests at "The Christmas Banquet," there was a man whose misfortune it was "to cherish within his bosom a diseased heart, which had become so wretchedly sore, that the continual and unavoidable rubs with the world . . . made uclers in it. . . . he found his chief employment in exhibiting these miserable sores to any who would give themselves the pain of viewing them"; there was a man of "nice conscience" as well, "who bore a blood-stain in his heart"; then there was an aged lady, "who had lived from time immemorial with a constant tremor quivering through her frame"; and then again, a certain Mr. Smith, "afflicted with a physical disease of the heart, which threatened instant death on the slightest cachinnatory indulgence, or even that titillation of the bodily frame, produced by merry thoughts" (X:287–88, 294–95).

That Hawthorne is so often concerned with the psychosomatic reveals to what extent his fiction is grounded in the situation. His oeuvre, in fact, secures this from the beginning; for the structure of the image already expresses the dual, reciprocal horizons of being in its affective foundation. His understanding of this phenomenon has put itself ahead of the subject-object dichotomy, and its concomitant conceptual schema: form-content. As a structure, this phenomenon transpires alongside two simultaneous horizons, two horizons moreover which are neither parallel nor conjoined in infinity. Grounded in a space neither physico-geometric nor expressive, but both, the phenomenon thus undercuts the entire arsenal of machinery which representation has at its command. Furthermore, because its form is purely phenomenal, its "truth" is discovered solely in the appearance, in what is both revealed and concealed. And this essential ambiguity remains its truth: the "subject" of this phenomenon is at once its own "object." Against an insatiable gap between the biological need (object) and its demand (expression), against the outline of this perpetual inadequation appears the silhouette of the subject—the void in which it is carved out at the level of desire.[15]

Now in the register of the psychosomatic, Hawthorne's villains do not want to desire; they *do not want to be* (in what is "other" to the self). In fact, they deny it. This nevertheless constitutes a form of desire which, because it closes itself off to the dialectic of the other, requires that the subject (of/as desire) appear elsewhere (as an object). This it does in the body, where the subject now turns up in the form of an absolute (in-itself)—that is, ironically, as the object of its own (lack of) desire. The subject becomes slave to a solitary authority, and is completely *written by it* (sub-scribed). In this circumscription, the subject "satisfies" (feeds on) itSelf, and yet demands (expresses) its own need as something radically Other. The body becomes this Alien. That this is generally so of alienation in Hawthorne bespeaks "the world" as *exposition*. Here the body *is* its "truth," a single configuration of simultaneous horizons—that is, the trans-figuration of self and other, of subject and object.[16] Together, head and heart express the interval between the factual and the factical, that gap in being to which the subject is given over in desire.

The psychosomatic expresses the textuality of being; it attests to what extent Hawthorne implicitly understood its dialogical configuration. In protest to (the fullness of) reason as a whole, its "ratio," Hawthorne's oeuvre asserts its lack, the void of desire at its heart, the inscription of the subject as a (w)hole. Here the heart will have its "say" as well. The void which Hawthorne's villain experiences at the center of his being, and to which the body subsequently *bears testimony,* is the very emptiness of the subject itSelf. The circle, moreover, is vicious. Outside the heart, the villain denies the "other" (his own desire). In severing his relation to the other, however, he likewise cuts *(coup)* himSelf. Whenever the subject isolates itSelf from the other, it loses its self as well. Indeed, it becomes the other—not itself. The body will recoup this loss. As Sartre suggests, at the level of reflection there is no self(understanding) outside the conception of other selves. So too within the psychoanalytic register as well: at the level of desire, the subject is (the desire of) the other. Even prior to the psychosomatic, this ontological duplicity plays itself out in the form of alienation to the extent that it not only originates the self, but terminates it as well: witness Goodman Brown. The self-assertive domination of the subject, and its objectification of being, places Hawthorne's villains outside all solicitude and care—yet only from a "transcendental" point of view. The body cannot escape its situation, and thus rebels against the heartless proposition of reason, its unreasonable desire. The head can have no "reason" without the heart; conversely, the heart becomes a blind and willful imposition, void of its own "reason," without the head. Each without the other reduces itself to absurdity. Within the space of this reduction, the body itself becomes a thing, an object for the subject itSelf. In this "inadequate" design, in this abyss between the two, being emerges to meaning.

☐

From an existential point of view, this distinction takes the form, *en soi/pour soi:* in-itself/for-itself. In their ontological constitution they are the same, and delineate but two aspects of a single configuration. As Scheler remarks, the physiological and psychic processes "differ only as phenomena. . . . Thus, what we call 'physiological' and 'psychological' are but two ways of looking at one and the same process of life. There is a biology 'from within' and a biology 'from without.'"[17] Hawthorne's oeuvre discloses the Pascalian truth that we are always searching (without) for what we have already found (within). To put it another way: "The real is that which always comes back to the same place."[18] Thus Ethan Brand, for instance, spends eighteen years in search of a truth he is at last to discover, beside the blaze of the lime-kiln, within the "space" of his own heart. Against the infinite expanse revealed in measuring the distance between the self and its (objective) ideal, Hawthorne's villain deserts the very structure of his being. By seeking to be the *equal of* (identical to) this idea(l), he reduces being to the dull integrity of mere uniformity.[19] Indeed, he has already measured this distance mathematically or, better, "geometrically." Such is the supreme *reductio ad absurdum* which reason proposes, the reduction of being to quantification—and such is the issue that troubles Aylmer.

As the technological envoy of his age, Aylmer's destiny has always already arrived. The experiment on his wife reveals his absolute faith in science and its ultimate ability to transcend nature: "The higher intellect, the imagination, the spirit, and even the heart, might all find their congenial aliment in pursuits which . . . would ascend from one step of powerful intelligence to another, until the philosopher should lay his hand on the secret of creative force, and perhaps make new worlds for himself" (X:36). His wife becomes the *probability* of this new "world," for he had devoted himself too unreservedly to scientific studies "ever to be weaned from them by any second passion"—which is to say, by any passion whatsoever; his "love for his young wife might prove the stronger of the two; but it could only be by intertwining itself with his love of science, and uniting the strength of the latter to his own" (X:36–37). While Aylmer therefore seeks to make Georgiana more than she is *factually*, he likewise seeks to make himself more than he is *factically*. For Aylmer, the birthmark, this imperfection inscribed within the other, but signifies a lack. (So too, ironically, does his desire to erase it.) In striving to come up to perfection, to become its equal as "creator," he has already measured this dimension quantitatively. By definition, however, the idea(l) of perfection is infinitely remote from the factical, for only number as quantity can negotiate the idea of infinity (Kant aside). As Scheler has expressed it, "Man takes his own emptiness of heart for the 'infinite emptiness' of space and time," where "empty" means, to begin, "an expectation that is not satisfied"; the subject's original emptiness is, then, the emptiness of its own heart[20]—the emptiness (lack) of desire. In order to own (up to) this emptiness, moreover, the subject must measure this dimension with another metric, as Heidegger suggests, a *metron* which is "no mere geo-metry";[21] only thus will subjectivity bring being into its own, its ground plan. Aylmer, on the other hand, addresses an expectation which in itself makes no sense: to coincide with himSelf—to be an "in-itself." As such, the original emptiness of his heart is inhuman from the start, for its desire is already outside its own *possibility*.

Similarly, the void at the interior of Gervayse Hastings is beside itSelf: "he is such a being as I could conceive you to carve out of marble, and some yet unrealized perfection of human science to endow with an exquisite mockery of intellect; but . . . the demands that spirit makes upon spirit, are precisely those to which he cannot respond" (X:284). As Gervayse says of himself, "It is a chillness—a want of earnestness—a feeling as if what should be my heart were a thing of vapor—a haunting perception of unreality! Thus, seeming to possess all that other men have—all that men aim at—I have really possessed nothing, neither joys nor griefs" (X:304). Roderick's preface to the story of Gervayse hits upon a further irony: such a man is often never "conscious of the deficiency" (X:285). Neither, of course, is Ethan Brand, whose marble heart reflects the utter desolation of a consciousness grounded in objectification and manipulation.

Like all of Hawthorne's villains, Ethan "unreasonably" expects to come up to the ideal, to identify at some point in the future with what is infinitely removed from him (self). He thus becomes a fiend—in fact, began to be so from the moment that his heart had ceased to keep pace with his intellectual development, a development which in its progress,

> disturbed the counterpoise between his mind and heart. The Idea that possessed his life had operated as a means of education; it had gone on cultivating his powers to the highest point of which they were susceptible; it had raised him from the level of an unlettered laborer, to stand on a star-light eminence, whither the philosophers of the earth, laden with the lore of universities, might vainly strive to clamber with him. So much for the intellect! But where was the heart? That, indeed, had withered—had contracted—had hardened—had perished! It had ceased to partake of the universal throb. He had lost his hold of the magnetic chain of humanity. He was no longer a brother-man, opening the chambers or the dungeons of our common nature by the key of holy sympathy, which gave him a right to share in all its secrets; he was now a cold observer, looking on mankind as the subject of his experiment. (XI:98–99)

In this respect, Ethan typifies the unfettered disregard for the being of others which the rational attitude merely posits, using Heidegger's phrase, as "*quanta* of calculation."[22] To order its "world," reason "subjects" the existent as a whole to conform to the uni-formity of its view. It thereby levels down every *ordo* to that of the manipulatively objective.

Here is that very universe exposed by Scheler whenever the living being is taken as the sum of its parts: the resultant picture is that of a gigantic, strictly continuous and coherent system in which the totality of egos *(res cogitantes)* represent "nothing but thinking points in an immense mechanical process!"[23] Such is the nature of the integer (the One); it preserves "integrity"—what constitutes its very rationale, its *ratio* for being (Plato's "Hen" is here as well). Similarly, the *ratio* of reason would be (identical to) its purpose or end, without the slightest deviation—ever forgetful of its ground in aught, zero, nothingness. To this coincidence between its end and its self it owes its uni-versality (the One-ness of its domain). Precisely insofar as this *ratio* of manipulative consciousness perceives its end and self as synonymous, it precludes the very *experience* of itself and is, in its inclusiveness, everywhere the same *(das Man)*. To this extent, it must exclude deficiency or "difference," for in (self)division it admits of no "remainder." Here too subsists its greatest danger: it is unaware of itSelf. Hence the objectification of being toward which reason aspires consists of nothing less than the subject's blind and willful imposition, its self-assertion in everything.[24]

The "Paul Pry" attitude, inaugurated in "Sights from a Steeple," exposes those extremes of isolation and alienation to which such a position is inherently susceptible—a danger uncompromisingly characterized, in "Ethan Brand," as the Unpardonable Sin: "The sin of an intellect that triumphed over the sense of brotherhood with man . . . and sacrificed everything to its own mighty claims! The only sin that deserves a recompense of immortal agony" (XI:90). Here consciousness would make of the subject an object—an object, moreover, of "psychological experiment" (XI:94): "he was now a cold observer, looking on mankind as the subject of his experiment, and, at length, converting man and woman to be his puppets, and pulling the wires that moved them to such degrees of crime as were demanded for his study. Thus Ethan Brand became a fiend" (XI:99). Whenever and where the other becomes a thing, then and there the subject is subject, subjected, only to itSelf. For Hawthorne, the whence and whither of such a consciousness, one that would (itSelf) be beyond the scope of its own view, its ownmost enemy, is not to be discerned in the voyeur, as *Blithedale* seems to indicate, but rather in (the image of) Narcissus—that is, in the very nature of reflection itSelf, in self-reflection (witness "Monsieur du Miroir"). And if its abysmal structure takes the form of a circle, it does this insofar as the subject objectifies another subject and thereby subjects itSelf to objectification. Once again, by virtue of its view, the subject loses sight of itSelf.

It's not for nothing that Hawthorne recites the location of this scene within the structure of a tale whose very circularity might lead us to believe we have recovered an origin—that is, being as a *whole*. So too, the end (death) of Ethan Brand invokes excessive imagery of gold, a gold which echoes the alchemical tort, the philosopher's stone, and seemingly bespeaks the redemption and resurrection of (Mother) Nature as well:

> The early sunshine was already pouring its gold upon the mountain-tops. . . . Every dwelling was distinctly visible; the little spires of the two churches pointed upward, and caught a fore-glimmering of brightness from the sun-gilt skies upon their gilded weathercocks. . . . Old Greylock was glorified with a golden cloud upon his head. Scattered, likewise, over the breasts of the surrounding mountains, there were heaps of hoary mist, in fantastic shapes, some of them far down into the valley, others high up . . . and still others . . . hovering in the gold radiance of the upper at-

mosphere. . . . Earth was so mingled with sky that it was a daydream to look at it.

   To supply that charm of the familiar and homely, which Nature so readily adopts into a scene like this, the stage-coach was rattling down the mountain-road, and the driver sounded his horn; while echo caught up the notes and intertwined them into a rich, and varied, and elaborate harmony. (XI:100–101).

Indeed, the abundance of circular imagery throughout the tale would seem to reclaim this harmony, the unitary nature of Nature as a whole. For example, Ethan returns to where his quest began, "making himself at home in his old place" (XI:88). As he remarks of himself, "He has found what he sought, and therefore he comes back again" (XI:87). In the same way, the mountains reverberate back upon themselves the circular hollow of Ethan's laughter. The story itself moves from sunset to sunrise. Ethan's idea(l) pre-figures the disposition of his body at the end: each completes the circuit of the lime-kiln, that solitary structure seemingly beyond the ravages of time, the kiln which has "stood unimpaired, and was in nothing changed, since he had thrown his dark thoughts into the intense glow of its furnace, and melted them, as it were, into the one thought that took possession of his life" (XI:84). Little Joe repeats the circle in miniature: he travels to the village and back. Even the fire sends up "spouts of blue flame, which quivered aloft and danced madly, as within a magic circle" (XI:100).

   The mad dance of the flame, in turn, re-sites an earlier circle, where an elderly dog, suddenly, "began to run around after his tail, which, to heighten the absurdity . . . was a great deal shorter than it should have been. Never was seen such headlong eagerness in pursuit of an object that could not possibly be attained . . . as if one end of the ridiculous brute's body were at deadly and most unforgivable enmity with the other. Faster and faster . . . went the cur . . . until, utterly exhausted, and as far from the goal as ever, the foolish old dog ceased his performance" (XI:96). This tale of a circle but re-creates, in minimal concentric form, the vicious (abysmal) circularity of a tale that would be its own end, its own tail.

   Let's back up: at the end of this tale is a disappearing head. For isn't it the case that Ethan loses his head in the end, has—in fact—always already lost his head in the *impossible* "purpose" to which he aspires? The circularity of the lime-kiln to which Ethan surrenders towers head over heels above the smaller concentric circles of this tale. Here, heading into its head, Ethan will meet his end. Here too, the marble is burnt into another circle—a "perfect, snow-white" circle of lime against which Ethan's skeleton, "snow-white too," figures forth (XI:102). I'll return to this white-on-white—a most unusual image in Hawthorne, and not un-like that virgin, blank page (to) which the writer lays (siege). Lest it obscure the (primal) scene itSelf, I draw your attention to this site; it recapitulates the space of desire, the place of the phantasy itself: "The writer puts his dejecta on paper."[25] The question thus rears its head: what are we to make of all this circularity, the round-about way in which everything returns to itself? At the level of the image, at the level of the symbol, at the level of its very structure, the text agrees with Bachelard: being is round.[26]

Let's not be taken in by this, however, as though being could ever return to itself as (a) *whole*. The circle inscribes, circumscribes, a void, a location empty of any and all content—a *hole*. If nothing else, the ob-sessive imagery of fragmentation shatters any and all access to the whole. From the outset, we are in the realm of ruin, the shadow, the trace, (the bare bones of) what remains: the skeleton (death). The tale opens onto this (unimaginable) image. At its inception, "Bartram, the lime-burner . . . sat watching his kiln, at nightfall, while his little son played at building houses with the scattered fragments of marble" (XI:83). With this opus, being is sent on its way, dispatched, posted, to make its rounds. Then everything becomes broken, a blur: "the tender light of the half-full moon" strives "to trace out the indistinct shapes of the neighbor-ing mountains" while, "in the upper sky," there lingers "a flitting con-gregation of clouds, still faintly tinged with the rosy sunset, though, thus far down into the valley, the sunshine had vanished long and long ago" (XI:85); Ethan's laughter rolls "away into the night . . . indistinctly re-verberated among the hills" (XI:88); his crime, "in its indistinct black-ness," seems to "overshadow" Bartram (XI:88); all about the scene "lay the gigantic corpses of dead trees, decaying on the leaf-strewn soil" (XI:97); the upper surface of the kiln itself presents a view of an "im-mense mass of broken marble" (XI:99), while visitors to Bartram's hut resign themselves to sit on "a fragment of marble" (XI:84); even the dog's tail seems to be "a great deal shorter than it should have been" (XI:96). Upon this site, Ethan consigns himself to the fire, resolved that earth itelf should not resolve him; astride the lime-kiln he disclaims the maternal: "Oh, Mother Earth . . . who art no more my Mother, and into whose bosom this frame shall never be resolved" (XI:100). "Bosom" indeed: what bosom? Who ever saw a bosom shaped like this? This (lack of the) "breast" prefigures a later construction: the deflection of the ego through reflections of the Other.[27] This will come to a head. In the end, we're left in the lurch, left with nothing but left-overs whence the head of this tale began: "the relics of Ethan Brand were crumbled into fragments"

(XI:102). If relics, then Bartram's act can only be sacrilege: his pole disturbs these saintly remains.

For the moment, let's pile up the fragments. Three "locals," visitors to Ethan's original locale (the place from which he [dis]embarks upon his [im]possible quest, and which has always already been the scene of the crime), are singled out by the narrative consciousness; each is delineated by means of synecdoche: these locals are neither subjects nor objects— not even "partial"; rather, they are objects of the (partial) drive, characterized in terms of a single bodily part. In the case of the state-agent and the Doctor, that part is summed up simply as the remainder of a fire that burns within, a mere bodily extension—in fact, a pseudo-body part, a fetish, that has come to replace the life of the body itself: a cigar and a pipe. The Lawyer takes us one step further in this simple lesson in subtraction: "He had come to be but the fragment of a human being, a part of one foot having been chopped off by an axe, and an entire hand torn away by the devilish gripe of a steam-engine" (XI:91). Here we've left vitality (the fire of life) behind. We're in the precinct of the morgue, or— better—the butcher shop. (Faulkner read his Hawthorne well: "My, my. A body does get around.") These parts extend beyond the absence of life, the presence of death (of no-thing), and point to, in and of themselves, the region of de-parture. The culminating spectacle, the final scene of this tableau, but takes us from the butcher shop to the battle field.

This remarkable passage concludes with an image to which I would recall you once again. Having placed his diorama in proper position, the German Jew "invited the young men and girls to look through the glass orifices of the machine," where he exhibited cracked and wrinkled pictures of "cities, public edifices . . . ruined castles . . . Napoleon's battles, and Nelson's sea-fights"; in the very midst of these appears "a gigantic, brown, hairy hand—which might have been mistaken for the Hand of Destiny, though, in truth, it was only the showman's—pointing its forefinger to various scenes of the conflict" (XI:95). At the conclusion, "the German bade little Joe put his head into the box. Viewed through the magnifying glasses, the boy's round, rosy visage assumed the strangest imaginable aspect of an immense, Titanic child, the mouth grinning broadly, and the eyes, and every other feature, overflowing with fun at the joke. Suddenly, however, that merry face turned pale, and its expression changed to horror; for this easily impressed and excitable child had become sensible that the eye of Ethan Brand was fixed upon him through the glass" (XI:95). All "objective" distance has vanished. It comes as no surprise that, at the moment he fixes his gaze within the showman's box, Ethan sees nothing; his very subjectivity has long since disappeared—

erased, eradicated by the vanishing point of his objective idea(l). We are returned to Ethan's self-effacing act within the orifice of the kiln, the glaringly blank (white-on-white) page that encapsulates the story of his life, his existence, his being—the nothingness at the heart of the tale of "Ethan Brand."

One needn't search long for what occasioned this removal. It is reason itself, reason understood as "ratio," the integer, the One, the whole. Thus, Ethan's identification with the idea(l): he would coincide with himSelf; he would be the transcendental signified he seeks. In this way lies madness. His displacement of the primal phantasy thereby towers over the scene of this story as both its beginning and end, that haunting phantasm in which the idea(l) was forged and to which it must inevitably return: the lime-kiln, a perpetual erection. As transcendental signifier, the lime-kiln not only corresponds to Ethan's objective idea(l) as a *whole,* the transcendental signified, but is its very occasion. No wonder he has lost his head. Like Hamlet, rather than have the phallus, he would be it. For the moment, suffice it to say that Ethan not only represses the nature of himself as subject, but also the very nature of the signifier as signifier. Neither is self-sufficient. As a signifier itself, the phallus bespeaks an absence in the subject (desire): it represents the subject in its nullity, that *kern* of non-sense (non-being) at the heart of being itSelf.

Regarding its psychoanalytic reverberations, this is a game of hide-and-seek *(fort-da).* Very simply, Ethan doesn't play by the rules. He would simultaneously *be* "it" and that which *seeks* "it." He need only have heeded the simple lesson of the dog: in seeking its tail, it loses its head. So too, Ethan's tale proposes, from the beginning, the end of itSelf, itSelf as its own end, its own (point of) departure. One needn't solicit the conclusion for this end. If Ethan loses his head, he has already done so from the beginning. Of course it turns up in the end, re-turns to overtake him from behind. Let's not fall back on tradition. This "return-to-the-womb/origins" business makes sense here only up to a point. In one sense, Ethan (re)inserts himSelf into the *hole* of the lime-kiln—a return to (Mother) Nature as a *whole.* And on the surface (of the kiln) this would appear to be the case: he now is One and All. We needn't belabor the obvious: he is the de-parted One. Yet, this (w)hole affair returns us to the point itself: the lime-kiln. Ethan's remains attest to the very insufficiency of the integer, the One, the whole. His trace inscribes a remainder, what is always and everywhere left over and above the whole: a spare part, if you will. This final image puts logic beside itself. The signifier once again sends being on its way, beyond the realm of the logician, the mathematician, the geometrician. The part is greater than the whole. Dismemberment but celebrates the origin of this dis-stance, disintegrates the whole of the body (image)—the space (of the phantasy) in which desire takes (up) its place: the *objet (a)*. From the scene of this dissection, there can be no clean get-away.

What, then, would it mean to *be* returned to the womb? And what, exactly, is this lime-kiln? Flip a coin: heads it's a penis; tails it's a vagina. For Ethan, it's neither: ne-uter: neuter. It's neutered of being, just as he. For in being the phallus, he chooses not to be (sexual). He would be both signifier and signified at once: both being and its truth (meaning), both beginning and end. From this "star-light eminence, whither the philosophers of the earth . . . might vainly strive to clamber after him" (XI:99), Ethan's being is destined to end in failure, destined to fall toward this (in)significant abyss. With no-where else to go but down, we're hardly surprised should he fail to get (it) up. From here, we can jump ahead quickly.

I've deferred that white-on-white image of Ethan's skeleton against the circle of lime (the bosom of [Mother] Nature) and Bartram's (unholy?) act which disturbs these remains, the relics of this "saint." To recapitulate: those who take the primal scene for what it is, a phantasm, will take the lime-kiln as a *hole*—will take it, not overtake it. It's that missing scene, the scene that Ethan missed, what never took "place" as such, the very scene that Ethan rejects, forgets: forgets, that is, on purpose. The kiln provokes interpretation; here nothing takes place, takes up *its* place in the subject. Ethan forecloses this event (and hence himSelf), refuses its possibility. His life "remains" a blank. The reader, on the other hand, is offered this scene anew. The final image in the lime-kiln recuperates a writing effect. What is this white-on-white if not the nothingness of being, that empty page which offers no reflection (of itSelf), which offers back to the subject the possibility of its own inscription, of writing itSelf? Bartram rises to this occasion. What is his pole if not a pen, the knife that cuts into, opens the wound of, being? What is this final inscription if not the subject making sense of itSelf, creating its own significance?

Nature, on the other hand, will coincide with itself, can therefore have no self, must thus be meaningless. Nature, like Ethan, is a bonehead. How else are we to understand its final scene (tantrum), its childish masquerade at sex, its ultimate boner? Let's have another look.

The early sunshine was already pouring its gold upon the mountaintops. . . . Every dwelling was distinctly visible; the little spires of the two churches pointed upward, and caught a fore-glimmering of brightness from the sun-gilt skies upon their gilded weathercocks. . . . Old Graylock was glorified with a golden cloud upon his head. Scattered, likewise, over the breasts of the surrounding mountains, there were heaps of hoary mist, in fantastic shapes, some of them far down into the valley, others high up . . . and still others . . . hovering in the gold radiance of the upper atmosphere. . . . Earth was so mingled with sky that it was a daydream to look at it. (XI:101)

This is chaos, child's play, a messy room at best: a surrealistic collage of (body) parts scattered everywhere: a penis here, a penis there, some breasts, and sperm all over the place. Here nothing "fits." Narration, too, has lost its head—inscribes or circulates these (body) parts as but the scene of its (anal) retention. Sub-scribed by its dejecta, narration here underwrites its own (hysteric) failure to give them up, surpass them—to "pass" them. Thus in the end it seeks to keep them whole, "One." And yet these (body) parts will have their "say," will speak, wag their tails, bat an eye, come to a head: darting tongues, (cunni)lingus, dry in the end, cotton-mouthed, Peter-cotton-tail. Where everything is yet to come, nothing is left behind: it's hard just keeping up with what's ahead (what's a head). Ethan/Nature: is this what comes of being One? Doesn't any "body" know what to do with "it," where to put it? Bartram does: or so it seems. Against the backdrop of this phantastic scenario, these "fantastic shapes," the real (scene) unfolds before our eyes. Thus Bartram, "his long pole in his hand . . . ascended to the top of the kiln," then "lifted his pole, and letting it fall upon the skeleton, the relics of Ethan Brand were cumbled into fragments" (XI:102). Here sexuality cuts into being, carves out the subject as a *hole:* the *not* of itSelf. Sex is but the fore-play of death. Bartram knows: or so it seems. A hint of necrophilia nevertheless disturbs this scene: putting it to a corpse—although the body itself has once more disappeared. Only "little Joe"—the boy of the (diorama) scene—enacts the "truth" of this site, recites the (primal) scene of its significance, knows how to stick his head into a box. On the hither side of this event, Ethan (silly boy) goes whole hog, dives right on in, sticks in himself, the *whole* of his being. This just won't work. At the tail of this tale, the repressed returns to overtake him from behind, in the very place the subject runs ahead of itSelf only to be taken in the end. The simple logic of the geometrician will never articulate the (lack of) meaning of Ethan's desire (not to desire), for he would be (nothing—less than) the mouth that eats itself.

□

The subject is, therefore, both a being *for-itself* and yet a being *for-others* (the otherness of its own desire), for being is always situated. Accordingly, as Jean Normand remarks, "The word 'heart' is for Hawthorne the supreme mirror-word, the word enclosing all others: it is sphere, house, temple, prison, cave, grave, lake, fountain, and furnace. The word 'head,' its antithetical homologue, is, in comparison, lackluster, indigent, barren. And both the attic and the aerie, images of the observing and sovereign consciousness, refer us back yet again to the central organ that symbolizes better than any other all man's hidden inclinations. For Hawthorne, consciousness was not a brain but a heart. . . . And poetic language is not a language of the brain but of the heart."[28] In this spherical domain, the heart must likewise have its "reason(s)." The subject here takes to itSelf the other as its own (desire), its "rationale" for being. This "balance" alone secures the spaciousness of the world.[29] For Hawthorne, love inclusively expresses, within the horizon of its space, the dual metaphysical postures of head and heart, self and other, and does so over and against the "emptiness" of desire, the horizon of temporality. Love brings about the future precisely to the extent that it bestows upon the actual the possible (the freedom "to be").

Objective consciousness, on the other hand, in (and of) itself, can only be within the delimitations of the actual—its present. In the end, the logic of the head imagines nothing more than an eternal presence to its self (in-itself)—the ultimate, and only, logical consequence of the *cogito:* from this phantastic coincidence of subject and self emerges that timelessness of mind which the Cartesian doctrine inaugurates. Accordingly, as Merleau-Ponty observes, "eternity understood as the power to embrace and anticipate temporal developments in a single intention, becomes the very definition of subjectivity."[30] It is, in fact, this temporal abyss—stretching out between an equally opaque past and future—that the villain would abridge to a transparent present. Hawthorne's work disowns the ingenuineness of this actual (present) in favor of an authenticity grounded in the possibility of (not) being itSelf; it therefore gives the subject back its time. The villain, on the other hand, encapsulated by the god-like transparency of an ideal eternally present (in-itself), represents a form of subjectivity that "kills" its very own time. Because this self-ideal would be its very ideal self, would coincide with itSelf, it is anything (and everything) but its own. Hawthorne's villains would be timeless. Thus the watchmaker, Owen Warland, for example, "would turn the sun out of its own orbit, and derange the whole course of time" (X:448), "and cared no more for the measurement of time than if it had been merged into eternity" (X:451). So too, the sundial placed over the door of the House of the Seven Gables functions as an ironic reminder that time *will* enter here—and Judge Pyncheon will lie dead with his timepiece in his hand, as Claudia Johnson observes: "Death, which struck as soon as the house was complete, is the one constant reality of the edifice erected to isolate the Pyncheons from a time-affected world."³¹ In contrast, the narrator of "Earth's Holocaust" remarks, "And as for ripeness—and as for progress—let mankind always do the highest, kindest, noblest thing, that at any given period, it has attained to the perception of; and surely that thing cannot be wrong, *nor wrongly timed*" (X:393, italics mine). Above all, this characterizes the villain in his insignificance: he is untimely.

Over and against a present condemned to (be) itSelf—a timeless present hypnotically fixed in the past, transfixed toward an impossible future—Hawthorne's work recites a present which holds a finite future in it, a present whose very past comes out of the future (possibility), is transfigured in it. Reuben Bourne begins "to be" only when the burden of his past has been returned to him as (the possibility of) his future (X:360); Roderick Elliston initiates a new life with Rosina only when the eternal moment of his morbid egotism has been disrupted (X:283): Owen Warland inaugurates a new beginning for his art only when the superficial motivation of his past has been nullified or transcended (X:475); Matthew and his bride embark upon a new life only when their impossible quest has been foresaken (XI:165); Peter Goldthwaite launches a realistic future only when the pretense of his "castle in the air" had been exposed (IX:383, 406); Robin discovers he is his own person only when his immature dependence upon his kinsman has been displaced (XI:231); Pearl comes into her own only when the truth of her birth has been laid bare (I:256); the two "owls" disengage themselves from a stifling past only when the House has been abandoned (II:318). Hawthorne's world attests the bankruptcy of all who would live a present grounded in the sterile fixation of its past, the impossibility of its future: "In this world, we are the things of a moment, and are made to pursue momentary things, with here and there a thought that stretches mistily towards eternity, and perhaps may endure as long. All philosophy, that would abstract mankind from the present, is no more than words" (XI:133). Against the horizon of temporality, existence appropriates the present as its own, a present which *can be* only insofar as its future is finite. To live for and in the present, therefore, becomes meaningful solely to that self who understands that "once upon a time" it will not be; this alone confers upon the present its meaning and value.³²

Within the heart, that "little, yet boundless sphere" (X:403), the subject holds both a past and a future within the present. Only in the space of this precinct can being transform the existent: "Purify that inner sphere; and the many shapes of evil that haunt the outward, and which now seem almost our only realities, will turn to shadowy phantoms, and vanish of their own accord. But, if we go no deeper than the Intellect, and strive, with merely that feeble instrument, to discern and rectify what is wrong, our whole accomplishment will be a dream" (X:404). For Hawthorne, the present is authentic only for that subject open to itSelf, the possibility of its own not-being. In this domain, the logic of the head declines to represent its self ("I"); its presence, rather, is felt, affected as that void (the desire of the other) toward which it always runs ahead of itself and which remands it to its own and only self-constancy: being-toward death. The head would yet avoid this constancy, this resolution, toward which it is perpetually preempted by means of constantly repeating to itSelf *(cogito)* "I think" *(ergo sum)*. It's but a backward gaze toward eternity, as Aylmer's life attests: "The momentary circumstance was too strong for him; he failed to look beyond the shadowy scope of Time, and living once for all in Eternity, to find the perfect Future in the present" (X:56). Hawthorne's villains thus maniacally attach themselves to the idea *(eidos)*, an ideal grounded in impossibility, an unattainable future. Forever closed off to possibility, the villain thereby lives an eternal present in which existence has already escaped his grasp. "Dr. Heidegger's Experiment" bears witness to this phenomenon, and the absurdity of its four "melancholy old creatures who had been unfortunate in life, and whose greatest misfortune it was, that they were not long ago in their graves" (IX:227). While Dr. Heidegger accepts the situation, his four friends "had taught no such lesson to themselves. They resolved forthwith to make a pilgrimage to Florida, and quaff at morning, noon, and night, from the Fountain of Youth" (IX:238).

In opposition to that existence founded on hypocrisy (hiding the self behind the *presence* of eternity, perpetually false to the *present*), Hawthorne's world exhorts the daring venture *to be* (open to being).[33] Against the fear and ultimate despair, in Kierkegaard's words, of "every human existence which supposedly has become or merely wills to become infinite,"[34] Hawthorne's world sets forth a resolute anxiety grounded in the world's inner space—Pascal's logic of the heart. At home with itSelf, the subject here confers upon the other an embouchure, a life hypothecated in finitude and solicitude. In contrast, whoever would be an absolute consciousness, coincident with itSelf, would be an absolute object (in-itself) as well. Outside the heart, the subject cannot figure itSelf; for subjectivity configures being-for-others (intersubjectivity). Without the other, the subject is *de trop*.

Accordingly, to make one's private sins "public" can sometimes cure the psychosomatic illness itself: witness Roderick Elliston. So too, *The*

Scarlet Letter employs an explicit alternation between public and private scenes, between pillory and pulpit on the one hand, and the interior drama of conscience and guilt on the other. The avowed brotherhood at Blithedale likewise reflects the morally untenable nature of those distinctions which separate subject from subject in society, just as the relation between Zenobia and Priscilla mirrors an implicit sisterhood decisively more significant than the playful masquerade Zenobia would make of it.[35] In this respect, Westervelt epitomizes to what extent the "intellectual" attitude, resigned to avoid (the void of) itSelf, manipulatively devastates the (w)hole of being. As a phenomenon, Westervelt's control over both Zenobia and Priscilla constitutes a peculiarly sinister variation of the technological imposition, which makes a delusive show of "spirituality" while really imbued throughout with a cold and dead materialism: "it suggests the exploitative power which technology was putting into the hands of men: the power to bring individuals into total bondage while leaving them outwardly free and untouched. . . . against the brotherhood of voluntary love, which is based upon the magnetic chain of human sympathy, Westervelt's mesmeric union is enforced bondage, destructive of true individuality as well as true community."[36] Regarding its power of "remote control," the hyperopic gaze, here typified by Westervelt, prefigures the technological focus of the twentieth century. And yet this abolition of "distance" brings nothing near. Counterposed against the remote, Hawthorne's work "nears" being; it accommodates both being for-itself and being for-others as reciprocal dimensions of subjectivity within the space of the heart. In turn, being secure "by heart" makes being spacious.

Those characters who fail ("fall") in love do so because they would make of the other an object, a possession. We take it for granted: the lover's most significant gift to the beloved is that of the self. This average understanding of love ironically proclaims itself "self-less"—and properly so. For it the lover forfeits the self, what remains for the beloved to love? Here the structure of narcissism once again informs the implicit duplicity of all relationships. In its everyday form, loving another is thus identical to loving one's self. And for this reason, the narrator of *The Scarlet Letter* sets forth the essential similarity between love and hate, for both expose the master-slave relationship in its most radical configuration: "It is a curious subject of observation and inquiry, whether hatred and love be not the same thing at bottom. Each, in its utmost development, supposes a high degree of intimacy and heart-knowledge; each renders one individual dependent for the food of his affections and spiritual life upon another; each leaves the passionate lover, or the no less passionate hater, forlorn and desolate by the withdrawal of his object. Philosophically considered, therefore, the two passions seem essentially the same" (I:260). The price of possession necessarily entails the dispossession of the self. Over and against this ordinary form of love—always already doomed from the outset insomuch as it incurs resentment for what the other possesses (one's self)—Hawthorne's work proposes an extraordinary form of love for the future: "at some brighter period, when the world should have grown ripe for it, in Heaven's own time, a new truth would be revealed, in order to establish the whole relation between man and woman on a surer ground of mutual happiness" (I:263). In its regenerated structure, love gives the other over to *its self*, its inalienable subjectivity: love confers upon the other *the freedom to be* (itSelf).[37] It is the form of love which Dimmesdale's "gift" to Pearl inaugurates—one which equally maps out the integral boundary between Miriam and Donatello. This finally accounts for Hawthorne's aversion to both the reformer and altruism in general. As Scheler observes of such relations:

> This love is not directed at a previously discovered positive value, nor does any such value flash up in the act of loving: there is nothing but the urge to turn away from oneself and to lose oneself in other people's business. We all know a certain type of man frequently found among socialists, suffragettes, and all people with an ever-ready "social conscience"—the kind of person whose social activity is quite clearly prompted by inability to keep his attention focussed on himself, on his own tasks and problems. Looking away from oneself is here mistaken for love! Isn't it abundantly clear that "altruism," the interest in "others" and their lives, has nothing at all to do with love? . . . Conversely, there is a form of genuine "self-love" which has nothing at all to do with "egoism." It is precisely the essential feature of egoism that it does not apprehend the full value of the isolated self. The egoist sees himself only with regard to the others, as a member of society who wishes to possess and acquire *more* than the others.[38]

I recall you not only to Hollingsworth, but also to Coverdale, whose very being seeks to live (in) the being of others. In Hawthorne's most inward, unaccommodated domain, on the other hand, the self is handed over to its freedom. With this event, the other is given over to itSelf.

□

If the logic of the heart sets out the freedom and openness to being of the *for-itself*, it likewise points us to the basic meaning of the *in-itself* and the essential comportment of each to the other. Here we seek to understand the "heart" *of things*. Science usurps this fundamental value; it strives to

dominate its object-world as it does the other: witness Aylmer, Chillingworth, Westervelt, Rappaccini or, elsewhere, Judge Pyncheon. For the
Judge, moreover, the House (and everything in it) but represents the
accumulation of possessions. That so much is made of the deed to property serves to indicate the technological swindle of subject and object in
general. If the property in Maine, for example, returns the Judge to the
quest for an inaugural "deed," it nevertheless originates as an "expression" (a written document). Here too, the right to property—to possess
some-thing by means of confiscation—obscures its fundamental value.
How else are we to understand that *its expression has been lost?* With this
dumb-founding ruse, the subject's imposition silences (represses) what
the thing itself has "to say." Conversely, the House assumes an elemental
physiognomy—its "character"—only to the extent that *it expresses itself.*
For the Judge, however, this expression falls upon deaf ears (and blind
eyes—to which the vacancy of his stare at death attests) long since closed
to anything other than his will to master his environment, where everything is standing by for duty: "trampling on the weak, and, when essential to his ends, doing his utmost to beat down the strong" (II:123).
Hawthorne's villains consistently fail to *read* the existent. Rather, they
"take" the thing (everything) literally. The figuration of being forever
eludes them. Indeed, these villainous figures figure Hepzibah's own disfiguration of reading, "holding a book in close contiguity to her nose; as
if with the hope of gaining an olfactory acquaintance with its contents,
since her imperfect vision made it not very easy to read them" (II:98).
This scene, the scene of (mis)reading (itSelf), prefigures a later remark by
Phoebe—and, indeed, the problematic of reading (in) Hawthorne in general: "Cousin Hepzibah is not quick at figures" (II:215). We've seen this
scene before. Little wonder that Judge Pyncheon's attempts at speech are
characterized by an "aukward ingurgitation" in the throat, habitual and
yet "indicative of nothing," which serves to repeat in meaningless noise
the very form of death attributed to his ancestors—"the popular notion,
that this miraculous blood might now and then be heard gurgling in their
throats" (II:124).

This blood itself but signifies an initial absence of expression—one,
furthermore, to which the missing signature(s) of the deed yet testifies in
full: he is origin-ally inarticulate. The Judge thus fails to be articulated
from the beginning—and this is what he would ironically re-cover in the
deed. In fact, his very existence begins and ends amid the dumb impotence of this deed which fails to purchase him at every turning. Rather
than stand out, his existence, like his physiognomy, belies the single-
minded insistence of his will to will. It is meaningless and says no-thing:

"it seemed not to express wrath or hatred, but a certain hot fellness of purpose, which annihilated everything but itself" (II:129). In his blind and purposeful self-assertion in every-thing, Judge Pyncheon constructs a world of his own. Like the House, this world is misappropriated at the expense of, with the eradication of, the other. With this in view, the narrator ironically comments on the Judge's advances toward Phoebe, his literal (mis)reading of (her) figure: "He is apparently conscious of having erred, in too energetically pressing his deeds of loving-kindness on persons unable to appreciate them. He will await their better mood, and hold himself as ready to assist them, then, as at this moment. As he draws back from the door, an all-comprehensive benignity blazes from his visage, indicating that he gathers Hepzibah, little Phoebe, and the invisible Clifford, all three, together with the whole world besides, into his immense heart, and gives them a warm bath in its flood of affection" (II:129–30). In fact, one might say that he drowns them: his inarticulate gurgle drowns out the other.

Regarding the construction of the House, moreover, we excavate the meaning of the thing (in-itself) within the structure of its design. To begin, a written deed (expression) stands before the actual deed (construction) as the occasion for building—an expression, however, which lies *hidden* in the very "heart" of the construction (House) itself. Indeed, the House recalls us to the general significance attached to building in Hawthorne's oeuvre. It's more than curious that the narrative constructions of all the major novels negotiate a threshold: *The Scarlet Letter* with the prison-door and, beside it, the rose, "so directly on the threshold of our narrative, which is now about to issue from that inauspicious portal" (I:48)—not to ignore the Custom-House itself; *The House of the Seven Gables* with the entrance to Hepzibah's shop, where "All this time, however, we are loitering faint-heartedly on the threshold of our story" (II:34); *The Blithedale Romance* with Silas Foster's house in which, one by one, the figures enter Coverdale's story while (the knot of) dreamers sit inside, awaiting each new guest and "contrasting our own comfort with the chill and dreary situation of the unknown person at the threshold" (III:25); *The Marble Faun* with the entrance into, and exit out of, the various rooms of the Capitoline museum whence the four main characters ultimately emerge "from the gateway of the palace" (IV:19) and into the story. To this there is conjoined the significance of that "aesthetic" space or threshold between Hawthorne's prefaces and the faces of the texts themselves.

Now while construction here builds for and toward the threshold, a passageway between "within" and "without," the threshold itself is not constructed first—but rather stands "before" the work as that which provokes it, calls it forth. Though building holds its threshold before it, it does so as something that is constructed later. It's taken for granted: construction is pre-liminary to the threshold *(limen)* itself. At the threshold of building, for example, Hawthorne recounts the "history" of another building (the House) as the pre-text to the construction of his own text *(The House).* Here the speaker lingers, facing (both forward and back) this narrative sight (site/cite). It is the place to which we are invited. Each locus of inauguration is one of departure also; every entrance is itself pro-visional, a pro-spective region of retrospect: a pre-text.

In the same way, the thing too precedes building as that which building "borrows" in order to build for itself—a borrowing, moreover, which in no way constitutes a possession, but rather a return, just as the House returns to its original builder, a Maule (Holgrave). In one sense, building re-enacts an originary event: insofar as it borrows, it indicates the locus of a transfer. Yet the topology of this locus suggests nothing of a spatial location. It is originally a place of indebtedness; to recover its primordial dimensions, we must initially recognize that "presence" lacking to it(self). Erupting from the "text" (sight) of the thing, for example, consciousness seeks a "cite" (site) for itSelf—a home or context for its own textuality which is no longer a simple (sense) impression, but one which reads into experience an *imprimatur.* This event brings with it the question of authority—the author-ization of one's self. Building carries with it a corresponding need to secure a place of one's own: it provokes the subject to itSelf. In this abode, things too are given to "cite" (site)— for each object has its own "thing" to say. In contrast, science envisages the thing as "dumb": objects but accumulate as part of its collection. By means of objectification, as Heidegger observes, the technological frame *(Ge-stell)* would thereby seek to dominate the object as "standing-reserve" *(Bestand),* that which "stands by" (for duty): something payable on demand.[39] Here the object no longer even ob-jects. Against this attitude which confiscates the thing, which professes the right to plunder and possess it, Hawthorne's oeuvre gives both the being of the thing (in-itself) and the subject (for-itself) back to the world: the situated structure of existence.

Not only as a possession, however, but in its everydayness as well, the thing is given over to the habitual, to the familiar, to that which has been lost to sight (and sound)—that is, to *sense,* to significance, to meaning. In this way, being itself disappears.[40] Hawthorne's world, on the contrary, seeks to recuperate the thing (in) itself, its *kern:* to recover (the "subject" of) the object. And this recalls us to an essential function of imagination:

> Moonlight, in a familiar room, falling so white upon the carpet, and show-
> ing all its figures so distinctly,—making every object so minutely visible,
> yet so unlike a morning or noontide visibility,—is a medium the most
> suitable for a romance-writer to get acquainted with his illusive guests.
> There is the little domestic scenery of the well-known apartment; the chairs,
> with each its separate individuality; the centre-table, sustaining a work-
> basket, a volume or two, and an extinguished lamp; the sofa; the book-case;
> the picture on the wall;—all these details, so completely seen, are so spir-
> itualized by the unusual light, that they seem to lose their actual substance,
> and become things of intellect. Nothing is too small or too trifling to
> undergo this change, and acquire dignity thereby. A child's shoe; the doll,
> seated in her little wicker carriage; the hobby-horse;—whatever, in a word,
> has been used or played with, during the day, is now *invested with a quality of
> strangeness and remoteness.* (I:35, italics mine)

Yet for the object to come to "life," it equally requires the warmth of the fire-light which gives to things their heart: "This warmer light mingles itself with the cold spirituality of the moonbeams, and communicates, as it were, a heart and sensibilities of human tenderness to the forms which fancy summons up. It converts them from snow-images into men and women" (I:36). While these "forms which fancy summons up" specifi-cally refer to Hawthorne's "illusive guests," his characters, his "figures," the passage invokes a new regard for things themselves. In this "neutral territory," the thing dwells as its own, in itself.[41] The author constructs his work for dwelling so that both subject and object might *belong* to one another, each as its own. Imagination authorizes this belonging together: it lets the thing appear (to sight) as something cited in the construction. In this "recitation" of the thing, the subject thus allows for *its expression.* For Hawthorne, the thing is always and everywhere a figure of speech.

The House, for example, specifically provokes personification; it returns the subject's gaze with its own "dark, alien countenance" (II:294). Indeed, while Judge Pyncheon lies dead at its center, its very "heart," the House itself is serenaded by the Italian organ-grinder who knows the "heart's language" and seeks to make it open up, to *respond.*[42] Through-out Hawthorne's oeuvre, in fact, the object harbors an expressive phys-iognomy. Yet, over and above this surplus, there is another sense in which the thing "matters." As Heidegger suggests, the thing *gathers:* "Gathering or assembly, by an ancient word of our language, is called 'thing.'"[43] For Hawthorne, the mirror (or any reflecting surface) embodies this elemental structure, which gathers every-thing to itself: "Glancing at the looking-glass, we behold—deep within its haunted verge—the smouldering glow of the half-extinguished anthracite, the white moonbeams on the floor, and a repetition of all the gleam and shadow of the picture, with one remove farther from the actual, and nearer to the imaginative. Then, at such an hour, and with this scene before him, if a man, sitting all alone, cannot dream strange things, and make them look like truth, he need never try to write romances" (I:36).

Still other things, too, partake of this facility to gather each to its own. The brook, for instance, with Hester's Letter lying displaced beside it, has yet the power to reassemble into a single image those isolated aspects standing upon both extremes of its banks: "Pearl, without responding in any manner to these honey-sweet expressions, remained on the other side of the brook. Now she fixed her bright, wild eyes on her mother, now on the minister, and now included them both in the same glance; as if to detect and explain to herself the relation which they bore to one another. . . . At length . . . Pearl stretched out her hand, with the small forefinger extended, and pointing evidently towards her mother's breast. And beneath, in the mirror of the brook, there was the flower-girdled and sunny image of little Pearl, pointing her small forefinger too" (I:209). By means of its expressive configuration, therefore, the brook gathers each to the other; in this "assembly," the brook incorporates a "correspondence." It happens as no accident that this "babbling" brook is also given to articulate speech—that with its "never-ceasing loquacity," it should "whisper tales out of the *heart* of the old forest whence it flowed" (I:186, italics mine).

Indeed, in this most "vocal" of Hawthorne's chapters, amid the heart of things, everything is given over to speech. Thus, "one solemn old tree groaned dolefully to another, as if telling the sad story of the pair that sat beneath, or constrained to forebode evil to come" (I:195); and elsewhere, "A partridge . . . with a brood of ten behind her, ran forward threateningly, but soon repented of her fierceness, and clucked to her young ones not to be afraid. A pigeon, alone on a low branch, allowed Pearl to come beneath, and uttered a sound as much of greeting as alarm. A squirrel, from the lofty depths of his domestic tree, chattered either in anger or merriment" (I:204); even the flowers "whispered, as she passed, 'Adorn thyself with me, thou beautiful child'" (I:205). And once this fateful interview amid the heart of the forest has come to its close, "The dell was to be left a solitude among its dark, old trees, which, with their multitudinous tongues, would whisper long of what had passed there, and no mortal be the wiser. And the melancholy brook would add this

other tale to the mystery with which its little heart was already overbur-
dened, and whereof it still kept up a murmuring babble, with not a whit
more cheerfulness of tone than for ages heretofore" (I:213).

Amid this "con-vocation" of objects, every "thing" expresses itself;
it *matters* in a twofold "sense": not only as a figure of perception, but also
as a figure of speech—an expression in and of itself. The thing therefore
pro-vokes an occasion for deliberation, something under discussion, a
contested matter: what the Romans called "res"—*a matter for discourse*.[44]
For Hawthorne, the thing is thus an *expression* which in-cites a response:
it is originally an occasion for re-sponsibility. Expression inscribes that
bridge between both subject and object we call "the world"; amid the
heart of things, amid the (dia)logic of affective situations, subject and
thing (for-itself and in-itself) belong to one another. Here, language
secures the very threshold or passageway between the two insofar as it
provides the opportunity for co-respondence. Thus, in *The Marble Faun*,
for example, artist (subject) and art work (object) coalesce, as John Caldwell Stubbs observes: "The characters merge into the art objects they
create and own. The result is the reduction of the characters toward the
quality of art objects and the raising of the art objects toward the human
level."[45]

Regarding the House, moreover, we further observe that while expression (the written deed) stands before construction (the actual deed) as
the occasion for building, it nevertheless appears that temporality itself
invalidates its "private" significance. For when this lost expression is at
last recovered, it is no longer meaningful:

> A recess in the wall was thus brought to light, in which lay an object so
> covered with a century's dust, that it could not immediately be recognized as
> a folded sheet of parchment. Holgrave opened it, and displayed an ancient
> deed, signed with the hieroglyphics of several Indian sagamores, and con-
> veying to Colonel Pyncheon and his heirs, forever, a vast extent of territory
> at the eastward.
>
> "This is the very parchment, the attempt to recover which cost the
> beautiful Alice Pyncheon her happiness and life," said the artist, alluding to
> his legend. "It is what the Pyncheons sought in vain, while it was valuable;
> and now that they find the treasure, it has long been worthless." (II:316)

Thus what the individual deed would seem to convey "forever," has been
already annulled by time. Dispossessed of any and all authority, void of
its meaning, it stands for the "remainder" of an originary intention.
Ironically, its initial authority (the deed as expression) abides as incomplete (a hieroglyphic signifier). Throughout the course of history, in

fact, it comes to be displaced by that very thing it would provoke to fulfillment: the con-vocation of "signatures" (other signifiers) that have "endorsed" a settlement by means of dwelling. Indeed, those settlers "would have laughed at the idea of any man's asserting a right—on the strength of mouldy parchments, signed with faded autographs of governors and legislators, long dead and forgotten—to the lands which they or their fathers had wrested from the wild hand of Nature, by their own sturdy toil" (II:19).

Thus while authority is grounded in itself, its act of author-ization (a text), it nonetheless implies another (context) in the enactment ("decipherment") of its significance. Neither the initial deed of expression nor the final deed of construction are, in and of themselves, complete. Rather, both acquire their meaning across the span of human history: the relation of significance accrues in time. With respect to its initial expression, the validity of authority subsequently depends upon a "community of subjects" which, together, inhabit the same territory, the same "frame" (text). Likewise, Hawthorne's "history" of the House stands before his actual "story" *(The House)* as that occasion which calls him to construct the framework for his own authority. Upon the threshold of this narrative design authority requires for its con-firmation an intersubjective consent.[46] If, in the register of this configuration, Hawthorne's "story" here becomes the figure against an "historical" ground, there is yet another sense in which a "story" can be said to constitute the very ground of "history" itself—in which authority is but a beginning intention "to mean." Regarding the na(rra)tivity of this event, Hawthorne's Letter points to the primordial dimension across which signs signify.

☐

When Hawthorne "discovers" the Letter in the attic of the Custom-House, he does precisely what reason demands—he seeks to understand the object by means of analysis: "This rag of scarlet cloth . . . on careful examination, assumed the shape of a letter. It was the capital letter A. By an accurate measurement, each limb proved to be precisely three inches and a quarter in length" (I:31). Yet this solitary mark, discovered in the attic, refuses to resign itself to rational design: "Certainly, there was some deep meaning in it, most worthy of interpretation . . . but evading the analysis of my mind" (I:31). For its sign-ificance, Hawthorne must go from the "attic," or head, to what science would deem the "cellar," its heart: "While thus perplexed,—and *cogitating,* among other hypotheses . . . *I happened to place it on my breast.* It seemed to me,—*the reader* may smile, but *must not doubt my word,*—it seemed to me, then, that *I experi-*

enced a sensation not altogether physical, yet almost so, as of burning heat" (I:31–32, italics mine). Here Hawthorne positions author-ity in opposition to the traditional logic of the head. It is understood—and not to be doubted—from the outset, that the meaning of the sign is excavated from the logic of the heart: the correspondence between subject and object is primordially inscribed (with)in the (con)text of the body.

Moreover, in its "initial" design, the Letter falls (even further) away from its (origin-al) space, falls out of (its) place, its location as circumscribed by Surveyor Pue's manuscript: "In the absorbing contemplation of the scarlet letter, I had hitherto neglected to examine a small roll of dingy paper, around which it had been twisted. This I now opened, and had the satisfaction to find, recorded by the old Surveyor's pen, a *reasonably* complete explanation of the whole affair" (I:32, italics mine). We needn't be reminded of the extent to which these "half a dozen sheets of foolscap" (I:33) constitute the authority and domain of explanation in its entirety: so much for reason. This too accounts for the emphasis Hawthorne gives to the Imaginary which returns the Actual to the logic (affective significance) of the heart. Imagination provokes subjective correspondence to the "heart" of *things*. The Letter invokes this (co)responsibility. Indeed, one might say that in its very *fall* from (the grace of) this "original" manuscript, the Letter itself is thereby inaugurated into "si(g)n"—that in falling out of his-story (Surveyor Pue's), from the place in which its initial inscription is circumscribed, the Letter thus stands in *need*. It needs to be recovered elsewhere: as Hawthorne's *own* (story). For in this slippage, this sliding *(glissement)* of the signifier[47] from the inscriptions on the page, the Letter itself does nothing less than fall into the white space, the empty space, of a "margin"—a fall, moreover, from black to red: it is already (blissfully) "wounded" *(blessure).*

We are recalled to Hester's own predicament beside the brook: "By this time Pearl had reached the *margin* of the brook, and stood on the farther side, gazing silently at Hester and the clergyman, who still sat together on the mossy tree-trunk, waiting to receive her" (I:207–8, italics mine). When Hester hastens Pearl to retrieve the Letter, and is refused, she remarks to Dimmesdale:

> "Was ever such a child! . . . O, I have much to tell thee about her. But, in very truth, she is right as regards this hateful token. I must bear its torture yet a little longer. . . ."
>
> With these words, she advanced to the *margin* of the brook, took up the scarlet letter, and fastened it again into her bosom. Hopefully, but a moment ago, as Hester had spoken of drowning it in the deep sea, there was a sense of inevitable doom upon her, as she thus received back this deadly symbol

from the hand of fate. She had flung it into infinite space!—she had drawn an hour's free breath!—and here again was the scarlet misery, glittering on the old spot. (I:211, italics mine)

As of her desire to return to Europe (origins) with Dimmesdale, here we stand witness to the return of the repressed; the Letter comes back to Hester once again from out of the Other: its original source (of meaning). Here too issues forth the locus of what Lacan refers to as the "real"—that which always comes back to the same place, and before which all symbolic discourse falters—what is at all times held in abeyance; it is "another locality, another space, another scene": the encounter inasmuch as it is missed, "in so far as it is essentially the missed encounter."[48] So with the forest scene: its significance resides in what is missing, in what is missed (an-Other scenario). Likewise, in (the) place of the Letter, Pearl but indicates its absence—as Hester observes: "Pearl misses something which she has always seen me wear" (I:210). Amid a circular round of pointing [Pearl to Hester: "Pearl stretched out her hand, with the small forefinger extended, and pointing evidently towards her mother's breast" (I:209); Hester to the Letter: " 'Pearl,' she said, sadly, 'look down at thy feet! There!—before thee!—on the hither side of the brook!' " (I:210); and so in turn to Pearl: "she extended her hand to Pearl" (I:211)], amid this encapsulated round of substitution and displacement of the signifier, the margin of the stream similarly returns the Letter in its absence, reflecting only the margin of the Letter itself—"The child turned her eyes to the point indicated; and there lay the scarlet letter, so close upon the margin of the stream, that *the gold embroidery was reflected in it*" (I:210, italics mine). Only with Hester's Letter finally back in (the) place (of what is missing) does Pearl acknowledge her as mother: "Now thou art my mother indeed! And I am thy little Pearl" (I:211).

It is further to be remarked, amid this round of nomination, and in the very presence of Dimmesdale, that the name of the father is here occluded—and this, despite the many lessons in catechism in response to which Pearl repeatedly demands her origins:

"Tell me, then, what thou art, and who sent thee hither?"

"Tell me, mother!" said the child, seriously, coming up to Hester, and pressing herself close to her knees. "Do thou tell me!"

"Thy Heavenly Father sent thee!" answered Hester Prynne.

But she said it with a hesitation that did not escape the acuteness of the child. Whether moved only by her ordinary freakishness, or because an evil spirit prompted her, she put up her small forefinger, and touched the scarlet letter.

"He did not send me!" cried she, positively. "I have no Heavenly Father!"

"Hush, Pearl, hush! Thou must not talk so!" answered the mother, suppressing a groan. "He sent us all into this world. He sent even me, thy mother. Then, much more, thee! Or, if not, thou strange and elfish child, whence didst thou come?"

"Tell me! Tell me!" repeated Pearl, no longer seriously, but laughing, and capering about the floor. "It is thou that must tell me." (I:98)

Without a history, Pearl lacks a story of her own. And yet it's "logically" appropriate that, here, beside the brook, she should omit (the name of) the father, for it is she who—by upholding the (Puritan) Law, by laying it down, demanding with her "singular air of authority" (I:209) that Hester return the Letter to *its* place—usurps the very place of the Letter (of the law) itself. In (the) place of the father (the Law), she presumes to fill the gap—and does so as an impostor, outside any and all authority of her own, as but "the freedom of a broken law" (I:134). Indeed, desire emerges in this very margin where demand becomes separated from need.[49]

For Hawthorne, also, who—on the margin of discourse, upon the threshold of "The Custom-House"—seeks to father the Letter as his own (story), to re-cover its history, there arises the question of Authority. Regarding the Letter, which has fallen out of another manuscript (the discourse of the Other), Hawthorne is acutely sensitive to the demands of authorship. When first he broaches this issue in conjunction with the meaning of "historical" Authenticity, he disclaims responsibility for the "story" by assuming the posture of editor: "it should be borne carefully in mind, that the main facts of that story are authorized and authenticated by the document of Mr. Surveyor Pue" (I:132). The history of the Letter represents an in(ter)ruption *in* (the) *place of* Hawthorne's story. Here, the other displaces his *récit*, providing the occasion for Hawthorne to re-nounce his own author-ity. This "false" submission to the authorization of another inhabits the very place we would expect to see appear the author's signature itself. If he disowns the Letter, however, he must disown *The Letter* as well: "The original papers, together with the scarlet letter itself,—a most curious relic,—*are still in my possession,* and shall be freely exhibited to whomsoever, *induced by the great interest of the narrative,* may desire a sight of them" (I:32–33, italics mine). Thus in the very next breath he now disclaims his initial disclaimer so that he might reclaim the story as his own: "I must not be understood as affirming, that, in the dressing up of the tale, and imagining the motives and modes of passion that influenced the characters who figure in it, I have invariably confined myself within the limits of the old Surveyor's half a dozen sheets of foolscap. On the contrary, I have allowed myself, as to such points, nearly or altogether as much license as if the facts had been entirely of my own invention. What I contend for is the authenticity of the out-line" (I:33).

What then is the truth of history (his-story)? As Lacan cautions, "Any statement of authority has no other guarantee than its very enunci-ation, and it is pointless for it to seek it in another signifier, which could not appear outside this locus in any way."[50] Within the register of the symbolic, the Letter is itself the very "cutting edge"[51] of the (Oedipal) Law: the "cut" in Hawthorne's discourse, the eradication (erasure) of the phallus, which allows it to (re)emerge as the signifier of desire. It is this wounded, this "fallen," signifier which dis(inter)rupts the discourse of the manuscript (history) and confers upon Hawthorne the responsibility of authorship (fatherhood) for his story. This authorial "I" occasioned by Surveyor Pue's history cannot accede to itself by means of being desig-nated in its (own) story, but is the constant rem(A)inder of the (w)hole text *(The Scarlet Letter)*. Hawthorne's authority is (nothing) less than the white page which stands before him: it remains to be written. In this event, he fa(e)ces up to himself, divellicating this "roll of dingy paper" (I:32) for his own use.[52] Here he will mark out his own paternity—the authority by which he will transcend the law "external" to himself (the threat of castration), that ominous shadow of both his ancestral (Pu-ritanical) and societal (political) constraints.

The entire Custom-House moves away from this oppressive impo-tence toward manhood. Heretofore, and indicative of his tenure as Custom-House "official," Hawthorne's signature has never been his own, but rather the mark of Uncle Sam's *seal*. At the same time, he is everywhere circumscribed by a paternity of impotent old men: "I doubt greatly—or rather, I do not doubt at all—whether any public functionary of the United States, either in the civil or military line, has ever had such *a patriarchal body* of veterans under his orders as myself" (I:12, italics mine). Amid this limp, debilitating context (conscription), Hawthorne would carve out or inscribe the text of himself:

> An effect—which I believe to be observable, more or less, in every individ-
> ual who has occupied the position—is, that, while he leans on the mighty
> arm of the Republic, his own proper strength departs from him. He loses, in
> an extent proportioned to the weakness or force of his original nature, the
> capability of self-support. . . . Conscious of his own infirmity,—that his
> tempered steel and elasticity are lost,—he for ever afterwards looks
> wistfully about him in quest of support external to himself. . . . Uncle
> Sam's gold . . . has, in this respect, a quality of enchantment like that of the

Devil's wages. Whoever touches it should look well to himself, or he may find the bargain to go hard against him, involving, if not his soul, yet many of its better attributes; its sturdy force, its courage and constancy, its truth, its self-reliance, and all that gives the emphasis *to manly character.* (I:38–39, italics mine)

And though his own prognosis confirms that he has taken a turn for the worse, Hawthorne is nevertheless able to prescribe the cure: "I had ceased to be a writer of tolerably poor tales and essays, and had become a tolerably good Surveyor of the Customs. That was all. But, nevertheless, it is any thing but agreeable to be haunted by a suspicion that one's intellect is *dwindling away*" (I:38, italics mine). That is, as an official representative of Customs or conventional authority, Hawthorne's very own manhood—his "head"—is shrinking to aught: "I began to grow melancholy and restless; continually *prying into my mind,* to discover which of *its poor properties were gone,* and what degree of detriment had already accrued to the remainder. I endeavored to calculate how much longer I could stay in the Custom-House, and yet go forth *a man*" (I:39–40, italics mine). As things stand (or, in this case, fall), he is not even the remainder of himself.

Herein, too, we discern the very trace of the signifier as the desire of an-Other (signifier): in this bind, Hawthorne is divided against himSelf. On the one hand, he would like to resign: "In view of my previous weariness of office, and vague thoughts of resignation, my fortune some-what resembled that of a person who should entertain an idea of commit-ting suicide" (I:42). On the other hand, he feels compelled to sign himself as his own (man), to inscribe his own sign-ature, to (A)rise from the "deadly" political (mis)fortune of his dismissal from office—"*My own head* was the first that *fell*" (I:41, italics mine)—and therefore employs the Custom-House pre-text as the very ground from which he will figure forth as his own author(ity), his own text. As a (w)hole, he offers his public this autobiographical sketch as the "POSTHUMOUS PAPERS OF A *DECAPITATED* SURVEYOR" (I:43, italics mine), and this he understates with self-effacing mockery: "The moment when *a man's head drops off* is seldom or never, I am inclined to think, precisely the most agreeable of his life" (I:41, italics mine). Indeed, the public voice of conventional authority (the One—*das Man*) would have it no other way: "Meanwhile, the press had taken up my affair, and kept me, for a week or two, careering through the public prints, in my decapitated state, like Irving's Headless Horseman; ghastly and grim, and longing to be buried, as a politically dead man ought" (I:42–43). Over and against his decapita-tion by the public as a (w)hole, however, Hawthorne would yet "stand up." And toward this climax he therefore inserts his own private part: "The real human being, all this time, with *his head safely on his shoulders,* had *brought himself to the* comfortable *conclusion,* that every thing was for the best; *and, making an investment in* ink, paper, and *steel-pens,* had *opened his* long-disused *writing-desk, and was again a* literary *man*" (I:43, italics mine). Thus Hawthorne bears the (re)construction of himSelf—bares, indeed, his very own erection.

Unlike the blissful couple of Edward and Ellen in *Fanshawe,* who, at the end of the romance and the beginning of Hawthorne's career, were content to leave "no name behind them" (III:460), Hawthorne is now committed to the opposite. It is the problem of nomination repeated again in Dimmesdale's failure to admit his own paternity to Pearl: an occlusion in (the place of) the name of the Father. Although for Dimmesdale it is a matter of seven years, for Hawthorne it is simply a matter of several pages before he confesses to the lie of editorship—the truth of authorship (fatherhood). At the conclusion of the Custom-House sketch, Hawthorne is therefore ready publicly to stand up for (the erection of) (the name of) himSelf: "Now it was, that the lucubrations of my ancient predecessor, Mr. Surveyor Pue, came into play" (I:43). In effect, Hawthorne will leave this past behind, will put his own past behind him, will put it in the rear. Indeed, with the arrival of these lucubrations (lubrications?) Hawthorne himself comes (into play):

> The life of the Custom-House lies like a dream behind me. . . . Soon, likewise, my old native town will loom upon me through the haze of memory. . . . Henceforth, it ceases to be a reality in my life. I am a citizen of somewhere else. My good townspeople will not much regret me; for— though it has been as dear an object as any, in my literary efforts, to be of some importance in their eyes, and to win myself a pleasant memory in this abode and burial-place of so many of my forefathers—there has never been, for me, the genial atmosphere which a literary man requires, in order to ripen the best harvest of his mind. I shall do better amongst other faces; and these familiar ones, it need hardly be said, will do just as well without me. (I:44–45)

If the public was incensed with this introductory sketch (its indictment of an impotent community and a decrepit bureaucracy), clamoring for an apology, Hawthorne's Preface to the second edition will leave it kicking and screaming:

> As the public disapprobation would weigh very heavily on him, were he conscious of deserving it, the author begs leave to say, that he has carefully read over the introductory pages, with a purpose to alter or expunge what-

ever might be found amiss, and to make the best reparation in his power for the atrocities of which he has been adjudged guilty. But it appears to him, that the only remarkable features of the sketch are its frank and genuine good-humor, and the general accuracy with which he has conveyed his sincere impressions of the characters therein described. . . . *The sketch might,* perhaps, *have been wholly omitted, without loss to the public,* or detriment to the book; but, having undertaken to write it, he conceives that it could not have been done in a better or a kindlier spirit, nor, so far as his abilities availed, with a livelier effect of truth.

    The author is constrained, therefore, *to republish* his introductory sketch *without the change of a word.* (I:1–2, italics mine)

I needn't add that this "constraint" is now of his own making, the progeny of his own authority: for this reason, what might have been "wholly" omitted (without loss to the public) has been "hole-ly" included (at the public exclusion)—and this, for the sake of "fathering" (a private part) itSelf.[53] Indeed, against the shadow of this monstrous erection ("his head . . . on his shoulders"), there can be little doubt that (not for the first time) Hawthorne has stuck it to the public, his Gentle Reader.

    Furthermore, we detect, in this bind, a structure not unlike that which Derrida calls "differance," and which Gayatri Spivak transcribes as "*pre*monition" and "*post*ponement."[54] If the sign might both be said to defer itself and differ from itself, the same might be said of that signifier named "Hawthorne," who in the Custom-House sketch would clearly seek to understand the significance of his own existence. Toward this end, however, he is divided in his dual role as editor and author. Similarly, the ambivalent tone of "The Custom-House" discloses Hawthorne's ambiguous attitude toward his Puritan ancestry; as both story and family "line," he would simultaneously recognize and disown it. At the same time, he repeatedly delays the fact that he must stand up to this story as his own, as that to which he must at last sign his name—one which nominates him in the role of "father." He is, of course, aware from the outset that his story excludes a privileged authorial position, that its beginning, in fact, originates elsewhere—a location whose origin is ultimately inaccessible: "As regarded its origin, there were various explanations, all of which must necessarily have been conjectural" (I:258). Regarding this genealogy, we are repeatedly cautioned: if he is ever to come into his own, Hawthorne realizes that he must recognize his source (of identity) in the Other, just as the source of his story is not his own (un)doing; yet if one tries to follow it back to an absolutely certain origin, the trace of its historical inscription becomes irrevocably lost in prehistorical discourse—that is, in gossip, in what is passed down or passed along by word of mouth. Such is his original source of indebtedness: "The authority which we have chiefly followed—a manuscript of old date, drawn up from the verbal testimony of individuals, some of whom had known Hester Prynne, while others had heard the tale from contemporary witnesses" (I:259–60). And such is the testimony to which Hawthorne's signature at last bears witness: from the beginning, his story is inscribed within the Other.

If Hawthorne's story immediately obtains from Surveyor Pue's history (fact)—"half a dozen sheets of foolscap" (I:33)—history itself nevertheless appears all the more problematic when we recall its intimate resemblance to story (fiction); for while Hawthorne initially remarks its status as "official" (documentary), a closer examination reveals "more traces of Mr. Pue's mental part, and the internal operations of his head, than the fizzled wig had contained of the venerable skull itself. They were documents, in short, not official, but *of a private nature,* or, at least, *written* in his private capacity, and apparently *with his own hand*" (I:30, italics mine). Hawthorne here undermines that easy epistemology which relegates knowledge to the simple accumulation of facts. In doing so, he also speaks against the authority of his Puritan ancestors whose judgment would comdemn him to insignificance: "an idler like myself. . . . A writer of story-books" (I:10). Indeed, from the beginning, the fact itself is put in doubt: for when he measures the Letter (three inches and a quarter in length) it tells him nothing. While the proper measurement of a thing gives us its "correct" form, its meaning remains absent. The signifier considered in and of itself is nothing but the isolated subject "taken by itself" (narcissism): the subject objectified. Thus would reason reduce (castrate) meaning to the integer of self-"identity." A fact is therefore meaningless precisely to the extent that it coincides with itself; identity does not give rise to meaning, but rather—like meaning itself—arises from discrepancy.

Similarly, the question of "self"-identity returns every character in *The Scarlet Letter* to an-other: Chillingworth returns to Dimmesdale (in whom he forecloses on himSelf); Pearl returns to Dimmesdale (in whom she finds herSelf); Hester returns to Dimmesdale (in whom she sustains herSelf); and Dimmesdale returns to each (for whom he names himSelf). It happens as no accident, moreover, that each and everyone desires to know the name of the father, in whom there resides the locus of authority as the source of any and all identity. In this regard, identity itself is always a fiction, a text whose con-text, whose very pre-text, needs to be de-line-ated: a story whose knot demands to be (un)tied—one, moreover, which might also "induce the beholder to attempt unravelling it" (IV:306).

History too reveals its origins in story, in fiction, in "narration," as Arthur Danto observes: "To exist historically is to perceive the events one lives through as part of a story later to be told."[55] Thus Hawthorne cautions his Gentle Reader in *The Marble Faun,* for example, about the fragile structure of his woven narrative, the tapestry of his-story: "If any brilliant or beautiful, or even tolerable, effect have been produced, this pattern of kindly Readers will accept it at its worth, without tearing the web apart, with the idle purpose of discovering how its threads have been knit together; for the sagacity, by which he is distinguished, will long ago have taught him that any narrative of human action and adventure—whether we call it history or romance—is certain to be a fragile handiwork, more easily rent than mended. The actual experience of even the most ordinary life is full of events that never explain themselves, either as regards their origin or their tendency" (IV:455).

In this way, too, Hawthorne's superficial observance of historical objectivity often merely constitutes an ironic posture; like Goethe and Tieck, he delighted in destroying this objectivity at every opportunity. Indeed, he frequently satirizes the past as a value in itself. Whereas, for example, only one glass of whiskey suffices to produce the rather doubtful "Edward Randolph's Portrait," the story of Lady Eleanor represents the product of three glasses of madeira.[56] Likewise, the stamp of historical authority lies in the personal or private register, the individual domain of an author—though for its institutionalization (that is, in order to become a "fact") it clearly requires the public consent. That Hawthorne appreciates the problematics of this bind becomes all the more ironic insofar as he too, like Surveyor Pue, has author-ized official governmental transactions by means of a meaningless stamp, an imprimatur which bears his name—"imprinted . . . with a stencil and black paint" (I:27)—but not his signature. By an ironic *dédoublement* of perspective, furthermore, he speculates that his fiction alone, and not the fact of his official public activities, may lead to the discovery and preservation of any meaningful identity—that his stories might become, in turn, *"materials of* local *history"* (I:28, italics mine).[57] If, then, "the main facts of the story are authorized and authenticated by the document of Mr. Surveyor Pue" (I:32), Hawthorne nevertheless realizes that he must expose the irony of these facts, the fictive (narrative) ground of history in general: "I have allowed myself . . . nearly or altogether as much license *as if the facts had been entirely of my own invention.* What I contend for is the authenticity of the outline" (I:33, italics mine).

By the time that Hawthorne finally signs his name to the work, we are aware that his ironic signification already contains within it the possibility of meaning its opposite—that, indeed, as Foucault repeatedly observes, authority belongs to discourse itself. Through his ironic (mis)construction, then, Hawthorne blazons the significance of his pen(*manship*)—the authority for a discourse of which he is the father. Discourse, by nature, displaces the insignificant certitude ("correctness") of fact with the "sign" of fiction: in language, *there is* (Dasein)[58] inscribed the na(rra)tivity of being itSelf. Witness, for example, Hawthorne's "conclusion" (in which nothing is concluded) regarding the further adventures of the Letter in the transformed shape of Pearl: "But, in no long time after the physician's death, the wearer of the scarlet letter disappeared, and Pearl along with her. For many years, though a *vague report* would now and then find its way across the sea,—like a shapless piece of driftwood tost ashore, with the *initials of a name* upon it,—*yet no tidings of them unquestionably authentic were received*" (I:261, italics mine). In contrast to these vague reports bearing but the initials of a name, Hawthorne's final signature commends us to the discursive fabric of all authority: it is from the beginning devoid of propositional logic. Insofar as no text (much less one which claims authority for itself) can ever be said to supply its whole field—or even its intention—in advance of itself, as Edward Said points out, it can properly be said to begin, therefore, only with a large *supposition;* if meaning is to be produced in writing, this beginning intention remains always and everywhere a fiction.[59]

Regarding its claim to authority, moreover, the text refers us purely and simply to the domain of (good) faith and interpretation. So Hawthorne concludes with respect to Pearl's correspondence with Hester, letters that locate Pearl within another story, another context, yet one for which he implicitly claims authority as well: "In fine, the gossips of that day believed,—and Mr. Surveyor Pue, who made investigations a century later, believed,—and one of his recent successors in office, moreover, faithfully believes,—that Pearl was not only alive, but married, and happy, and mindful of her mother" (I:262). Authority therefore displaces the *lineage* of fatherhood with the discursive *knot* of textuality. The signifier inaugurates this dis-location; it opens being to meaning—a series of substitutions; language constitutes the beginning of another enterprise, a temporal structure signifying a series of displacements: language replaces genesis with paragenesis, origins with beginnings, continuity (the line) with contiguity (the knot), genetics with textuality. Textuality transforms an original object whose (in)significance is fixed (factual) into a beginning intention (to mean) whose significance is open and multiple (fictive), permitting the possible forms of discourse to merge one into the other.[60] From this tangle of supposition there arises the inosculation and metamorphosis of *history* into *story* and finally into *legend:* "The story of the scarlet letter grew into a legend" (I:261)—and this, moreover, in (its own) time. Authority is nothing less than this inaugural "position" of the text.

Authority, in turn, refers us back to the site of this displacement, its recitation of repression. As Freud observes of the Hexateuch, there is a violence in texts:

> almost everywhere noticeable gaps, disturbing repetitions and obvious contradictions have come about—indications which reveal things to us which it was not intended to communicate. In its implications the distortions of a text resemble a murder: the difficulty is not in perpetrating the deed, but in getting rid of its traces. We might well lend the word "Entstellung" [distortion] the double meaning to which it has a claim but of which today it makes no use. It should mean not only "to change the appearance of something" but also "to put something in another place, to displace." Accordingly, in many instances of textual distortion, we may nevertheless count upon finding what has been suppressed and disavowed hidden away somewhere else, though changed and torn from its context.[61]

This textual dis(inter)ruption is traceable to the discrepancy and substitutability of the sign itself. As the Letter in another form, for example, Pearl's nature articulates this broken law of signification: "it lacked reference and adaptation to the world into which she was born. The child could not be made amenable to rules. In giving her existence, a great law had been broken" (I:91). Meaning emerges from this (violent) gap in signification. A consciousness of the facts can therefore never account for the fact of consciousness: the self-reflexive subject reveals that its identity in no way coincides with itSelf, but rather is constituted by an-Other in its origin. This otherness represents the boundary or limit of the self as signifier (of desire). The Letter (of the law) originates here, just as the brook—this "boundary between two worlds" (I:208), between signifier and signified—conceals its source: "Letting the eyes follow along the course of the stream, they could catch the reflected light from its water, at some short distance within the forest, but soon lost all traces of it" (I:186). If origins, however, remain forever inaccessible, beginnings do not: beginnings inaugurate the signifier to meaning (the "spirit" of the law).

It is precisely this missing or *absent* beginning which makes *present* the crisis of Pearl's identity: she would know the other by whom she has "initially" been authorized. Lacking this, she nevertheless occasions the significance of those Other lives surrounding her by means of substitution. With respect to her parents, for example, Pearl knots the chain of signification, "herself a symbol, and the connecting link between those two" (I:154). She is the other whose substitution will guarantee the bond of (self)identity for both Hester and Arthur: "In her was visible the tie that united them. She had been offered to the world, these past seven years, as *the living hieroglyphic,* in which was revealed the secret they so darkly sought to hide,—*all written in this symbol,*—all plainly manifest,— had there been a prophet or magician skilled *to read* the character of flame! And Pearl was the oneness of their being" (I:206–7, italics mine). Significance here emerges from the insertion of one signifier in (the) place of another. When Hester discards the Letter (Pearl) in the forest, this alters the relationship insofar as Dimmesdale takes its (her) place: "The stigma gone, Hester heaved a long, deep sigh. . . . O exquisite relief! She had not known the weight, until she felt the freedom" (I:202). Here Hester assumes the very freedom she had for so long postponed, "the freedom of a broken law" (I:134) which Pearl represents and yet dissembles in herself. Similarly, Hester's self-expression occasions the premonition of Dimmesdale's self-repression, how the return of the repressed exposes the lacuna of his own desire. Thus, when Hester returns the Letter to its initial place, when Pearl once again occupies the place next to her mother, Dimmesdale is, in turn, recalled to the displacement of himSelf—the way in which the real, as Lacan defines it, always comes back to the same place: "As the minister departed, in advance of Hester Prynne and little Pearl, he threw a backward glance; half expecting that he should discover only some faintly traced features or outline of the mother and the child, slowly fading into the twilight of the woods. So great a vicissitude in his life could not at once be received as real. . . . And there was Pearl, too, lightly dancing from the margin of the brook,—now that the intrusive third person was gone,—and taking her old place by her mother's side. So the minister had not fallen asleep, and dreamed" (I:214).

By the same "token"—that is, the displacement of the Letter/Pearl insofar as both are the same (thus different, not identical)—Dimmesdale feels "this indistinctness and duplicity of impression" (I:214) within himself, though it has yet to be expressed: "the *intervening space* of a single day *had operated on his consciousness* like the lapse of years. . . . Before Mr. Dimmesdale reached home, his inner man gave him other evidences of a revolution in the sphere of thought and feeling. In truth, nothing short of a total *change of* dynasty and moral *code,* in that interior kingdom, was adequate to account for the impulses now communicated to the unfortunate and startled minister. At every step he was incited to do some strange, wild, wicked thing or other, *with a sense that it would be at once*

involuntary and intentional; in spite of himself, yet growing out of a pro-
founder self than that which opposed the impulse" (I:217, italics mine).
In this regard, he stands witness to the Freudian subject and its (de)termi-
nation (in language): to write itSelf off. "Now, during a conversation of
some two or three moments between the Reverend Mr. Dimmesdale and
this excellent and hoary-bearded deacon, it was only by the most careful
self-control that the former could refrain from uttering certain blasphe-
mous suggestions that rose into his mind, respecting the communion-
supper. He absolutely trembled and turned pale as ashes, *lest his tongue
should wag itself,* in utterance of these horrible matters, and plead his own
consent for so doing, without his having fairly given it. And, even with
this terror in his heart, he could hardly avoid laughing to imagine how
the sanctified old patriarchal deacon would have been petrified by his
minister's impiety" (I:218, italics mine). And to "the eldest female mem-
ber of his church" (I:218), who seeks the "heaven-breathing Gospel truth
from his beloved lips" (I:219), he once again consigns himself to this
other voice: "on this occasion, up to the moment of putting his lips to the
old woman's ear, Mr. Dimmesdale, as the great enemy of souls would
have it, could recall no text of Scripture, nor aught else, except a brief,
pithy, and, as it then appeared to him, unanswerable argument against
the immortality of the human soul. . . . What he really did whisper, the
minister could never afterwards recollect. There was, perhaps, a fortunate *disorder in his utterance,* which failed to impart any distinct idea to the
good widow's comprehension, or which Providence interpreted after a
method of its own" (I:219, italics mine). Need I add that this "Providen-
tial" method is nothing less than the province of the analyst's couch?

Once Dimmesdale reaches home, he is again confronted with this
disordered Self—the way in which his very meaning has been disrupted,
his significance broken: "There was the Bible, in its rich old Hebrew,
with Moses and the Prophets speaking to him, and God's voice through
all! There, on the table, with the inky pen beside it, was an unfinished
sermon, *with a sentence broken in the midst,* where his thoughts had ceased
to gush out upon the page two days before. He knew that it was himself,
the thin and white-cheeked minister, who had done and suffered these
things, and written thus far into the Election Sermon! But he seemed to
stand apart, and eye this former self with scornful, pitying, but half-
envious curiosity. That self was gone! Another man had returned out of
the forest" (I:223, italics mine). No longer the scribbler of another's
authority (the Divine Word), Dimmesdale is momentarily compelled to
relinquish his role as scribe. Like Hawthorne in "The Custom-House,"
Dimmesdale too experiences the double-cross (the chiasm, self-other) of

his discourse, the duplicity of a demand to "eye" his "I," to pen himSelf what has been hitherto inscribed within the other and therefore express that authority which is his own—though yet it "lies" repressed. In this regard, moreover, "it would appear natural, that a part of it should be expressed. It is singular, however, how long a time often passes before words embody things" (I:224). Thus "flinging the already written pages of the Election Sermon into the fire, he forthwith began another, which he wrote with such an impulsive flow of thought and emotion, that he fancied himself inspired" (I:225). Yet with the first sign of sunrise, he still sub-sists—resigned to his task(master), "the pen still between his fingers, and a vast, immeasurable tract of written space behind him" (I:225). What lies ahead, however, constitutes the measurable tract (of discursive space) of his own authority, the inscription of himSelf as (not in the name of) the father. These "blank pages" which lie before him, and which have heretofore been *writing him* (and into his flesh, his very body), reveal the letter of the law (of signification) in its concealment: what is absent (the phallus) cannot hide—what is present can.

From the structure of repression, there emerges the (lack of) meaning in Pearl's existence as well. While she refuses the ideal—"I have no Heavenly Father" (I:98)—she nevertheless repeatedly invokes the name of the (real) father. Without this name, of course, she lacks a history: she is a story begun, yet neither origin-al nor signed—she is anonymous. Until Dimmesdale's final confession, she remains a character in search of an <u>A</u>uthor (<u>A</u>rthur): a letter takes the place of a name, an initial the place of a signature. Though she lives with Hester as her mother, she must abide the Letter in (the) place of the father. This substitution confers upon Pearl the status of an inauthentic document. It happens as no coincidence, then, that the central character (signifier) in the novel possesses the Letter as the central (though hidden) letter in her name (Pe<u>A</u>rl);[62] for so long as Dimmesdale refuses to nominate himself as the father (author) of this (art) work, Pearl's (missing) identity resides purely in the Letter (of the law). While Arthur conceals his Letter behind conventional clothes, Hester ironically wears his secret (and hypocrisy)—the occluded name— as her very garment. In this respect, Pearl's identification with the Letter is made all too easy: "she *is* the scarlet letter" (I:113, italics mine). Her own attire but mimics this (con)fusion, arrayed "in a certain velvet tunic, of a peculiar cut, abundantly embroidered with fantasies and flourishes of gold thread" (I:102). From birth, Pearl seeks to decipher the enigmatic significance of the Letter as that which holds the key to her existence; she even places eel-grass on her own breast in its form—now "freshly green, instead of scarlet" (I:178):

"I wonder if mother will ask me what it means!" thought Pearl.

"My little Pearl," said Hester, after a moment's silence, "the green letter, and on thy childish bosom, has no purport. But dost thou know, my child, what this letter means which thy mother is doomed to wear?"

"Yes, mother," said the child. "It is the great letter A. Thou hast taught it me in the horn-book." (I:178)

As an *initial* (original) trace, the Letter "marks" Pearl's missing name—it takes the place of a (de)nomination which demands to be AnNOUNced: there is a (proper) name involved in its sound for which no other substitution can bequeath to Pearl her meaning without (the loss of) significance. As Derrida remarks, "every signified whose signifier can neither vary nor be translated into another signifier without loss of significance, suggests a proper-name effect."[63] While the "A" appears in different places, different forms, and while it meaningfully weaves or inscribes itself into the existence of others, for Pearl it lacks any and all signification "proper" to herSelf. She is an unaccomplished (art) work, missing the other (letters of her name). In relation to the other, she stands as a meaningless phoneme—although not insignificantly as the first letter of both the Alphabet and Arthur's name. Isolated as "the great letter A" of her horn-book, she implies the missing part of a whole (text) and subsequently constitutes "a law unto herself, without her eccentricities being reckoned to her for a crime" (I:134–35). Not until the end, when Dimmesdale discloses his co-responding Letter and gives to her his name, is Pearl at last authorized and authenticated. Only now does she become a meaningful signifier able to write her own existence.

At the conclusion, moreover, her substitution in (the) place of the Letter confers upon *The Letter* a significant displacement—a self-reflexive and therefore bifurcated commentary on itself. Pearl's name, in fact, is interchangeable with Hawthorne's title for the book; we might read into her various "properties" the status of the art work (romance) in general. Thus from America, where Pearl "became the richest heiress of her day, in the New World" (I:261)—a circumstance which "wrought a very material change in the public estimation" (I:261)—Hawthorne cleverly dispatches his "child" *(The Scarlet Letter)* to Europe, where it "grew into a legend" (I:261). The reader is invited to this "christening," permitted to be in on this inaugural intention (authorization): the birth of American Art—its first great literary work. In this beginning, there is the promise that others will follow—a situation as pregnant with possibilities as Pearl herself: "And, once, Hester was seen embroidering a baby-garment" (I:262). At last, having come into her own (authority), Pearl's correspondence with Hester—"Letters came" (I:262)—here parallels her co-respondence with *The Letter.* Regarding both, the end of Hawthorne's story holds forth the birth of other beginnings. An author in her own right, bequeathed by Dimmesdale's confession the other letters of her (proper) name, Pearl now initiates her correspondence with the other as one who has come into the fullness of the alphabet: thus, to Hester, *other* "Letters came" (B, C, D, E, F, G, H, I, J, K, L, M, N, O, P, Q, R, S, T, U, V, W, X, Y, and Z?). And with her "signature," *The Letter* too begins its round of nomination, the proselytization of American letters in Europe: "through the remainder of Hester's life, there were indications that the recluse of the scarlet letter was the object of love and interest with some inhabitant of another land" (I:262).

Furthermore, Pearl's signature returns the Letter to its initial configuration. Though Hester is sentenced to wear the sign of the Letter (of the law), she nevertheless transfigures it by way of embroidery. Indeed, what the pen is to Hawthorne, so the needle is to Hester: with it, she *trans-forms* her *subjectivity to discourse.* By means of her needle-work, Hester confers upon the existent "*a fictitious value* even to common or worthless things; . . . Hester really *filled a gap* which must otherwise have remained vacant" (I:82, italics mine): that is, she weaves (inscribes) herSelf (signifier) into the status of a text. Her sentence is becoming to her: she becomes a sentence. Upon entering a church, for example, "it was often her mishap to find herself the text of the discourse" (I:85). Thus, while she often fancies "that the scarlet letter had endowed her with a new sense" (I:86), she nonetheless defers its final significance. Only with her return from abroad is she at last bequeathed a textuality (author-ity) of her own figuration, a threshold which freely opens onto other figures (contextuality): "But there was a more real life for Hester Prynne, here, in New England, than in that unknown region where Pearl had found a home. . . . She had returned, therefore, and resumed,—of her own free will, . . . the symbol of which we have related so dark a tale. Never afterwards did it quit her bosom. . . . the scarlet letter ceased to be a stigma . . . and became a type. . . . And, as Hester Prynne had no selfish ends . . . people brought all their sorrows and perplexities, and besought her counsel" (I:262–63). Bequeathed to dialogue (intertextuality), the Letter thence transforms itself toward "revelation," the "sacred scripture" of love—a text whose very nature is destined to unfold, unknot itself, "in Heaven's own time" (I:263) and therefore doomed to remain forever un(dis)closed:

> Hester comforted and counselled them, as best she might. She assured them, too, of her firm belief, that, at some brighter period, when the world

should have grown ripe for it, in Heaven's own time, a new truth would be revealed, in order to establish the whole relation between man and woman on a surer ground of mutual happiness. Earlier in life, Hester had vainly imagined that she herself might be the destined prophetess, but had long since recognized the impossibility. . . . The angel and apostle of the coming revelation must be a woman, indeed, but lofty, pure, and beautiful; and wise, moreover, not through dusky grief, but the ethereal medium of joy; and showing how sacred love should make us happy, by the truest test of a life successful to such an end. (I:263)

And so the harbinger of the new sexuality must be a woman—one, we might conjecture, who would dismiss the epithalamion as superfluous. In all of this, however, there is again the ironic bifurcation of significance: for insofar as Hawthorne's own child *(The Scarlet Letter)* is female (Pearl), his book will not perpetuate his (paternal) *name*. Writing (existence) is a dead end. This too suggests that writing does not simply play at childbirth across the abyss of paternity alone, but rather articulates the androgynous abyss across which signs signify, that continually problematic status of being as a (w)hole which combines the absence of the (dead) father with the presence of the (living) mother: "Writing leaps back and forth across this impossible interval, doubling, multiplying, with no escape save annihilation."[64]

Just as the Letter multiplies its meaning across the otherness of itself (Adultery, Angel, Apostle, Able, Authority, Authenticity, Alpha, Alphabet, American, Art, Alterity), so too with the subject: the signifier acquires its meaning (self-"identity") from out of the other (signifiers), its resistance to A (transcendental) signified.[65] Regarding its ultimate destination, the Letter which goes abroad is finally returned to its "initial" place. In spite of its deviation from itself, from an initial design—"many people refused to interpret the scarlet A by its original signification" (I:161)—the otherness of the Letter always and everywhere returns its bearer to the place in which it inaugurates the subject to assume responsibility for itself, to speak back or reply as one's own, to inscribe the text of the Self upon the margin of an-Other text (desire). For, as Geoffrey Hartman remarks, "the word that is given up is not given up: it must inscribe itself somewhere else, as a psychosomatic or mental symptom."[66] Thus, for example, while Hester is tempted—should Pearl be taken from her—to enter the forest, where souls are consigned to the devil, and sign her name in "the Black Man's book" (I:117), she yet refuses to resign herself to this text. Rather than submit to either this or the Puritan conscription—"she will be a living sermon against sin" (I:63)—she chooses to embroider a discourse of her own. In this event, she reassigns the letter (of the [Puritan] law) to herSelf, thereby returning it to the Puritan community at the very point from which it originated—but in reverse form: for *her needle* (work) *now clothes the community* in garments of her own making. By means of her embroidery, Hester rewrites their history as (her) story, reversing the (short) circuit wherein those who would initially "write her" (off) are finally "written" (on) by her: a discourse signed, sealed, and delivered, moreover, with her very signature. It is no wonder, then, that this initial (Letter) symptom shows up on the blank page of the night sky to (dis)cover the entire community.

Dimmesdale, on the other hand, re( )signs himself to the "A." By its absence (repression), the Letter is destined to presence elsewhere; its symptomatic manifestation, in turn, inscribes itself upon his very body in the form of his psychosomatic illness: he is entirely written by it. Until his confession, the Letter bespeaks him. Condemned to conscription in the authority of another, the Puritan law, the Letter is destined to finish him upon the very point at which it began—a point not unlike Hester's needle, yet one for which he lacks any and all authority of his own. He is cut up by this (double) edge, carved out *in spite of* (despite) his impotent "pen"(manship), just as his sermons but represent a "paranoid" form of dictation: the divine writing that (re)calls him to remember a "Dead Letter" and thereby forget himSelf. For Dimmesdale, the Letter must be uncovered, laid bare: he must expose the self to its "A" version—his aversion to himSelf. Hawthorne's A-diction to the truth—"Be true! Be true! Be true! Show freely to the world, if not your worst, yet some trait whereby the worst may be inferred!" (I:260)—simply underscores the "sentence" whereby human existence is provoked to express the intertextuality of self and other, the inter-subjective dimension of being itSelf. In this con-text, truth knows nothing of fact but rather exposes the facticity of being—the fictive significance of its origin, its na(rra)tivity in language. To be true means simply to discover a voice of one's own, to fabricate a version, to rehearse the dialogic interval of existence: "to open an intercourse with the world" (IX:6). To be false, on the other hand, is to be missing a version of one's self—to be, rather, the One self *(das Man):* it is to be in such a way that One averts itSelf. To repress a version therefore constitutes the very per-version of being to which Dimmesdale is given over until the end. Perversion here but represents that mode of being in which the subject no longer signifies: it is to have no version (phallus) of one's own.

Like Hester's Letter, furthermore, Dimmesdale's final scene allows a multiplicity of scenarios to figure forth. With his disclosure, the Letter's significance has yet to be discerned. For some, it represents his self-inflicted penance; for others, it represents the (im)potent token of Chillingworth's necromancy; for others, still, it represents "the ever active tooth of remorse, gnawing from the inmost heart outwardly" (I:258). A special few, moreover, who "professed never once to have removed their eyes from the Reverend Mr. Dimmesdale, denied that there was any mark whatever on his breast" (I:259). Except for this last (blind) version, which obviously misses the mark, the narration permits each version to stand side by side with the others: "The reader may choose among these theories" (I:259). Herein subsists that genuine conversion of consciousness which Hawthorne's oeuvre provokes, the intertextuality of existence: being-together in the open, in the freedom of each to the other—of each to all, each to its own. The problematic status of the sign invites interpretation, as Donatello remarks to Kenyon: "'My dear friend,' exclaimed Kenyon, 'how strangely your eyes have transmuted the expression of the figure! It is divine Love, not wrath!' 'To my eyes,' said Donatello stubbornly, 'it is wrath, not Love! Each must interpret for himself'" (IV:306). Regarding *The Letter* also, Hawthorne's open(ended)ness allows us to choose, and thereby releases us from the narrative authority: the reader is called upon to authorize (begin) the text in terms of its significance to Self.[67] And while the narrative announces its desire, once the Letter has done its office, to "erase its deep print out of our own brain" (I:259), the trace of this effacement must nonetheless remain forever upon the heart: indeed, its *ghostly presence* now prohibits all interpretation precisely insofar as it cuts across it. To this extent, the narrative wish to disembody the Letter serves merely to revive the deadly trace that marks it—the (dis)appearance of a dead-*line* which *knots the historical* (w)hole *to the very center of a* (ghost) *story,* the maternal cathexis (narrativity) in place of the (missing) phallus (nativity): by handing over to the reader the "potential" of this lack, Hawthorne entrusts the task of further inscription—that in the overabundance of this Other(ness), the reader would write itSelf all the more.[68]

All of this suggests the ontological import of narration, the very textuality of being itSelf—"The page of life" (I:37)—as the narrator of *The Marable Faun* observes regarding Miriam's existence: "In weaving these mystic utterances into a continuous scene, we undertake a task resembling, in its perplexity, that of gathering up and piecing together the fragments of a letter, which has been torn and scattered to the winds. Many words of deep significance—many entire sentences, and those possibly the most important ones—have flown too far, on the winged breeze, to be recovered. If we insert our own conjectural amendments, we perhaps give a purport utterly at variance with the true one. Yet, unless we attempt something in this way, there must remain an unsightly gap, and a lack of continuousness and dependence in our narrative" (IV:92–93). Narration occupies both story and history at their point of embarkation, that locus of authorization which makes existence a "work." Meaning is born through exposition, the temporal fabrication *(poiēsis)* in which existence is made to stand out (ek-sist): there must be a narrator. Narration enables existence to stand out/in itSelf. Hawthorne's pre-text ("The Custom-House"), Pearl's correspondence, Dimmesdale's confession, Hester's embroidery—each inscribes the "figure" (text) of the Self against the "frame" (context) of the Other to which it co-responds; each discourse makes the Other its own. While Hester, for example, initially rejects her needle-work as sin, she learns its joy as *"a mode of expression,* and therefore soothing, the passion of her life" (I:84, italics mine). Both Chillingworth and the Puritans in general, on the other hand, deny being its exposition. Repression therefore circumscribes the subject as an impostor, without a position of its own: an imposition of being. Precisely and ironically to the extent that Chillingworth, for instance, entirely subscribes to or underwrites the text of Dimmesdale's life, he serves as but an annotation to the authority of another. What is the Letter, if not the cutting edge of this bifurcated, asymmetrical structure: self-other? If at its origin the self is always already written by another, it nevertheless is called upon to inaugurate the manner and meaning of its significance. In its intention to secure a beginning, the self thus authorizes its emergence into the world as an authentic (art) work—one of its own making. The world (of the work) becomes the work (of the world) exposed. With this exposition, being is provoked to itSelf. Hawthorne 's villains, however, revoke the self to the failure of being, entirely spoken for and written by the other—upon this line of resistance to the self at the insistence of another, existence is repressed. Authentic existence would yet tie this original line with a significant knot, its own story: the subject itSelf is always a fiction.[69]

Hawthorne's *Letter* exposes this duplicity of being within the very structure of the work: his authorial switch from the first-person "Custom-House" to the third-person "romance" enacts the abyss between self and other, subject and object, "fiction" and "fact," individual and community, private and public. Here the pronoun not only reveals the transposition of subject and object within narration (reflection), but also its reciprocal means of being present/absent to itSelf. The configuration of a consciousness articulated both within and without implies the very subversion of its ground: the otherness of discourse. Insofar as existence, moreover, is bequeathed to language, to the abysmal structure

of the sign—the irreducible discrepancy between signifier and signified—the subject transacts both speech and writing as separate aspects
of the same phenomenon, the otherness of being itSelf. Each is the horizon of the other. Discourse too defers and differs from itself: speech and
writing correspond to this event.[70] The narrative discourse comes from
out of the manuscript of Surveyor Pue, although this manuscript, in turn,
originates in the gossip of the age; Hester's discourse comes to her from
out of the spoken judgment of the Puritan tribunal; Pearl's discourse
comes to her from out of Dimmesdale's confession; Dimmesdale's discourse, on the other hand, comes to him from out of the unspoken
name—the written mark inscribed upon his very flesh, the mere ghost of
a divine insignia. In every case, discourse is called to assume responsibility both for the other as its own and for its own otherness. Hawthorne assumes his pen in order to write his romance; Hester utilizes her
needle in order to embroider her garments; Pearl takes up her armorial seals in order to post her letters of correspondence; Dimmesdale
employs his voice in order to sing the song of himself. In every case, the
subject is provoked to sign the other with a discourse which encircles
the (w)hole of its (in)significance: a circle of de-negations which recovers
the self by means of exposition.

Exposition recuperates the subject from the abyss of nothingness
across which the signs signify and for significance itself, just as Hepzibah,
for example, is "redeemed from insignificance" (II:41) by her scowl.
Expression, here, articulates the heart of exposition—the subject's co-
respondence to the heart of things: a matter for discourse. Dimmesdale's
voice suggests such correspondence: "it breathed passion and pathos, and
emotions high or tender, in a tongue native to the human heart" (I:243).
The logic of the heart exposes this intertextuality, the narrative dimension of being. While Hawthorne "undoes meaning"[71] at the level of
reason, he nonetheless secures it to a significance which occasions the
very possibility of (self) expression—the greatest danger imaginable to
the Puritan community as a whole. Both Dimmesdale's voice and
Hester's needle disrupt the communal "ratio" *(das Man)*, as Nina Baym
observes: "Disguised as a social document, the work of art secretly expresses the cry of the heart. Doing this, it covertly defies society in
response to hidden but universal needs. . . . *The Scarlet Letter* makes it
clear that imagination serves the self."[72] Imagination, in turn, returns the
subject to an irreducible locus of signification, what—at the very center
of its existence, as a repressed signifier—inheres as its irreducible kernel
or *kern,* its *heart* of non-sense.[73] Around this (k)not, the subject inscribes
itSelf. What Hawthorne's narrator in *The Marble Faun* observes of the

image in painting equally bespeaks the core of textuality in general: *"that indefinable nothing, that inestimable something, that constitutes the life and soul"* (IV:60, italics mine). As Lacan suggests, all discourse harbors within it this locus of the imaginary by means of which the subject constructs (the object of) itSelf: "The *I* is not a being, it is a presupposition with respect to that which speaks."[74]

How else do we account for Hawthorne's final tombstone "inscription" which would efface its very discourse, displace the symbolic with the imaginary? Indeed, the very *lack of* a tombstone *inscription* returns the reader to the heart of all significance, its center of non-sense (non-being) around which the subject would tie the (k)not of textuality: "All around, there were monuments carved with armorial bearings; and on this simple slab of slate—as the curious investigator may still discern, and perplex himself with the purport—there appeared the semblance of an engraved escutcheon. It bore a device, a herald's wording of which might serve for a motto and brief description of our now concluded legend; so sombre is it, and relieved only by one ever-glowing point of light gloomier than the shadow:—'On a Field, Sable, the Letter A, Gules'" (I:264). In one sense, of course, Hawthorne re-returns this final image back to the symbolic (discourse) insomuch as he translates its significance into the "language" of heraldry: "On a Field, Sable, the Letter A, Gules." In another sense, however, there remains only the image itself—or rather its ghost: the after-image of an image whose absence can now only suggest the presence of a dead Letter. If anything, this "reading" of the (lack of) "inscription" is reinforced by Hawthorne's narrative de-scription: for here the (invisible) motto—the visible image—is "relieved only by one ever-glowing point of light gloomier than the shadow." The oxymoron expresses in the register of the symbolic what must remain forever unimaginable: existence is a dead end.

It also seems that in the lack of a verse upon the (tomb)stone, this (writing) tablet fails once again to sign the name. The missing epitaph reverses the point of origin and the end of this (ghost) story, the space of the Freudian *fort-da;* now the present absence of the father "playing" with the absent presence of the mother engenders the possibility of discourse: "Writing oscillates between a name that cannot be inscribed and the dead body, a corpse-effect whose intrusion into the real is the sign and signature of this impasse. . . . the tomb is the point at which name and body are wed in their common impasse."[75] Narration encircles this (w)hole which would draw everything into it. It should come as no surprise that in the failure of adequation, in this very lack, in the trace or mark of the signifier as remainder of another—that which represents a subject *for another signifier*—death has already taken place, has taken up its place in the beginning. Death has secured the end at the front. This (double) crossing of signifiers constitutes, in effect, the very locus of significance as that which comes between: the gap or void of being—(inter)subjectivity—itSelf. As the skeleton at "The Christmas Banquet" betokens: "And if, in their bewildered conjectures as to the purpose of earthly existence, the banqueters should throw aside the veil, and cast an inquiring glance at this figure of death, as seeking thence the solution otherwise unattainable, the only reply would be a stare of the vacant eye-caverns, and a grin of the skeleton-jaws. Such was the response that the dead man had fancied himself to receive, when he asked of Death to solve the riddle of his life; and it was his desire to repeat it when the guests of his dismal hospitality should find themselves perplexed with the same question" (X:287). From no-thing to nothing, the subject comes and goes upon its round of nomination, and reads in advance this missing inscription. "Death . . . is an idea that cannot easily be dispensed with, in any condition between the primal innocence and that other purity and perfection, which, perchance, we are destined to attain, after travelling round the full circle" (X:393).

Here reading and writing are one and the same: for in the end, regarding its ultimate design, the Letter which goes abroad is finally returned to its "initial" place. Lacan observes the same of Poe's "Purloined Letter," in which the sender receives from the receiver his own message in reverse form: "Thus it is that what the . . . 'letter in sufferance' means is that a letter always arrives at its destination."[76] Throughout its circular course, in fact, the Letter elicits the reader to respond to it(self)—indeed, *repeats* the very trauma of interpretation which inaugurates the self to meaning. *The Letter* thus prefigures the (primal) scene of psychoanalysis itself: "the traumatic deferred interpretation not *of* an event, but *as* an event which never took place as such. The 'primal scene' is not a scene but an *interpretive infelicity*. . . . Psychoanalysis has content only insofar as it repeats the dis-content of what never took place"; similarly, every reader is destined to have the Letter "addressed" to itSelf: the Letter's destination *is* "wherever it is read."[77] Hawthorne's Letter signs the reader itself—assigns the reader to itSelf. The Letter (The *Letter*) reads the reader: it both conceals and reveals its truth (meaning) at once. In this event, there also appears the arrival of meaning (truth): its path returns us to *The Letter* as the very remnant of the Letter (itself a remnant of Surveyor Pue's manuscript) (itself a remnant of gossip) (ad infinitum). This open(ended) text refers us to the infinite regress of (self) referentiality—the abyss *(mise-en-abyme)* of Hawthorne's narrative frame *(récit)*. The source of (his) story is always another (story). Each and every discourse on/of the Letter bears the trace of another (repressed/forgotten [on purpose]) signifier, another letter: *a dead letter*. We are recalled to Hawthorne's pre-text in "The Custom-House," where the Letter turns up as simply one of the innumerable pieces of *dead weight* which clutter the House itself: the mere ghosts of men who through the repetition and redundancy of bureaucratic scribbling have come to occupy this *dead letter office*. It is indeed their office to repress—by means of idle chit-chat and procrastination—the very thing bureaucracy perpetually defers: the *dead-line*. Here it is (mis)construed, of course, that life goes on forever. How else are we to understand the overpowering lethargy that befalls Hawthorne in "the" place of dead being *(l'être morte/lettre morte)*,[78] these dead letters (being(s)-of-no-consequence) who because they always talk can therefore never write (a thing): a veritable *dead end* which by its impotence leaves everything unfinished?

Within this House of (dead) letters, the subject is provoked to build, to dwell, to construct "A" text (of) itSelf—the meaning of its being. The office of (the) "custom" (house) but serves to distinguish Hawthorne from both the Other (readers) and himSelf, to inaugurate the repetition of *The Letter* as it goes its various rounds within the symbolic structure of discourse. Hawthorne's writing *is* this house, the House of Fiction, which constructs a passage(way/*weg*) between self and other: intercourse with the world: "thoughts are frozen and utterance benumbed, unless the speaker stand in some true relation with his audience" (I:4). Upon the threshold of this (Custom) House, Hawthorne's discourse exposes the world as the work *(poiēsis)* of reading and writing (its own) inscription. It silences the idle chatter of custom *(das Man)*, provokes the reader to itSelf. As he expressed it in a letter to his publisher, James T. Fields, "'The Custom-House' is merely introductory,—an entrance-hall to the magnificent edifice which I throw open to my guests."[79] Hawthorne's prefaces are thus significant precisely insofar as they function as various thresholds to this single house. Edgar Dryden brilliantly seizes the significance of this event when he observes that the Custom-House sketch "endows the familiar house-of-fiction metaphor with an important ontological dimension."[80] Indeed, Hawthorne's House of Fiction is nothing less than Language, what Heidegger refers to as the house or temple of being. Thus Hawthorne could refer to fiction as the very "kingdom of *possibilities*" (XII:119, italics mine). This figure, moreover, solicits the ontological structure of existence at its *kern* or heart: for being itSelf *can* figure forth only against the frame(work: *récit*) of that being for whom the meaning of being *can be* an issue in the first place—that being who *cannot be/can not-be* itSelf. What, then, does it mean to be? To recite the question by heart reveals a final (dis)solution: the possibility of not being one's own *is* the possibility of one's own not being. The subject already resonates this silence, this gap or void, as that configuration around which being, in turn, inscribes or entombs itSelf. Meaning here constitutes the play of presence and absence, disclosure and concealment, whereby the ghost of substitution (desire) assumes its port of entry—its "in" (the place of). Language exposes this silent co-respondence: the insertion of the subject in (the place of) being as a (w)hole.

The structure of signification thus plays across a silent abyss in which the Letter is both its cutting edge and knot. For Hawthorne, this abyss opens upon and structures every dimension of being—from the image [being(-)in(-)*the-world*], through the other [being(-)*in*(-)thc-world], to the subject itSelf [*being*(-)in(-)the-world]. There is *(Dasein)* the gap, the ch(i)asm which yawns—waiting for the subject to insert itSelf, to uncover its meaning: to inscribe the text of existence with its (k)not. Here being shelters this absence, this nullity, within the house of language. *There is* the interval of discourse: amid this interval, the Other is exposed; from out of this abyss, it calls. If in the Other, there arises to being its exposition, discourse sounds the silent co-respondence between this being and its meaning: the very heart of non-being (non-sense) at its center. Narration implies an ontology wherein both presence and absence equiprimordially obtain: the construction and repetition of a story in which the subject is at all times missing from itSelf, and thereby stands in need of interpretation. Interpretation, in turn, returns us to Hawthorne's own obsession for "masquerade," the persona of textuality—disclosure in concealment: *being* (exposed or unmasked) *in* (the very face of) *the* (masked) *text*. Over and against the irresponsible imposition of being as repression, responsibility re-(A)-signs the subject to itSelf. In re-sponse-ability, *there is* given to being its exposition. And in the roundness of this correspondence, the subject is bequeathed to its de-sign. Herein dwells the genuine work of Hawthorne's world, the tangle whence emerges its na(rra)tivity. In this fabrication, this construction, this weaving, is inscribed, in (the) place of the missing phallus, the magic "limen"—the thread of a story designed to be, from the outset, fated to end: the very (k)not of being itSelf. When Hawthorne posts his *Letter,* it is for nothing (less than this): to send being on its way, its destination—to be (more than) the k(not).

☐

It's been a long way back. But I at last return you to that track *(weg)* regarding whose destination our path has found its way *(Holzweg)*, turns back upon itself, short-circuits its "intercourse with the world" (its "intercourse" with "the world"). The Gentle Reader's destiny will bear upon this site, will (over)take it in "the end." Hawthorne's work (scenario) recites the very space (scene) of this phantastic matrix ("The Gentle Reader") upon the site of another (primal) scene: Plato's "One" (the "Hen") returns to (its) roost. Here Hawthorne figures as a family affair, the oneness of the *Reader* with (its) *Author*, the "one" inscribed within the (hen) House of (family) Romance. *The House* itself has always already (pre)figured the Gentle Reader as one of its birds. Within "a hen-coop, of very reverend antiquity, that stood in the farther corner of the garden" (II:88), the Pyncheon hens appear "wise as well as antique," as if "they had existed, in their individual capacity, ever since the House of the Seven Gables was founded, and were somehow mixed up with its destiny" (II:89). As Holgrave remarks, "the chicken itself was a symbol of the life of the old house. . . . It was a feathered riddle; a mystery hatched out of an egg, and just as mysterious as if the egg had been addle" (II:152). So too, the Gentle Reader has inhabited Hawthorne's house of fiction since its incubation (I recall you to all the talk of birds in "The Custom-House"), its destiny scrambled with its origin, its mystery hatched from a rotten egg, its being "crack-brained" (II:151).

With (dis)respect to its reversible gestalt (chicken/egg), and for the sake of (the very pleasure of) its "figure" (the text), I'll now attempt to lay (out) that configuration of texts we designate as "Hawthorne." What does this proper name provoke? It calls forth (nothing: less than) the dead. Such is the case whenever the scene overtakes the scenario, wherever it takes over, takes the narration from behind. This it does with a vengeance in *The Marble Faun,* where "death becomes the companion of the author," of the narration itself.[81] By confering a shape and temporality upon *The Faun,* I seek to gather that text within another narration that both recollects backward its historical genesis toward origin and recollects forward or repeats (Kierkegaard) its own performance as story, recites the future of its own fabrication. The event I would locate is, by definition, its primal scene: that scenario by means of which it will defenestrate the frame of its own *récit,* by means of which it enunciates itSelf. This annunciation is, of course, a noun. I might as well announce it in advance, dismissing all suspense from the outset despite (in spite of) the fact that everything remains suspended upon the tenuous *text*ure of this name. "Pearl" is but another name for "Donatello." It's not by chance that "Hawthorne" lays "felonious hands upon a . . . statue of a Pearl-Diver" (IV:4) in order to re-site Akers at the scene of Kenyon's studio: "the statue of a beautiful youth, a pearl-fisher, who had got entangled in the weeds at the bottom of the sea, and lay dead among the pearl-oysters (IV:117). *The Faun* will serve to resuscitate this figure (Pearl/letter/*Letter* transfigured to faun/Donatello/"a beautiful youth") regarding which Miriam observes, "the form has not settled itself into sufficient repose" (IV:117). Remarking this trans-formation, I repeat: "Donatello"—that is, the marble faun as both the site of an object/cite of a text *(The Marble Faun)*—is but another name for "Pearl." Just as the preface revises its previous cite(s), so too *The Faun* repeats *The Letter,* posts it to a future site, The End ("Postscript"), its after-cite (Post Crypt): a dead letter office. To sight this location is to recite that event (primal scene) by means of which the textual configuration called "Hawthorne" is able to appear in the first place. For this, we'd be well-advised to begin at the end—the tail of this tale, if you will, and under whose very cover is revealed that layer which conceals the egg, one whose mystery can only be further scrambled in any tale of mixed and mixed up metaphors (symptoms).

Resurrected by the designation "Postscript," "Hawthorne" resumes himSelf to once more stick it to the Gentle Reader in the end. The point is this: do Donatello's ears have points? Since the Gentle Reader is dying to know this point—to get it, to take it all in—and since Hawthorne has already conceded the state of his own abysmal ignorance regarding any such points where knowledge is concerned—"How excessively stupid in me not to have seen it sooner!" (IV:465)—Hawthorne is forced to depend upon his characters with a faith no less suspect than that with which he would invest the very character of the Real, and in whose name he would now address the circuitous character of the Imaginary (character) itself. Dis-placing Hawthorne—"the Subject who is Supposed to Know"[82]—it thus befalls Kenyon to stick it to the Gentle Reader for whom this issue constitutes the only point: "I know, but may not tell," replies Kenyon: "On that point, at all events, there shall be not one word of explanation" (IV:467). Reduced to this exclusion, the Gentle Reader is left but one arena, one roost, it would seem, for sympathy. Identification resigns itSelf to the following form: "Poor Hawthorne!" For the moment, how-ever, let's not confuse the dark in which "Hawthorne" remains, in which he seems to be remaindered (dismembered), with the dark of the hen house from which he has barely escaped this tale: his tail is intact. Moreover, the point on which the Gentle Reader has now been skewered is not at all the point.

Let's bear in mind the beginning of this tale, the head of its tail, the very front of Donatello, the marble faun. Here everything would seem to be revealed: its only garment "falls half-way down his back, leaving the limbs and entire front of the figure nude" (IV:8). Thus, while the front is laid bare from the beginning of this tale, its end conceals the real tale—the tail at its end. We'd best be alerted to this frontal scene at the head of this tale lest we attack it from the rear. Let's keep a cool head here: there's something hanging there. But this is clearly not the point. Here we are compelled to admit to two points, regarding which Miriam assures Donatello, "your tender point—your two tender points, if you have them—shall be safe, so far as I am concerned" (IV:12–13). However, those Gentle Readers who have managed to stay awake to this point (I remind you of Phoebe's "remarkable drowsiness" in *The House*, "wholly unlike that with which the reader possibly feels himself affected [II:211]) can rest assured that Donatello's two ears are themselves but one point regarding a point which is itself divided into two. The two points upon which Donatello's secret depends entail not only the secret of his ears, but also that of his tail. And that points to the significant question at the end of this tale: does Donatello have a tail; does Donatello's tale have a tail—or, better, *can* it end? This possibility of its being-able-to-end depends entirely upon its "time": the tail is that upon which everything depends. We are inveterately deceived should we, for a moment, believe the tail depends upon—that is, hangs from—the body. The body, rather, the very body of this tale depends upon its tail.

To hell with the ears; they merely pose the "riddle" of the phallus—although I see no logical reason to exclude them as its possible site. After all, if one can find it in the nose, why not the ears? There must be something there (a woman's shape?)—something, perhaps, to do with all its "folds." We hear its labial lament in keys of major and minor, its scopic reverberations in Shakespeare's *Lear* ("Look with thine ears") and Kierkegaard's *Irony* ("Speak that I might see you").[83] Van Gogh's obsession with the ear, moreover, recalls its phallic dimension.[84] Why else would he cut it off? Regarding its size, most prefer dainty. The Greeks, we are told, preferred them small: the smaller, the better. I hasten this ellipsis. Having scrambled these body parts (ears/penis), I'd best cook up this omelette while it's firm. Or, to scramble my metaphor at the expense of reason, a madman's cuisine (Brillat-Savarin, forgive me), I'd better fold in the yoke at this point. The point is neither penis nor ear as such, but rather "folds"—regarding which our formula is equally simple: the more, the better. And here's the irony of the phallic soufflé(e): the smaller the penis—that is, the greater its number of folds—the larger it is when erect: its life to come. Nor can we hide this point: folds recall us to the ancient art of embalming, as Saul Steinberg suggests: "Folds embalm reality and thereby deify or sublimate it."[85] The phallus is, of course, the very fold of death, the cut, the incision of desire.

I would recall you to Miriam's studio (butcher shop: a.k.a. "return of the repressed": re-member "Ethan Brand"?), where one can hardly stand without encountering a plethora of mutilated and severed heads: "Jael, driving the nail through the temple of Sisera. It was dashed off with remarkable power"; "The head of Holofernes . . . screwing its eyes upward and twirling its features into a diabolical grin of triumphant malice, which it flung right at Judith's face. On her part, she had the startled aspect that might be conceived of a cook, if a calf's head should sneer at her, when about to be popt into the dinner-pot"; "the daughter of Herodias, receiving the head of John the Baptist in a charger. . . . Miriam had imparted to the Saint's face a look of gentle and heavenly reproach, with sad and blessed eyes fixed upward at the maiden; by the force of which miraculous glance, her whole womanhood was at once awakened to love and endless remorse" (IV:43–44). It is nothing less than this string of severed heads that Hilda "inherits" at the end of this tale—an epithalamium by means of which she is finally strung up: "a bracelet . . . composed of seven ancient Etruscan gems, dug out of seven sepulchres, and each one of them the signet of some princely personage" (IV:462). Narration strings together a series of (family) jewels (Romance) in light of whose princely (paternal) "shade" the Gentle Reader—hanging by its tail/tale—is now exhorted to substitute, for "sepulchral gems," "ghostly balls." For the moment, however, amid the carnage of Miriam's studio, there now appears the image of an object regarding which not only its head, but body as well, is absent—an image that echoes the "fold" of desire which *is* its very subject: "a drawing of an infant's shoe, half-worn out, with the airy print of the blessed foot within" (IV:45). I needn't echo this ghostly rem(a)inder: we may be speaking of further meat for the shop (studio). And by a most circuitous route, this missing infant's cries reverberate, in turn, another scene, the belated image of a peasant's shoe beside which, severed from its head, a painter's ear has fallen—folded in silence.

Lest we stray too far, we'd best return to the matter at hand, the statue of the faun. To quote Saul Steinberg, "classical painters, educated by statues, endow their male figures with undersized phalluses, and this causes confusion in girls educated by museums."[86] Regarding its frontal view, the faun's exposure would appear to be its very exposition. Yet, while the Gentle Reader may linger over this sight/site/cite (its sole commitment to re-reading), let's not jump to conclusions. You will forgive me, but this is not a phallus (it may be a pipe). From the front it should be clear: the penis is an appendage: it is, in effect, that is, after the fact, his tail/tale. For the moment, it just hangs there. The same might be said of the head of any tale; it depends, for its very life, upon the end. The voyeur, moreover, who lingers before this scene, will see nothing whatsoever—will be compelled to peek around the back to find the answer to his phantasy. Unlike the Gentle Reader, who cannot get off this page, he has already skipped to the end.

But this too misses the mark. The question is about the point of this tale, its end, its time. I've already suggested that its name is always already inscribed elsewhere, that the marble faun, "Donatello," is but another name for "Pearl." Better yet, the shape of Pearl trans-figured in/as/by the scarlet letter (itSelf the site/cite of both object and text) transforms the very place we would expect to see appear the body of Donatello. When Donatello approaches Miriam in the Capitoline Museum, the narrator observes: "So full of animal life as he was . . . so handsome, so physically well-developed, he made no impression of incompleteness, of maimed or stinted nature. . . . these familiar friends of his . . . instinctively allowed for him, as for a child or some other lawless thing, exacting no strict obedience to conventional rules. . . . There was an indefinable characteristic about Donatello, that set him outside of rules" (IV:14). This scene symmetrically mirrors an earlier one, the reader's introduction to Pearl: "By its perfect shape, its vigor, and its natural dexterity . . . the infant was worthy to have been brought forth in Eden . . . to be the plaything of the angels"; and like Donatello, "The child could not be made amenable to rules" (I:90–91). In their reflection of—their perfect coincidence with—the letter and faun, respectively, both Pearl and Donatello mirror an originary, unified being, a being identical to itself, a whole, an origin. If Pearl requires the name of the Father to come into her own, Donatello likewise re-enacts this scene, yet at a further remove: the level of the Phallus. His story both subjects him to itSelf and yet objects to this intolerable subjectification. Upon this very point, his story introduces the object of desire as other than its own: "I did what your eyes bade me do, when I asked them with mine, as I held the wretch over the precipice" (IV:172). In this regard, the primal scene reflects the otherness of itSelf. The other, here, is not a subject but a site: the scene of the crime—a murder. It is the birth of the time of this tale, that which bears the mark of the signifier. Here, too, the signifier is destined "to be" wherever and only where it is read. The subject itSelf emerges at the cite of this reading, and henceforth carries with it the mortal wound of the grave, the hole of its being to which it has always already arrived. Hawthorne's letter (Pearl), Lacan's letter (Poe), Derrida's letter (Lacan): they are the same: a letter always arrives (can always not arrive) at its destination.

While Hawthorne's *Letter* repeats this scene as the site of the Father (the Law), the letter itSelf has yet to return. *The Faun* recites this circuit once again, enacts this interpretive infelicity as its very felicity. Hawthorne's myth of the fall removes us to the site of the Phallus (the Law of the Law), that textual citation wherein the signifier ("Donatello") emerges to its (k)not: the tail of its tale, the not of its being whereby it's able to knot the story of itSelf, the story of its not, its demise, its *dénouement*. Hawthorne's "fortunate fall" recites (the fall of) the signifier as (the very scene of) the crime by means of which the subject is bequeathed the scenario of itSelf, its essential freedom. And let's make no mistake: it's freedom that's at stake, at issue, in this hen house of Gentle Readers.

It's not for nothing that Hawthorne's preface mirrors this problematic, and does so with a crow (hen) to pluck. His feigned despair at finding a Gentle Reader for *The Faun*—"If I find him at all, it will probably be under some mossy grave-stone, inscribed with a half-obliterated name, which I shall never recognize" (IV:2)—seems imbricated amid the same topography whence the romance itself originates—the very city (Rome) of "headless . . . torsos, and busts that have invariably lost . . . the nose" (IV:37)—since both "need Ruin to make them grow" (IV:3). In both instances, the nature of the origin suggests that "once upon a time" there existed a unitary whole to which the trace ("half-obliterated name"/"Ruin") testifies. The archaeology of Rome, however, unearths the part (ruin) as greater than the whole. Where nothing but (body) parts remain, narration forecloses both orgin and end. Around these objects of the partial drive, desire must fabricate (condense) a story whose knots conceal the (w)hole with which it is riddled. For "even the most ordinary life is full of events that never explain themselves, either as regards their origin or their tendency" (IV:455). Here everything turns on its head, the locus of displacement, its mislaid desire. While nature may appear as whole (One), the fullness of the in-itself, it too "falls" into the very crack of the ruin it seems to (ful)fill. Thus, for instance, in the place we would expect to see appear the presence of Miriam's fountain, its site/sight (representation) but speaks the locus of absence: "the patches of moss, the tufts of grass, the trailing maiden-hair, and all sorts of verdant weed that thrive in the cracks and crevices of moist marble, tell us that Nature takes the fountain back into her great heart" (IV:38). Instead of "heart," read (its) "lips": the Gentle Reader is invited to read these lips, between whose crack Nature will "take in" (to its fold) the very (crack of the) ruin (of) itself. Its heart (desire) is where its head is (missing).

In (the) place of the whole, the One, the Gentle Reader will assume this position (the site of that Idea(l) with which it identifies) at whose expense *(jouissance)* the text will plug its hole. As with the statue unearthed by Kenyon—"I seek for Hilda, and find a marble woman" (IV:423)—the text would seem to do the work of restoration:

> The head was gone; both arms were broken off at the elbows. Protruding from the loose earth, however, Kenyon beheld the fingers of a marble hand . . . still appended to its arm. . . . Placing these limbs in what the nice adjustment of the fractures proved to be their true position, the poor, fragmentary woman forthwith showed that she retained her modest instincts to the last. . . .
>
> In a corner of the excavation, lay a small, round block of stone. . . . the sculptor lifted it . . . brushed off the clinging soil, and finally placed it on the slender neck of the newly discovered statue. The effect was magical. It immediately lighted up and vivified the whole figure, endowing it with personality, soul, and intelligence. (IV:423)

In reality, however, this whole is mere illusion, the unity of a reflected ideal. Precisely where it finds itself (identical to itself), the mirror will crack—as does the Gentle Reader, whose very image this statue reflects, virginal to the end: "The beautiful Idea at once asserted its immortality, and converted that heap of forlorn fragments into a whole, as perfect to the mind, if not to the eye, as when the new marble gleamed with snowy lustre; nor was the impression marred by the earth that still hung upon the exquisitely graceful limbs, and even filled the lovely crevice of the lips" (IV:423–24). Between this crevice (abyss), the Gentle Reader eats dirt.

While in the preface, its pre-text, the author is missing (lacks) its corresponding "other" (The Gentle Reader), so too the text is missing its originary reality and "demands" (to use Lacan's terminology) an imaginary substitute as the locus of its desire—"a sort of poetic or fairy precinct" (IV:3). The text itself *(The Marble Faun)* does nothing whatsoever to restore this absent unity; indeed, its initial and final meaning are perpetually deferred—that is, consigned to the symbolic register and therefore closed off to unequivocal significance: to which the obsessive imagery of fragmentation again bears witness. At the conclusion, its narrative ghost ("Author"/"Hawthorne") admonishes the Gentle Reader regarding the lure of such a phantasy:

The Gentle Reader, we trust, would not thank us for one of those minute elucidations, which are so tedious, and, after all, so unsatisfactory, in clearing up the romantic mysteries of a story. He is too wise to insist upon looking closely at the wrong side of the tapestry, after the right one has been sufficiently displayed to him, woven with the best of the artist's skill, and *cunningly* arranged with a view to the harmonious exhibition of its colours. If any brilliant or beautiful, or even tolerable, effect have been produced, this pattern of kindly Readers will accept it at its worth, without tearing the web apart, with the idle purpose of discovering how its threads have been knit together; for the sagacity, by which he is distinguished, will long ago have taught him that any narrative of human action and adventure—whether we call it history or romance—is certain to be a fragile handiwork, more easily rent than mended. (IV:455, italics mine)

"Cunningly arranged," indeed: we here stand witness to the tangled skein, the disarray, (dis)cord, mishmash, botch, farrago, hodgepodge, imbroglio, dishevelment, litter, what the cat brought in (hens), *disjecta membra*—the very love knot, nuptial knot, Gordian knot—from which the Gentle Reader is strung (up) by its pubic hair.

Like the Monte Beni frescoes—the genealogy of "Sunshine"— linked together by allegorical "threads" impossible, "or, at least, very wearisome to unravel" (IV:227), narration (Romance) is similarly fated to conjecture and fragmentation: "In weaving these mystic utterances into a continuous scene, we undertake a task resembling, in its perplexity, that of gathering up and piecing together the fragments of a letter, which has been torn and scattered to the winds. Many words of deep significance— many entire sentences, and those possibly the most important ones— have flown too far, on the winged breeze, to be recovered. If we insert our own conjectural amendments, we perhaps give a purport utterly at variance with the true one" (IV:93). As Donatello (signifier) must fall if he is ever to mean, so too must the narration. Chapter XI, "Fragmentary Sentences," thematizes this event. The "weave" of any text is but a tapestry of fragments, "threads," which seem to constitute a whole, but whose structure, at bottom, more nearly resembles "a heap of worthless fragments" (IV:424)—the very ghost of another scene, that Pearl-Diver, who "got entangled in the weeds at the bottom of the sea, and lay dead among the pearl-oysters."

Like Rome, narration falls in(to) ruin. In order to mean, it must (re)collect these ghostly ruins, repeat the scene of its absence to itSelf. For what is ruin if not the inscription of time, its bodily remains, the signature of death? *The Faun* has memorized the narrative suggestion in *The House* to "sport with the idea" of ghosts (II:279). Similarly, Dryden remarks the "spectral figure" (IV:432) of Miriam's Model as that which generates the very narration of *The Faun*, "for it is his 'death' that is the enabling energy of 'the Romance of Monte Beni.' "[87] Narration but represents that duplicitous or "doubled" inscription of the absence of its "subject" (matter) to itself, the absence of the subject to itSelf. In this respect, it more closely resembles those artificial ruins so artfully scattered about "The Suburban Villa," the ghost of a ghost: "What a strange idea—what a needless labour—to construct artificial ruins in Rome, the natural soil of Ruin! But even these sportive imitations, wrought by man in emulation of what Time has done to temples and palaces, are perhaps centuries old, and, beginning as illusions, have grown to be venerable in sober earnest" (IV:73). These inscriptions belong more genuinely to the past the further they extend toward the future. Narration likewise recollects forward the past as future, repeats an absence as the sight of its future, its future site (death). Over and against the scene of *The Faun*, which sets its sights on the fullness of the image (the presence of the object), the very past of Rome reflects the specular nature of its present, the presence of its present as spectral, imaginary, doubled, a (k)not, a ghost story. The meaning of *The Letter*—"gathering up and piecing together the fragments of a letter"—has always already been posted to this site, disseminated, "scattered to the winds." Like those sugar-plums dispersed among the crowd at Carnival, concocted with a "worthless kernel in the midst" (IV:439), a *kern* of nonsense inhabits the very heart of sense, the fabric of meaning, as that around which narration weaves its web— the tapestry of the text.[88] And if it looks as though the scene of *The Faun* erases its scenario, it is because that scene (ancient Rome) is itself a scenario.

The story of *The Faun* repeats the past of Rome (its ruin) as *the* scene (primal) that sees before (in front of) itself (that sees ahead of itself before it sees itSelf) in *(the)* place of fullness only absence—that sees *(in fact)* nothing. This is its very content. *The Letter* inaugurates that problematic of interpretation in terms of which *The Faun* concludes: meaning is in(con)clusive, the inclusion of (being "with"/"con") others, Other than itSelf. Thus Hilda's response to Kenyon's interpretation—"I will not accept your moral"—provokes, in turn, yet a further response from the sculptor: "Then, here is another; take your choice" (IV:460). In its contingency, meaning includes, by necessity, other versions. It "lies" at the point on which an axis of ruin ("history") intersects an axis of (re)construction ("fiction"). Interpretation gathers this conflation as its own dispersion. No less than *The Letter*, the meaning of *The Faun* depends upon this intersection, the knot by means of which the reader will knit or fabricate its threads.

Make no mistake, it's knitting itself that's at stake in this (hen)house of fiction. The (art) work has always already "wrought itself out, and come fairly to an end" (IV:124) around this issue.

> There is something extremely pleasant, and even touching . . . in this pecu-liarity of needlework, distinguishing women from men. Our own sex is incapable of any such by-play, aside from the main business of life; but women . . . have always some little handiwork ready to fill the tiny gap of every vacant moment. A needle is familiar to the fingers of them all. . . . The slender thread of silk or cotton keeps them united with the small, familiar, gentle interests of life. . . . A vast deal of human sympathy runs along this electric line . . . especially as they are never more at home with their own hearts than while so occupied. (IV:39–40)

What—after all—is the "history" of Miriam if not the (missing) "story" of Pearl in Europe: the woven "fragments of a letter" *(The Letter)?* The needle will knot the (short) circuit of this return. Precisely at this point, where Hester picks up her needle, Miriam will let it drop: "And when the work falls in a woman's lap, of its own accord, and the needle involun-tarily ceases to fly, it is a sign of trouble" (IV:40). The scenario will unknot itself here for the sake of which Miriam must substitute paint brush for needle in order to sever those heads whose tale (the very content of her paintings) prefigures the tail of this story. Similarly, re-garding the masquerade of the Carnival, in whose anonymity the revelers would seem to be One—"bear-headed, bull-headed, and dog-headed individuals" (IV:446)—we would be well advised to read, instead, "be-headed." Here, everything is lopped off.

The art work represents the act of representation (narration) in its abysmal de-sign: for if it is to knot the tail of its tale, the head must have been severed (missing) from the beginning—and this is what, like Miriam's needle, falls into its lap at the end. Thus everything comes undone. We have already been cautioned by Miriam. Speaking *to*—that is, *of* (the story of)—Donatello, whose resemblance to Praxiteles' Faun contains within "itSelf" the very phantasy of representation (identity), Miriam portends the way in which the image must always and every-where escape its capture: "If I can catch you on my canvas, it will be a glorious picture; only I am afraid you will dance out of it, by the very truth of the representation, just when I shall have given it the last touch" (IV:47). Narration enacts the mirror in which identity imagines itSelf (identical to itself) and thereby escapes itSelf. Its semblance as a whole (One) dissembles the hole of its fabrication, the void around which it re(a)sembles (knots) the path (line) by whose circuitous route it will unravel. The heart or "kern" of Romance (story) conceals a "dead" line (history), an "out" line (ruin), the ghost (of a ghost), just as the skeleton of Rome (its ruin) contains within itself the ruins of human ruin (skeletons).[89] Here death inhabits the very heart of the "Eternal City." *The Faun* recites this scene as that scenario which "takes place" between two sites: while Donatello will dance out of his picture at the end, the Model has already "stept out of a picture" (IV:19) from the beginning. In the "mean" time, the story *(récit)* of the faun will "occupy" that place in whose very name ("Rome") this Romance will unravel itself—that is, come into its own, its demise, its ruination.

To this effect, the tail of (the tale of) *The Faun* dis-places that view by means of which the Gentle Reader and Author are One. For now the One (who is supposed to know) itself defenestrates the view, steps out of the picture, beyond the frame of the *récit,* beyond the body of this tale, in order to hang itSelf at the end, to hang itSelf outside the tale as its tail, an appendage—its postscript, a post crypt *to which* it now re-signs itself (a dead letter, a block-head, a dummy), *in which* it now consigns itself to the margin of this text (the One who doesn't know), and in whose absence the Gentle Reader, if it is ever to be One, to know, is subsequently compelled to identify with the Imaginary (a character) itself, Kenyon, who tells us (1) that he knows, and (2) that he will not tell us what he knows. "On that point, at all events, there shall be not one word of explanation." This withheld secret but marks the place of containment ("hysteria") to which the Gentle Reader has always already been dispatched, and in whose very structure (identification) it betrays itSelf ("if only *you* had told *me:* I can keep a secret").[90] *The Faun* entrusts this secret to its (post) crypt, its very "shrine" (a container for books or papers). So too the text enshrines (inters) itSelf in the Pantheon at its end (in The End): the temple of "A̲rtists," the tomb of "A̲uthors." Such is the scenario to which the identity of the Gentle Reader has been appended from the head of this tale. For with the disappearance (death) of the author, the Gentle Reader likewise loses its head.

Out of its mind from the beginning, the disembodied head of this tale (Hawthorne's preface) consigns the Gentle Reader, this Ideal "other," to the grave, "to the Paradise of Gentle Readers"; it is, in any case, "extremely short-lived" (IV:2). In returning, it does so as a ghost ("under some mossy grave-stone"), a dead letter ("inscribed with a half-obliterated name"), and from some point in time so prior that the author, the name "Hawthorne," can be only the belated image of itSelf—"I cannot precisely remember the epoch" (IV:2, 1). This epoch is, of course, the very scene of its own decapitation: The (Custom) House of *The Letter.*

And while he "never personally encountered, nor corresponded through the Post, with this Representative Essence of all delightful and desirable qualities which a reader can possess" (IV:1), Hawthorne's *Letter*—or, better, Pearl, "the scarlet letter in another form; the scarlet letter endowed with life," its "living hieroglyphic" (I:102, 207)—has nevertheless been posted: to Europe no less. And in its own circuitous (discontinuous) time, it now returns to haunt him. Prefiguring Lacan's purloined letter from (to) Poe, Hawthorne (A)luringly remarks, "Unquestionably, this Gentle, Kind, Benevolent, Indulgent, and most Beloved and Honoured Reader, did once exist for me, and (in spite of the infinite chances against a letter's reaching its destination, without a definite address) duly received the scrolls which I flung upon whatever wind was blowing" (IV:2). The letter, here, recites the function of the signifier which, against all odds, arrives, in fact, at its destination. Its destination, moreover, repeats that circuit of subjectivity by means of whose whence and whither the Gentle Reader—belonging to that "Golden Age, before mankind was burthened with sin and sorrow" (IV:84)—has always already been "ruined," withdrawn to "the Paradise of Gentle Readers," since, for "Golden Age," we might just as well read "imaginary"/"phantasm"/ "origin"/"primal scene." "The Custom-House" already prefigures this phantasy: "Some authors . . . indulge themselves in such confidential depths of revelation as could fittingly be addressed, only and exclusively, to the one heart and mind of perfect sympathy; as if the printed book, thrown at large on the wide world, were certain to find out the divided segment of the writer's own nature, and complete his circle of existence by bringing him into communion with it. It is scarcely decorous, however, to speak all, even where we speak impersonally" (I:3–4). Such "communion" cannibalizes those writers "who serve up their own hearts delicately fried, with brain-sauce, as a tidbit for their beloved public" (X:33)—to which the Gentle Reader graciously consents: "it's good to eat meat that talked with us."

If "Hawthorne" skirted this issue in the youthful days of *The Letter*, he now (un)dresses these chickens with a *coup (de grâce)* regarding which this flirtation, this courtship, this seduction is cut off—regarding which the Gentle Reader is itSelf (vis-à-vis) disregarded, taken from behind, stuffed from the rear. Thus he finally lays (to rest) this illusion, the Gentle Reader's delusion of itself as one "whose apprehensive sympathy has so often encouraged me to be egotistical in my Prefaces" (IV:2)—that is, as the One whose plenary identification with the Author thereby guarantees its being (identical to) itSelf. Hawthorne will inter this presumptuous familiarity, dispatch this "familiar," dispose of this ghostly double once and for all with but a single gesture of formality. Here, night falls like a curtain: "I stand upon ceremony, now, and, after stating a few particulars about the work which is here offered to the Public, must make my most reverential bow, and retire behind the curtain" (IV:2). Amid their cackling, however, the hens will never hear this swan song.

If in *The Letter* the ghost of the letter returns to life in Pearl, she is, in turn, the very ghost of *The Faun* (text)/the faun (Donatello), its final destination. The forest scene secures this scenario in advance: the forest, and all those "wild things which it nourished, all recognized a kindred wildness in the human child"; "A wolf, it is said,—but here the tale has surely lapsed into the improbable,—came up, and smelt of Pearl's robe, and offered his savage head to be patted by her hand" (I:205, 204). Rest assured that at the tail of this tale, at its end—as at the end of this "tight shot"—the cite has shifted: beyond this hand, at the end of its arm, appears the body of Donatello, "like a wolf that meets you in the forest" (IV:229). The image of the wolf, here, turns on its head: its tale (scenario) has changed; yet once again the scene remains the same: "The animal nature, indeed, is a most essential part of the Faun's composition; for the characteristics of the brute creation meet and combine with those of humanity." "Neither man nor animal," the faun is thus "a being in whom both races meet, on friendly ground" (IV:9, 10). Regarding the *récit* of this myth, moreover, "the idea may have been no dream, but rather a poet's reminiscence of a period when man's affinity with Nature was more strict, and his fellowship with every living thing more intimate and dear" (IV:10–11). If the faun thus seems to "mediate" this scene, patting the head of the wolf while shaking the hand of the human, it's but illusion once again, the delusion of a sight, the site of unified being—that is, being as a whole. As for the wolf: it too has been transfigured by this text, yet still remains the self-same scene. Transformed to she-wolf—the mother of Romulus and Remus—the riddle bears the mark of its insistence: who is the Father? The name is "Rome." The scene would seem to have changed. It hasn't. It but further reverberates the etymological space of the origin of this "Romance," of the name of the Father's ("Hawthorne's") own *jouissance* beyond instinct, beyond orgasm, beyond life itself—where a plethora, a veritable fullness, of objects, "antique, pictorial, and statuesque . . . fill the mind, everywhere in Italy, and especially in Rome, and cannot easily be kept from flowing out upon the page, when one writes freely, and with self-enjoyment" (IV:3). Forget "easily": *cannot*—that is to say, *will not*—be kept from flowing out. Hawthorne, my dear, you've messed up yet another page! We're in the realm of the Real; for what else is this register if not the full coincidence of the object with itself—the very thing-in-itself, a being outside, without desire?

Over and against these objects, Hawthorne observes: "Italy, as the site of his Romance, was chiefly valuable . . . as affording a sort of poetic or fairy precinct, where actualities would not be so terribly insisted upon" (IV:3). The question of the Father inhabits this precinct, despite all appearance to the contrary, and intersects the origin at that most simple, discontinuous space (0, 1) of the Freudian *fort-da,* where the ghosts of authority and paternity return to be revised; where Hawthorne's Romance, sited in Rome, needs—that is, desires—Ruin to make it grow; where its art works "have been dug up out of the deep grave in which old Rome lies buried" (IV:17); where their resus-citation recalls us to those stolen art works (Akers, Story, Rogers, Hosmer), now returned, "restored," to their "proper" owners, their proper names—a theft Promethean in its risk, and one that gathers the Prometheus Complex,[91] the issue of authority, within the self-same register as the Oedipal, the issue of paternity; where the issue of Donatello is itself the issue: what's at stake here is a dead line.

And this returns us to the head of the tale of Donatello: his own identity. Let's get it straight up front. His resemblance to the marble faun is so uncanny that Kenyon remarks the two to be identical. It nearly seems he *is* the faun which the marble faun of Praxiteles represents (which the bust by Kenyon represents) (which *The Marble Faun* of Hawthorne represents . . .). As things stand, or—in this case—fall, Donatello is but the ghost (of a ghost) (of a ghost . . .). The paradox of being, it would seem, must come to nothing less than this: he must fall if he is ever to get it up. Yet prior to the scene of the crime itself, another scene has layed the way, way-laid by a ghostly apparition, another murder, where death has always already taken up its place in the end, the tail of this tale, and done so from the beginning. Just as Miriam reaches to reveal the ears of Donatello in the Capitoline Museum—to know the point(s), missing the mark as usual—Donatello himself entreats her: "take the tips of my ears for granted"; and even as he speaks, "the young Italian made a skip and jump, light enough for a veritable Faun; so as to place himself quite beyond the reach of the fair hand that was outstretched. . . . 'I shall be like a wolf of the Apennines,' he continued, taking his stand on the other side of the Dying Gladiator, 'if you touch my ears ever so softly'" (IV:12). Note well the spatial arrangement of this scene, where Donatello now lines up opposite the Faun, aligns himself over and against it, in (the) place of the wolf, a line now intersected by an axis whose origin recites the scene of death, the Dying Gladiator, as its source. The site of this ghostly dilemma, this abyss, this ch(I)asm (self-other), this double-cross(ing), recuperates that original scene—wherein Kenyon would equate the two, Faun and Donatello, as One—and alters the scenario at once. It happens as no coincidence that this vector now points from the Faun (Nature) through death toward Donatello, the Faun tranformed to Wolf (Civilization), and in whose name will be enacted the very birth of (human) existence. Here Donatello but echoes an earlier birth: Pearl, the birth of language.

Let me make it simple. I'm speaking of two primal scenes: (1) the romance called *The Marble Faun,* and (2) that configuration of Romances called "Hawthorne"—the "family romance," if you will. Regarding the first, its narration recovers, by way of inversion, the literal as the figural, the object as the subject, the signified (that absolute coincidence of Nature and Civilization) as the signifier (subjectivity, Donatello), the whole of being as a hole; it recollects forward the history (genealogy) of the faun as the very time of its future: in this, it will have the time of its life.[92] Regarding the second, that configuration of Romances called "Hawthorne," *The Faun* recites *The Letter,* recuperates—indeed, reverses—the circuit, the very circuit of the letter, the tail of the tale of the return of the repressed. And this is the point of the (counter)transference, for which the Gentle Reader has served its final purpose, and regarding which it may, at last, be dismissed—having paid, I might add, by way of inversion once again, its final debt to the analysand ("Hawthorne") for its discourse, and having paid it up the nose, the ears, wherever you desire to place it. Having posted *The Letter* (his original Romance) to Europe in the trans-figured shape of Pearl, he now returns *The Faun* (his final Romance) to America in the trans-figured shape of Donatello. Having posted America's past, its history, to Europe, he now returns Europe's past, its history, to America—and as its very own: the history of itself, but in reverse form. There is always this reversal of effect: now Europe's past, the past of Western civilization, arises out of America's future: Europe—or, better, "Rome"—is as it always was, a dead letter. Having posted *The Letter,* the story of the origin of myth, he now returns *The Faun,* the story of the myth of origin. They are, however, the same. Having posted *The Letter,* the story of language, he now returns *The Faun,* the story of being (subjectivity). They are, however, the same: the self-same scene. Only now, the scenario has been changed to protect the guilty: those guilty for being. And this is always the case where the transference succeeds; cause and effect become blurred.[93]

Is *The Faun* the effect of *The Letter;* or is it the cause? They are the same: the myth of origin is the origin of myth.[94] So too with being (subjectivity) and language. Cause and effect are displaced, doubled, in that short-circuit called "Hawthorne" which I've laid bare in order to exhume its skeleton. This is the reversible gestalt of chicken/egg I held before you as a carrot at the outset of this fairy tale, this family romance—or, to further mix the metaphor—this Easter egg I've laid before you in order to resurrect what will be, always and everywhere, nothing less than a mythic causality. If genealogy demands the father as the Law (a line of descent, the whole history), narration (Romance) demands the phallus as the Law of the Law (a knot of dissent, the [hi]story riddled with holes, the fiction of the subject itSelf). There's more than one rooster in this hen house. No, there's less than One: it's hen-pecked from the start. This is the very "kernel" on which the hens will choke: the history of fiction is the fiction of history, the story of a subject that *can* not beget itSelf/*cannot* (not) beget itSelf. To phrase Lukacher paraphrasing Althusser: "there is no subject to the primal scene; it is the primal scene itself which is a subject insofar as it does not have a subject."[95] Its scenario must, in effect, be scrambled—so much, that the question of the egg always already betrays the question of the chicken, the layer: a mixed up tale, this yoke (zeugma), this *hommelette,*[96] this tail upon which is appended the head (the subject itSelf). Nietzsche observed as much: the subject is not a given; it's added to—stuck onto—the tail.[97] Here layer and laid are one and the same, the very self-same of an obverse image in whose name that configuration of Romances called "Hawthorne" so rapaciously delights to stick it: that illusion (delusion—paranoid, by definition) of the Gentle Reader who can be nothing more or less than itSelf.

Epilogue

○

The structure of *The Letter* conceals another design beneath the tripartite foundation of its scaffold scenes, one which underpins the entire oeuvre and functions on a level closely approaching that of an obsession. For throughout Hawthorne's work, a single theme persistently surfaces—that of the journey and return (of the repressed). It is the theme of repetition (itSelf): "You are aware, my dear Sir—you must have observed it, in your own existence—that all human progress is in a circle; or, to use a more accurate and beautiful figure, in an ascending spiral curve. While we fancy ourselves going straight forward, and attaining, at every step, an entirely new position of affairs, we do actually return to something long ago tried and abandoned. . . . The past is but a coarse and sensual prophecy of the present and the future" (II:259–60). Thus Dimmesdale returns to the spot from which he strayed seven years prior. So too, Coverdale enters the experiment at Blithedale only to return once again to the "world"; Goodman Brown journeys forth from the clearing at dusk and returns again at sunrise; the narrator of "The Celestial Rail-Road" re-enters the space of his dream only to dismiss it at the end with the "light" of reason whence it originated; the narrator of "The Procession of Life" comes back to his own situation—it is not time for death; Feathertop commences the world only to return to the lifeless heap from which he began; Roderick finds salvation in being restored to the love of Rosina, the wife whom he had originally deserted so many years past; the Christmas banquet returns to itself each year, terminated only with the death of Gervayse Hastings; Drowne's art reverts to its dull mechanical style after his brief interlude with the lady of the wooden image; Roger Malvin's curse is lifted only by Reuben's return to the site whence it was incurred; the narrator of "A Virtuoso's Collection" forsakes the illusive museum for the "real" world from which he entered; the Gray Champion disappears as suddenly as he appeared; the revellers at the may-pole disperse once again to the gloomy world forced upon them when driven from their classic groves of fable; the gentle boy, cast aside by his mother, is again reunited only to lose her in the end; Dr. Dolliver and his great granddaughter meet each other at the two extremities of life, her sunrise serving as his sunset; Ethan Brand returns to the place whence his quest for the Unpardonable Sin began; Wakefield comes home twenty years later to discover that the final joke is on him; David Swan interrupts his journey with a nap, only to return to the highway of life refreshed but unaware; Dr. Heidegger's guests become the shriveled victims of their age prior to the

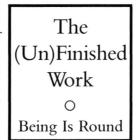

The
(Un)Finished
Work

○

Being Is Round

experiment; Robin returns from his labyrinthian sweep of the town to the ferryman who brought him hence; Nurse Toothaker returns to the bedside of the dying man who had originally disclaimed her; the wanderer of the "Night Sketches" returns to the fireside; the wives of the dead return to their beds; the Haunted Mind returns to its sleep. The list goes on. This obsession with circularity in Hawthorne, to come round again to the beginning, at once attests to both the roundness of his oeuvre and the inevitable end which it implies, for roundness ends wherever it begins. In the "mean" time, the circle transports the subject.

☐

Being is round.[1] Hawthorne's work was his life; and as his work, Hawthorne's life was round, for it came full circle and by a most uncanny, symmetrical route. "My journey, as thou callest it, forth and back again, must needs be done 'twixt now and sunrise" (X:74). Hawthorne's European travels were circular, and nearly perfectly so. For from the States (Wayside), he proceeded to England, France, and Italy; he returned from Italy, to France, then to England, and finally back to the States (Wayside). It is a curious fact, also, that the very same ship captain, a Captain Leitch, who took him over to England, brought him back again—and yet a more curious fact that Hawthorne's absence from home reflects the same amount of time that Dimmesdale avoided the pillory: seven years.

Like Dimmesdale, too, Hawthorne's natural bent betrayed his own personal tendencies toward introspection, what Melville called his "indoor cast of mind." As Harry Levin observes, "Where openness, expansion, and a hankering after infinitude are characteristic of his contemporaries, Hawthorne sticks to his secretiveness, and to the atmosphere of enclosure, the awareness of things closing in. The journey ends in a house and within a locked room, with the rediscovery of another self for whom it has all been a dream; he has never left home. But this does not mean that he has never adventured; for there can be cosmic adventure in introspection, as much as in exploration."[2] Torn between "without" and "within," public and private, Hawthorne's life, like his work, mirrors his struggle with the single-minded injunction: to be responsible for itSelf. How difficult it may have been, for example, for Hawthorne to underplay his gravitation toward Melville, and the exotic world this nomad offered, in the interest of his family and its commitments. Since he often confided to his journals those experiences which affected him most, the very absence of any detailed commentary on Melville bespeaks a world of supposition. Yet, Sophia's insistence upon reading everything he committed to paper accounts, at least in part, perhaps, for Hawthorne's reticence. He would keep many such secrets. And so the journey *(weg)* ends for Hawthorne—as in his fiction—where it had begun, within his indoor cast of mind. Its shadows return to haunt him.

In *Our Old Home,* he recuperates once more the disjunction between fact and fiction: "Facts, as we really find them, whatever poetry they may involve, are covered with a stony excrescence of prose, resembling the crust of a beautiful sea-shell, and they never show their most delicate and divinest colors, until we shall have dissolved away their grosser actualities by steeping them long in a powerful menstruum of thought. And, seeking to actualize them again, we do but renew the crust" (V:135–36). Here Hawthorne retrieves the distinction made earlier in *The Letter* between the actual and the imaginary. Regarding this dichotomy, Nina Baym remarks of *Our Old Home:* "Because the actual is material, it lacks meaning and has no relation to human needs and desires. Actualities are given meaning and brought into relation with feelings by the act of the imagination, which recreates the actual in conformity with human pressures. The actual itself, lacking the human dimension, is basically empty even though it may be dense and crowded with events: it is empty of meaning."[3] So, too, now, is Hawthorne's life: he is unable to sustain the imaginative demands of fiction. As he expressed it at the Wayside in 1863, less than a year before his death: "The Present, the Immediate, the Actual, has proved too potent for me" (V:4). Against the horizon of temporality, Hawthorne exposes his diminishing potential to create *(poiēsis).*

It therefore happens as no accident that, during his final years, his gaze is able to focus on the fact alone, whereas his fiction can but envision an image blurred time and again—the double of itself. In a letter to Fields, for instance, he supports the prefatory letter of *Our Old Home*—dedicated to Franklin Pierce—"despite the fact" that it might damage not only the sale of the book but also his very reputation:

> I find that it would be a piece of poltroonery in me to withdraw either the dedication or the dedicatory letter. My long and intimate personal relations with Pierce render the dedication altogether proper, especially as regards this book, which would have had no existence without his kindness; and if he is so exceedingly unpopular that his name is enough to sink the volume, there is so much the more need that an old friend should stand by him. I cannot, merely on account of pecuniary profit or literary reputation, go back from what I have deliberately felt and thought it right to do; and if I were to tear out the dedication, I should never look at the volume again without remorse and shame. As for the literary public, it must accept my book precisely as I think fit to give it, or let it alone. (V:xxvi)

Similarly, in "Chiefly about War Matters," Hawthorne displays a steadfast courage to "face the facts," to live up to the single-minded injunction, *in spite of the fact* that his position runs counter to the public sentiment of the

North; of John Brown, he remarks: "Nobody was ever more justly hanged" and "any common-sensible man, looking at the matter unsentimentally, must have felt a certain intellectual satisfaction in seeing him hanged, if it were only in requital of his preposterous miscalculation of possibilities."[4]

Hawthorne's determination to set forth the facts of his persuasion regarding matters public and "external"—so entirely against the grain of public opinion *(das Man)* that these personal expressions directed toward an audience of "dolts and mean-spirited scoundrels" (V:xxvi) endanger his very (literary) existence—suggests a correspondence with the unfinished fiction itself. If at the end of his life he could so rigidly focus his energy upon the *actual* events surrounding him, might we not read into this "failure" to temper his position the mark of another discourse entirely unspoken? With respect to the "Present" which so obsessively burdens him, might there not be lurking, beneath this rhetoric of certainty, an unassailable doubt—one, furthermore, which takes the form of a more general question: "What does it matter in the end?" Is this not, "in fact," the very heart of his complaint against John Brown—"his preposterous miscalculation of *possibilities?*" It is this actual which overpowers Hawthorne, now, at the close of his life, and which suggests the ultimate, abysmal *implosion* of his imagination: that "kingdom of possibilities." We need not attribute this implosion to external circumstances such as the Civil War, however, since his oeuvre had steadfastly exposed *this* possibility from the beginning: the meaningless void which inhabits the very heart of any and all significance. Although the issues of the war weighed heavily upon his consciousness, it is once again to the heart of existence, the world's inner space, that Hawthorne turns his gaze. If anything, his unfinished works expose, more than ever, the *kern* of non-sense central to meaning, and upon which being makes sense of itSelf.

In *The Ancestral Footstep,* for example, Hawthorne initially and repeatedly provokes this abyss: "I spoke to you of a strange family-story, of which there was no denouement, such as a novel-writer would desire, and which had remained in that unfinished posture for more than two hundred years" (XII:15); "I suppose . . . the settlers in my country may have carried away with them traditions, long since forgotten in this country . . . but which now, only the two insulated parts of the story being known, remain a riddle, although the solution of it is actually in the world; if only those two parts could be united across the sea, like the wires of an electric telegraph" (XII:5–6); "English secrets might find their solution in America, if the two threads of a story could be brought together" (XII:15); "So here was Middleton, now at length seeing indistinctly a thread, to which the thread that he had so long held in his hand—the hereditary thread, that ancestor after ancestor had handed down—might seem ready to join in. He felt as if they were the two points of an electric chain, which being joined, an instantaneous effect must follow" (XII:8). Yet nothing will come of it; the knot of this line cannot be secured; the past can no longer be given a future—history no longer turned to story; the doubt extends beyond it: "The tradition had lost, *if it ever had,* some of its connecting links" (XII:10, italics mine). Around this (k)not of being, Hawthorne recuperates the black, impenetrable void of the "Night Sketches" in order to write himself off. He is no longer able to author-ize meaning. His aspirations in "The Custom-House"—"At some future day, it may be, I shall remember a few scattered fragments and broken paragraphs, and write them down, and find the letters turn to gold upon the page" (I:37)— have now expired. The "trace" or sign no longer even holds within it *the possibility of significance:* there is but resignation that the foot will never "fit that bloody footmark left of old upon the threshold" (XII:13). As he expressed his impotence to write *The Dolliver Romance:* "I linger at the threshold, and have a perception of very disagreeable phantoms to be encountered, if I enter" (XIII:574). The threshold upon which he lingers is, of course, the very threshold of death itself.[5]

The unfinished manuscripts stare vacantly into the void of these meaningless phantoms unable to secure the fictive knot which would seduce these "ghosts" to life. Here everything comes undone. If in *The American Claimant Manuscripts* the legendary bloody footprint "exists only as a rust-colored stain," the silver key "unlocks only a coffin, containing nothing of any use," and the novel in general "is filled with ominous but empty symbols," so too the hair-filled coffin in *Dr. Grimshawe's Secret* and the residue of dust in *The Ancestral Footstep* convey the same message: "there is no gold, no jewel; there is only evidence of mortality."[6] These works now purely and simply inhabit the abyss. Hawthorne has returned the world of his work to the borderland or boundary—the very limit—of the hypnagogic image: the Haunted Mind retrieves its ground in sleep. Between the actual and the imaginary, the fact and the fiction, *there is no* longer "A" *difference,* as Hawthorne remarked of the Civil War itself—that "hurricane that is sweeping us all along with it, possibly, into a Limbo where our nation and its polity may be as literally the fragments of a shattered dream as my unwritten Romance" (V:4). The fragments of a shattered dream: what once suggested a world, transcending the radical contour of incompletion, has now become the black, impenetrable (w)hole. The kingdom of possibilities has become the impossibility of meaning, the ghost or skeleton of what was once a house, a dead letter office. Where once he had suggested that "all that is higher and holiest in this life depend on death and the expectation of it" (XIII:511), his (un)final revisions of *Septimius Norton* bear no such possibility: death now constitutes nothing more or less than an empty sign, "a token of that contemptuous kindness . . . which Nature shows, . . . the last sensation of the body, . . . a thrill of the very highest rapture" (XIII:246).

In his final years, he could no longer sustain the thrust of that forward recollection, the kingdom of possibilities, which grounded the world of his work. As his final fragmentary pieces confirm, the issue most at stake had become the void itself. The fragmented consciousness of *Dr. Grimshawe's Secret* and the obsession with the impossibility of meaning in both *Septimius Felton* and *The Dolliver Romance* testify to the "untimely" consciousness with which Hawthorne quitted the world. The concerns of the haunted mind had become his only ones; he grew especially weary of the feeling that he had been here before—the *déjà vu* of going through the same (e)motions meaninglessly: as writers repeat their plots, thus man's life repeats itself, and at length grows stale.[7] Like the dream-scape of *Dr. Grimshawe's Secret,* in the end everything was comparable to a dream for Hawthorne, an unforgotten reality.[8] The "flight of time" in *Fanshawe* which characterizes Dr. Melmouth's study, that flight of time so "swift as the wind, and noiseless as the snow-flake . . . a sure proof of real happiness" (III:337), had run its course. Death was close, and he knew it. Yet it was no surprise; nor could he suddenly fear what had persistently inhabited the house of his entire oeuvre: "the only guest who is certain, at one time or another, to find his way into every human dwelling" (II:16).

Believing, or pretending to believe, that a change of air was his only hope for recovery, he determined upon a journey to the region of lakes and hills that had been his true native land all his life.[9] Having succumbed in those final barren years to the expectations and demands he had set upon himself throughout life, half-way between waking and dream, and unable to write, he summoned one last spurt of courage and set off, on 12 May 1864, with his dearest friend, Franklin Pierce, to die alone—far from the domestic complications of Sophia and his children. "Making their way up into the White Mountains, perhaps with the expectation of reaching Crawford Notch, the two friends stopped off at the little town of Plymouth. Hawthorne seemed to be having more and more difficulty in walking and using his hands. Was it paralysis or a heart attack? However, on the evening of May 18 he went off to sleep peacefully enough. Between three and four o'clock in the morning of the nineteenth, Pierce went into his friend's room, and upon touching him discovered that he was already cold. That was how Hawthorne died, . . . in the completest solitude, his last thoughts, his torments, his doubts, and the mystery of his genius locked up forever in his heart."[10] At the gravesite, *The Dolliver Romance* was placed upon his breast. His heart embraced in death what it could never complete in life.

☐

Being is round. The world is round around the round being.[11] Being is around the world. We come from nothing and return to nothing: from the darkness of the womb to the darkness of the tomb. In the "mean" time, the subject transports its center, side-steps its tracks.[12] It encircles the void of its center—its central void—as its own, embraces this void with its inscription, the inscription of temporality (being), the ripeness of its own time (non-being). The movement in Hawthorne's oeuvre, both in and toward the heart's interior, creates a safety for being itSelf, a security without care, a care-free *kern* which turns toward the open draught of being and into it. Beyond the objectification of being, here being itSelf reposes in the logic of the heart: being makes *sense* of nothing. This unguardedness, outside the protective defenses of the head, intimately secures the (w)hole of being within: being makes sense of *nothing*.

Dimmesdale secures a safety in (being responsible for) himSelf: "I am a dying man. So let me make haste to take my shame upon me" (I:254). His gesture lights up the void of being and makes it present in its widest orbit, wider by far than that of the comet, which illumines the night sky and yet conceals it. To Chillingworth, moreover, Dimmesdale now is hidden more than ever: "'Hadst thou sought the whole earth over,' said he, looking darkly at the clergyman, 'there was no one place so secret,—no high place nor lowly place, where thou couldst have escaped me,—save on this very scaffold'" (I:253). Under rational analysis the gesture of the heart has already taken flight. It is gone: "'Thou hast escaped me!' he repeated more than once. 'Thou hast escaped me!'" (I:256). Being thus shatters every attempt to penetrate it, to lay it bare; it turns the calculating imposition back toward its destruction. Reciprocally, Dimmesdale acknowledges where being touches him most; his death becomes the constant. His death sets being on the way of its orbit once again: the Letter goes abroad. It too will "die." Yet while it is, it exceeds the calculation of reason, secures the inner surplus of itSelf, the interior of the heart.[13] Dimmesdale's exposition recalls the objectness of objects back into the space of the heart. It rescues the thing from objectness and rescues it for being. Dimmesdale's (con)version returns the Letter to the world, the path on which is traced its own diminishing return(s). It gives both object and subject back to one another in such a way that the (w)hole of being comes up and into its own within (the logic of) the heart.

In the saying of the inner recall, Dimmesdale exposes the mark of his

complicity. His exposition remarks this (re)turn, the roundness of its path
(weg). "Language is the precinct *(templum)*, that is, the house of Being."[14]
Dimmesdale accomplishes the return from voiceless subjection back to his
re-sponsibility only in this precinct, the exposition of being. The Letter
flees from its objectification, from its confinement, toward itSelf. By
opening inward, it opens out:

> People of New England! . . . I stand upon the spot where, seven years since, I
> should have stood. . . . Lo, the scarlet letter which Hester wears! Ye have all
> shuddered at it! Wherever her walk hath been . . . it hath cast a lurid gleam of
> awe and horrible repugnance roundabout her. But there stood one in the
> midst of you, at whose brand of sin and infamy ye have not shud-
> dered! . . . But he hid it cunningly from men, and walked among you with
> the mien of a spirit, mournful, because so pure in a sinful world!—and sad,
> because he missed his heavenly kindred! Now, at the death-hour, he stands up
> before you! He bids you look again at Hester's scarlet letter! He tells you, that,
> with all its mysterious horror, it is but the shadow of what he bears on his own
> breast, and that even this, his own red stigma, is no more than the type of
> what has seared his inmost heart. (I:254–55)

Dimmesdale's saying punctuates the silence of the crowd more piercingly
than even the meteor punctures the dark fissure of the night; it rends the
jagged edge of silence away from the void and back to the soundness of the
wor(l)d, the knot of existence, the story of being itSelf To this, the Letter
corresponds: "The multitude, silent till then, broke out in a strange, deep
voice of awe and wonder, which could not as yet find utterance, save in this
murmur that rolled so heavily after the departed spirit" (I:257). In itSelf,
this co-respondence exposes being to a (dai)logic that accomplishes the
con-version of the two realms (head and heart), the inversion of (their)
logic, "by circling through all beings, in-finitely unbounding them."[15]
Because the saying in-finitely unbounds all beings, it thus finitely binds
them to themSelves, and to themselves alone. Language thence encircles
in and through the crowd, bringing it before its own facticity, and at the
threshold of the temple as well—but only at the threshold: at best, it can
but murmur. And yet, there is a beginning; it begins to form the work of
language on its own, the gesture that returns the vision (of the head) to the
saying (of the heart). Dimmesdale's articulate utterance, on the other hand,
has come round to the temple full circle and back into it. It has already
pronounced the round sound itself and brought it to repose: being is
round.[16]

Dimmesdale's exposition recuperates the Letter for the (w)hole of
discourse. Out of the silence comes the sound. The silence and the spoken
come together; yet what is spoken is never, and in no language, what is

said.[17] The "A" becomes alphabet, becomes alpha, becomes beginning; and yet it is itself the end as well. It is beginning and end. It has already come round the full circle to itself. Dimmesdale's conversion occurs in the poetry of language, its figuration: the exposition of being. It is therefore uncommon; it is exceptional. In turning toward the freedom and openness of its finitude, it denies the customary imposition of the Oneself *(das Man)* in its everyday, eternal imposture of the "they." Dimmesdale's saying makes being safe, secure; it makes it sound. It is a saying that follows something to be said, a saying said solely in order to turn itSelf toward the world: "The more venturesome are those who say in a greater degree, in the manner of the singer. Their singing is turned away from all purposeful self-assertion. . . . Their song does not solicit anything to be produced. In the song, the world's inner space concedes space within itself."[18] Song is existence.[19] The more venturesome is thus the singer; the singer makes space—does not confine it, frame it. He makes the round space for being (temporality). The singer takes the first breath that makes the round space of being *there,* so that when being is there, it *is* the singer *(Da-sein).* Being and the singer are in the breath which dares to say, and "those who are more daring by a breath dare the venture with language."[20] And who is this singer who ventures more than any other?

He is the poet, but only the poet "whose song turns our protected being into the Open"; in the saying of the inner recall, Dimmesdale takes up the song of the singer and dares to venture forth from the everyday nature of the subject (repression) into the round realm of (its) being (exposition).[21] Dimmesdale is thus the poet whose song sings the round being itSelf *(poiēsis).* And yet, this round being is in no sense thereby handed over to the geometrician, whose thinking is exterior to thinking.[22] For being always comes into its completion within the finitude of its own time, and so can never enter onto the single, infinite horizon of the geometrician's eternally vacant stare. Rather, the simple song which Dimmesdale sings teaches a profound lesson in both finitude and solitude, but only to those who listen. It is outside the noisy chatter of the "they," and therefore to the point. Dimmesdale's song is near and to the point because it sounds, amid the interval of silence, the interrogation, "What does it *mean* to be?" It echoes a response as well, which is itself but yet another question—for this correspondence is itSelf what *can not-be.* Dimmesdale's saying echoes the song: "What does it mean to be (able to die)?" It echoes this song with such resounding silence that those who are talking cannot hear. Silence is itself most sound. The saying is therefore like the singer itSelf: *tout rond.*[23] The roundness of the poet is the roundness of his song: "in being sounded it dies away."[24] The poet Dimmesdale thus sings the saying of the inner recall: here the question, like its meaning, comes round full circle in the solitude of the poet who sings it. And the roundness of the question comes back to us in his death.

Being is round. The time of Hawthorne's oeuvre is present in its future. Those with ears may hearken to the intimate silence of its void. The silent void of this world unnerves us with its strange and alien listening. It is the silence of the dark, the silence that echoes a saying, a saying out of a silence which is, as night is to darkness, the disembodied shade of silence itself. Hawthorne's work informs a single question; it answers none. It is silent. The question is the saying which has long been forgotten because it is too near. For this "reason," it has been forgotten on *purpose*. Hawthorne's work disrupts the talkative chit-chat of forgetfulness with a silence that remembers what has become remote, and which is near to us whenever nothing is (in) the way. It takes in a single breath the question of being and, in an aspiration singly full of sound, sends it (A)round. The world of Hawthorne's work inverts the technological subversion (subjection) of "the world" understood as a view (spectacle); it therefore makes *(poiēsis)* the subject timely.[25] Its ex-position speaks, today, to those who hear, and does so within the silence of its listening—a listening which echoes the saying of the inner recall, the void at its heart. It says nothing/"nothing." It gathers the subject into the (w)hole of (its) being. Hawthorne's world is his work *(récit);* it opens onto the very frame that would contain it. Along the margin, the work of this world abides.

☐

The Letter passes beyond the scene of itSelf, beyond its Puritan frame *(récit),* goes (on) its circuit, its (own) way *(weg).* It goes abroad; it returns; it "stays." It corresponds with itself, "here" and "there" *(fort-da).* So too, its Puritan surveillance—policing the subject/restricting the post *(poste de police)*—is thus undone; the veil of the voyeur is rent, shredded, a tattered remnant, a thread. The image comes apart at the seams *(parergon):* "On a field, sable, the letter A, gules" (I:264). It "bleeds" beyond the "*tex*ture" of itself, its very fabric of embodiment. Author-ity no longer offers to vision the pro-position of its (ultimate) frame. The spectacle returns to the scene of its ghostly apparition, its "style," the mark of the gaze: "the semblance of an engraved escutcheon," regarding which "a herald's wording" can only serve as substitution (in [the] place of), as "a motto and brief description of our now concluded legend" (I:264). The scene thus interferes with itself. Its corporality reduces everything to silence—including the narrative frame. Narration here becomes an icon of itSelf. Its final tombstone scene disfigures its own "con"-figuration—an unaccountable phantasm, doubled in itself, "relieved only by one ever-glowing point of light gloomier than the shadow" (I:264)—where meaning is no longer "with"-held (held "together"), but is impossible: the scene of ("double") writing, the ghost of meaning. Iconology is for epitaphs.[26] The phrase itself ("the phrase itself")—"On a field, sable, the letter A, gules"—is in dispute.[27] The Letter alone will skirt this circular abyss,[28] become an open book *(The Letter):* the book an open letter—the very open letter which fiction is.[29]

As the Letter falls from (out of) the pages of—escapes the very frame of—Surveyor Pue's manuscript, so too *The Letter* escapes the *(mise-en-)scene* of itself: its own writing, its own reading. The Letter will echo this silent differ(a)nce between writing and reading—between its colossal (A) inscription (scenario) and the space (scene) in which it is read, that margin in which it becomes an object (a) of desire. *The Letter,* in (re)turn, will frame that very other *(objet a)* by means of which it doubles itSelf *(droit de regards),* the double-cross of self-regard—and in whose name ("Hawthorne") the event *(das Ereignis)* will always and everywhere (dis)figure (pass over) itself, pass beyond the very possibility of ever happening. When Hawthorne posts his Letter (A)/*Letter* (a), it is for this: to send it on being's (own) way. It's (not) for nothing that he sends The Letter (a letter) a way, (away), (a)(way), a(w)(a)y: ay, it's but a supplement, an extra letter. Being is "a spelling mistake in the text of death."[30] Death is being's desire *(fort-da),* its circuit *(weg).* Here (there) being is on its (own) way; death is (on) its own, being's o(w)n: it's fitting, proper. Upon the site of this economy, in sight of its end (purpose), being recites (the name of) the Law (the Father)—(ex)changes its name, has always already given it up.[31] (Nietzsche re-marks its "spur," its *style.*[32]) In this event, it signs itSelf (off). In any event, it passes away.[33]

Notes

PROVISION
In Retrospect: Looking A/head

1. Maurice Merleau-Ponty, "Reflection and Interrogation," *The Visible and the Invisible*, trans. Alphonso Lingis (Evanston: Northwestern University Press, 1968), p. 9.

2. Rodolphe Gasché, "Deconstruction as Criticism," *Glyph* 6 (1979): 185.

3. Ibid., 188; and Merleau-Ponty, "Interrogation and Dialectic," *The Visible and the Invisible*, p. 95.

4. Jacques Derrida, "The Voice That Keeps Silence," *Speech and Phenomena*, trans. David B. Allison (Evanston: Northwestern University Press, 1973), pp. 78–79.

5. Ibid., p. 79. In a later work, Derrida returns to the relation between perception and reflection—specifically in terms of narrative and the Kantian "sublime"; see Jacques Derrida, "Parergon," *The Truth in Painting*, trans. Geoff Bennington and Ian McLeod (Chicago: University of Chicago Press, 1987), p. 142: "But does not the distance required for the experience of the sublime open up perception to the space of narrative? Does not the divergence between apprehension and comprehension already appeal to a narrative voice? Does it not already call itself, with a narrative voice, the colossal?" We'll run into this "colossal" up ahead.

6. Jean-François Lyotard, *Discours, Figure* (Paris: Klincksieck, 1971), p. 56.

7. For an overview of what's at stake, I refer you to Gasché, "Deconstruction as Criticism," 177–215.

PROLOGUE
Perspective and Frame: The Daguerreotype

1. Erwin Panofsky, "Artist, Scientist, Genius: Notes on the 'Renaissance-Dämmerung,'" in *The Renaissance: Six Essays* (New York: Harper Torchbooks, 1962), pp. 124, 131–32.

2. Ibid., pp. 133, 124.

3. Ibid., pp. 148, 153–55; and George Sarton, "The Quest for Truth: Scientific Progress during the Renaissance," in *The Renaissance*, p. 70.

4. Maurice Merleau-Ponty, *Phenomenology of Perception*, trans. Colin Smith; rev. trans. Forrest Williams (London: Routledge and Kegan Paul, 1962), pp. 90–92.

5. Marshall McLuhan and Harley Parker, *Through the Vanishing Point: Space in Poetry and Painting* (New York: Harper and Row, 1968), p. 16.

6. I refer you to Derrida's reworking of the frame *(parergon)* in Kant's Third Critique; see Derrida, "Parergon," *The Truth in Painting*, pp. 17–147.

7. *The Life and Letters of Sir Henry Wotton*, ed. Logan Pearsall Smith, 2 vols. (London: Oxford University Press, 1907), II:205, 206.

8. Marjorie Hope Nicolson, *Newton Demands the Muse* (Princeton: Princeton University Press, 1966), pp. 78–79.

9. See Jacques Lacan, "Of the Subject who is Supposed to Know, of the first Dyad, and of the Good," *The Four Fundamental Concepts of Psycho-Analysis*, trans. Alan Sheridan (New York: W. W. Norton, 1978), pp. 230–43.

10. John Locke, *An Essay Concerning Human Understanding*, ed. Peter H. Nidditch (London: Oxford University Press, 1975), p. 163.

11. Gottfried Wilhelm Von Leibniz, "Discourse on Metaphysics," in *The European Philosophers: From Descartes to Nietzsche*, ed. Monroe C. Beardsley (New York: Modern Library, 1960), pp. 254–55. I specifically refer you, here, to his argument against the possibility of a series of events whose contour cannot be represented mathematically.

12. See David Hume, "A Treatise of Human Nature," in *David Hume: The Philosophical Works*, ed. Thomas Hill Green and Thomas Hodge Grose, 4 vols. (Darmstadt: Scientia Verlag Aalen, 1964), I:317–18.

13. Ibid., II:205–6.

14. Ibid., II:209–10.

15. Immanuel Kant, *Critique of Judgment*, trans. J. H. Bernard (New York: Hafner, 1968), p. 79, hereafter cited in the text, with page numbers, as CJ.

16. Between imagination and understanding, there is subjective agreement only: "Now, if in the judgment of taste the imagination must be considered in its freedom, it is in the first place not regarded as reproductive, as it is subject to the laws of association, but as productive and spontaneous (as the author of arbitrary forms of possible intuition)" (CJ:77).

17. See, for example, "Tuché and Automaton," *The Four Fundamental Concepts of Psycho-Analysis*, especially p. 62.

18. See Derrida, "Parergon," *The Truth in Painting*, p. 111.

19. Martin Heidegger, "The Age of the World View," trans. Marjorie Grene, *Boundary 2* 4 (1976): 350.

20. Martin Heidegger, "The Question Concerning Technology," *The Question Concerning Technology and Other Essays*, trans. William Lovitt (New York: Harper and Row, 1977), p. 27. The exposition set forth in this essay will "frame" the entirety of my own work, most conspicuously the notions of *technē* and *poiēsis*. These are not to be thought in opposition, but rather as configuration: each (dis)figures the other. Derrida subsequently reinscribes *technē* as but a "subset" of—and subject to—the "post" itself. I rely upon this relay (Heidegger-Derrida) in my exposition of both the daguerreotype and Hawthorne's work.

21. Derrida, "Parergon," *The Truth in Painting*, p. 128.

22. Immanuel Kant, *Critique of Practical Reason and Other Writings in Moral Philosophy*, trans. L. W. Beck (Chicago: University of Chicago Press, 1949), p. 191.

23. Ibid., pp. 181–88.

24. Heidegger, "The Age of the World View," 354.

25. Ibid., 351–52.

26. "Hence can be explained what Savary remarks, in his account of Egypt, viz. that we must keep from going very near the Pyramids just as much as we keep from going too far from them, in order to get the full emotional effect from their size" (CJ:90).

27. Derrida, "Parergon," *The Truth in Painting*, p. 140.

28. Cf. Derrida's figuration of column/colossus in ibid., pp. 119ff.

29. See Fredric Jameson, "Imaginary and Symbolic in Lacan: Marxism, Psychoanalytic Criticism, and the Problem of the Subject," in *Literature and Psychoanalysis; The Question of Reading: Otherwise*, ed. Shoshana Felman (Baltimore: Johns Hopkins University Press, 1982), p. 370: "This view of ethics would seem to find confirmation in Lacan's essay, 'Kant avec Sade'. . . . Yet this structural result turns out to be homologous with perversion, defined by Lacan as the fascination with the pleasure of the Other at the expense of the subject's own, and illustrated monotonously by the voluminous pages of Sade." Thus Jameson turns the table on Lacan: psychoanalysis itself can be a perversion.

30. Derrida suggests as much in the second section of "Parergon," *The Truth in Painting:* "The deterioration of the *parergon,* the perversion, the adornment, is the attraction of sensory matter" (p. 64). In the final section, this will come to the fore(play): "pleasure only 'gushes indirectly.' It comes after inhibition, arrest, suspension *(Hemmung)* which keep back the vital forces. This retention is followed by a brusque outpouring, an effusion *(Ergiessung)* that is all the more potent" (p. 128); and again: "in view of the faculty of judging, the natural sublime, the one which remains privileged by this analysis of the *colossal,* seems to be formally contrary to an end *(zweckwidrig),* inadequate and without suitability, inappropriate to our faculty of representation. It appears to do violence to the imagination. And to be all the more sublime for that" (p. 129).

31. Cf. Jameson, "Imaginary and Symbolic in Lacan," p. 373.

32. I refer to Freud's case study. See Sigmund Freud, "From the History of an Infantile Neurosis (1918)," *Three Case Histories*, ed. Philip Rieff (New York: Collier Books, 1963), pp. 187–316. See also Nicolas Abraham and Maria Torok, *The Wolf Man's Magic Word: A Cryptonomy*, trans. Nicholas Rand, foreword by Jacques Derrida (Minneapolis: University of Minnesota Press, 1986), especially pp. 29–40.

33. Derrida, "Parergon," *The Truth in Painting*, p. 142.

34. Heidegger, "The Age of the World View," 353.

35. Ibid.

36. See Derrida, "Parergon," *The Truth in Painting*, pp. 24–27, 143–45. I'm also indebted, for my discussion of Kant's Third Critique, to Mary Warnock, *Imagination* (Berkeley: University of California Press, 1976), pp. 41–66.

37. Heidegger, "The Age of the World View," 352.

38. McLuhan and Parker, *Through the Vanishing Point*, p. 121.

39. Journal entry for May–September, 1871, *The Journals and Miscellaneous*

Notebooks of Ralph Waldo Emerson, ed. Ronald A. Bosco and Glen M. Johnson, vol. XVI (Cambridge: Belknap Press, 1982), p. 242.

40. "Rhymes and Chimes," quoted in Richard Rudisill, *Mirror Image: The Influence of the Daguerreotype on American Society* (Albuquerque: University of New Mexico Press, 1971), pp. 74–75.

41. Rudisill, *Mirror Image,* p. 73.

42. Panofsky, "Artist, Scientist, Genius," p. 147.

43. This crossover (shutter/lens/eye) alludes to Derrida's critique of Husserl's *Phenomenology of Internal Time-Consciousness.* See Derrida, "Signs and the Blink of an Eye," *Speech and Phenomena,* p. 65: "As soon as we admit . . . continuity of the now and the not-now . . . we admit the other into the self-identity of the *Augenblick;* nonpresence and nonevidence are admitted into the *blink of the instant.* There is a duration to the blink, and it closes the eye. This alterity is . . . the condition for presence . . . for *Vorstellung* in general." Derrida plays on this notion again as it appears in Kant's sublime, at pleasure's "point" of inhibition; see "Parergon," *The Truth in Painting,* p. 128: "This retention is followed by a brusque outpouring. . . . The maximum pressure lasts only an instant *(augenblicklich),* the time it takes to blink an eye, during which the passage is strictly closed and the stricture absolute."

44. Quoted in Rudisill, *Mirror Image,* p. 85.

45. Heidegger, "The Age of the World View," 346.

46. Edward Hitchcock, *The Religion of Geology and Its Related Sciences* (Boston: Phillips, Sampson, and Co., 1851), p. 410.

47. Hitchcock, *The Religion of Geology,* pp. 410, 418, and 426, respectively. There's no essential difference between Hitchcock's view and Whitman's interior picture gallery; cf. Walt Whitman, *Pictures: An Unpublished Poem* (New York: June House, 1927).

48. Heidegger, "The Age of the World View," 349. For a brilliant Heideggerian reading of "the (true) world" as fiction, see John Sallis, "Meaning Adrift," *Heidegger Studies* 1 (1985): 91–100.

49. *Nature,* in *The Complete Works of Ralph Waldo Emerson,* ed. Edward Waldo Emerson, Centenary Edition, 12 vols. (Boston: Houghton Mifflin, 1903–21), "Language," I:29, 26. All subsequent references to this essay are hereafter parenthetically cited in the text by section title and page number. I will grant, in advance, that my reading of Emerson as idealist is traditional; nevertheless, his entire oeuvre seems implicated in dominance, manipulation, and the will to power.

50. Rudisill, *Mirror Image,* p. 17.

51. *The Journals and Miscellaneous Notebooks of Ralph Waldo Emerson,* ed. Linda Allardt and David W. Hill, vol. XV (Cambridge: Belknap Press, 1982), p. 261.

52. McLuhan and Parker, *Through the Vanishing Point,* p. 13.

53. Cf. Heidegger, "The Age of the World View," 349ff., for a commentary on the Cartesian "picture" and its history.

54. Maurice Merleau-Ponty, "Eye and Mind," *The Primacy of Perception*, ed. James Edie (Evanston: Northwestern University Press, 1964), p. 169.

55. Roland Barthes, *Camera Lucida: Reflections on Photography*, trans. Richard Howard (New York: Hill and Wang, 1981), p. 30.

56. Ibid., pp. 26–27.

57. Ibid., pp. 47, 96.

58. Ibid., p. 42.

59. Sontag disavows this "possibility," this alternate circuit, as something that comes later. She argues that, while Fox Talbot did photographic close-ups in the 1840s, these objects are entirely recognizable. It was only later that photography sought to isolate the detail from its familiar context—that is, the space of the real. See Susan Sontag, *On Photography* (New York: Dell, 1977), pp. 90ff.

60. Cf. ibid., pp. 13–14.

61. See Barthes, *Camera Lucida*, pp. 40–41.

62. Quoted in Carol Shloss, *In Visible Light: Photography and the American Writer: 1840–1940* (New York: Oxford University Press, 1987), p. 32.

63. Quoted in M. A. Root, *The Camera and the Pencil* (Philadelphia: J. B. Lippincott, 1864), p. 391.

64. In a letter to William Dunlap, for example, Thomas Cole denounces Turner's later works: "in pictures, representing scenes in this world, rocks should not look like sugar candy, nor the ground like jelly." Quoted in William Dunlap, *A History of the Rise and Progress of the Arts of Design in the United States*, ed. Frank W. Bayley and Charles E. Goodspeed, rev. ed., 3 vols. (Boston: C. E. Goodspeed, 1918), III:152, 153.

65. Rudisill, *Mirror Image*, p. 12.

66. Ibid., p. 39.

67. Quoted in ibid., p. 41.

68. Ibid., p. 38.

69. S. G. Goodrich, *Recollections of a Lifetime*, quoted in *Hawthorne: The Critical Heritage*, ed. J. Donald Crowley (New York: Barnes and Noble, 1970), p. 6.

70. Nathaniel P. Willis, "The Pencil of Nature," *The Corsair* 1 (1839): 71.

71. A passage from the *Leipziger Anzeiger* amusingly reflects an extreme reaction to the daguerreotype. Having failed to make a daguerreotype of its own, the *Anzeiger* denounced Daguerre in the following terms:

> Wanting to hold fast to transitory mirror-pictures is not only an impossibility, as has been shown by basic German research, but even the wish to do so is blasphemy. Man is created in the image of God, and God's image cannot be captured by any man-made machine. . . . God has, to be sure, tolerantly forborne the mirror in His creation as a vain toy of the Devil. Most likely, however, He is regretting this tolerance, especially because many women are using mirrors to look at themselves in all of their vanity and pride. But no mirror, neither of glass nor of quicksilver, has yet received permission from God to hold fast the image of the human face. . . . Now: Should this same God, who for thousands of years has never allowed that mirror-pictures of men should be

fadeless, should this same God suddenly become untrue to His eternal principles and allow that a Frenchman from Paris should set loose such a devilish invention into the World!!?? We must make clear, after all, how unChristian and Hellishly vain mankind would become if everyone could have his own mirror-pictures made for filthy money and reproduced by the dozen. There would be such a mass epidemic of vanity that mankind would become godlessly superficial and godlessly vain. And if this "Monsewer" Daguerre in Paris maintains a hundred times that his human mirror-pictures can be held fast on silver plates, this must a hundred times be called an infamous lie, and it is not worthwhile that German masters of optics concern themselves with this impertinent claim. (quoted in Rudisill, *Mirror Image*, p. 50)

72. Quoted in Van Deren Coke, "Camera and Canvas," *Art in America* 49 (1961): 68. Ironically such is not the case with the tales of ratiocination—specifically, "The Purloined Letter," where scrutiny does not reveal the truth.

73. J. M. Whittemore, prospectus for *The Daguerreotype: A Magazine of Foreign Literature and Science,* quoted in Rudisill, *Mirror Image,* p. 73.

74. See Merleau-Ponty, *Phenomenology of Perception,* pp. 60–61.

75. Rudisill, *Mirror Image,* pp. 224, 225.

76. Ibid., p. 32.

77. Barthes, *Camera Lucida,* p. 80.

78. Quoted in Samuel Prime, *The Life of Samuel Morse* (New York: Appleton, 1875), p. 400.

79. James F Ryder, *Voigtlander and I in Pursuit of Shadow Catching* (Cleveland: Cleveland Printing and Publishing Co., 1902), p. 16.

80. See Sontag, *On Photography,* p. 54.

81. Barthes, *Camera Lucida,* p. 34.

82. See Sontag, *On Photography,* p. 130.

83. See ibid., pp. 14–15.

84. Heidegger, "The Age of the World View," 352.

85. For a detailed analysis of the role of dialectic in Emerson's historical thinking, see Gustaaf Van Cromphout, "Emerson and the Dialectics of History," *PMLA* 91 (1976): 54–64.

86. Cf. Charles Feidelson, Jr., *Symbolism and American Literature* (Chicago: University of Chicago Press, 1959), p. 318.

87. Sontag, *On Photography,* p. 71.

88. Oliver Wendell Holmes, "The Stereoscope and the Stereograph," *Atlantic Monthly* 3 (1859): 102.

89. Quoted in Sontag, *On Photography,* p. 207.

90. Barthes, *Camera Lucida,* p. 90.

91. See Susan Stewart, *On Longing: Narratives of the Miniature, the Gigantic, the Souvenir, the Collection* (Baltimore: Johns Hopkins University Press, 1984), p. 135.

92. Marshall McLuhan, *Understanding Media: The Extensions of Man* (New York: Signet, 1964), p. 170.

93. Herman Melville, *Pierre, or the Ambiguities* (Evanston: Northwestern University Press, 1971), p. 254.

94. Rudisill, *Mirror Image,* p. 161.

95. Quoted in James D. Horan, *Mathew Brady: Historian with a Camera* (New York: Bonanza Books, 1955), p. 18.

96. Gabriel Harrison, "Lights and Shadows of Daguerrean Life," *Photographic and Fine Art Journal* 7 (1854): 8. Harrison deliberately emphasized this potentially "dramatic" aspect of the daguerreotype as a literary technique in his own writings. Indeed, the literary world at large was quick to adopt the daguerreotype for its own purposes. As Rudisill observes, nearly ten years prior to Hawthorne's use of the daguerreotype as an organizing metaphor in *The House of the Seven Gables,* Frances Osgood had employed it as a kind of framing device for a series of character sketches in her short story, "Daguerreotype Pictures." And in 1847, a new literary magazine, *The Daguerreotype,* was established in order to create "verbal pictures," a new visual approach to literature, suggesting to what extent the literary world was willing to appropriate the new technology to its own domain. Henceforth, the daguerreotype appeared in numerous short stories and novels either as some kind of plot device or metaphor for moral commentary. Such works as Fred Hunter's *The Daguerreotype: or Love at First Sight,* Dion Boucicault's *The Octoroon,* Augustine Duganne's *The Daguerreotype Miniature or Life in the Empire City,* and others, made extensive use of the daguerreotype as a literary *technē,* especially as a "framing" device for characterization or "portraiture" (Rudisill, *Mirror Image,* pp. 221–22).

I hate to keep you on this note, to linger in the rear; but we'll make head-way in a moment. At this juncture, however, I draw your attention to the passage opened up in the chiasmus "literature"/photography. The twentieth-century photo-text will recollect this scene both (1) backward: in its desire to separate mechanical reproduction from intentional "art," and (2) forward: as envoy of its (later) desire to conflate image and sign. See Stuart Culver, "How Photographs Mean: Literature and the Camera in American Studies," *American Literary History* 1 (1989): 203.

For further discussion of this phenomenon, see Ralph F. Bogardus, *Pictures and Texts: Henry James, A. L. Coburn and New Ways of Seeing in Literary Culture* (Ann Arbor: UMI Research Press, 1984), and Jefferson Hunter, *Image and Word: The Interaction of Twentieth-Century Photographs and Texts* (Cambridge: Harvard University Press, 1987).

97. Cf. Sontag, *On Photography,* p. 175.

98. Ibid., p. 95.

99. I here repeat Lacan's analysis of repetition. See "Tuché and Automaton," *The Four Fundamental Concepts of Psycho-Analysis,* pp. 53–64.

100. See Derrida's remarks in Marie-Françoise Plissart, *Droit de regards: Avec une lecture de Jacques Derrida* (Paris: Minuit, 1985), pp. v, xxiv.

101. See Jacques Derrida, "Envois," *The Post Card: From Socrates to Freud and Beyond,* trans. Alan Bass (Chicago: University of Chicago Press, 1987), pp. 65–66, and David Wills, "Supreme Court," *Diacritics* 18 (1988): 27–29.

102. See Derrida, "Parergon," *The Truth in Painting,* pp. 1ff.; Derrida, "Envois," *The Post Card,* pp. 104–5; Derrida, *Droit de regards,* pp. vi, xxii; and Wills, "Supreme Court," 27–29.

103. Wills, "Supreme Court," 28, note 10.

104. Barthes, *Camera Lucida*, p. 31.

105. Ibid., p. 76.

106. Guy Debord, *Society of the Spectacle* (Detroit: Black and Red, 1977), section 218 (no page numbers).

107. Sontag, *On Photography*, p. 57.

108. Stewart, *On Longing*, p. 110.

109. Walter Benjamin, "The Work of Art in the Age of Mechanical Reproduction," *Illuminations*, trans. Harry Zohn (New York: Harcourt, Brace and World, 1968), p. 253.

110. Ibid., p. 253, note 21.

111. Ibid., p. 238.

112. Ibid., p. 222.

113. Stewart, *On Longing*, p. 133.

114. See, for instance, Michael Lesy, *Wisconsin Death Trip* (New York: Pantheon Books, 1973).

115. Barthes, *Camera Lucida*, pp. 9, 15.

116. Debord, *Society of the Spectacle*, section 160: "One who has renounced using his life can no longer admit his death. Life insurance advertisements suggest merely that he is guilty of dying without ensuring the regularity of the system after this economic loss; and the advertisement of the *American way of death* insists on his capacity to maintain in this encounter the greatest possible number of *appearances* of life. On all other fronts of the advertising onslaught, it is strictly forbidden to grow old. Even a 'youth-capital,' contrived for each and all and put to the most mediocre uses, could never acquire the durable and cumulative reality of financial capital. This social absence of death is identical to the social absence of life."

117. Ibid., sections 167, 217.

118. See Derrida, *Droit de regards*, p. ix.

119. John Steinbeck, *A Russian Journal with Pictures by Robert Capa* (New York: Viking Press, 1948), p. 5; quoted in Shloss, *In Visible Light*, p. 20, to whom I'm indebted for this observation.

120. See Joseph P. Fell, "The Crisis of Reason: A Reading of Heidegger's *Zur Seinsfrage*," *Heidegger Studies* 2 (1986): 59; see also Fell, *Heidegger and Sartre: An Essay on Being and Place* (New York: Columbia University Press, 1979), p. 261.

121. See Derrida, "Parergon," *The Truth in Painting*, p. 87.

122. Panofsky, "Artist, Scientist, Genius," pp. 140, 133.

123. McLuhan, *Understanding Media*, p. 181. See also Derrida, "+R (Into the Bargain)," *The Truth in Painting*, p. 181: "Picking out the enlarged detail comes in any case from cinematographic and psychoanalytic technique. The two powers, the two techniques, the two situations, another of Benjamin's demonstrations, are indissociable. One and the same mutation."

124. Debord, *Society of the Spectacle*, section 220.

THE WORLD OF HAWTHORNE'S WORK
Being(-)in(-) *THE-WORLD*

1. McLuhan and Parker, *Through the Vanishing Point*, p. 235.
2. Ibid., pp. xxiii and 241, respectively.
3. Merleau-Ponty, "Eye and Mind," *The Primacy of Perception*, p. 168.
4. Nathaniel Hawthorne, "Monsieur du Miroir," in *The Centenary Edition of the Works of Nathaniel Hawthorne*, ed. William Charvat, et al., 20 vols. to date (Columbus: Ohio State University Press, 1962–present), X:169–70. Subsequent references to Hawthorne, unless otherwise noted, will be exclusively to this edition, hereafter parenthetically cited in the text by volume and page number only. For a different treatment of the double or "ghost" of one's self, see "Graves and Goblins" (XI:289–97).
5. Cf. also, for example, "Fancy's Show Box" (IX:221), where Mr. Smith gazes at his own reflection in the madeira glass.
6. Jean Normand, *Nathaniel Hawthorne: An Approach to an Analysis of Artistic Creation*, trans. Derek Coltman (Cleveland: Press of Case Western Reserve University, 1970), p. 41.
7. Malcolm Cowley, "Hawthorne in the Looking-Glass," *Sewanee Review* 56 (1948): 545.
8. Normand, *Nathaniel Hawthorne*, p. 121.
9. "Apparent" and "opaque" are not contradictory, here, but point to the phenomenal nature of the appearance itself. The appearance is all the "reality" we have; there is no transparent, noumenal vision beyond. It is therefore destined to remain opaque.
10. Henry David Thoreau, *Walden* (1854; New York: Holt, Rinehart and Winston, 1961), p. 86.
11. Reprinted in Crowley, *Hawthorne: The Critical Heritage*, p. 508.
12. Reprinted in ibid., p. 329.
13. Normand, *Nathaniel Hawthorne*, p. 245.
14. Ibid., p. 173.
15. An unsigned essay, "Modern Novelists—Great and Small," *Blackwood's Magazine*, 1855, reprinted in Crowley, *Hawthorne: The Critical Heritage*, p. 313.
16. "Tale Writing—Nathaniel Hawthorne," *Godey's Lady's Book*, 1847, reprinted in Crowley, *Hawthorne: The Critical Heritage*, p. 150.
17. Reprinted in Crowley, *Hawthorne: The Critical Heritage*, p. 327.
18. Normand, *Nathaniel Hawthorne*, p. 173.
19. Ibid., p. 172.
20. An unsigned review, *Southern Review*, 1870, reprinted in Crowley, *Hawthorne: The Critical Heritage*, pp. 465–66.
21. "Nathaniel Hawthorne," *National Review*, 1860, reprinted in Crowley, *Hawthorne: The Critical Heritage*, p. 372.
22. Cf., for example, *The American Notebooks* (VIII:219)—"The sun shone

strongly in among these trees, and quite kindled them; so that the path seemed brighter for their shade, than if it had been quite exposed to the sun."

23. Harry Levin, *The Power of Blackness* (New York: Alfred A. Knopf, 1958), p. 39. Cf. Merleau-Ponty, *Phenomenology of Perception*, p. 317: "moonlight and sunlight, present themselves in our recollection, not pre-eminently as sensory contents, but as certain kinds of symbiosis, certain ways the outside has of invading us and certain ways we have of meeting this invasion, and memory here merely frees the framework of the perception from the place where it originates."

24. Normand, *Nathaniel Hawthorne*, p. 163.

25. D. H. Lawrence, *Studies in Classic American Literature* (New York: Viking Press, 1964), p. 83.

26. Normand, *Nathaniel Hawthorne*, p. 304.

27. Cf. also: "Hepzibah spread out her gaunt figure across the door, and seemed really to increase in bulk" (II:129).

28. "Their voices are encompassed and re-echoed by the walls of a chamber, the windows of which were rattling in the breeze; the regular vibration of a clock, the crackling of a fire, and the tinkling of the embers as they fell among the ashes, rendered the scene almost as vivid as if painted to the eye" (IX:201). See Leland Schubert, *Hawthorne the Artist* (New York: Russell and Russell, 1963), p. 24, for an interesting structural comparison between "The Hollow of the Three Hills" and Grant Wood's painting *American Gothic*.

29. Cf. Gaston Bachelard, *The Poetics of Space*, trans. Maria Jolas (Boston: Beacon Press, 1969), p. 37. "Concentration of intimacy" refers, here, to "the world" of (human) desire, to its "construction" in (the house of) language.

30. Merleau-Ponty, *Phenomenology of Perception*, p. 24.

31. Ibid., p. 309; cf. also: "Reflections and lighting in photography are often badly reproduced because they are transformed into things" (p. 309).

32. Cited in ibid., p. 305; cf. also: "The eye is not the mind, but a material organ. How could it ever take anything 'into account'? It can do so only if we introduce the phenomenal body beside the objective one, if we make a knowing-body of it, and if, in short, we substitute for consciousness, as the subject of perception, existence, or being in the world through a body" (p. 309, note 1).

33. Cf. ibid., p. 305.

34. Merleau-Ponty, "Eye and Mind," *The Primacy of Perception*, p. 167; cf. also *Phenomenology of Perception*, p. 310: "We perceive in conformity with the light, as we think in conformity with other people in verbal communication. . . . [P]erception presupposes in us an apparatus capable of responding to the promptings of light in accordance with their sense. . . . This apparatus is the gaze, in other words the natural correlation between appearances and our kinaesthetic unfoldings . . . the involvement of our body in the typical structures of a world. Lighting and the constancy of the thing illuminated, which is its correlative, are directly dependent on our bodily situation."

35. See, respectively, Kurt Koffka, *Principles of Gestalt Psychology* (New York: Harcourt, Brace and Co., 1935), pp. 254ff., and Merleau-Ponty, *Phenomenology of Perception*, p. 312.

36. Cf. Bachelard, *The Poetics of Space*, pp. 211–31.

37. Normand, *Nathaniel Hawthorne*, p. 308. By "diorama," I mean not only a three-dimensional, translucent scene *in miniature*, but any such scene produced with similar effects, including those displayed before a collective audience— e.g., Daguerre's diorama *à double effet*.

38. Already by 1842, he had observed in a journal entry: "A Father-Confessor—his reflections on character, and the contrast of the inward man with the outward, as he looks round on his congregation—all whose secret sins are known to him" (VIII:235). Similarly, Hilda's confession in *The Marble Faun* enables her to discard the personal burden of guilt, which she attaches to her own identity, by welcoming the anonymity of the enclosing dark. Only afterwards, in the determinate world of the cathedral, is she compelled to discuss it face to face (IV:357–58).

39. V. F. Perkins, *Film as Film* (London: Penguin Books, 1972), p. 134.

40. Wladimir Jankelevitch, "Le Romantisme allemand," quoted in Normand, *Nathaniel Hawthorne*, p. 318.

41. Cf. Raymond Durgnat, *Films and Feelings* (London: Faber and Faber, 1967), p. 99.

42. Jules Supervielle, "The Man Who Stole Children," trans. Alan Pryce-Jones, in *Selected Writings* (New York: New Directions, 1967), pp. 194–95.

43. Georges-Michel Bovay, "Poésie et réalisme," *Cinéma: un oeil ouvert sur le monde*, ed. Georges-Michel Bovay (Lausanne: La Guilde du Livre, 1952), p. 95.

44. Benjamin Lease, "Diorama and Dream: Hawthorne's Cinematic Vision," *Journal of Popular Culture* 5 (1971): 321.

45. Comte de Lautréamont, *Le Chants de Maldoror*, trans. Guy Wernham (New York: New Directions, 1965), p. 306. Cf. Goodman Brown who cannot bring himself to accept the (moral) darkness he discovers in the forest.

46. Normand, *Nathaniel Hawthorne*, p. 311.

47. Thus, in the preface to *A Wonder Book*, Hawthorne explains that he felt no reluctance to shape anew, "as his fancy dictated, the forms that have been hallowed by an antiquity of two or three thousand years" (VII:3). His perceptual and reflective habits naturally gravitated toward our "interior" facticity rather than our external factuality. Correspondingly, in the preface to *Biographical Stories for Children*, he advances the personal and intimate approach to the history of a life: "It is here attempted to give our little readers such impressions as they might have gained, had they themselves been the playmates of persons, who have long since performed important and brilliant parts upon the stage of life" (VI:213).

48. Merleau-Ponty, "Eye and Mind," *The Primacy of Perception*, p. 181.

49. Merleau-Ponty, *Phenomenology of Perception*, p. 283.

50. See ibid., pp. 100–101.

51. Rudisill, *Mirror Image*, p. 85.

52. Albert S. Southworth, "An Address to the National Photographic Association of the United States," *The Philadelphia Photographer* 8 (1871): 322.

53. "But I wonder that the late Judge . . . should not have felt the propriety of embodying so excellent a piece of domestic architecture in stone, rather than in

wood. Then, every generation of the family might have altered the interior, to suit its own taste and convenience; while the exterior, through the lapse of years, might have been adding venerableness to its original beauty, and thus giving that impression of permanence, which I consider essential to the happiness of any one moment" (II:314–15).

54. *The Knickerbocker,* reprinted in Crowley, *Hawthorne: The Critical Heritage,* p. 52.

55. *New York Tribune Supplement,* reprinted in Crowley, *Hawthorne: The Critical Heritage,* p. 159.

56. *Literary World,* reprinted in Crowley, *Hawthorne: The Critical Heritage,* p. 238.

57. *North American Review,* reprinted in Crowley, *Hawthorne: The Critical Heritage,* p. 417.

58. Levin, *The Power of Blackness,* pp. 63, 28, and 36, respectively.

59. *Atlantic Monthly,* quoted in the "Explanatory Notes" to Hawthorne's *American Notebooks* (VIII:621).

60. See Roman Jakobson, "Two Aspects of Language: Metaphor and Metonymy," in *European Literary Theory and Practice: From Existential Phenomenology to Structuralism,* ed. Vernon W. Gras (New York: Dell Publishing Co., 1973), pp. 124–25. In Hawthorne, one of these tight shots will carry the *affective* "significance."

61. See Béla Balázs, *Theory of the Film,* trans. Edith Bone (London: Dennis Dobson, 1952), p. 35. See also Perkins, *Film as Film,* pp. 72–73.

62. Cf. Normand, *Nathaniel Hawthorne,* p. 244. For a more liberal attitude toward Hawthorne's use of allegory, see Q. D. Leavis' classic essay, "Hawthorne as Poet," *Sewanee Review* 59 (1951): 179–85, 198–205, 456–58. I wish to stress that I employ the term "allegory" in reference to traditional Hawthorne criticism—clearly not in the sense de Man has rewritten this term.

63. Merleau-Ponty, *Phenomenology of Perception,* pp. 277 and 13, respectively.

64. Cf. Henry Tuckerman, "Nathaniel Hawthorne," *Southern Literary Messenger,* 1851, reprinted in Crowley, *Hawthorne: The Critical Heritage,* p. 215: "The imagination is a wayward faculty, and writers largely endowed with it, have acknowledged that they could expatiate with confidence only upon themes hallowed by distance. . . . To clothe a familiar scene with ideal interest . . . requires an extraordinary power of abstraction and concentrative thought. . . . It is otherwise in a new and entirely practical country; the immediate encroaches too steadily upon our attention; we can scarcely obtain a perspective." In the register of the psychoanalytic, for example, this emblematic aspect of Hawthorne's gaze corresponds to "overdetermination"; cf. Merleau-Ponty, "Working Notes," *The Visible and the Invisible,* p. 270.

65. *North American Review,* reprinted in Crowley, *Hawthorne: The Critical Heritage,* p. 391.

66. "Hawthorne," *American Whig Review,* 1846, reprinted in Crowley, *Hawthorne: The Critical Heritage,* pp. 130–31.

67. *The Journals and Miscellaneous Notebooks of Ralph Waldo Emerson,* ed. A. W. Plumstead and William H. Gilman, vol. XI (Cambridge: Belknap Press:

1975), pp. 230–31. Cf. Emerson's "Natural History of Intellect," *The Complete Works of Ralph Waldo Emerson,* Centenary Edition, XII:93, for a "daguerrean" analogy to memory: "as if the mind were a kind of looking-glass, which . . . receives on its clear plate every image that passes; . . . our plate is iodized so that every image sinks into it, and is held there."

68. Feidelson, *Symbolism and American Literature,* p. 52.

69. Normand, *Nathaniel Hawthorne,* p. 94.

70. *Hawthorne's Lost Notebook, 1835–1841,* intro. Hyatt H. Waggoner (University Park: Pennsylvania State University Press, 1978), p. 82.

71. Henry Cornelius Agrippa, *Of the Vanitie and Vncertaintie of Artes and Sciences,* ed. Catherine M. Dunn (Northridge: California State University, 1974), p. 80. Cf. Hawthorne's use of Agrippa in "A Virtuoso's Collection" (X:482, 490–91, and 492); cf. also *The French and Italian Notebooks:* "the most delicate . . . charm of a picture is evanescent; . . . we continue to admire pictures prescriptively and by tradition, after the qualities that first won them their fame have vanished" (XIV:176).

72. In the same entry Hawthorne observes that "when a great squash or melon is produced, it is a large and tangible existence, which the imagination can seize hold of and rejoice in" (VIII:330).

73. Quoted in James R. Mellow, *Nathaniel Hawthorne in His Times* (Boston: Houghton Mifflin, 1980), p. 523.

74. Mellow, *Nathaniel Hawthorne in His Times,* p. 523. So too Mellow remarks that Hawthorne's "thefts" of art works "give a realistic texture to his studio scenes, they are works of sculpture: Akers' *Dead Pearl Diver,* Story's *Cleopatra,* as well as the works he avoided borrowing—Hosmer's *Zenobia* and Randolph Rogers' bronze Columbus doors for the Capitol in Washington" (p. 523).

75. Within the realm of imagination, the echo is, of course, the audible correspondence to the visible trace. This "trace" ("sketch," "outline," "aspect," "track," "print," "tint," "ruin"), moreover, will figure prominently in Hawthorne's understanding of the *sign,* and of signification in general. What follows is intended as a limited list of references, in the major romances only, to this all-important notion. Cf. I:21, 22, 28, 31, 43, 47, 56, 109, 147, 151, 169, 175, 186, 206, 214, 216, 226; II:5, 6, 34, 41, 46, 58, 72, 95, 107, 108, 111, 122, 240, 276, 299, 314; III:11, 56, 109, 111, 118, 146, 155, 162, 185, 187, 190, 194, 197, 201, 208, 211, 213, 231, 237; IV:2, 3, 6, 8, 9, 24, 25, 28, 32, 37, 38, 41, 43, 45, 55, 75, 94, 107, 111, 114, 118, 137, 138, 139, 144, 150, 153, 154, 165, 181, 193, 213, 227, 232, 248, 263, 292, 296, 302, 306, 348, 372, 379, 381, 388, 414, 420, 444, 450, 453, 465.

76. For further references to portraits, pictures, engravings, etchings, and the like, cf. the following pages in *The American Notebooks,* VIII:53, 65, 130, 149, 212, 214–15, 218, 226, 227, 231, 233–34, 235, 242, 254, 255, 259, 260–61, 263, 293, 321, 331, 366, 383, 385–86, 394, 396, 399, 400, 401, 403, 407–8, 416, 417, 418–19, 444, 490, 491, 492, 495, 498–99.

77. Henry James, *Hawthorne* (1879; Ithaca: Cornell University Press, 1966), p. 79.

78. *Francis Bacon's Essays,* intro. Oliphant Smeaton (1906; rpt. London:

J. M. Dent & Sons, 1958), pp. 15–16. Cf. Hawthorne: "A life, generally of a grave hue, may be said to be *embroidered* with occasional sports and fantasies" (VIII:235).

79. "Hawthorne and His Mosses," reprinted in Crowley, *Hawthorne: The Critical Heritage*, pp. 115–16.

80. James, *Hawthorne*, p. 99.

81. Cf. William V. Spanos, "Heidegger, Kierkegaard, and the Hermeneutic Circle: Towards a Postmodern Theory of Interpretation as Dis-closure," *Boundary 2* 4 (1976): 479. Cf. also Merleau-Ponty, "Working Notes," *The Visible and the Invisible*, p. 261:

> The flesh of my fingers = each of them is phenomenal finger and objective finger, outside and inside of the finger in reciprocity, in chiasm, activity and passivity coupled. The one encroaches upon the other, they are in a relation of real opposition (Kant)—Local *self* of the finger: its space is felt-feeling.—
>
> There is no coinciding of the seer with the visible. But each borrows from the other, takes from or encroaches upon the other, intersects with the other, is in chiasm with the other. In what sense are these multiple chiasms but one: not in the sense of synthesis, of the originally synthetic unity, but always in the sense of *Uebertragung,* encroachment, radiation of being therefore—
>
> The things touch me as I touch them and touch myself: flesh of the world— distinct from my flesh: the double inscription outside and inside. The inside receives without flesh: not a 'psychic state,' but intra-corporeal, reverse of the outside that my body shows to things.

And again, cf. Merleau-Ponty, "Eye and Mind," *The Primacy of Perception*, p. 163: "Visible and mobile, my body is a thing among things; it is caught in the fabric of the world, and its cohesion is that of a thing. But because it moves itself and sees, it holds things in a circle around itself. Things are an annex or prolongation of itself; they are incrusted into its flesh, they are part of its full definition."

82. Cf. the following passages in *The American Notebooks:* "At a distance, mountain summits look close together, and almost forming one mountain, though in reality, a village lies in the depth between them" (VIII:101); "It is amusing to see all the distributed property, the aristocracy and commonality, the various and conflicting interests of the town, the loves and hates, compressed into a space which the eye takes in as completely as the arrangement of a tea-table" (VIII:102); "the prospect from the top of Wachusett is the finest that I have seen— the elevation being not so great as to snatch the beholder from all sympathy with the earth. The roads that wind along at the foot of the mountains are discernable; and the villages, lying separate and unconscious of one another, each with their little knot of peculiar interests, but all gathered into one category by the observer above them" (VIII:259–60); "the beholder takes in at a glance the estates on which different families have long been situated . . . acting out the business of their life, which looks not so important when we can get up so high as to comprehend several men's portions in it at one glance" (VIII:274).

83. "It is a singular thing, that at the distance, say, of five feet, the work of

the greatest dunce looks just as well as that of the greatest genius,—that little space being all the distance between genius and stupidity" (VIII:16).

84. Levin, *The Power of Blackness*, p. 50.

85. *The Letters of Herman Melville*, reprinted in Crowley, *Hawthorne: The Critical Heritage*, p. 190.

86. Cf. Merleau-Ponty, *Phenomenology of Perception*, p. 330.

87. Ibid., p. 316. For another dimension of Hawthorne's "corporeality," see Sharon Cameron, *The Corporeal Self: Allegories of the Body in Melville and Hawthorne* (Baltimore: Johns Hopkins University Press, 1981), pp. 77–157.

88. In a journal entry of 1 June 1842, he expressed it thus: "The greater picturesqueness and reality of back-yards, and everything appertaining to the rear of a house; as compared with the front, which is fitted up for the public eye. There is much to be learnt, always, by getting a glimpse at rears. When the direction of a road has been altered, so as to pass the rear of farm-houses, instead of the front, a very noticeable aspect is presented" (VIII:239). Eight years later, Hawthorne indulged in just such a sketch (VIII:496–97).

89. Merleau-Ponty, "Eye and Mind," *The Primacy of Perception*, p. 180.

90. Ibid.

91. Ibid., pp. 183–84: "There is a painting by Klee of two holly leaves, done in the most figurative manner. At first glance the leaves are thoroughly indecipherable, and they remain to the end monstrous, unbelievable, ghostly, *on account of their exactness* [*à force d'exactitude*]. And Matisse's women (let us keep in mind his contemporaries' sarcasm) were not immediately women; they became women. It is Matisse who taught us to see their contours not in a 'physical-optical' way but rather as structural filaments [*des nervures*], as the axes of a corporeal system of activity and passivity."

92. Quoted in ibid., pp. 185–86. As Merleau-Ponty suggests, the same may be true of modern painting:

> Figurative or not, the line is no longer a thing or an imitation of a thing. It is a certain disequilibrium . . . a certain constitutive emptiness—an emptiness which, as Moore's statues show decisively, upholds the pretended positivity of the things. The line is no longer the apparition of an entity upon a vacant background, as it was in classical geometry. It is, as in modern geometries, the restriction, segregation, or modulation of a pre-given spatiality. . . . But the immobile canvas could suggest a change of place in the same way that a shooting star's track on my retina suggests a transition, a motion not contained in it. The painting itself would offer to my eyes almost the same thing offered them by real movements: a series of appropriately mixed, instantaneous glimpses along with, if a living thing is involved, attitudes unstably suspended between a before and an after—in short, the outsides of a change of place which the spectator would read from the imprint it leaves. . . . Movement is given, says Rodin, by an image in which the arms, the legs, the trunk, and the head are each taken at a different instant, an image which therefore portrays the body in an attitude which it never at any instant really held and which imposes fictive linkages between the parts, as if this mutual confrontation of incompossibles could, and could alone, cause transition and duration to arise in bronze and on canvas. . . . The picture makes movement visible by its internal discordance. Each member's position, precisely by virtue of its

incompatibility with the others' (according to the body's logic), is otherwise dated or is not 'in time' with the others; and since all of them remain visibly within the unity of a body, it is the body which comes to bestride time. (pp. 184–85)

93. Merleau-Ponty, *Phenomenology of Perception*, p. 6.

94. Jean-Paul Sartre, *L'Imaginaire* (Paris: Gallimard, 1940), p. 19.

95. Mikel Dufrenne, *The Phenomenology of Aesthetic Experience,* trans. Edward S. Casey, et al. (Evanston: Northwestern University Press, 1973), pp. 355 and 357, respectively. For Dufrenne, imagination's correlate is the possible, "and this is why it can get carried away at times. . . . But when imagination functions normally—and especially when it functions aesthetically—the possible constitutes a prereal. It is for this reason that imagination is constantly in touch with the real, surpassing the given toward its sense" (p. 357). Cf. also Ernst Cassirer, *The Philosophy of Symbolic Forms,* trans. Ralph Manheim, 3 vols. (New Haven: Yale University Press, 1957), III:69:

> The image must assert a peculiar primacy over the thing. For what 'is' in the object in its expressive character is not taken up and destroyed in the image; on the contrary, it is set in high relief and intensified. The image frees this expressive reality from all merely accidental determinations and concentrates it in a single focus. In the empirical world view we determine and know the 'object' by dissecting it backward into its conditions and following it forward into its effects. It is what it is only as a single link in a system of such effects, as part of a causal structure. Where, however, an occurrence is not thus viewed as a mere factor in a thoroughgoing and universal order of law but is experienced in its physiognomic individuality so to speak; where instead of the analysis and abstraction that are the precondition of all causal understanding, pure vision prevails— it is the *image* which opens up the true essentiality and makes it knowable. All 'image magic' rests on the presupposition that in the image the magician is not dealing with a dead imitation of the object; rather, in the image he possesses the essence, the soul, of the object.

96. Kurt Koffka, *The Growth of the Mind* (New York: Harcourt, Brace and Co., 1925), p. 320. See also Merleau-Ponty, *Phenomenology of Perception,* p. 322: "The thing and the world . . . are offered to perceptual communication as is a familiar face with an expression which is immediately understood."

97. Merleau-Ponty, *Phenomenology of Perception,* pp. 239–40; cf. also: "My set of experiences is presented as a concordant whole, and the synthesis takes place not in so far as they all express a certain invariant, and in the identity of the object, but in that they are all collected together, by the last of their number, in the ipseity of the thing. The ipseity is, of course, never *reached:* each aspect of the thing which falls to our perception is still only an invitation to perceive beyond it, still only a momentary halt in the perceptual process. If the thing itself were reached, it would be from that moment arrayed before us and stripped of its mystery. It would cease to exist as a thing at the very moment when we thought to possess it. What makes the 'reality' of the thing is therefore precisely what snatches it from our grasp. The aseity of the thing, its unchallengeable presence and the perpetual absence into which it withdraws, are two inseparable aspects of transcendence" (p. 233).

98. Ibid., p. 284.

99. Cassirer, *The Philosophy of Symbolic Forms*, III:68.

100. Ibid., III:70.

101. Cf. Merleau-Ponty, *Phenomenology of Perception*, p. xvi, regarding intentionality and Husserl's "eidetic reduction."

102. Ibid., p. 320. See also H. Conrad-Martius, *Realontologie*, cited in *Phenomenology of Perception*, p. 319: "The perceived world is . . . a set of symbols of human life, as is proved by the 'flames' of passion, the 'light' of the spirit and so many other metaphors and myths."

103. Merleau-Ponty, "Eye and Mind," *The Primacy of Perception*, pp. 186–87; see also *Phenomenology of Perception*, pp. 83–84, 215, and the following: "The ideal of objective thought is both based upon and ruined by temporality. The world, in the full sense of the word, is not an object, for though it has an envelope of objective and determinate attributes, it has also fissures and gaps into which subjectivities slip and lodge themselves, or rather which are those subjectivities themselves" (p. 333).

104. See, respectively, Geoffrey H. Hartman, "Romantic Poetry and the Genius Loci," *Beyond Formalism: Literary Essays, 1958–1970* (New Haven: Yale University Press, 1970), pp. 333–35, and J. Hillis Miller, *Hawthorne and History: Defacing It* (Oxford: Basil Blackwell, 1991), p. 99.

Cf. also Cassirer, *The Philosophy of Symbolic Forms*, III:68: "When water is sprinkled in rain magic, it does not serve as a mere symbol or analogue of the 'real' rain; it is attached to the real rain by the bond of an original sympathy. The demon of the rain is tangibly and corporeally alive and present in every drop of water." We should be reminded, however, as Cassirer warns, that personification

> does not signify a mere transposition of the objective world view into a subjective view, for this would require both of these two aspects to be present and determined. . . . Reality—corporeal or psychic—has not yet become stabilized but preserves a peculiar 'fluidity'. . . . A whispering or rustling in the woods, a shadow darting over the ground, a light flickering on the water; all these are demonic in their nature and origin; but only very gradually does this pandemonium divide into separate and clearly distinguishable figures. . . . Everything is connected with everything else by invisible threads; and this connection, this universal sympathy, itself preserves a hovering, strangely impersonal character. 'There is a fitting in; there is an omen; there is a warning'—but behind these there is not necessarily a personal subject, the shape of any recognizable warner. It is the whole of reality rather than any separate part of it that constitutes this subject. (III:70–72)

105. See Merleau-Ponty, *Phenomenology of Perception*, p. 215; see also: "We now understand why things . . . are not meanings presented to the intelligence, but opaque structures, and why their ultimate significance remains confused. The thing and the world exist only in so far as they are experienced by me or by subjects like me, since they are both the concatenation of our perspectives, yet they transcend all perspectives because this chain is temporal and incomplete" (p. 333).

106. McLuhan and Parker, *Through the Vanishing Point*, p. 2.

107. Ibid., p. 77.

108. See Susanne K. Langer, *Feeling and Form* (New York: Charles Scribner's Sons, 1963), p. 412.

109. Merleau-Ponty, *Phenomenology of Perception*, p. 215.

110. Langer, *Feeling and Form*, p. 413.

111. McLuhan and Parker, *Through the Vanishing Point*, p. 137.

112. Langer, *Feeling and Form*, p. 415.

113. See Joseph C. Pattison, "Point of View of Hawthorne," *PMLA* 82 (1967): 365–66.

114. Gotthold Ephraim Lessing, *Laocoön: An Essay Upon the Limits of Painting and Poetry*, trans. Ellen Frothingham (New York: Farrar, Straus and Giroux, 1969), p. 91: "All bodies . . . exist not only in space, but also in time. They continue, and, at any moment of their continuance, may assume a different appearance and stand in different relations."

115. For example, Kant's position from the outset is tantamount to "One knows. . . . " Thus the transcendental unity of apperception is *no one's in particular.* Insofar as both rationalism and idealism demand the same "objective" frame, they repress the *point of view.* In other words, "one knows" in the same way "one sees"—by virtue of a uni-form mental space, the space of "perspective." In Heideggerian terms, Kant's unity of apperception is therefore "inauthentic"; it constitutes a care-less mode of the "they-self." Because it is no one's in particular, it belongs to everyONE *(das Man).* For this observation, I'm indebted to Forrest Williams.

116. As Pascal observed: "Take away *probability,* and you can no longer please the world; give *probability,* and you can no longer displease it"—see Blaise Pascal, *Pensées,* in *"Pensées" and "The Provincial Letters,"* trans. W. F. Trotter and Thomas M'Crie (New York: Modern Library, 1941), p. 318.

117. Pascal, *Pensées,* p. 23.

118. Martin Heidegger, "What Are Poets For?" *Poetry, Language, Thought,* trans. Albert Hofstadter (New York: Harper and Row, 1975), p. 131; see also: "Only what we thus retain in our heart *(par coeur),* only that do we truly know by heart" (p. 130). Cf. Pascal's observation that the heart has reasons of which reason itself knows nothing *(Pensées,* p. 95). Cf. also, Claude Lévi-Strauss, *The Savage Mind* (Chicago: University of Chicago Press, 1966), p. 252: "Language, an unreflecting totalization, is human reason which has its reasons and of which man knows nothing." I'll (over)take this notion up ahead.

119. See Merleau-Ponty, *Phenomenology of Perception*, p. 340.

120. See McLuhan and Parker, *Through the Vanishing Point*, pp. 99–101.

121. See Max Scheler, "Idealism and Realism," *Selected Philosophical Essays,* trans. David R. Lachterman (Evanston: Northwestern University Press, 1973), p. 331:

> We cannot represent to ourselves any sort of spatiality in which the peculiar phenomenon of the 'void' does not appear, the phenomenon of that intuitive *mē on,* that 'lack' which proceeds from the factual datum itself. This phenomenon is, in any event, prelogical and certainly has nothing to do with the function of negative judgment.

The phenomenon of the void is of the greatest interest. It arises, in the last analysis, from the experience that occurs when a driving hunger [*Triebhunger*] for spontaneous movement has not been satisfied or fulfilled. This hunger in the end conditions all perceptions [*Perzeptionen*] as well as representations and the spontaneous images of fantasy, which are independent of external perceptions. Thus, the phenomenon of the void, which is bound up with the power of self-movement (insofar as the latter is connected with the unsatisfied hunger), must be given as a stable background prior to all changing perceptions and even the material images of fantasy. The 'emptiness' of the heart is, remarkably, the principal datum for all concepts of emptiness (empty time, empty space). The emptiness of the heart is, quite seriously, the source from which all emptiness springs.

Cf. Merleau-Ponty, *Phenomenology of Perception*, p. 285:

The phantasms of dreaming, of mythology, the favourite images of each man or indeed poetic imagery, are not linked to their meaning by a relation of sign to significance; . . . they really contain their meaning, which is not a notional meaning, but a direction of our existence. . . . The bird which hovers, falls and becomes a handful of ash, does not hover and fall in physical space; it rises and falls with the existential tide running through it. . . . The level of this tide at each moment conditions a space peopled with phantasms, just as, in waking life, our dealings with the world which is offered to us condition a space peopled with realities. There is a determining of up and down, and in general of place, which precedes 'perception'. Life and sexuality haunt their world and their space. Primitive peoples, in so far as they live in a world of myth, do not overstep this existential space, and this is why for them dreams count just as much as perceptions. There is a mythical space in which directions and positions are determined by the residence in it of great affective entities. . . . In dreaming as in myth we learn *where* the phenomenon is to be found, by feeling that towards which our desire goes out, what our hearts dread, on what our life depends.

122. Heidegger, "What Are Poets For?" *Poetry, Language, Thought*, p. 138.

123. Joseph C. Pattison, "'The Celestial Rail-Road' as Dream-Tale," *American Quarterly* 20 (1968): 236.

124. Gaston Bachelard, *The Psychoanalysis of Fire*, trans. Alan C. M. Ross (Boston: Beacon Press, 1968), p. 82.

125. See Pattison, "'The Celestial Rail-Road' as Dream-Tale," p. 227.

126. Ibid.

127. Normand, *Nathaniel Hawthorne*, p. 107.

128. In a journal entry, 1842, Hawthorne expressed it thus: "To write a dream, which shall resemble the real course of a dream, with all its inconsistency, its strange transformations, which are all taken as a matter of course, its eccentricities and aimlessness—with nevertheless a leading idea running through the whole. Up to this old age of the world, no such thing ever has been written" (VIII:240).

129. Normand, *Nathaniel Hawthorne*, p. 294.

130. Ibid., p. 298.

131. Ibid., p. 300.

132. Werner Wolff, *The Dream: Mirror of Conscience* (New York: Grune and Stratton, 1952), pp. 299–300.

133. Sigmund Freud, *The Interpretation of Dreams*, trans. A. A. Brill (New York: Macmillan Co., 1937), p. 304.

134. Pattison, "Point of View in Hawthorne," p. 369.

135. See Claire Sprague, "Dream and Disguise in *The Blithedale Romance*," *PMLA* 84 (1969): 596–97. Lauren Berlant takes the step "beyond": "he—he himself—was in love—with—Hollingsworth"; see Lauren Berlant, "Fantasies of Utopia in *The Blithedale Romance*," *American Literary History* 1 (1989): 36.

136. See Normand, *Nathaniel Hawthorne*, p. 329.

137. See, respectively, F. O. Matthiessen, *American Renaissance* (New York: Oxford University Press, 1941), p. 232, and Sergei M. Eisenstein, *The Film Sense*, trans. Jay Leyda (New York: Harcourt, Brace and World, 1942), p. 33. Cf. also Ernest Lindgren, *The Art of the Film* (London: Allen and Unwin, 1948), p. 92: "It is the spectator's own mind that moves." Regarding Hawthorne's own ambiguous narratives, see Lease, "Diorama and Dream: Hawthorne's Cinematic Vision," 321: it is the disembodied voice of the dream, the secret witness whose vision we share; thus, what made dioramic effects particularly significant to the implementation of Hawthorne's descriptive gaze was their singular appropriateness to the world he characteristically evoked—"a dream world halfway between reality and fantasy in which truth is simultaneously, maddeningly, graspable and evanescent."

138. Franklin B. Newman, "'My Kinsman, Major Molineux': An Interpretation," *University of Kansas City Review* 21 (1955): 205.

139. Ibid., p. 209.

140. Normand, *Nathaniel Hawthorne*, p. 329.

141. Bachelard, *The Psychoanalysis of Fire*, p. 18.

142. Normand, *Nathaniel Hawthorne*, p. 21.

143. Bachelard, *The Psychoanalysis of Fire*, p. 16.

144. Cf. ibid., pp. 17–19.

145. Normand, *Nathaniel Hawthorne*, p. 350.

146. Merleau-Ponty, *Phenomenology of Perception*, p. 287.

147. Cf. ibid., p. 291: "What protects the sane man against delirium or hallucination, is not his critical powers, but the structure of his space: objects remain before him, keeping their distance and, as Malebranche said speaking of Adam, touching him only with respect. What brings about both hallucinations and myths is a shrinkage in the space directly experienced, a rooting of things in our body, the overwhelming proximity of the object, the oneness of man and the world, which is, not indeed abolished, but repressed by everyday perception or by objective thought, and which philosophical consciousness rediscovers."

148. Normand, *Nathaniel Hawthorne*, p. 236.

149. Merleau-Ponty, *Phenomenology of Perception*, p. 293.

150. Cf. ibid., p. 294: "It has often been said that consciousness, by definition, admits of no separation of appearance and reality, and by this we are to understand that, in our knowledge of ourselves, appearance is reality. . . . Here reality appears in its entirety, real being and appearance are one, and there is no

reality other than the appearance"; and again, p. 296: "Consciousness is neither the positing of oneself, nor ignorance of oneself, it is *not concealed* from itself, which means that there is nothing in it which does not in some way announce itself to it, although it does not need to know this explicitly. In consciousness, appearance is not being, but the phenomenon."

151. Pierre Schneider, *Louvre Dialogues*, trans. Patricia Southgate (New York: Atheneum, 1971), p. 201. Here, too, is Miró's fascination with the line in handwriting/painting—"as if the line were breathing" (quoted in Schneider, *Louvre Dialogues*, p. 30). Hawthorne/Giacometti/Miró: it is the cult of the detail.

152. Jean Piaget, *The Construction of Reality in the Child*, trans. Margaret Cook (New York: Ballantine Books, 1954), pp. 354ff.

153. See, respectively, Max Scheler, *Man's Place in Nature*, trans. Hans Meyerhoff (New York: Noonday Press, 1961), p. 52, and Merleau-Ponty, *Phenomenology of Perception*, p. 343.

154. Cf. Merleau-Ponty, *Phenomenology of Perception*, p. 84: "Just as we speak of repression in the limited sense when I retain through time one of the momentary worlds through which I have lived, and make it the formative element of my whole life—so it can be said that my organism, as a prepersonal cleaving to the general form of the world, as an anonymous and general existence, plays, beneath my personal life, the part of an *inborn complex*"; cf. also p. 83; "All repression is, then, the transition from first person existence to a sort of abstraction of that existence . . . until finally only the essential form remains. Now as an advent of the impersonal, repression is a universal phenomenon, revealing our condition as incarnate beings by relating it to the temporal structure of being in the world. . . . In so far as I inhabit a 'physical world', in which consistent 'stimuli' and typical situations recur—and not merely the historical world in which situations are never exactly comparable—my life is made up of rhythms which have not their *reason* in what I have chosen to be, but their *condition* in the humdrum setting which is mine."

There is a correlation here between the registers of the psycho-analytic and Heidegger's existential analytic in *Being and Time*—between perception, repression, and consciousness in its average everydayness which Heidegger calls the "they-self" *(das Man)*, and against which authentic existence is able to figure forth. For Heidegger, *das Man* (the "One": Plato's "hen" is here as well) articulates that inauthentic mode in which human existence covers over the responsibility to be *its own*. It is the very "discourse of the Other," as Lacan defines the unconscious itself. I explore this notion further up ahead.

155. See Scheler, *Man's Place in Nature*, p. 55; cf. also "Idealism and Realism," *Selected Philosophical Essays*, pp. 336–37: "In no other single aspect does man prove himself so much a repressor of drives and 'nay-sayer' than in the fact that he objectifies the always deficiently filled emptiness of his heart into an infinitely empty being and allows this emptiness to precede things and their causal relations. That it is his own 'nay,' the emptiness of his own heart, which yawns before him seemingly from the outside and awakens the dread which

Pascal so frighteningly depicted, is a wisdom which reason was late in discovering. Once it was found, it was immediately buried again in oblivion by an automatic compulsion of the human constitution."

156. Schneider, *Louvre Dialogues,* p. 87.

157. Charles Campbell, "Representing Representation: Body as Figure, Frame, and Text in *The House of the Seven Gables,*" *Arizona Quarterly* 47 (1991): 15.

158. Ibid., 12.

159. See ibid., 18.

THE WORLD OF HAWTHORNE'S WORK
Being(-)*IN*(-)the-world

1. Merleau-Ponty, *Phenomenology of Perception,* p. 363.

2. Cf. A. F. Lingis, "On the Essence of Technique," in *Heidegger and the Quest for Truth,* ed. Manfred S. Frings (Chicago: Quadrangle Books, 1968), pp. 126–38.

3. Merleau-Ponty, *Phenomenology of Perception,* p. 361.

4. See, respectively, ibid., "Eye and Mind," *The Primacy of Perception,* p. 187, and "Working Notes," *The Visible and the Invisible,* p. 269.

5. Jacques Lacan, "The Split between the Eye and the Gaze," *The Four Fundamental Concepts of Psycho-Analysis,* p. 72.

6. As Heidegger has expressed this paradox: "the frantic abolition of all distances brings no nearness; for nearness does not consist in shortness of distance. What is least remote from us in point of distance . . . can remain far from us. What is incalculably far from us in point of distance can be near to us. Short distance is not in itself nearness. Nor is great distance remoteness" ("The Thing," *Poetry, Language, Thought,* p. 165).

7. Merleau-Ponty, "Working Notes," *The Visible and the Invisible,* pp. 263–64; this, in turn, points once again to the emblematic quality of existence: "the other is a relief as I am" (p. 269).

8. Søren Kierkegaard, *The Concept of Irony,* trans. Lee M. Capel (Bloomington: Indiana University Press, 1968), pp. 56–57.

9. Lacan, "Anamorphosis," *The Four Fundamental Concepts of Psycho-Analysis,* pp. 82–83; cf. also: "The privilege of the subject seems to be established here from that bipolar reflexive relation by which, as soon as I perceive, my representations belong to me" (p. 81).

10. See Martin Heidegger, "Aletheia (Heraclitus, Fragment B 16)," *Early Greek Thinking,* trans. David Farrell Krell and Frank A. Capuzzi (New York: Harper and Row, 1975), pp. 102–23.

11. Ibid., pp. 106–7.

12. Ibid., p. 104.

13. Cf. Lacan's observation on Freud's case history of the Wolf Man ("From Interpretation to the Transference," *The Four Fundamental Concepts of Psycho-Analysis,* p. 251): "the sudden appearance of the wolves in the window in the

dream plays the function of the *s*, as representative of the loss of the subject. It is not only that the subject is fascinated by the sight of these wolves. . . . It is that their fascinated gaze is the subject himself."

14. See Lacan, "Anamorphosis," *The Four Fundamental Concepts of Psycho-Analysis*, p. 85. In addition to Hawthorne's *Blithedale*, of course, "The Minister's Black Veil" (IX:37–53) constitutes another brilliant variation on the theme of voyeurism.

15. See also, for example, the following references in *Blithedale* to "spying out"—III:207; to the "glance"—III:82, 173, 185, 187, 203; to the "glimpse"—III:88, 102, 165, 195, 228; and to the "Paul Pry" attitude in general—III:71, 84, 97, 148–59, 160, 163.

16. Lacan, "The Partial Drive and Its Circuit," *The Four Fundamental Concepts of Psycho-Analysis*, p. 182.

17. Merleau-Ponty, "The Child's Relations with Others," *The Primacy of Perception*, p. 137.

18. Cf. Lacan, "Anamorphosis," *The Four Fundamental Concepts of Psycho-Analysis*, p. 80.

19. Cf. Merleau-Ponty, "The Child's Relations with Others," *The Primacy of Perception*, p. 142.

20. Jean-Paul Sartre, *Being and Nothingness*, trans. Hazel E. Barnes (New York: Philosophical Library, 1956), p. 221; cf. also: "By the mere appearance of the Other, I am put in the position of passing judgment on myself as an object, for it is as an object that I appear to the Other. . . . Shame is by nature *recognition*. I recognize that I *am* as the Other sees me. There is however no question of a comparison between what I am for myself and what I am for the Other as if I found in myself, in the mode of being of the For-itself, an equivalent of what I am for the Other. In the first place this comparison is not encountered in us as the result of a concrete psychic operation. Shame is an immediate shudder which runs through me from head to foot without any discursive preparation" (p. 222).

21. See ibid., p. 262.

22. Lacan, "The Partial Drive and Its Circuit," *The Four Fundamental Concepts of Psycho-Analysis*, p. 182: "What the voyeur is looking for and finds is merely a shadow, a shadow behind the curtain. There he will phantasize any magic of presence, the most graceful of girls, for example, even if on the other side there is only a hairy athlete. What he is looking for is not, as one says, the phallus—but precisely its absence, hence the pre-eminence of certain forms as objects of his search."

23. Cf. Sartre, *Being and Nothingness*, p. 264.

24. Ibid., p. 267. Here, in fact, Coverdale's relation to Zenobia approximates that between analysand and analyst. As Lacan explains, "the subject, in so far as he is subjected to the desire of the analyst, desires to betray him for this subjection, by making the analyst love him, by offering of himself that essential duplicity that is love" ("From Interpretation to the Transference," *The Four Fundamental Concepts of Psycho-Analysis*, p. 254).

25. Merleau-Ponty, "The Child's Relations with Others," *The Primacy of Perception,* p. 143.

26. Ibid., p. 144.

27. Ibid., p. 143.

28. See Sigmund Freud, "Psychoanalytic Notes upon an Autobiographical Account of a Case of Paranoia (Dementia Paranoides)," *Three Case Histories,* pp. 165ff. See also Merleau-Ponty, "The Child's Relations with Others," *The Primacy of Perception,* p. 144:

> Freud admits that a jealousy which seems to be directed toward one person is in reality directed toward another. A man's jealousy of his wife is the rivalry between that man and that woman in the presence of a third person who is the occasion of the jealousy. This leads us to say that in all jealous conduct there is an element of homosexuality. Wallon takes this kind of view when he admits that the jealous man is the one who lives, as his own, not only his own experiences but those of others as well, when he assumes the attitudes of the other (and, for example, the attitudes toward a third). . . . Relations between two people are in reality more extensive relations, since they extend across the second person to those with whom the second person is vitally related. Likewise when Wallon writes of jealousy, 'This feeling is the feeling of a rivalry in a person who does not know how to react except as a spectator possessed by the action of the rival,' he is very close to the psychoanalytic considerations of the attitude of the 'voyeur.'

29. See Martin Heidegger, *Being and Time,* trans. John Macquarrie and Edward Robinson (New York: Harper and Row, 1962), pp. 163ff.

30. Cf. Frederick Crews, *The Sins of the Fathers: Hawthorne's Psychological Themes* (London: Oxford University Press, 1966), pp. 207ff. Cf. also Leonard F. Manheim, "Outside Looking In; Evidences of Primal-Scene Fantasy in Hawthorne's Fiction," *Literature and Psychology* 31 (1981): 4–15.

31. See Lacan, "Aphanisis," pp. 227–28, and "Of the Subject who is Supposed to Know," p. 235, respectively, in *The Four Fundamental Concepts of Psycho-Analysis.*

32. Cf. Lacan, "In You More Than You," *The Four Fundamental Concepts of Psycho-Analysis,* p. 268: "I love you, but, because inexplicably I love in you something more than you—the *objet petit a*—I mutilate you."

33. Edward W. Said, *Beginnings: Intention and Method* (Baltimore: Johns Hopkins University Press, 1975), p. 22.

34. Lacan, "Presence of the Analyst," *The Four Fundamental Concepts of Psycho-Analysis,* p. 129.

35. Kierkegaard, *The Concept of Irony,* p. 155; for a full explication of this concept, see Kierkegaard's *Repetition: An Essay in Experimental Psychology,* trans. Walter Lowrie (New York: Harper and Row, 1964).

36. This is, of course, the very starting point for Heidegger's existential analytic of Dasein in *Being and Time.*

THE WORLD OF HAWTHORNE'S WORK
BEING(-)in(-)the-world

1. Heidegger, "What Are Poets For?" *Poetry, Language, Thought,* p. 130.

2. Heidegger, "The Thing," *Poetry, Language, Thought,* p. 177.

3. Heidegger, "What Are Poets For?" *Poetry, Language, Thought,* p. 131: "this inner recalling of the already immanent objectness of consciousness into the heart's innermost region . . . concerns every being inasmuch as it is a being."

4. Pascal, *Pensées,* p. 314.

5. Ibid., p. 73.

6. Ibid., p. 96.

7. Cf. also "The Man of Adamant" (XI:161–69) and "The Ambitious Guest" (IX:324–33).

8. R. W. B. Lewis, *The American Adam: Innocence, Tragedy, and Tradition in the Nineteenth Century* (Chicago: University of Chicago Press, 1955), p. 119.

9. Pascal, *Pensées,* p. 118. Cf. Heidegger, "Poetically Man Dwells," *Poetry, Language, Thought,* p. 221: "Man, as man, has always measured himself with and against something heavenly. Lucifer, too, is descended from heaven."

10. Pascal, *Pensées,* p. 151.

11. Ibid., p. 217.

12. Heidegger, "What Are Poets For?" *Poetry, Language, Thought,* pp. 127–28.

13. Cowley, "Hawthorne in the Looking-Glass," 562.

14. Alfred H. Marks, "German Romantic Irony in Hawthorne's Tales," *Symposium* 7 (1953): 284.

15. I employ these terms in their explicit Lacanian determination; here "need" inosculates the function of "desire."

16. See Lacan, "Aphanisis," p. 227 and "From Love to the Libido," p. 198, respectively, in *The Four Fundamental Concepts of Psycho-Analysis.* Lacan states as much when he observes that the psychosomatic itself is not a signifier.

17. Scheler, *Man's Place in Nature,* pp. 74–75.

18. Lacan, "Of the Network of Signifiers," *The Four Fundamental Concepts of Psycho-Analysis,* p. 49.

19. Heidegger, "Poetically Man Dwells," *Poetry, Language, Thought,* p. 219.

20. Scheler, *Man's Place in Nature,* pp. 44–45.

21. Heidegger, "Poetically Man Dwells," *Poetry, Language, Thought,* p. 221.

22. Heidegger, "What Are Poets For?" *Poetry, Language, Thought,* p. 129.

23. Max Scheler, *Ressentiment,* trans. William W. Holdheim (New York: Schocken Books, 1972), p. 164.

24. See Heidegger, "What Are Poets For?" *Poetry, Language, Thought,* p. 116.

25. Catherine Clément, "The Guilty One," in Hélène Cixous and Catherine Clément, *The Newly Born Woman,* trans. Betsy Wing (Minneapolis: University of Minnesota Press, 1986), p. 37.

26. Bachelard, *The Poetics of Space,* p. 234.

27. "Glossary," *The Newly Born Woman,* p. 166.

28. Normand, *Nathaniel Hawthorne,* p. 341.

29. As Albert Hofstadter argues, "Enownment," *Boundary 2* 4 (1976): 374, this openness to being characterizes perception itself: "Perception, for instance, is an enownment between man, Being, and time, in which the world opens up for man in his seeing, hearing, touching, smelling, tasting. In perception, what is other to the individual human being appears as enowned in its otherness. The house we see over there is seen as the dwelling place, whose entrance beckons or repels, which harbors within it the family, the hidden place of love and hate, conflict and healing." Thus Hofstadter interprets what Heidegger calls "the event" *(das Ereignis)* of Being as *enownment:* "If we were to give the most literal possible translation of *das Ereignis* it would have to consist of *en-, -own-,* and *-ment: enownment.* Enownment is the letting-be-own-to-one-another of whatever is granted belonging-together. . . . The second important facet of the meaning of enownment is also reflected by the root portion of the word, *eig-,* seen from a different vantage point. . . . *Eräugen* is, as it were, to en-eye." In this way, too, although belonging together is being own to one another, enownment is more than simply the belonging together of beings (of one to the other), for the subject belongs to itSelf as well. To this resolute anticipation of one's own not-being, Heidegger assigns the ontological structure of "care" *(Sorge); see Being and Time,* pp. 225ff.

30. Merleau-Ponty, *Phenomenology of Perception,* p. 372.

31. Claudia D. Johnson, *The Productive Tension of Hawthorne's Art* (University: University of Alabama Press, 1981), pp. 72–73.

32. Cf. Pascal, *Pensées,* pp. 60–61: "We do not rest satisfied with the present. We anticipate the future as too slow in coming, as if in order to hasten its course; or we recall the past, to stop its too rapid flight. So imprudent are we that we wander in the times which are not ours, and do not think of the only one which belongs to us; and so idle are we that we dream of those times which are no more, and thoughtlessly overlook that which alone exists. For the present . . . is never our end. The past and the present are our means; the future alone is our end. So we never live, but we hope to live; and, as we are always preparing to be happy, it is inevitable we should never be so."

33. Cf. Heidegger, "What Are Poets For?" *Poetry, Language, Thought,* p. 130: "Here everything is inward: not only does it remain turned toward this true interior of consciousness, but inside this interior, one thing turns, free of all bounds, into the other. The interiority of the world's inner space unbars the Open for us."

34. Søren Kierkegaard, *The Sickness Unto Death,* in *"Fear and Trembling" and "The Sickness unto Death,"* trans. Walter Lowrie (Princeton: Princeton University Press, 1968), p. 163.

35. A. N. Kaul, "The Blithedale Romance," in *Hawthorne: A Collection of Critical Essays,* ed. A. N. Kaul (Englewood Cliffs: Prentice-Hall, 1966), p. 158.

36. Ibid., p. 159.

37. Husserl addresses this issue (intersubjectivity) in another context when he recognizes subjectivity as an *inalienable fact,* and the world to which it intends its self as *omnitudo realitatis;* see Merleau-Ponty, *Phenomenology of Perception,* p. 398, note 1.

38. Scheler, *Ressentiment*, pp. 95–96.

39. Martin Heidegger, "The Question Concerning Technology," *The Question Concerning Technology*, pp. 3–35.

40. The familiar, for example, is that which has been lost to sight because we "take it" *for granted;* in the same way, we lose sight of being itSelf—that is, the being-question, the meaning of being: "What does it mean to be?" Moreover, we forget it as we do a lover who has left us, a dear friend who has died: *on purpose*—to which, of course, psychoanalysis gives the name "repression."

41. Cf. Heidegger, "Building Dwelling Thinking," *Poetry, Language, Thought*, pp. 149 and 151: "To dwell, to be set at peace, means to remain at peace within the free, the preserve, the free sphere that safeguards each thing in its nature. *The fundamental character of dwelling is this sparing and preserving*. . . . dwelling itself is always a staying with things. Dwelling, as preserving, keeps the fourfold in that with which mortals stay: in things."

42. Joel Porte, "Redemption through Art," in *Nathaniel Hawthorne: A Collection of Criticism*, ed. J. Donald Crowley (New York: McGraw-Hill, 1975), p. 76.

43. Heidegger, "Building Dwelling Thinking," *Poetry, Language, Thought*, p. 153.

44. Heidegger, "The Thing," *Poetry, Language, Thought*, p. 174.

45. John Caldwell Stubbs, "*The Marble Faun:* Hawthorne's Romance of the Adamic Myth," in Crowley, *Nathaniel Hawthorne: A Collection of Criticism*, p. 105.

46. Cf. Brook Thomas, "*The House of the Seven Gables:* Reading the Romance of America," *PMLA* 97 (1982): 207.

47. See Jacques Lacan, "The Subversion of the Subject and the Dialectic of Desire in the Freudian Unconscious," *Écrits*, trans. Alan Sheridan (New York: W. W. Norton, 1977), p. 303.

48. Lacan, "Tuché and Automaton," *The Four Fundamental Concepts of Psycho-Analysis*, pp. 55–56.

49. Lacan, "The Subversion of the Subject and the Dialectic of Desire in the Freudian Unconscious," *Écrits*, p. 311: "this margin being that which is opened up by demand, the appeal of which can be unconditional only in regard to the Other, under the form of the possible defect, which need may introduce into it, of having no universal satisfaction (what is called 'anxiety')."

50. Ibid., pp. 310–11: "which is what I mean when I say that no meta-language can be spoken, or, more aphoristically, that there is no Other of the Other."

51. Cf. Gayatri Spivak's Lacanian interpretation of Coleridge's *Biographia Literaria*, "The Letter as Cutting Edge," in *Literature and Psychoanalysis; The Question of Reading: Otherwise*, pp. 208–26.

52. This "roll of dingy paper?"—cf. Lacan, "The Subversion of the Subject and the Dialectic of Desire in the Freudian Unconscious," *Écrits*, p. 315: "Ask the writer about the anxiety that he experiences when faced by the blank sheet of paper, and he will tell you who *is* the turd of his phantasy."

53. For another reading of Hawthorne's "manliness" in "The Custom-House," see John T. Irwin, *American Hieroglyphics* (New Haven: Yale University Press, 1980), pp. 276–84.

54. See Jacques Derrida, "Differance," *Speech and Phenomena*, pp. 129–30:

The verb "to differ" [*différer*] seems to differ from itself. On the one hand, it indicates difference as distinction, inequality, or discernibility; on the other, it expresses the interposition of delay, the interval of a *spacing* and *temporalizing* that puts off until "later" what is presently denied, the possible that is presently impossible. Sometimes the *different* and sometimes the *deferred* correspond [in French] to the verb "to differ." This correlation, however, is not simply one between act and object, cause and effect, or primordial and derived. In the one case "to differ" signifies nonidentity; in the other case it signifies the order of the *same*. Yet there must be a common, although entirely differant [*différante*], root within the sphere that relates the two movements of differing to one another. We provisionally give the name *differance* to this *sameness* which is not *identical*: by the silent writing of its *a*, it has the desired advantage of referring to differing, *both* as spacing/temporalizing and as the movement that structures every dissociation.

See also Spivak, "The Letter as Cutting Edge," pp. 209–10. If postponement recollects forward *there being* a future, premonition recollects backward the future as that which *has* already *been*. Postponement "knows" behind itself from out of the future; premonition "knows" ahead of itself from out of the past.

55. Arthur C. Danto, "Narration and Knowledge," *Philosophy and Literature* 6 (1982): 18.

56. Marks, "German Romantic Irony in Hawthorne's Tales," 278.

57. See Marshall Van Deusen, "Narrative Tone in 'The Custom House' and *The Scarlet Letter*," in Crowley, *Nathaniel Hawthorne: A Collection of Criticism*, pp. 53–62.

58. *Dasein* ("there-is," "there-being," "being-there") is, of course, Heidegger's term for that being for whom the meaning of Being can be an issue in the first place. There is, in this sense, a correspondence, an internal relation, between Being itself and being itSelf *(Dasein)*.

59. Said, *Beginnings: Intention and Method*, pp. 59–60.

60. Ibid., pp. 65–67.

61. Freud, "Moses and Monotheism," *The Standard Edition of the Complete Psychological Works of Sigmund Freud*, trans. James Strachey (London: Hogarth Press, 1964), XXIII:43. See also Said, *Beginnings: Intention and Method*, p. 59.

62. I am indebted to one of my students, Lloyd Kirk, for this observation.

63. Jacques Derrida, "Coming into One's Own," in *Psychoanalysis and the Question of the Text*, ed. Geoffrey H. Hartman (Baltimore: Johns Hopkins University Press, 1978), p. 127.

64. Daniel Sibony, "Hamlet: A Writing-Effect," in Felman, *Literature and Psychoanalysis; The Question of Reading: Otherwise*, p. 74.

65. Cf. Merleau-Ponty on the physiognomy of this event: "Words have a physiognomy because we adopt towards them, as towards each person, a certain form of behaviour which makes its complete appearance the moment each word is given" (*Phenomenology of Perception*, pp. 235–36). So too, with reading: " 'The word as read is not a geometrical structure in a segment of visual space, it is the

presentation of a form of behaviour and of a linguistic act in its dynamic fullness.' Whether it is a question of perceiving words or more generally objects, 'there is a certain bodily attitude, a specific kind of dynamic tension which is necessary to give structure to the image; man, as a dynamic and living totality has to "pattern" himself in order to trace out a figure in his visual field as part of the psycho-somatic organism'" (Werner, *Untersuchung über Empfindung und Empfinden*, quoted in *Phenomenology of Perception*, p. 236).

66. Geoffrey H. Hartman, "Preface," *Psychoanalysis and the Question of the Text*, p. xviii.

67. See Richard H. Brodhead, *Hawthorne, Melville, and the Novel* (Chicago: University of Chicago Press, 1976), pp. 67–68.

68. See Philippe Sollers, "Freud's Hand," in Felman, *Literature and Psycho-analysis; The Question of Reading: Otherwise*, p. 337, note 1: "Freud makes the following suggestion: that writing was invented by women through the weaving and braiding of their pubic hairs."

69. Cf. Michael Ragussis, "Family Discourse and Fiction in *The Scarlet Letter*," *English Literary History* 49 (1982): 880.

70. The myth of the incarnation plays out this advent of language to being, the advent of being in language, both in its structure and origin: "In the begin-ning was the Word." The void of the *Logos* always already stands in need, and would redeem (demand) its own abysmal "sense" as some-"thing" other (desire). In this beginning, as but the trace of itself, it thus already embodies its "sound" (speech) in "sight" (writing)—that is, the way in which it is/will be carved out *in the flesh*. The incarnate word expresses the facticity of Being as a (w)hole, the place of its inscription as Other than itSelf, the very bio-logos of desire: "once upon a time," Being too will not be.

71. Jonathan Arac, "Reading the Letter," *Diacritics* 9 (1979): 49: "*The Scarlet Letter* offers the most famous example of the disjunction between things and words, or meanings." Yet Arac's reading ignores the con-"figuration" of subject and object within the logic of the heart. In Hawthorne, the thing itself occasions a matter for discourse: indeed, it is this matter, this expression.

72. Nina Baym, *The Shape of Hawthorne's Career* (Ithaca: Cornell University Press, 1976), p. 142.

73. See Lacan, "From Interpretation to the Transference," *The Four Funda-mental Concepts of Psycho-Analysis*, p. 250; see also Spivak, "The Letter as Cutting Edge," p. 223. We might read into this a correlation between an original signifier or *kern* of irreducible non-sense and the pervasive sense of an original "sin" in Hawthorne's oeuvre. If signification originates in a si(g)n or (fortunate) "fall" of the signifier into the "de-nominator" as zero, it constitutes the very possibility of value and signification, and "kills" all meaning. This is, of course, the very story of *The Faun*. The gap or fold of the subject (as represented by a signifier for another signifier) is therefore an infinity (of possibilities: $\frac{S}{0} = \infty$) against the fini-tude of desire. This, in turn, constitutes the subject in its freedom. See Lacan, "From Interpretation to the Transference," *The Four Fundamental Concepts of Psycho-Analysis*, pp. 250ff.

74. Lacan, "Ronds de ficelle," quoted in Spivak, "The Letter as Cutting Edge," p. 220.

75. Sibony, "*Hamlet:* A Writing-Effect," pp. 82 and 75, respectively.

76. Lacan, *Seminar on the Purloined Letter,* quoted in Barbara Johnson, "The Frame of Reference: Poe, Lacan, Derrida," in Felman, *Literature and Psychoanalysis; The Question of Reading: Otherwise,* p. 476.

77. Johnson, "The Frame of Reference: Poe, Lacan, Derrida," pp. 499 and 502, respectively.

78. For the punning on this phrase in French, see Sibony, "*Hamlet:* A Writing-Effect," p. 54.

79. Cited in James T. Fields, *Yesterdays with Authors* (Boston: James R. Osgood, 1874), p. 52.

80. Edgar A. Dryden, *Nathaniel Hawthorne: The Poetics of Enchantment* (Ithaca: Cornell University Press, 1977), p. 149.

81. Edgar A. Dryden, *The Form of American Romance* (Ithaca: Cornell University Press, 1988), p. 34.

82. Lacan, "Of the Subject who is Supposed to Know, of the first Dyad and of the Good," *The Four Fundamental Concepts of Psycho-Analysis,* pp. 230–43.

83. See Geoffrey H. Hartman, *Saving the Text: Literature/Derrida/Philosophy* (Baltimore: Johns Hopkins University Press, 1981), pp. 128ff., and Kierkegaard, *The Concept of Irony,* p. 52.

84. Saul Steinberg, quoted in Schneider, *Louvre Dialogues,* p. 91. See also Jacques Derrida, *Spurs: Nietzsche's Styles,* trans. Barbara Harlow (Chicago: University of Chicago Press, 1979), p. 43: "All of Nietzsche's investigations . . . are coiled in the labyrinth of an ear."

85. Schneider, *Louvre Dialogues,* p. 91.

86. Ibid.

87. Dryden, *The Form of American Romance,* p. 37.

88. Cf. Lacan, "From Interpretation to the Transference," *The Four Fundamental Concepts of Psycho-Analysis,* p. 250: "The fact that I have said that the effect of interpretation is to isolate in the subject a kernel, a *kern,* to use Freud's own term, of *non-sense,* does not mean that interpretation is in itself nonsense."

89. See Dryden, *The Form of American Romance,* p. 41: "For Hawthorne, material ruins always imply—often contain—decayed human ruins."

90. For an analysis of hysteria in terms of secrets and assertions of authority, see Neil Hertz, "Dora's Secrets, Freud's Techniques," *Diacritics* 13 (1983): 64–76. See also Henry Sussman, "*The Marble Faun* and the Space of American Letters," *Glyph Textual Studies* 1 (1986): 145.

91. See Bachelard, *The Psychoanalysis of Fire,* pp. 7–12.

92. For an opposite reading, see Sussman, "*The Marble Faun* and the Space of American Letters," 129–52.

93. In passing, I would mention two scenarios that further frame this scene, the re-"citation" of two poems by Andrew Marvell: "The Unfortunate Lover" ("In a field sable a lover gules") and "The Nymph Complaining for the Death of Her Fawn" ("Upon the roses it would feed, / Until its lips e'en seemed to

bleed / . . . For I would have thine image be / White as I can, though not as thee").

94. Irwin, *American Hieroglyphics*, p. 50.

95. Ned Lukacher, *Primal Scenes: Literature, Philosophy, Psychoanalysis* (Ithaca: Cornell University Press, 1986), pp. 13–14.

96. Lacan, "From Love to the Libido," *The Four Fundamental Concepts of Psycho-Analysis*, p. 197.

97. Friedrich Nietzsche, *Will to Power*, trans. Walter Kaufmann (New York: Vintage, 1968), p. 227.

EPILOGUE
The (Un)Finished Work: Being Is Round

1. Bachelard, *The Poetics of Space*, p. 234: "das Dasein ist rund." So too is that icon that "watches over" Derrida's text. See Derrida, "Envois," *The Post Card*, p. 122. Cf. also Peter Schwenger, "Circling Ground Zero," *PMLA* 106 (1991): 252.

2. Levin, *The Power of Blackness*, p. 100.

3. Baym, *The Shape of Hawthorne's Career*, p. 273.

4. Quoted in Dan McCall, "Hawthorne's 'Familiar Kind of Preface,'" in Crowley, *Nathaniel Hawthorne: A Collection of Criticism*, p. 128. I disagree with McCall's evaluation of Hawthorne's anonymous footnote "disclaimers" to his own text—that "he was compelled to take back at the bottom of the page what he had put on the page itself." On the contrary, these anti-notations serve rather to underscore the daring and conviction of his position, to make it stand out all the more.

5. See Rita K. Gollin, *Nathaniel Hawthorne and the Truth of Dreams* (Baton Rouge: Louisiana State University Press, 1979), p. 195.

6. Ibid., pp. 211 and 218, respectively.

7. Levin, *The Power of Blackness*, pp. 97–98. For another reading of Hawthorne's final years, see Agnes McNeill Donohue, *Hawthorne: Calvin's Ironic Stepchild* (Kent: Kent State University Press, 1985), pp. 310–37.

8. Levin, *The Power of Blackness*, p. 98.

9. Normand, *Nathaniel Hawthorne*, p. 77.

10. Ibid., pp. 77–78.

11. Bachelard, *The Poetics of Space*, p. 240.

12. The space of desire comes in between (the return of) the step itself, its passage around the circle. See Derrida, "To Speculate—on Freud," *The Post Card*, p. 397: "The step or the *trans-* always already have the form of the return. It begins by coming back [*revenir*], by tending toward the annulling of its own process. This is also the progress of the proper which lets itself be enmeshed by this circular ring. Pleasure is found en route, the place of passage and moment of the ring."

13. Heidegger, "What Are Poets For?" *Poetry, Language, Thought*, pp. 127–28: "The inner and invisible domain of the heart is not only more inward than the

interior that belongs to calculating representation, and therefore more invisible; it also extends further than does the realm of merely producible objects. Only in the invisible innermost of the heart is man inclined toward what there is for him to love. . . . the interior of uncustomary consciousness remains the inner space in which everything is for us beyond the arithmetic of calculation, and free of such boundaries, can overflow into the unbounded whole of the Open. This overflow beyond number arises, in its presence, in the inner and invisible region of the heart. . . . The widest orbit of beings becomes present in the heart's inner space."

14. Ibid., p. 132.

15. Ibid., p. 136.

16. See Bachelard, *The Poetics of Space*, p. 239: "What calm there is in the word round. How peacefully it makes one's mouth, lips and the being of breath become round."

17. Heidegger, "The Thinker as Poet," *Poetry, Language, Thought*, p. 11.

18. Heidegger, "What Are Poets For?" *Poetry, Language, Thought*, p. 138.

19. Rainer Maria Rilke, *Sonnets to Orpheus*, trans. M. D. Herter Norton (New York: W. W. Norton, 1962), pp. 20–21:

> Gesang, wie du ihn lehrst, ist nicht Begehr,
> nicht Werbung um ein endlich noch Erreichtes;
> Gesang ist Dasein.

> Song, as you teach it, is not desire,
> Not suing for something yet in the end attained;
> Song is existence.

20. Heidegger, "What Are Poets For?" *Poetry, Language, Thought*, p. 140.

21. See ibid.

22. Cf. Bachelard, *The Poetics of Space*, p. 233.

23. Cf. ibid.: in the society of the spectacle, Dimmesdale's exposition could not be "round"; it could only be "square." Cf. also Jacques Derrida, *Dissemination,* trans. Barbara Johnson (Chicago: University of Chicago Press, 1981), p. 297: "In the *frame* of the text, one side of the square . . . will *represent:* it will be the opening to the classical representative scene. In representing representation, it will reflect and explain it in a very singular mirror. It will speak representation, proffering its discourse through a kind of 'square mouth,' 'oblivion closed by the frame.'"

24. Derrida, "Differance," *Speech and Phenomena*, p. 154.

25. Cf. Sallis, "Meaning Adrift," 99, for a reading of Nietzsche/Heidegger which lines up neatly with Hawthorne's exposition of *The Letter:* "Suppose that the originary, which can be called truth and world, were now to be called the true world. And suppose that one were to tell then of how the true world drifts along in the drift of language, in the ways that words have of telling, in their *Sage-weisen,* or—letting the translation itself now drift ever so slightly—in the styles *(Weisen)* in which a fable *(Sage)* can be told. One would then have begun again to tell—though with an ever so decisive twist—the story of how the true world finally became a fable."

26. Schneider, *Louvre Dialogues*, p. 213.

27. See Lyotard's (re)working of *differance* (the *differend*): Jean-François Lyotard, *The Postmodern Condition: A Report on Knowledge*, trans. Geoff Bennington and Brian Massumi (Minneapolis: University of Minnesota Press, 1984), and *The Differend: Phrases in Dispute*, trans. Georges Van Den Abbeele (Minneapolis: University of Minnesota Press, 1988).

28. I refer you back to Derrida's critique of the Kantian frame in *The Truth in Painting*: "Circle of circles, circle in the encircled circle. How could a circle place itself *en abyme?*" ("Parergon," p. 24); "the inscription of a circle in the circle does not necessarily *give* the abyss, onto the abyss, *en abyme*. In order to be abyssal [*sic*], the smallest circle must inscribe in itself the figure of the largest" ("Parergon," p. 27).

29. I refer specifically to Derrida's discussion of Poe's *Letter* in "Le facteur de la vérité," *The Post Card*, pp. 413–96.

30. Schneider, *Louvre Dialogues*, p. 213.

31. The work of Hawthorne's world thus *courts* the "other," the reader, defers its change of name (to whom it nevertheless has always already been wedded)—action at a distance: (its) truth is (A) woman.

32. "The enchantment and the most powerful effect of woman . . . is, to use the language of philosophers, an effect at a distance . . . , an *actio in distans;* there belongs thereto, however, primarily and above all—*distance!*" (quoted in Derrida, *Spurs: Nietzsche's Styles*, p. 47).

33. "Hathorne": I leave you in this margin.

Works Cited

Abraham, Nicolas, and Maria Torok. *The Wolf Man's Magic Word: A Cryptonymy.* Trans. Nicholas Rand. Minneapolis: University of Minnesota Press, 1986.

Agrippa, Henry Cornelius. *Of the Vanitie and Vncertaintie of Artes and Sciences.* Ed. Catherine M. Dunn. Northridge: California State University, 1974.

Arac, Jonathan. "Reading the Letter." *Diacritics* 9 (1979): 42–52.

Bachelard, Gaston. *The Poetics of Space.* Trans. Maria Jolas. Boston: Beacon Press, 1969.

———. *The Psychoanalysis of Fire.* Trans. Alan C. M. Ross. Boston: Beacon Press, 1968.

Bacon, Francis. *Francis Bacon's Essays.* Intro. Oliphant Smeaton. London: J. M. Dent & Sons, 1958.

Balázs, Béla. *Theory of the Film.* Trans. Edith Bone. London: Dennis Dobson, 1952.

Barthes, Roland. *Camera Lucida: Reflections on Photography.* Trans. Richard Howard. New York: Hill and Wang, 1981.

Baym, Nina. *The Shape of Hawthorne's Career.* Ithaca: Cornell University Press, 1976.

Benjamin, Walter. *Illuminations.* Trans. Harry Zohn. New York: Harcourt, Brace and World, 1968.

Berlant, Lauren. "Fantasies of Utopia in *The Blithedale Romance.*" *American Literary History* 1 (1989): 30–62.

Bogardus, Ralph F. *Pictures and Texts: Henry James, A. L. Coburn and New Ways of Seeing in Literary Culture.* Ann Arbor: UMI Research Press, 1984.

Bovay, Georges-Michel, ed. *Cinéma: un oeil ouvert sur le monde.* Lausanne: La Guilde du Livre, 1952.

Brodhead, Richard H. *Hawthorne, Melville, and the Novel.* Chicago: University of Chicago Press, 1976.

Cameron, Sharon. *The Corporeal Self: Allegories of the Body in Melville and Hawthorne.* Baltimore: Johns Hopkins University Press, 1981.

Campbell, Charles. "Representing Representation: Body as Figure, Frame, and Text in *The House of the Seven Gables.*" *Arizona Quarterly* 47 (1991): 1–26.

Cassirer, Ernst. *The Philosophy of Symbolic Forms.* 3 vols. Trans. Ralph Manheim. New Haven: Yale University Press, 1957. Vol. 3.

Cixous, Hélène, and Catherine Clément. *The Newly Born Woman.* Trans. Betsy Wing. Minneapolis: University of Minnesota Press, 1986.

Coke, Van Deren. "Camera and Canvas." *Art in America* 49 (1961): 68–73.

Cowley, Malcolm. "Hawthorne in the Looking-Glass." *Sewanee Review* 56 (1948): 545–63.

Crews, Frederick. *The Sins of the Fathers: Hawthorne's Psychological Themes.* London: Oxford University Press, 1966.

Crowley, J. Donald, ed. *Hawthorne: The Critical Heritage*. New York: Barnes and Noble, 1970.

———, ed. *Nathaniel Hawthorne: A Collection of Criticism*. New York: McGraw-Hill, 1975.

Culver, Stuart. "How Photographs Mean: Literature and the Camera in American Studies." *American Literary History* 1 (1989): 190–205.

Danto, Arthur C. "Narration and Knowledge." *Philosophy and Literature* 6 (1982): 17–32.

Debord, Guy. *Society of the Spectacle*. Detroit: Black and Red, 1977.

Derrida, Jacques. "Coming into One's Own." *Psychoanalysis and the Question of the Text*. Ed. Geoffrey H. Hartman, 114–48. Baltimore: Johns Hopkins University Press, 1978.

———. *Dissemination*. Trans. Barbara Johnson. Chicago: University of Chicago Press, 1981.

———. *Speech and Phenomena*. Trans. David B. Allison. Evanston: Northwestern University Press, 1973.

———. *Spurs: Nietzsche's Styles*. Trans. Barbara Harlow. Chicago: University of Chicago Press, 1979.

———. *The Post Card: From Socrates to Freud and Beyond*. Trans. Alan Bass. Chicago: University of Chicago Press, 1987.

———. *The Truth in Painting*. Trans. Geoff Bennington and Ian McLeod. Chicago: University of Chicago Press, 1987.

Donohue, Agnes McNeill. *Hawthorne: Calvin's Ironic Stepchild*. Kent: Kent State University Press, 1985.

Dryden, Edgar A. *Nathaniel Hawthorne: The Poetics of Enchantment*. Ithaca: Cornell University Press, 1977.

———. *The Form of American Romance*. Ithaca: Cornell University Press, 1988.

Dufrenne, Mikel. *The Phenomenology of Aesthetic Experience*. Trans. Edward S. Casey, et al. Evanston: Northwestern University Press, 1973.

Dunlap, William. *A History of the Rise and Progress of the Arts of Design in the United States*. 3 vols. Ed. Frank W. Bayley and Charles E. Goodspeed; rev. ed. Boston: C. E. Goodspeed, 1918. Vol. 3.

Durgnat, Raymond. *Films and Feelings*. London: Faber and Faber, 1967.

Eisenstein, Sergei M. *The Film Sense*. Trans. Jay Leyda. New York: Harcourt, Brace and World, 1942.

Emerson, Ralph Waldo. *The Complete Works of Ralph Waldo Emerson*. Centenary Edition. 12 vols. Ed. Edward Waldo Emerson. Boston: Houghton Mifflin, 1903–21. Vols. 1 and 12.

———. *The Journals and Miscellaneous Notebooks of Ralph Waldo Emerson*. 16 vols. Ed. William H. Gilman et al. Cambridge: Belknap Press, 1960–82. Vols. 11, 15, and 16.

Feidelson, Charles, Jr. *Symbolism and American Literature*. Chicago: University of Chicago Press, 1959.

Fell, Joseph P. *Heidegger and Sartre: An Essay on Being and Place*. New York: Columbia University Press, 1979.

————. "The Crisis of Reason: A Reading of Heidegger's *Zur Seinsfrage.*" *Heideg-ger Studies* 2 (1986): 41–65.

Felman, Shoshana, ed. *Literature and Psychoanalysis; The Question of Reading: Otherwise.* Baltimore: Johns Hopkins University Press, 1982.

Fields, James T. *Yesterdays with Authors.* Boston: James R. Osgood, 1874.

Freud, Sigmund. "Moses and Monotheism." *The Standard Edition of the Complete Psychological Works of Sigmund Freud.* 24 vols. Trans. James Strachey. London: Hogarth Press, 1964. Vol. 23.

————. *The Interpretation of Dreams.* Trans. A. A. Brill. New York: Macmillan Co., 1937.

————. *Three Case Histories.* Ed. Philip Rieff. New York: Collier Books, 1963.

Frings, Manfred S., ed. *Heidegger and the Quest for Truth.* Chicago: Quadrangle Books, 1968.

Gasché, Rodolphe. "Deconstruction as Criticism." *Glyph* 6 (1979): 177–215.

Gollin, Rita K. *Nathaniel Hawthorne and the Truth of Dreams.* Baton Rouge: Louisiana State University Press, 1979.

Gras, Vernon W., ed. *European Literary Theory and Practice: From Existential Phenomenology to Structuralism.* New York: Dell Publishing Co., 1973.

Harrison, Gabriel. "Lights and Shadows of Daguerrean Life." *Photographic and Fine Art Journal* 7 (1854): 8–9.

Hartman, Geoffrey H. *Beyond Formalism: Literary Essays, 1958–70.* New Haven: Yale University Press, 1970.

————. "Preface." *Psychoanalysis and the Question of the Text.* Ed. Geoffrey H. Hartman, vii–xix. Baltimore: Johns Hopkins University Press, 1978.

————. *Saving the Text: Literature/Derrida/Philosophy.* Baltimore: Johns Hopkins University Press, 1981.

Hawthorne, Nathaniel. *The Centenary Edition of the Works of Nathaniel Hawthorne.* 20 vols. to date. Ed. William Charvat, et al. Columbus: Ohio State University Press, 1962–present.

————. *Hawthorne's Lost Notebook, 1835–1841.* Intro. Hyatt H. Waggoner. University Park: Pennsylvania State University Press, 1978.

Heidegger, Martin. *Being and Time.* Trans. John Macquarrie and Edward Robinson. New York: Harper and Row, 1962.

————. *Early Greek Thinking.* Trans. David Farrell Krell and Frank A. Capuzzi. New York: Harper and Row, 1975.

————. *Poetry, Language, Thought.* Trans. Albert Hofstadter. New York: Harper and Row, 1975.

————. "The Age of the World View." Trans. Marjorie Grene. *Boundary 2* 4 (1976): 341–55.

————. *The Question Concerning Technology and Other Essays.* Trans. William Lovitt. New York: Harper and Row, 1977.

Hertz, Neil. "Dora's Secrets, Freud's Techniques." *Diacritics* 13 (1983): 64–76.

Hitchcock, Edward. *The Religion of Geology and Its Related Sciences.* Boston: Phillips, Sampson, and Co., 1851.

Hofstadter, Albert. "Enownment." *Boundary 2* 4 (1976): 357–77.

Holmes, Oliver Wendell. "The Stereoscope and the Stereograph." *Atlantic Monthly* 3 (1859): 738–48.

Horan, James D. *Mathew Brady: Historian with a Camera.* New York: Bonanza Books, 1955.

Hume, David. "A Treatise of Human Nature." *David Hume: The Philosophical Works.* 4 vols. Ed. Thomas Hill Green and Thomas Hodge Grose, Vol. 1: 301–560 and Vol. 2: 1–374. Darmstadt: Scientia Verlag Aalen, 1964.

Hunter, Jefferson. *Image and Word: The Interaction of Twentieth-Century Photographs and Texts.* Cambridge: Harvard University Press, 1987.

Irwin, John T. *American Hieroglyphics.* New Haven: Yale University Press, 1980.

Jakobson, Roman. "Two Aspects of Language: Metaphor and Metonymy." *European Literary Theory and Practice: From Existential Phenomenology to Structuralism.* Ed. Vernon W. Gras, 119–29. New York: Dell Publishing Co., 1973.

James, Henry. *Hawthorne.* Ithaca: Cornell University Press, 1966.

Jameson, Fredric. "Imaginary and Symbolic in Lacan: Marxism, Psychoanalytic Criticism, and the Problem of the Subject." *Literature and Psychoanalysis; The Question of Reading: Otherwise.* Ed. Shoshana Felman, 338–95. Baltimore: Johns Hopkins University Press, 1982.

Johnson, Barbara. "The Frame of Reference: Poe, Lacan, Derrida." *Literature and Psychoanalysis; The Question of Reading: Otherwise.* Ed. Shoshana Felman, 457–505. Baltimore: Johns Hopkins University Press, 1982.

Johnson, Claudia D. *The Productive Tension of Hawthorne's Art.* University: University of Alabama Press, 1981.

Kant, Immanuel. *Critique of Judgment.* Trans. J. H. Bernard. New York: Hafner, 1968.

———. *Critique of Practical Reason and Other Writings in Moral Philosophy.* Trans. L. W. Beck. Chicago: University of Chicago Press, 1949.

Kaul, A. N. "The Blithedale Romance." *Hawthorne: A Collection of Critical Essays.* Ed. A. N. Kaul, 153–63. Englewood Cliffs: Prentice-Hall, 1966.

Kierkegaard, Søren. *Repetition: An Essay in Experimental Psychology.* Trans. Walter Lowrie. New York: Harper and Row, 1964.

———. *The Concept of Irony.* Trans. Lee M. Capel. Bloomington: Indiana University Press, 1968.

———. *The Sickness Unto Death. "Fear and Trembling" and "The Sickness unto Death."* Trans. Walter Lowrie. Princeton: Princeton University Press, 1968.

Koffka, Kurt. *Principles of Gestalt Psychology.* New York: Harcourt, Brace and Co., 1935.

———. *The Growth of the Mind.* New York: Harcourt, Brace and Co., 1925.

Lacan, Jacques. *Écrits.* Trans. Alan Sheridan. New York: W. W. Norton, 1977.

———. *The Four Fundamental Concepts of Psycho-Analysis.* Trans. Alan Sheridan. New York: W. W. Norton, 1978.

Langer, Susanne K. *Feeling and Form.* New York: Charles Scribner's Sons, 1963.

Lautréamont, Comte de. *Le Chants de Maldoror.* Trans. Guy Wernham. New York: New Directions, 1965.

Lawrence, D. H. *Studies in Classic American Literature.* New York: Viking Press, 1964.

Lease, Benjamin. "Diorama and Dream: Hawthorne's Cinematic Vision." *Journal of Popular Culture* 5 (1971): 315–23.

Leavis, Q. D. "Hawthorne as Poet." *Sewanee Review* 59 (1951): 179–85, 198–205, 456–58.

Leibniz, Gottfried Wilhelm Von. "Discourse on Metaphysics." *The European Philosophers: From Descartes to Nietzsche.* Ed. Monroe C. Beardsley, 250–86. New York: Modern Library, 1960.

Lessing, Gotthold Ephraim. *Laocoön: An Essay upon the Limits of Painting and Poetry.* Trans. Ellen Frothingham. New York: Farrar, Straus and Giroux, 1969.

Lesy, Michael. *Wisconsin Death Trip.* New York: Pantheon Books, 1973.

Levin, Harry. *The Power of Blackness.* New York: Alfred A. Knopf, 1958.

Lévi-Strauss, Claude. *The Savage Mind.* Chicago: University of Chicago Press, 1966.

Lewis, R. W. B. *The American Adam: Innocence, Tragedy, and Tradition in the Nineteenth Century.* Chicago: University of Chicago Press, 1955.

Lindgren, Ernest. *The Art of the Film.* London: Allen and Unwin, 1948.

Lingis, A. F. "On the Essence of Technique." *Heidegger and the Quest for Truth.* Ed. Manfred S. Frings, 126–38. Chicago: Quadrangle Books, 1968.

Locke, John. *An Essay Concerning Human Understanding.* Ed. Peter H. Nidditch. London: Oxford University Press, 1975.

Lukacher, Ned. *Primal Scenes: Literature, Philosophy, Psychoanalysis.* Ithaca: Cornell University Press, 1986.

Lyotard, Jean-François. *Discours, Figure.* Paris: Klincksieck, 1971.

———. *The Differend: Phrases in Dispute.* Trans. Georges Van Den Abbeele. Minneapolis: University of Minnesota Press, 1988.

———. *The Postmodern Condition: A Report on Knowledge.* Trans. Geoff Bennington and Brian Massumi. Minneapolis: University of Minnesota Press, 1984.

McCall, Dan. "Hawthorne's 'Familiar Kind of Preface.'" *Nathaniel Hawthorne: A Collection of Criticism.* Ed. J. Donald Crowley, 115–31. New York: McGraw-Hill, 1975.

McLuhan, Marshall, and Harley Parker. *Through the Vanishing Point: Space in Poetry and Painting.* New York: Harper and Row, 1968.

———. *Understanding Media: The Extensions of Man.* New York: Signet, 1964.

Manheim, Leonard F. "Outside Looking In; Evidences of Primal-Scene Fantasy in Hawthorne's Fiction." *Literature and Psychology* 31 (1981): 4–15.

Marks, Alfred H. "German Romantic Irony in Hawthorne's Tales." *Symposium* 7 (1953): 274–305.

Matthiessen, F. O. *American Renaissance.* New York: Oxford University Press, 1941.

Mellow, James R. *Nathaniel Hawthorne in His Times.* Boston: Houghton Mifflin, 1980.

Melville, Herman. *Pierre, or the Ambiguities.* Evanston: Northwestern University Press, 1971.

Merleau-Ponty, Maurice. *Phenomenology of Perception.* Trans. Colin Smith; rev. trans. Forrest Williams. London: Routledge and Kegan Paul, 1962.

———. *The Primacy of Perception.* Ed. James Edie. Evanston: Northwestern University Press, 1964.

———. *The Visible and the Invisible.* Trans. Alphonso Lingis. Evanston: Northwestern University Press, 1968.

Miller, J. Hillis. *Hawthorne and History: Defacing It.* Oxford: Basil Blackwell, 1991.

Newman, Franklin B. "'My Kinsman, Major Molineux': An Interpretation." *University of Kansas City Review* 21 (1955): 203–12.

Nicolson, Marjorie Hope. *Newton Demands the Muse.* Princeton: Princeton University Press, 1966.

Nietzsche, Friedrich. *Will to Power.* Trans. Walter Kaufmann. New York: Vintage, 1968.

Normand, Jean. *Nathaniel Hawthorne: An Approach to an Analysis of Artistic Creation.* Trans. Derek Coltman. Cleveland: Press of Case Western Reserve University, 1970.

Panofsky, Erwin. "Artist, Scientist, Genius: Notes on the 'Renaissance-Dämmerung.'" *The Renaissance: Six Essays,* 123–82. New York: Harper Torchbooks, 1962.

Pascal, Blaise. *Pensées.* *"Pensées" and "The Provincial Letters."* Trans. W. F. Trotter and Thomas M'Crie. New York: Modern Library, 1941.

Pattison, Joseph C. "Point of View in Hawthorne." *PMLA* 82 (1967): 363–69.

———. "'The Celestial Rail-Road' as Dream-Tale." *American Quarterly* 20 (1968): 224–36.

Perkins, V. F. *Film as Film.* London: Penguin Books, 1972.

Piaget, Jean. *The Construction of Reality in the Child.* Trans. Margaret Cook. New York: Ballantine Books, 1954.

Plissart, Marie-Françoise. *Droit de regards: Avec une lecture de Jacques Derrida.* Paris: Minuit, 1985.

Porte, Joel. "Redemption through Art." *Nathaniel Hawthorne: A Collection of Criticism.* Ed. J. Donald Crowley, 75–85. New York: McGraw-Hill, 1975.

Prime, Samuel. *The Life of Samuel Morse.* New York: Appleton, 1875.

Ragussis, Michael. "Family Discourse and Fiction in *The Scarlet Letter.*" *English Literary History* 49 (1982): 863–88.

Rilke, Rainer Maria. *Sonnets to Orpheus.* Trans. M. D. Herter Norton. New York: W. W. Norton, 1962.

Root, M. A. *The Camera and the Pencil.* Philadelphia: J. B. Lippincott, 1864.

Rudisill, Richard. *Mirror Image: The Influence of the Daguerreotype on American Society.* Albuquerque: University of New Mexico Press, 1971.

Ryder, James F. *Voigtlander and I in Pursuit of Shadow Catching.* Cleveland: Cleveland Printing and Publishing Co., 1902.

Said, Edward W. *Beginnings: Intention and Method.* Baltimore: Johns Hopkins University Press, 1975.

Sallis, John. "Meaning Adrift." *Heidegger Studies* 1 (1985): 91–100.

Sarton, George. "The Quest for Truth: Scientific Progress during the Renaissance." *The Renaissance: Six Essays,* 55–76. New York: Harper Torchbooks, 1962.

Sartre, Jean-Paul. *Being and Nothingness.* Trans. Hazel E. Barnes. New York: Philosophical Library, 1956.

———. *L'Imaginaire.* Paris: Gallimard, 1940.

Scheler, Max. "Idealism and Realism." *Selected Philosophical Essays.* Trans. David R. Lachterman, 288–356. Evanston: Northwestern University Press, 1973.

———. *Man's Place in Nature.* Trans. Hans Meyerhoff. New York: Noonday Press, 1961.

———. *Ressentiment.* Trans. William W. Holdheim. New York: Schocken Books, 1972.

Schneider, Pierre. *Louvre Dialogues.* Trans. Patricia Southgate. New York: Atheneum, 1971.

Schubert, Leland. *Hawthorne the Artist.* New York: Russell and Russell, 1963.

Schwenger, Peter. "Circling Ground Zero." *PMLA* 106 (1991): 251–61.

Shloss, Carol. *In Visible Light: Photography and the American Writer: 1840–1940.* New York: Oxford University Press, 1987.

Sibony, Daniel. "*Hamlet:* A Writing-Effect." *Literature and Psychoanalysis; The Question of Reading: Otherwise.* Ed. Shoshana Felman, 53–93. Baltimore: Johns Hopkins University Press, 1982.

Smith, Logan Pearsall, ed. *The Life and Letters of Sir Henry Wotton.* 2 vols. London: Oxford University Press, 1907. Vol. 2.

Sollers, Philippe. "Freud's Hand." *Literature and Psychoanalysis; The Question of Reading: Otherwise.* Ed. Shoshana Felman, 329–37. Baltimore: Johns Hopkins University Press, 1982.

Sontag, Susan. *On Photography.* New York: Dell, 1977.

Southworth, Albert S. "An Address to the National Photographic Association of the United States." *The Philadelphia Photographer* 8 (1871): 315–23.

Spanos, William V. "Heidegger, Kierkegaard, and the Hermeneutic Circle: Towards a Postmodern Theory of Interpretation as Dis-closure." *Boundary 2* 4 (1976): 455–88.

Spivak, Gayatri. "The Letter as Cutting Edge." *Literature and Psychoanalysis; The Question of Reading: Otherwise.* Ed. Shoshana Felman, 208–26. Baltimore: Johns Hopkins University Press, 1982.

Sprague, Claire. "Dream and Disguise in *The Blithedale Romance.*" *PMLA* 84 (1969): 596–97.

Steinbeck, John. *A Russian Journal with Pictures by Robert Capa.* New York: Viking Press, 1948.

Stewart, Susan. *On Longing: Narratives of the Miniature, the Gigantic, the Souvenir, the Collection.* Baltimore: Johns Hopkins University Press, 1984.

Stubbs, John Caldwell. "*The Marble Faun:* Hawthorne's Romance of the Adamic Myth." *Nathaniel Hawthorne: A Collection of Criticism.* Ed. J. Donald Crowley, 101–14. New York: McGraw-Hill, 1975.

Supervielle, Jules. *Selected Writings.* Trans. Alan Pryce-Jones. New York: New Directions, 1967.

Sussman, Henry. "*The Marble Faun* and the Space of American Letters." *Glyph Textual Studies* 1 (1986): 129–52.

Thomas, Brook. "*The House of the Seven Gables:* Reading the Romance of America." *PMLA* 97 (1982): 195–211.

Thoreau, Henry David. *Walden.* New York: Holt, Rinehart and Winston, 1961.

Van Cromphout, Gustaaf. "Emerson and the Dialectics of History." *PMLA* 91 (1976): 54–64.

Van Deusen, Marshall. "Narrative Tone in 'The Custom House' and *The Scarlet Letter.*" *Nathaniel Hawthorne: A Collection of Criticism.* Ed. J. Donald Crowley, 53–62. New York: McGraw-Hill, 1975.

Warnock, Mary. *Imagination.* Berkeley: University of California Press, 1976.

Whitman, Walt. *Pictures: An Unpublished Poem.* New York: June House, 1927.

Willis, Nathaniel P. "The Pencil of Nature." *The Corsair* 1 (1839): 70–72.

Wills, David. "Supreme Court." *Diacritics* 18 (1988): 20–31.

Wolff, Werner. *The Dream: Mirror of Conscience.* New York: Grune and Stratton, 1952.

Index

ABOUT THE AUTHOR

John Dolis is Associate Professor of English at Pennsylvania State University, Scranton. He received his bachelor's degree from Saint Louis University and his master's and doctorate from Loyola University of Chicago.